Cash Flow Forecasting

Essential Capital Markets

Books in the series:

Cash Flow Forecasting
Corporate Valuation
Credit Risk Management
Finance of International Trade
Mergers and Acquisitions
Portfolio Management in Practice
Introduction to Project Finance
Syndicated Lending

Cash Flow Forecasting

Edited by
Andrew Fight

ELSEVIER

AMSTERDAM · BOSTON · HEIDELBERG · LONDON · NEW YORK · OXFORD
PARIS · SAN DIEGO · SAN FRANCISCO · SINGAPORE · SYDNEY · TOKYO

Butterworth-Heinemann is an imprint of Elsevier

Butterworth-Heinemann is an imprint of Elsevier
Linacre House, Jordan Hill, Oxford OX2 8DP
30 Corporate Drive, Suite 400, Burlington, MA 01803

First published 2006

British Library Cataloguing in Publication Data
A catalogue record for this book is available from the British Library

Library of Congress Cataloging in Publication Data Control Number: 2005923901

ISBN-13: 978-0-7506-6136-2
ISBN-10: 0-7506-6136-4

For information on all Butterworth-Heinemann publications
visit our website at http://books.elsevier.com

Composition by Charon Tec Pvt. Ltd, Chennai, India
www.charontec.com
Printed and bound in Great Britain

06 07 08 09 10 11   10 9 8 7 6 5 4 3 2 1

Contents

Preface   ix

1   Overview of cash flow forecasting   1
Introduction   1
What is a healthy cash flow?   3
What are the uses of cash flow forecasting?   6

2   Summary of financial statements   8
Introduction   8
The annual report and accounts   10
The profit and loss account   33
Problems with financial statements and auditors   35
Conclusion   38

3   Factors impacting financial performance   41
Introduction   41
Strategic analysis – the external environment   42
Strategic analysis – the value chain   46
Management   49
Profitability and performance   50
Asset management   54
Capital structure   58
Cash flow   63

Cash flow forecasting   66
Corporate failure   70

4   Cash flow forecasting of financial statements   76
Why cash flow analysis?   76
Purpose of projections   79
Historical performance and variable input analysis   81
Profit and loss statement projections   86
Balance sheet projections   109
Assets   112
Liabilities   119
Completed AmaOS forecasted balance sheet   131
Cash flow projections   134
Cash flow ratio analysis   144
Sensitivity analysis   146
Protection and control in term lending   150
Conclusion   153
Chapter self-test   155
Chapter self-test answers   158

5   Cash flow forecasting of project finance   160
Introduction   160
Cash flow forecasting   163
Conclusion   171

6   Pro forma forecasts using AMADEUS electronic databases   172

Appendices   185
1 Credit rating agency rating scales   186
2 Country risk criteria   189
3 Summary of lending types   199
4 Complete AmaOS spreadsheet   200

Suggested reading   209

Glossary   210
Profitability indicators   237
Turnover and efficiency indicators   238

Financial position indicators   239
Cash flow terms   240
Cash ratios   240

Index   **243**

Preface

Welcome to this book on cash flow forecasting.

This book is presented in six chapters, each of which treats a specific aspect of cash flow forecasting. The individual chapters cover the following topics:

- Overview of cash flow forecasting
- Summary of financial statements
- Factors impacting financial performance
- Cash flow forecasting of financial statements
- Cash flow forecasting of project finance
- Pro forma forecasts using Amadeus electronic databases.

It also includes appendices, suggested reading, and a glossary.

This book aims to explain the background and *raison d'être* of cash flow forecasting as one of the techniques used in the capital markets to provide finance to companies, multinational corporations and large-scale projects.

Since most large loans and project financings are structured with a view to syndication in the international capital markets, cash flow forecasting also offers the possibility of structuring financings to satisfy the particular pricing, size and tenor appetites of the market.

It is suggested that this book be read in conjunction with the *Syndicated Lending* and *Introduction to Project Finance* books in this series, thereby linking the structuring of the cash flow forecasting facility to the marketing issues involved in loan syndication.

For newcomers to credit and financial analysis, the *Credit Risk Management* book in this series sets the analytical groundwork for understanding the concepts in *Cash Flow Forecasting*.

We hope that this book *Cash Flow Forecasting*, in the Essential Capital Markets Series, will be informative and instructional, and an indispensable and practical aid to persons seeking to understand this important area of banking.

Andrew Fight
www.andrewfight.com

Chapter 1

Overview of cash flow forecasting

Introduction

What is cash flow forecasting? The term features prominently in the press, more specifically with respect to infrastructure, and public and private venture capital needs. The press often refers to huge projects such as building infrastructure projects like highways, the Eurotunnel, metro systems or airports. It is a technique that has been used to raise huge amounts of capital and promises to continue to do so, in both developed and developing countries, for the foreseeable future.

Cash flow forecasting, however, is also useful for more mundane applications. In many countries, the SME sector can account for as much as 40–50 per cent of economic activity. Small and medium-sized enterprises often require access to growth capital during their expansion phase, and the greatest single problem facing SMEs in an expansion role is insufficient liquidity. It is unfortunate that in many countries the SME sector is overlooked in the quest for more lucrative, albeit higher-risk, credit scenarios. National economic growth can also be fostered by the growth in the economic activity of SMEs, and it is therefore important to understand the techniques that can be used to provide funding to this sector. It is crucial for potential lenders to understand the financial situation, liquidity and cash flow situation of SMEs in order optimally to practise good lending principles.

This book on cash flow forecasting will therefore explore some of the mechanisms used in preparing cash flow forecasts, with a view to using them for sensitivity analysis and designing appropriate financial structures and loan covenants to protect the bank's position in an adverse environment. Accordingly, this book will touch upon a number of issues *en passant*, such as the interrelations between items in a standard set of company accounts, ratio analysis, projection methodologies, debt runoff schedules, loan documentation, and the drafting of effective financial covenants in order to illustrate how to use the projections usefully.

The purpose of cash flow projections after all is not to construct elaborate mathematical models or predict the future, but rather to identify potential weaknesses in a given credit situation and point the way to adopt measures to enhance, correct or protect the bank's exposure.

Understanding the key risks and *practical applications* of cash flow forecasting and how it differs from other financing techniques is critical to all the major players in large capital projects (such as commercial and investment bankers), but also other players in lending situations (such as project finance, general contractors, subcontractors, insurance companies, suppliers and customers). All these participants will participate into an interlocking financing structure with mutual and multiple interdependencies.

In term lending, cash flow is the primary and usual source of loan repayment. The major credit issues are:

- Will the firm's projected cash flow – under various scenarios ranging from realistic to worst case – be sufficient to pay the interest and amortize the principal on existing long-term debt obligations? How do we measure the adequacy of cash flow to service debt, and what do we mean by a healthy cash flow?
- Does the projected asset structure and earnings stream indicate a potential need for additional financing in the future, and is there sufficient cash flow to service the near debt?
- What type of facility is appropriate, and how should the loan be structured? What would be the most appropriate amortization schedule for the new debt? What financial covenants should be included to provide

the bank sufficient protection against loss – that is, to preserve and control the cash flow and overall financial strength of the firm?

In the following sections we will explore each of these issues, beginning with a discussion of how to determine the relative 'health' and debt-servicing ability of a cash flow.

What is a healthy cash flow?

In term lending, we look to future cash flow for loan repayment. The objective of an analysis of cash flow as the primary repayment source is to ensure there will be sufficient cash to meet financing payments. Before considering future cash flow and determining its adequacy, it is useful to look at historical cash flow and pose the question: what constitutes a healthy cash flow? Whether a particular cash flow is healthy depends not only on the present financial condition of the company, but also on how it achieved its present position and the external and internal conditions it faces.

Consider Examples 1.1–1.5

Example 1.1

A company in the mature phase of its life cycle, where there is no expectation of continued growth, exhibits the following characteristics:

- earnings retained can finance permanent working investment
- cash 'throw-off' from depreciation (that is, the non-cash charge of depreciation on the income statement) is sufficient to maintain fixed assets
- the firm can pay down its short-term borrowings without riding the trade and without refinancing at the seasonal low point by borrowing from another bank
- there is sufficient cash to amortize existing long-term debt and pay dividends.

Here, the firm has a healthy cash flow.

Example 1.2

Considering Example 1.1, if the company had used its retained earnings to pay heavy dividends in excess of profits, with the following results:

■ cash throw-off from depreciation was used to amortize the term loan
■ the firm is increasingly riding the trade to finance permanent trading asset levels
■ bank lines of credit could not be cleaned up

then this would be an unhealthy cash flow.

Example 1.3

A company in a growth situation has, because competition has reduced profitability, introduced a new product that requires new plant and increased working investment.

If the present situation was anticipated before erosion of profits became serious and:

■ the company has had a conservative dividend policy
■ a significant portion of long-term debt has been replaced with equity through the retention of profits
■ plant can be maintained in efficient condition without reinvestment of the full amount of depreciation so that a significant portion of cash throw-off from depreciation may be used for other purposes
■ working investment has not been increased by offering longer credit terms or by reducing credit standards in order to generate sales
■ inventory turnover has been maintained at the maximum efficient level by careful planning and by control of both costs and the level of investment in each component

then so far, despite declining profitability, it would appear that the firm has been able to maintain a healthy cash flow and thus might have some additional debt capacity to support the growth in assets necessary to introduce the new product. The decision to provide that financing hinges on an assessment of the firm's future cash flows as affected by the introduction of the new product.

Example 1.4

A company with proven growth potential in which:

■ high profits have been retained
■ there is excess capacity in a well maintained plant
■ equity capital supports fixed assets and permanent working investment
■ financial leverage is modest
■ trade has been paid promptly

has a healthy cash flow.

Example 1.5

Considering Example 1.4, if:

■ the company has no safety stock of inventory, and vital materials are scarce
■ poor labour relations threaten strikes
■ skilled labour is not available and training is a two-year process

then although at present the firm has a strong cash flow, its prospects for the future indicate that it may not be able to maintain its present strength.

An analysis of a firm's cash flow and a determination of whether management has successfully and efficiently managed the sources and uses of cash must be based on an understanding of the nature of business, and on its position in the normal life cycle of a business – whether it is a newly developing business, in the growth stage, at maturity or in decline.

As a basic proposition, however, the bank as a creditor defines a healthy cash flow as one in which net cash inflow from the normal operations of the firm is sufficient to cover both financing payments and the maintenance of the quality and efficiency of its assets. Depending on where the firm is in its business life cycle, the bank would also like to see some percentage of the growth in assets (increasing working investment and gross plant expenditure) covered by internally generated funds.

Analysis of cash flow concentrates, then, on the debt servicing ability of the firm. By isolating, in a firm's cash flow, an amount of cash available for debt servicing, however, it is important to remember that:

- this is not an identifiable pool of cash earmarked solely for debt servicing, and
- from the corporation's point of view there may be a number of other needs equally urgent and necessary to ensure solvency of the business that are competing for the limited cash available.

Analysis of cash flow, then, cannot merely isolate debt capacity but must also consider all the factors producing major changes in cash inflows and outflows. The primary hazard of too much debt compared to cash generated is the risk of insolvency, and debt servicing is given top priority as far as the bank is concerned. However, all decisions involving cash outflows vital to the survival of the firm need to be considered when evaluating cash solvency.

What are the uses of cash flow forecasting?

Cash flow forecasting is subject to several types of risks. It is useful, therefore, to look at these risks by category and identify their salient features and characteristics.

- *Credit worthiness* – a company's financial condition can be analysed and tested under various scenarios to assess and enhance the intrinsic credit worthiness

- *Project feasibility* – a project can be tested using various assumptions in order to establish whether or not the project is feasible, and what measures can be adopted to enhance the project's feasibility
- *Loan structuring* – specific weaknesses in the credit can be identified, thereby enabling the loan facility to be optimally structured in terms of amount, tenor, pricing
- *Financial covenanting* – specific financial covenants can be created and tailored to the borrower's financial condition
- *Security perfection* – specific shortfalls can be identified and the resulting credit risk enhanced via the perfection of security arrangements, including assets and guarantees
- *Loan document drafting* – financial projections can be used to identify the parameters of specific issues and problems, which can subsequently be managed via the appropriate drafting of loan documentation.

Chapter 2

Summary of financial statements

Introduction

This is not a treatise on financial analysis, but rather a consideration of the interrelations existing between the various components of the balance sheet and income statement and financial ratios which it is essential to understand in the preparation of cash flow forecasting.

In particular, we are concerned with the interrelationships existing between the income statement, balance sheet, and various financial ratios summarizing their interrelationships, and which can be manipulated with 'cash drivers' to project key accounts.

We therefore touch upon these topics as they relate to the manipulations required in effecting financial analysis.

The accounting process is divided into two basic elements, recording and reporting of financial information. The emergence of the large-scale limited liability company has been the single most important factor stimulating the need for financial reports. The larger and more complex the company, the more remote the management can become from day-to-day operations, and the more reliant they have to become on accounting information. In addition, the company that borrows money will need to demonstrate its financial solidity to its bankers, and financial statements are used by bankers and others as part of the basis for lending decisions.

In recent years, there has been recognition that there may be a large number of different parties with a legitimate interest in a company's performance:

- the equity investors – existing and potential shareholders
- the loan creditors – including existing and potential holders of debentures and loan stock, and providers of short-term unsecured loans and finance
- the company's bankers
- the company's employees
- the analysts/advisers – this will include financial analysts and journalists, economists, researchers, stockbrokers etc.
- customers, trade creditors and suppliers
- tax authorities, supervisory bodies, local authorities
- the general public – including taxpayers, consumers, political parties, and consumer and environmental groups.

Each of the groups will have a common interest in the financial statements of a company, but will use the information as the basis for different types

Table 2.1 Comparison between continental European and Anglo-Saxon accounting systems

	Continental European	*Anglo-Saxon*
Capital markets	Mainly from banking sector	Mainly stock markets
Culture	State-focussed	Individualistic
Legal system	Law provides detailed accounting rules	Rules from standard setting bodies
Fiscal system	Accounting/tax closely connected	Accounting not influenced by tax rules
Examples of countries	Belgium	Australia
	Germany	Great Britain
	France	Ireland
	Italy	The Netherlands
	Japan	Singapore
	Switzerland	USA
Users of information	Creditors, taxman, investors	Notably investors
Accounting principles	Prudence	True and fair principle dominates

of decisions. There are differences in the amount of financial information made available to each of these groups, caused by different legal requirements and the company's management decisions as to what they wish to make available.

The annual report and accounts

The publication of an annual report and accounts by a company supposedly provides its shareholders and others with a means to keep themselves informed on the activities and financial position of the company.

The style and content of the annual report and accounts will vary from company to company, depending on the directors' design ideas and the financial resources available for the printing and designing of the report. Many companies will use their report and accounts as a marketing tool. However, there is a minimum amount of information that the law requires a company to print in the report and accounts. These requirements include four basic components:

1 The directors' report
2 A report by the company's auditors
3 A balance sheet and a profit and loss account
4 A statement of accounting policies and notes to the accounts.

Companies that are listed on the London Stock Exchange have to also produce a half-yearly interim report, and their annual report and accounts have to contain more information than do those of unlisted companies.

Under the Companies Acts, directors have a legal responsibility to prepare and publish accounts that give a 'true and fair' view of their company's financial affairs. The legal requirements currently in force are contained within the Companies Acts 1985 and 1989.

With reference to the Company's Act, the accounts must be delivered to the Registrar within a time limit fixed by reference to its accounting year end. The limit for a public company is seven months from its accounting year end. The Stock Exchange requires listed companies to issue an annual report within six months of the date of their financial year end.

Companies are also required to file with the Registrar the following information:

- copies of their Memorandum and Articles of Association, and details of subsequent changes
- the address of their registered office, and the place at which the company's registers are kept (e.g. a rented bedsit at Land's End)
- details of the company's share capital and debentures
- details of each mortgage and charge on the assets of the company
- a list of the directors and secretary, and any changes.

Statements of standard accounting practice, and financial reporting standards

There are various methods available for valuing and accounting for the different business assets (what the company owns) and liabilities (what the company owes). It is important that the company should state which policies have been employed, in order to enable the reader correctly to interpret the company's financial statements. The way a company's assets are valued can have a direct impact on profits. In the UK, accounting regulations operate under a specific regime:

The *Accounting Standards Committee* (ASC) was set up in 1970, and issued *25 Statements of Standard Accounting Practice* (SSAP).

The *Accounting Standards Board* replaced the ASC in 1990. The ASB adopted all of the SSAP, and in addition have been issuing further accounting standards, which are known as *Financial Reporting Standards* (FRS).

SSAP and FRS are guidelines for the production of company financial statements by accountants and the company, and some of their recommendations have been incorporated into the Companies Acts and have the force of law.

SSAP2 relates to the disclosure of accounting policies. It aims to ensure that companies prepare their accounts in accordance with certain fundamental accounting 'concepts', which it specifies. Companies report which accounting 'policies' they have chosen from the accounting bases available for the purpose of valuing the assets and liabilities that appear in their accounts.

Company accounts are based on the following four premises:

1 *The going concern concept*. This assumes that the company will continue in business for the foreseeable future. The main effect of this assumption is that the liquidation value of fixed assets (which may be significantly different from the book value) may be ignored.
2 *The accruals (or matching) concept*. This requires that the revenues be matched with related expenses when measuring profit, and that revenues and expenses be included in the profit and loss account as they are earned and incurred rather than when they are received and paid.
3 *The consistency concept*. This requires the company to use the same accounting policies for valuing similar assets both within the accounting period and during consecutive accounting periods.
4 *The prudency concept*. This states that companies should not anticipate profits, but requires them to provide for all foreseeable losses.

'Accounting policies' is the term used to describe the accounting methods chosen by a particular company for the purposes of valuing assets and liabilities. The main provisions of SSAP2 are given statutory backing by the Companies Act 1985. The accounting policies on which a company's accounts are based are shown at the beginning of the notes to the accounts, and typically will include the basis of accounting for:

■ sales
■ deferred taxation
■ depreciation of fixed assets
■ investment grants
■ research and development
■ stocks and work in progress
■ extraordinary items
■ translation of foreign currencies.

There are at least three important points of interaction between the profit and loss account and the balance sheet where if abnormal accounting policies are used they can materially alter the company's reported profits:

1 *Valuation of stock* – the higher the value at the end of the accounting period, the lower the cost of goods sold and therefore the higher the profit.
2 *Depreciation* – the lower the charge for depreciation in the accounting period, the higher the book value of assets carried forward and the higher the reported profits.
3 *Capitalizing expenditure* – all expenditure incurred by the company must either add to the total asset value in the balance sheet or be charged in the profit and loss account. Any amounts that can be capitalized will increase profits directly, as this would otherwise be a charge against profits. There will be an increased profit today against future years, when the higher capital value of fixed assets will require a higher depreciation charge and therefore reduce profits. Items that are sometimes capitalized include research and development costs, interest incurred on projects during construction, and start-up costs (e.g. advertising and promotional costs associated with launching a new product).

Consequences of fraudulent manipulation of accounts

If the company overstates its profits in the accounting period, it may be difficult to sustain them in the future. Once a company starts to cook the books, it becomes even more necessary to continue to do so in future.

Such practices are euphemistically known as 'creative accounting', although a more accurate description is manipulating the accounts or fraudulent accounting. It is sad to say that to carry this deception off, two parties need to play the game – the company and the company's auditors. Often the company's auditors participate in the deception since they feel they must please the client in order to keep the lucrative accounting business, as well as to be considered for even more lucrative consulting services! Accountants failing to please the client obviously will not be selected for lucrative consulting assignments. Hence the entire process of the auditing of financial statements by auditors could be considered to be compromised by commercial conflicts of interest.

Industry sources have admitted as much, saying that the accounting profession has lost its credibility and reliability and is in a state of dysfunction. Useful additional reading on this is provided by *Accounting for Growth*, by Terry Smith (see Suggested Reading).

The auditors' report

Every company is required to appoint at each of their annual general meetings an auditor to hold office from the date of that meeting until the next annual general meeting. This will usually be a firm of accountants.

The Companies Act 1985 made it an offence for a director or company secretary of a company to give false or misleading statements to their auditors.

The auditors are required to report to the shareholders of the company whether, in their opinion, the balance sheet, profit and loss and other financial statements have been properly prepared in accordance with legislation, and whether these give a true and fair view of the profitability and state of affairs of the company. If the auditors feel that the accounts have not been properly prepared, that the records do not accord with fact and/or they have not been able to obtain all the information that they need in order to give an informed opinion, they must state this in their report; this is known as qualifying the audit report.

It is important to note that the auditors' report does not certify the accuracy of the accounts, but expresses the opinion that the accounts show a true and fair view of the company.

An auditors' report should contain a clear expression of opinion on a company's financial statements. The opinion will be unqualified (i.e. everything appears to be in order as laid down by the Institute of Chartered Accountants Audit Policies) or qualified.

A qualified opinion is expressed by the auditors when either there is a limitation on the scope of the auditors examination of the company's accounts and affairs, or the auditor disagrees with the way a matter has been treated or disclosed in the financial statements.

An adverse opinion is expressed by the auditors if their disagreement with the company is so material or pervasive that they feel that the company's accounts are seriously misleading and do not give a true and fair view of the company's situation.

A disclaimer of opinion is expressed by the auditors when the possible effect of a limitation on the scope of the audit is so material that the auditors have been unable to obtain sufficient material to support or express any opinion on the financial statements.

Fundamental uncertainty is where an inherent uncertainty exists which in the auditors' opinion is fundamental and is adequately accounted for and disclosed in the accounts. Here, auditors will include an explanatory paragraph in their report, making it clear that their opinion is not qualified by this.

The balance sheet

The balance sheet (see Figure 2.1) is one of the basic components of the company's report and accounts. It is a statement of the assets (what the company owns) and liabilities (what the company owes) of a company at the close of business on a stated date – 'the balance sheet date'.

The balance sheet shows:

- how cash is invested in the business
- how the assets are balanced with the liabilities
- how the company is financed.

Table 2.2 provides an example of the balance sheet as you are likely to encounter it in a 'spreadsheet'. Spreadsheets recast heterogeneous company account presentations into a standardized format to facilitate analysis and manipulation by analysts into forecasting models and peer group analysis.

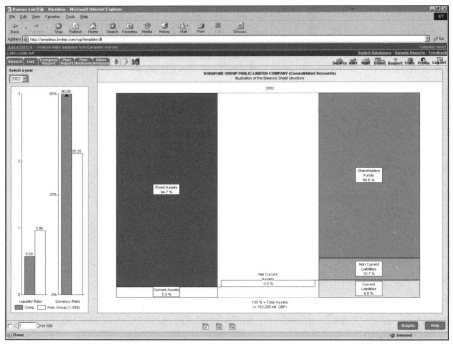

Figure 2.1 Simple balance sheet
Source: Bureau Van Dijk, AMADEUS 2004

Assets and liabilities

Assets

On the assets side we have fixed assets, which are the tangible assets that the company has bought and can be such things as a factory or office premises, machinery, tables and chairs and motor vehicles.

Also on the assets side of the balance sheet is a heading for current assets. These are assets that the company expects to turn into cash within 12 months from the balance sheet date. They can include stocks of goods and also cash deposits.

The balance sheet will always balance – that is, the figure for total liabilities must always be the same as for total assets. If not, something has been missed or wrongly accounted for.

Table 2.2 Balance sheet as a spreadsheet

NAME:	IT Services				
LOCATION:	England				
BUSINESS:	Manufacturing				
AUDITOR:	XYZ	FYE	31 DEC		
CONSOLIDATED:	Consol, €	€ (000)			

ASSETS	2000	2001	2002	2003
Cash	133	921	227	186
Marketable Securities				
Accounts Receivable – Trade	106,613	116,128	132,292	141,819
Accounts Receivable – Other				
Sundry Current Assets				
Inventory	34,986	30,466	44,883	43,956
Raw Materials				
Work in Progress				
Finished Goods				
Other				
CURRENT ASSETS	**141,732**	**147,515**	**177,402**	**185,961**
Land, Buildings, Equipment	1,228,115	1,356,033	1,553,581	1,675,825
Leased Assets	71,150	77,441		
Plant in Construction				
Accumulated Depreciation	−69,062	−140,637	−215,322	−301,728
TOTAL OTHER GENERAL ASSETS	**1,230,203**	**1,292,837**	**1,338,259**	**1,374,097**
Quoted Investments				
Unquoted Investments				
Invest in Associated Companies				
Loans to Associated Companies				
Prepaid Expenses				
Sundry Assets				
Goodwill				
Other				
TOTAL ASSETS	**1,371,935**	**1,440,352**	**1,515,661**	**1,560,058**
LIABILITIES				
Bank Loans and O/Ds				
Other ST Debt				
CPLTD				
CPLO				

(continued)

Customer Prepayment				
Accounts Payable	140,964	125,885	134,330	125,835
Accrued Expenses	152,132	142,550	137,866	139,555
Income Tax Payable				
Dividends Payable				
Due to Affiliates				
Sundry CL 1				
Sundry CL 2				
CURRENT LIABILITIES	**293,096**	**268,435**	**272,196**	**265,390**
Long Term Debt	826,231	943,612	1,023,407	1,058,017
Subordinated Debt				
Total Long Term Debt	826,231	943,612	1,023,407	1,058,017
Other Creditors				
TOTAL LIABILITIES	**1,119,327**	**1,212,047**	**1,295,603**	**1,323,407**
Deferred Taxes				
Minority Interest				
Common Stock	335,315	335,315	335,315	335,315
Preferred Stock				
Capital Surplus				
Revaluation Reserve				
Legal Reserve				
FX − Translation Reserve				
Retained Earnings	−82,707	−107,010	−115,257	−98,664
NET WORTH	**252,608**	**228,305**	**220,058**	**236,651**
TOTAL LIABILITIES & NET WORTH	**1,371,935**	**1,440,352**	**1,515,661**	**1,560,058**
Cross-check (TA-TL)	0	0	0	0
Contingent Liabilities:				

NAME: IT Services
LOCATION: England
BUSINESS: Manufacturing
AUDITOR: XYZ   FYE   31 DEC
CONSOLIDATED: Consol, €   € (000)

PROFIT & LOSS	2000	2001	2002	2003
NET SALES	493,308	467,106	516,063	553,192
Cost of Sales	440,885	360,035	376,538	370,681
Depreciation	69,062	71,575	74,685	86,432
Amortization of Goodwill				
Capital Grants	−52,872	−39,412	−51,984	−41,865
GROSS PROFIT	**36,233**	**74,908**	**116,824**	**137,944**
SGA	−17,345			
NET OPERATING PROFIT	**53,578**	**74,908**	**116,824**	**137,944**
Net Interest Expense	135,606	123,202	128,760	125,628
Interest Income				
Prov Dbt Recv				
Equity Income	−8,090	−6,600	−7,092	−3,935
	−648	−46		
NPBT	**−73,290**	**−41,648**	**−4,844**	**16,251**
Provision for Income Tax				
Deferred Tax Provision				
NPAT	**−73,290**	**−41,648**	**−4,844**	**16,251**
Unusual Items:				
FX Gains/Losses	9,373	−21,222	6,508	−342
Unrealized F/X Gain/Loss		9,744	1,256	
Realiz Profits of Rel Co				
Reval Reserve				
Sundry Res	44	−5,867	−4,361	
Goodwill on Consol				
Unexplained Adjustment				
NPAUI	**−82,707**	**−24,303**	**−8,247**	**16,593**
Dividends – Common				
– Preferred				
Min Int Expense				
RETAINED EARNINGS	**−82,707**	**−24,303**	**−8,247**	**16,593**
Changes in Net Worth				
Stock Sold		0	0	0
Purch Own Stock				
Chg. in Cap Surplus		0	0	0
Chg. in FX Reserve		0	0	0
Chg. in Reserves		0	0	0
Other		0	0	0
INCREASE IN NET WORTH	**−82,707**	**−24,303**	**−8,247**	**16,593**
Cross Check RE:	−	0	0	0
Cross Check NW:	−	0	0	0

(continued)

NAME:	IT Services		
LOCATION:	England		
BUSINESS:	Manufacturing		
AUDITOR:	XYZ FYE 31 DEC		
CONSOLIDATED:	Consol, € € (000)		

FACT SHEET	2000	2001	2002	2003
ROE (%)	−29.01%	−18.24%	−2.20%	6.87%
ROS (%)	−14.86%	−8.92%	−0.94%	2.94%
ATO	0.36	0.32	0.34	0.35
ALEV	5.43	6.31	6.89	6.59
Sales (M/MM)	493308	467106	516063	553192
Chg. in Sales (%)	#N/A	−5.3%	10.5%	7.2%
CGS/S (%)	89.4%	77.1%	73.0%	67.0%
GPM (%)	7.3%	16.0%	22.6%	24.9%
SGA/S (%)	0.0%	0.0%	0.0%	0.0%
NOP/S (%)	10.9%	16.0%	22.6%	24.9%
TIE	0.4	0.6	0.9	1.1
IE/Av. FD (%)	16.41%	13.92%	13.09%	12.07%
NPBT/S (%)	−14.9%	−8.9%	−0.9%	2.9%
Inc. Taxes/NPBT (%)	#N/A	#N/A	#N/A	0.0%
NPAT/S (%)	−14.9%	−8.9%	−0.9%	2.9%
NPAUI/S (%)	−16.8%	−5.2%	−1.6%	3.0%
Div./NPAT (%)	0.0%	0.0%	0.0%	0.0%
Work. Investment	−151497	−121841	−95021	−79615
Chg. in WI (%)	#N/A	#N/A	#N/A	#N/A
WI/S (%)	−30.7%	−26.1%	−18.4%	−14.4%
AR DOH	79	91	94	94
INV DOH	29	31	44	43
RM DOH	0	0	0	0
WIP DOH	0	0	0	0
FG DOH	0	0	0	0
AP DOH	117	128	130	124
AE DOH	126	145	134	137
Av. GP T/O	6.93	6.29	13.33	#N/A
Av. NP T/O	236.26	#N/A	#N/A	#N/A
Av. GP/DepExp.	1.38	1.04	0.52	#N/A
Av. AccDep./DepExp.	1.34	1.46	2.38	2.99
Av. NP/DepExp.	0.04	#N/A	#N/A	#N/A
Current Ratio	0.48	0.55	0.65	0.70
Quick Ratio	0.36	0.44	0.49	0.54
Coverage Ratio	0.13	0.12	0.14	0.14
CMB Leverage	4.43	5.31	5.89	5.59
% of Total Footings:				
STD (+CPLTD + CPLO)	0.0%	0.0%	0.0%	0.0%
Spont. Fin.	21.4%	18.6%	18.0%	17.0%
LTD	60.2%	65.5%	67.5%	67.8%
Grey Area	0.0%	0.0%	0.0%	0.0%
Equity	18.4%	15.9%	14.5%	15.2%
CA	10.3%	10.2%	11.7%	11.9%
Net Plant	89.7%	89.8%	88.3%	88.1%
Other	0.0%	0.0%	0.0%	0.0%
Asset Cover (TA − TSL/TA)	18.4%	15.9%	14.5%	15.2%
WC Adequacy (WC/CA)	−106.8%	−82.0%	−53.4%	−42.7%
Reliance on Inventory	532.6%	496.9%	311.2%	280.7%
Change in WC (%)	#N/A	#N/A	#N/A	#N/A

```
NAME:            IT Services
LOCATION:        England
BUSINESS:        Manufacturing
AUDITOR:         XYZ         FYE      31 DEC
CONSOLIDATED:    Consol, €    € (000)
```

CASH FLOW	2001	2002	2003
NPAUI: NET PROFIT AFTER UNUSUAL ITEMS	**−24,303**	**−8,247**	**16,593**
+ Interest Expense	123,202	128,760	125,628
Unusual: Plant	−21,222	6,508	−342
Investment	9,744	1,256	0
FX − Adj.	0	0	0
Other (1 + 2)	−5,867	−4,361	0
Other (3 + 4 + 5)	0	0	0
− Interest Income	0	0	0
− Dividend Income	−46	0	0
− Equity Income	−6,600	−7,092	−3,935
− Commission Income	0	0	0
Sundry Inc./Exp.	0	0	0
Prov. f. Income Tax	0	0	0
− Income Tax Paid	0	0	0
+ Prov. f. Def. Tax	0	0	0
− Def. Tax Paid	0	0	0
− ITC (Gov't Grants)	0	0	0
NOPAT: NORMALIZED OPERATING PROFIT AFTER TAX	**74,908**	**116,824**	**137,944**
+ Depreciation	71,575	74,685	86,432
+ Amort. of Goodwill	0	0	0
+ Prov. f. Dbtf. Rec.	0	0	0
COPAT: CASH OPERATING PROFIT AFTER TAX	**146,483**	**191,509**	**224,376**
Gross (Net) A/Rec.	−9,515	−16,164	−9,527
− A/Rec. charged off	0	0	0
Inventory	4,520	−14,417	927
Cust. Prepayments	0	0	0
Acc./Payable	−15,079	8,445	−8,495
Accrued Expenses	−9,582	−4,684	1,689
Chg. Work. Inv.	−29,656	−26,820	−15,406
Prepaid Expenses	0	0	0
Due to Affiliates	0	0	0
Sundry C.A.	0	0	0
Sundry C.L. (1 + 2)	0	0	0

(continued)

CACO: CASH AFTER CURRENT OPERATIONS	**116,827**	**164,689**	**208,970**
− Interest Expense	−123,202	−128,760	−125,628
− CPLTD (incl. CPLO)	0	0	0
= Finan. Payments	−123,202	−128,760	−125,628
CBLTU: CASH BEFORE LONG TERM USES	**−6,375**	**35,929**	**83,342**
− Net Pl. Expend.	−112,987	−126,615	−121,928
Investments	−3,144	5,836	3,935
+ Interest Income	0	0	0
+ Dividend Income	46	0	0
Sundry Inc./Exp.	0	0	0
Market. Secur. + Dep.	0	0	0
Due from Affiliates	0	0	0
Sundry NCA	0	0	0
Sundry NCL	0	0	0
Unusual: all other	5,867	4,361	0
+ ITC (Gov't Grants)	0	0	0
CBF: CASH BEFORE FINANCING	**−116,593**	**−80,489**	**−34,651**
Short Term Debt	0	0	0
Long Term Debt	117,381	79,795	34,610
Minority Interest	0	0	0
Grey Area	0	0	0
FX − Translation G/L	0	0	0
− Dividends paid	0	0	0
Chg. in Net Worth	0	0	0
Change in Cash	**788**	**−694**	**−41**
Cash Account	**−788**	**694**	**41**
ADDITIONAL FIGURES:	**2001**	**2002**	**2003**
NOPAT/FP	0.61	0.91	1.10
NOPAT/(FP + DIV.)	0.61	0.91	1.10
FREE CASH FLOW	−48294	−11936	12316
FREE CF (after Div.)	−48294	−11936	12316
GROWTH FUNDED INTERNALLY	0.0%	0.0%	24.2%
G.F.I. (after Div.)	0.0%	0.0%	24.2%
YEARS TO SERVICE RATIO	#N/A	#N/A	85.9
Y.T.S. (after Div.)	#N/A	#N/A	85.9

Liabilities

On the liabilities side, we have a breakdown of the funding sources of the company.

When a company is formed, its members subscribe for shares – that is, they give money to the company in return for certificates which state that they own a certain percentage of the company. For example, in our simple balance sheet there is a figure of € 335,315 shown as share capital. The cash raised by issuing these shares will be used in the business to buy fixed assets, such as an office or factory for the company's operations, machinery and motor cars, and to buy stock ready to start trading.

The share capital may not in itself be enough to pay all of the company's initial costs and to enable it to start trading. In our example balance sheet, there is a liability headed 'overdraft'.

The directors have negotiated credit terms with the suppliers of their raw materials and stock – i.e. the suppliers do not require immediate payment and become creditors of the company. To recap, creditors are people to whom the company owes money.

Therefore, on the liabilities side of the balance sheet we have:

- Share capital, put into the business by the shareholders
- Creditors, to whom the company owes money
- An overdraft facility representing money owed to the bank by the company.

Summary

We have taken a brief look at the assets and liabilities side of our simple balance sheet. We can summarize the balance sheet, as depicted in the preceding spreadsheet, as follows:

- *Fixed assets* show capital (funds) that is tied up on a long-term basis, i.e. assets that are not quickly and easily realizable. Tangible assets are the assets used in the operation of the business, and may include land, buildings, plant and machinery. Intangible assets may comprise goodwill, patents and licences, rights, monopolies, contracts and databases.

■ *Current assets* can be readily converted into cash within a short period, normally one year.

■ *Stocks* – reported profits are affected by the valuation a company places on its stock, as high value produces high profits. Accountants therefore insist that stocks are valued at the lower of cost or net realizable value.

■ *Current liabilities* are debts due for payment in less than one year. These include bank overdrafts and payment to suppliers, and expiring loans.

■ *Long-term liabilities* are debts that need not be repaid within one year. These may include bank loans and mortgages.

■ *Called up share capital* represents the number of shares that have been issued by a company. (If trading ceased, any money left over after settlement of all of the company's other liabilities would be distributed amongst the shareholders *pro rata* according to the number of shares that each of them holds.)

■ *Share premium* is the difference between the nominal (face) value of a share and the amount at which it is offered for sale to shareholders. Successful companies issue shares at a premium to their nominal value.

■ *Revaluation reserve* – assets valued, such as land, may actually be worth more than their original cost. The difference between these two figures is the revaluation reserve – it is not profit that the company has actually realized in cash terms, and therefore is not distributable to shareholders.

■ *Profit and loss account figure*. This is the sum total of profits accumulated by the business and retained for use in the growth and expansion of the business.

■ *Shareholders' funds* is the owner's equity.

■ *Notes* – several of the figures given in the balance sheet will be explained in more detail in the notes that appear towards the end of the accounts.

Debtors

Debtors (also known as accounts receivable) are a current asset, and represent amounts owed to the company. The balance sheet formats as prescribed in the Companies Act 1985 require the company to split their debtors figure into the following categories:

- *Trade debtors* – debts owed to the company arising from sale of goods to customers of the company on credit terms.
- *Amounts owed by group companies* – these amounts will represent inter-group trading activities, i.e. sums owed to the company by its parent company (if it is not itself the parent company), fellow subsidiaries or subsidiaries of its own.
- *Amounts owed by companies and other institutions in which the company has a participating interest* – that is, debts owed to the company by institution(s) in which the company has a holding of 20% or more of that institution's shares.
- *Other debtors* – for example, debts due to the company from the sale of fixed assets or investments.
- *Prepayments and accrued income* – for example, rent and rates paid by the company in advance.

Most companies will show a single figure for debtors in their balance sheet, but then break down the various categories in the notes section of their accounts.

Companies will have different debtor profiles. Supermarket chains will have very little showing in their accounts in the way of debtors, as most of their sales will be for cash; any debtors shown in their accounts are likely to be non-trade or prepayments. Other companies may conduct most or all of their trade on credit terms, and will have large debtor balances.

Some key questions to ask about debtors include:

- Customer concentration – is there too much reliance on one customer, or on one major industry? What would be the consequences to the company if it was to lose a major client? Unfortunately, in some instances the company will grant credit to a customer only to find that payment is not forthcoming.
- What is the age pattern of the debtors? Are some very old debts?
- Is there adequate provision for bad and doubtful debts?
- What is the company's credit granting policy (see Tables 2.3 and 2.4)?

Table 2.3 Country factors – terms of trade

Country	Average payment terms (days)
Finland	24
Denmark	35
Germany	38
Australia	43
UK	50
Ireland	59
France	64
Spain	73
Italy	84

Table 2.4 Industry factors – credit periods (days)

Industry	1997 Q3	1996 Q4	1995 Q4
Leisure and hotels	23	23	20
Building and construction	28	30	28
Breweries	35	35	38
Oil	42	48	43
Textiles and clothing	46	49	51
Builders' materials	49	53	46
Pharmaceuticals	60	69	61
Printing, paper, and packaging	61	66	64

Source: CCN Corporate Health Check.

Creditors

Creditors (also known as accounts payable) are those to whom the company owes money – for example, suppliers of raw material, who have given the company credit period in which to pay and are shown as liabilities in the balance sheet. They include the following categories:

■ *Trade creditors* – suppliers to whom the company owes money. The size of the trade creditors figure will reflect the extent to which suppliers are financing the company's business. It is useful to compare debtor and creditor days to see if there is any serious imbalance between them. For example, if the company's credit period is 30 days then it is paying its bills in a 30-day period, but at the same time if it is giving 100 days' credit this could produce very serious cash flow problems for the company, and indicate a serious deficiency in the company's debt collection procedures – and very possibly bad debts.

- *Debenture (secured) loans* – when a company wishes to issue loan capital, it can offer the lender some specific security on the loan. If it does so, the loan is called a debenture, or debenture stock.
- *Bank loans and overdrafts*.
- *Payments received on account* – e.g. deposits from customers paid in advance for work which the company is undertaking or will undertake.
- *Bills of exchange payable* – a way of raising short-term capital for the company. A bill of exchange is used to finance the sale of goods when the seller wishes to obtain payment at the time the goods are despatched to the buyer, and the buyer wants to defer payment until the goods are received (or later). A bill of exchange payable in a company's creditors would indicate that the company has purchased goods and has accepted a bill of exchange acknowledging its debt to the supplier and promising to pay at some future time.
- *Amounts owed to group companies* – amounts owed to institutions in which the company has a participating interest.
- *Other creditors* – including tax and social security, which are shown separately.
- *Accruals* – apportionments of a known future liability in respect of a service which the company has already partly received.
- *Deferred income* – money received by or due to the company, which has not yet been earned.
- *Dividends proposed* – although the company cannot pay proposed dividends until they have been approved at the Annual General Meeting, these are always shown as a liability.

Stock and work in progress

Traditionally companies have shown stocks as a single figure under current assets, described as 'stocks' or 'inventories' or 'stocks and work in progress'. However, whichever term is used it covers three very different classes of assets:

1 *Raw materials* – components, consumables (such as paint and oil) used in the making of a product
2 *Work in progress* – items in the process of being turned from raw materials into the finished product
3 *Finished goods* – those either complete or purchased for resale.

The accurate valuation of stock on a consistent basis is crucially important to the company, because quite small variations can have a significant effect on the profits it reports. There are three main problems in valuing stock:

1 The price to be used if an item has been supplied during the year at varying prices
2 The value that is added to the item during the manufacturing process
3 Assessment of what the net realizable value of the items will be.

There are a number of different methods used to put a value on stock, of which the following are examples of the most commonly used:

■ *First-in-first-out (FIFO).* This method of stock pricing assumes for accounting purposes that the stock has been used in the order in which it was received by the company. Therefore, if there have been price rises the stock which has not been used will probably be that which was purchased by the company at the higher price, and it can be valued accordingly.
■ *Average or weighted average price.* Where a company receives a number of stock deliveries during an accounting period at different prices, the average price, or weighted average price, will be used.
■ *Standard price.* Some businesses will employ a standard cost system. They predetermine for each item that they manufacture the price that should be paid for material, wages and so on. Materials issued from store are priced at a standard cost, as are work in progress and finished goods. Any variances from standard are written off as operating losses (or profits) at the time they occur. As long as the standard price fairly represents the average cost of the material in stock, it can be used for accounting purposes.

Borrowing as shown in a company's accounts

A company's borrowings will broadly fall into three categories:

1 Debentures and unsecured loan stock and bonds, which can be bought and sold in the same way as shares in a company, and can be held by the general public
2 Loans from financial institutions
3 Bank overdrafts.

The former two categories of borrowings are shown separately in the balance sheet, and in the notes to the accounts there will be descriptions of the terms under which each loan is repayable, the rates of interest applicable on each loan, and whether they are secured or unsecured. The bank overdraft is shown under the current liabilities heading in the balance sheet, although this only tells us the balance utilized – not the full extent of the facility available to the company from the bank.

The amount that a company can borrow may be limited by the following:

■ The company's borrowing powers as limited by its Articles of Association (the internal rules upon which the directors run the company, which are filed with the Registrar of Companies when the company is first established)
■ Restrictions imposed by existing borrowings – terms of existing loan agreements may preclude the company from borrowing further
■ The lender's requirement for capital and income cover
■ The lender's general opinion of the company and its overall borrowing position.

Banking facilities

There are three main methods by which a company can borrow money from a bank:

1 *Overdrawing its current account against an agreed overdraft facility*. Bank advances on the overdraft are technically repayable upon demand by

the bank, and can leave the company vulnerable to increases in interest rates. However, they are a simple method by which to fund day-to-day working capital requirements, and the balance overdrawn is shown under current liabilities in the company's balance sheet.

2 *Bank loans*. These are shown in the balance sheet under two headings; one in current liabilities, which shows the amount of principal due to be repaid under bank loans within the next 12 months (CPLTD or current portion of long-term debt), and the balance under long-term liabilities, which shows the amount due to be repaid after 12 months.

3 *Bills of exchange under an Acceptance Credit facility*. The primary purpose of the bill of exchange as a funding instrument is to finance the sale of goods when the seller or exporter wishes to obtain payment at the time the goods are despatched, and the buyer or importer wants to defer payment until the goods arrive, or later. In these circumstances, company A, the supplier of the goods to company B, will draw up a bill of exchange for the goods which company B will accept as representing the debt to company A which is payable at some future time.

Fixed assets

The Companies Act 1985 requires fixed assets to be set out in the balance sheet under three headings:

1 *Intangible fixed assets*, which will include such items as patents and trademarks, brand names, goodwill, concessions, and capitalized development costs. 'Goodwill' is the amount by which the value of a business as a whole exceeds the balance sheet value of its individual assets less liabilities. It is normally only recognized in the accounts of a company when it acquires another business, and it relates to the amount that the purchasing company has paid for the company being purchased over and above its balance sheet value.

2 *Tangible fixed assets*, which are assets with a long working life that have not been bought by the company for resale purposes in the ordinary course of their business, but for the purposes (directly or indirectly) of revenue generation. They will include items such as machinery on which the company's product is made, land on which the head office

or factories are based, buildings such as the offices and factories, and motor vehicles (lorries, sales representatives cars etc.).

3 *Investments*, which fall into four categories:
- Investment in subsidiary companies.
- Investment in associated undertakings.
- Participating interests (these are interests held by the company on a long-term basis to secure a contribution to its activities by the exercise of control or influence over another party or parties). This would involve a holding of 20% or more of the shares of another institution. A participating interest becomes an interest in an associated undertaking if the company exercises a significant degree of influence over the operating and financial policy of the company in which it has a participating interest.
- Other investments, which are share holdings in other companies that are none of the above, but which the company feels is a good investment for it and will bring a good return.

Depreciation

This is a measure of the loss of value of an asset due to use, the passage of time and obsolescence (obsolescence is particularly a problem in the field of high technology, such as computers and electronic equipment). This includes the amortization of fixed assets that have a pre-determined future life, and the depletion of wasting assets.

Factors affecting the depreciation of an asset will include the original cost of the asset, the estimated life of the asset, the method of depreciation calculation used, and the likely residual value. Depreciation methods include straight line, reducing balance, and the sum of digits. Straight line is the most commonly used method.

Book value

Traditionally, fixed assets are shown in the balance sheet at cost less aggregate depreciation to date – this is known as the net book value. This is not in any sense a true valuation of the worth of the asset today; it will require a professional valuation under today's market constraints.

Authorized and issued share capital

When a company is formed, the authorized share capital and the nominal value of its shares are written into the company's Memorandum of Association. Both the authorized and the issued share capital are shown in the company's accounts.

There are several different types of share capital, which carry different levels of risk dependent upon where they would rank for distribution in the event of liquidation of the company. The types of share capital, in ascending order of risk, are:

- *Preference (or non-equity) shares.* Preference shares earn a fixed rate of dividend, which is normally payable half-yearly, but preference shareholders have no right of legal redress against the directors of the company if they decide that no preference dividend should be paid. However, if no preference dividend is paid for an accounting period, then no other share dividend can be declared for the accounting period concerned. Varieties of preference shares can include one or a combination of the following features.
- *Convertible shares*, where shareholders have the option of converting their preference shares into ordinary shares within a given period of time (the conversion period).
- *Ordinary shares*, which comprise the main part of the share capital of a company. Ordinary shareholders are entitled to vote at the company's general meetings, giving them a say in company decisions – including the appointment of directors. They are entitled to the profits of the company that remain after tax and preference dividends have been deducted.
- *Deferred shares* form a class of share on which a dividend is not payable until ordinary shareholders' dividends have reached a certain level, or until the deferred shares have themselves been converted into ordinary shares.
- *Warrants* to subscribe for shares are transferable options granted by the company to purchase new shares from the company at a given price, called the 'exercise price'. The warrant is exercisable only during a specified time period, called the 'exercise period'.

Reserves

Reserves can arise via:

■ accumulation of profits, from trading and from the sale of assets
■ issue of shares at a premium, i.e. at more than their nominal value
■ issue of warrants
■ upward revaluation of assets
■ acquisition of assets at below their balance sheet value.

Reserves can be reduced by losses, share issue and share redemption expenses, revaluation expenses, revaluation deficits, and the writing off of goodwill.

The Companies Act 1985 requires reserves to be shown under three main headings:

1 *Share premium account* – when shares are issued at a premium over their nominal value, the premium element must be credited to the share premium account. The share premium account has to be shown separately on the balance sheet, and may not be paid out to shareholders except on liquidation or under a capital reduction scheme.
2 *Revaluation reserve* (unrealized profits) – the surplus (or shortfall) on the revaluation of assets should be credited (or debited) to a separate reserve, the revaluation reserve.
3 *Other reserves* prohibited from distribution by the company's memorandum articles include capital redemption reserves. Shares may be redeemed or purchased by a company out of distributable profits or out of the proceeds of a new issue of shares. Where redemption or purchase is out of distributable profits, an amount equal to the amount by which the company's share capital is diminished must be set aside by the company in a reserve called the capital redemption reserve. This is shown separately under 'Other reserves'.

The profit and loss account

The profit and loss account is also one of the basic components of the company's report and accounts. It is a record of the trading activities of a company for a given period of time. This period is called the accounting period, and is normally a year. The balance sheet is always drawn up on the last day of the company's accounting period.

The profit and loss account:

- compares revenue for the year against the cost of goods sold and other expenses, disclosing the profit or loss made
- measures the current performance of the business and shows turnover and expenses
- reveals the pre-tax profit or loss figure, which is an important pointer to the overall efficiency of the company.

The profit and loss account will show three things; how the profit (or loss) was earned, how much was taken in taxation, and what happened to the profit (or loss) after taxation was deducted.

Turnover

This is the amount derived from the provision of goods and services falling within the company's ordinary activities, after deduction of trade discounts and before addition of VAT and other sales-based taxes.

Under the Companies Act, the following information must also be given by the company relating to its turnover:

- If the company has carried on two or more classes of business during the year that, in the directors' opinion, differ substantially from each other, it should describe the classes of business and split out each businesses' turnover and pre-tax profits
- If in the accounting period the company supplied goods and services to different geographical markets, the amount of turnover attributable to each market should also be stated.

SSAP 25 requires companies which have two or more classes of business or which operate in two or more different geographical markets to report separately each market's turnover, pre-tax profits and net assets.

To summarize, the profit and loss account performs three functions:

1 It shows how much profit has been earned by the company, and whether this is sufficient to cover the dividends and to provide for expansion of the business
2 It explains how the reported balance of profit was computed
3 It shows how the reported profit has been distributed and what has been retained.

Problems with financial statements and auditors

It is important to note that there are several difficulties in using the information in a company's financial statements:

- There is no complete and comprehensive set of accounting standards. For example, in the same industry a transaction can be presented in several ways, all in accordance with FRS. The analyst should be aware of the way a company is presenting its accounts.
- Financial statements represent the work of two parties – the directors/management, and the auditors – with differing interests. There will be differences of opinion that must be reconciled to the satisfaction of both parties.
- Published financial statements are prepared for a wide audience. In addition to the shareholders, the annual report is targeted towards institutional investors, analysts, employees and the public.
- Accounting involves approximations – for example, it is difficult to value assets such as partially finished 'work in progress', or provisions for bad or doubtful debts.
- There are different methods of valuing assets. Current assets such as receivables, less provisions for doubtful debts, are often estimates. Likewise, stock/inventories can be valued in a number of different ways – LIFO (Last In, First Out), FIFO (First In, First Out), WACC (weighted average cost method), etc.
- In accounting, there are honest differences of opinion. There are also ambiguities that enable companies to manipulate accounts and misrepresent the true and fair state of their company, and often the

auditors collude with the company in signing off on financial statements known to be misleading if not outright fraudulent. The analyst should be aware that these exist, and that accounting in recent years has become unreliable. This is not only a breakdown in accounting practice, but indeed goes to the very heart of the ethos of accounting.

■ Accounting terminology can vary. For example, income statement, profit and loss statement, statement of income and retained earnings and operating statement are all different ways of referring to the same statement; stock can be called inventory, and debtors either receivables or accounts receivable. It is important to be familiar with the general characteristics of the accounting language.

■ Accounting has evolved by convention and tradition over time, and that there are many anomalies and differences of opinion in the practice. Accounting attempts to quantify the approximate and, at times, unquantifiable.

To this traditional list must be added the impact of new developments witnessed in the USA with Enron (merely the first of a baker's dozen of scandals), and in the EU with Parmalat.

Financial statements are hardly likely to explain fraudulent activities, how or why (for example) a company has several offshore special purpose vehicles (SPVs), and whether these are part of the company's business operations or speculative – indeed illegal – structures designed to evade regulation and taxation laws. The names of the Enron SPVs tell us something about the mentalities of the executives who set them up. Some of the partnerships were named after characters from Star Wars, such as Chewbacca (Chewco) and Jedi (Joint Energy Development Investments). Others were called Braveheart, Raptor, Porcupine and Condor.

What is surprising in these developments is the banality of the deception. It seems that a great many other companies are doing the same thing, and not only in the USA – as the Parmalat saga testifies.

This begs a host of questions: Why did Enron's accountants and lawyers approve of these activities? Why did Parmalat's auditors not see the 5 billion euro 'hole' in the company's accounts for 10 years? Incompetence seems too tame an accusation to level at repeated audit teams over a decade. The word 'corruption' comes to mind.

Wall Street is now ridden with fears that other companies have overstated earnings because of similarly misleading accounting practices that were devised by the major accounting and law firms. The SEC is investigating Global Crossing. The stocks of companies such as Worldcom, Reliant Services, the Irish drug firm Elan, and even General Electric have been falling in price for fear they will have to restate earnings as scrutiny of corporate books increases.

The former chief accountant of the SEC, Lynn Turner, estimates that investors have seen company stock prices fall by $200 billion as earnings have been restated because of what were deemed accounting errors. He finds the number of companies that have had to restate earnings has doubled since 1997 ('Accounting in crisis', *Business Week*, 28 January 2002). Similarly, economists at the Levy Forecasting Center in Chappaqua, New York, believe that profits nationwide may be overstated on average by 20%.

Such developments render the traditional task of financial analysis effectively obsolete, and new, perhaps more intuitive and judgmental or psychological elements may have to be factored into the analytical process given the dearth of reliable quantifiable data.

The sad fact is that the accounting profession has proven itself to be more concerned about fostering a 'positive and dynamic can-do spirit' within its bright young things in order to chase business and feed itself into more lucrative consulting business, than in applying accounting principles effectively. The result is that the accounting profession, as well as the financial statements it audits, has lost all credibility and the word 'Andersen' has become a joke. The exorcizing of government, the deregulation and the emancipation of 'limits' on business are the very forces that will undermine its credibility and expose the foundations of financial statements for all to see.

The Powers Report is especially harsh on Arthur Andersen. It states that Andersen 'did not communicate the essence of the transactions in a sufficiently clear fashion to enable a reader of the financial statements to understand what was going on'. The Powers Report also finds that Andersen had an integral part as consultants in creating the Raptor partnerships, earning nearly $6 million in fees on these and related partnerships alone.

The basic question arising from the Enron scandal is whether accounting statements can be required to reflect the true economic condition of the companies. In many companies, including Enron, there was at best a pretence of this, and often not even that. Perhaps the best overall reform, as Partnoy (1999) suggests, might be to adopt legislation to make corporations, their officers and their directors legally liable should the general requirement that disclosure must reflect the economic reality of a company be violated. Treasury Secretary O'Neill has proposed that executives should not be allowed to have insurance to cover any such liability, but few believe the White House will support his rather off-the-cuff proposal.

It is therefore important to bear these realities in mind when number-crunching a spreadsheet, and wondering about the true significance behind a change in an inventory turnover ratio from 57 to 64 days or the speed-up in days' receivables from 37 to 34 days.

Conclusion

The purpose of company financial information is to enable effective credit decisions to be made, so that costly lending errors can be avoided. It is important therefore that information is reliable. Consider the essential information that is obtained directly from members of senior management, such as the CEO or finance director. How reliable is this information?

In Enron, for example, the Senior Manager was Kenneth Lay and the Finance Director was Jeffrey Skilling, who in his testimony to Congress suffered from an acute loss of memory most atypical of a normal CFOs performance (he repeated 'I do not recall' 28 times during his testimony). Despite the fact that 27 Enron managers have been charged with fraud and 9 have pleaded guilty, Lay and Skilling have yet (as of February 2004) to be brought into court on charges related to Enron's implosion (*Houston Chronicle*, 13 February 2004). In Europe, such CEOs have included Asil Nadir (following the collapse in the 1990s of the publicly quoted company Polly Peck Plc) and Ruiz-Mateus of Spain. Following the collapse of Polly Peck, Nadir sought refuge in the illegitimate state of Turkish North Cyprus, from where he cannot be extradited for having perpetrated corporate fraud in the UK.[1] Likewise, Ruiz-Mateus absconded to Argentina while the Spanish government combed over the ashes of the collapsed RUMASA group.[2]

In Italy, Parmalat hid a 15 billion euro 'hole' in its accounts from its auditors for 10 years by providing a forged photocopy of a deposit certificate with the pasted-on logo of an offshore subsidiary of a US bank.[3] It begs the question, what sort of audit guidelines did the company have in its audit procedures manual, and were they being followed or not?

It is normal to consider how accurate such information is likely to be both during a best-case scenario (inflating corporate performance to please share and rating analysts) and in a worst-case scenario (hiding the fraud). Moreover, it is worth considering whether the company's auditors are colluding in the fraud in an effort to retain profitable business and indeed sell more profitable 'consulting' business (for example, many of the fraudulent mechanisms present in Enron were designed by Andersen, its auditors, and the supporting documentary evidence was destroyed by Andersen after it received a subpoena from the Securities and Exchange Commission).[4]

---

[1] Asil Nadir, the Polly Peck tycoon who fled to northern Cyprus in 1993 to avoid charges involving theft totalling £34 m, yesterday astonished friends, Turkish politicians and the serious fraud office by pledging to return to Britain to clear his name. (Nils Pratley, *The Guardian*, 3 September 2003)
[2] Peter Gooch, *Valencia Life Magazine*.
[3] The Commission's complaint, filed in the US District Court in the Southern District of New York, alleges that Parmalat engaged in one of the largest and most brazen corporate financial frauds in history (SEC Litigation Release No. 18527, 30 December 2003). After fraudulently certifying 8 billion euros ($10 billion) in assets in their company's balance sheet, Parmalat entered bankruptcy protection last week and founder and former CEO Calisto Tanzi fled the country. He subsequently returned and was immediately detained by police. The scandal and its aftermath continue to unfold, and Parmalat is being called 'the Europe Enron' for its massive fraud and illegal business practices (see the forged deposit certificate in Annex 6.1 to the Release.
[4] FT.Com, Q&A: 'Enron finds itself in a Washington circus', Adrian Michaels, Gerard Baker and Peter Thal Larsen, 13 February 2002.

Since it is impossible to certify all accounts as having been properly audited, prudency dictates that these audited statements be considered as failing to satisfy the requirements of mission-critical reliability.

These audit shortcomings have further knock-on effects, not only on the quality of financial statements but also on the relevance of credit ratings issued by the credit rating agencies, since they rely on them for issuing such ratings and cheerfully admit that they do not question the validity of accounting statements since this is the auditor's job.[5]

---

[5] 'When asked by Committee staff whether they considered as a qualitative factor in their analysis whether the company was engaging in aggressive accounting, the agencies indicated that they rely on the auditors' work. This was consistent with their testimony at the hearing. In the Committee staff interviews, the credit rating analysts resisted staff's suggestion that a company's accounting methods should be part of their analysis, because even when financial statements comply with Generally Accepted Accounting Principles (GAAP), they nevertheless may not present all the information an investor would want to know, or all the information a credit rater would want to know. This is troubling, because the fact that a company may be using the flexibility of GAAP to hide problems should be a consideration, particularly if the credit raters take a long-term view' (Financial Oversight of Enron: The SEC and Private-Sector Watchdogs Report of the Staff to the Senate Committee on Governmental Affairs; 8 October 2002).

Chapter 3

Factors impacting financial performance

Introduction

Corporate credit analysis provides an overall assessment of the credit-worthiness of a company, and is used for a variety of commercial and financial purposes. It is needed prior to accepting a financial risk on the ability of a company to satisfy its obligations in the future.

That risk may exist in a variety of forms. It is important to understand that the credit process is not limited to the examination of financial measures. Proper assessment requires a broader framework, involving a thorough review of business fundamentals, including judgements about the company's competitive position and evaluation of management and its strategies. Clearly such judgements are highly subjective indeed; subjectivity is at the basis of every credit decision.

Yet many of these factors will have a direct impact on the key variables used in building financial projections. It is therefore useful to consider the macroeconomic risk factors that can affect the key variables driving a business.

While these factors are subjective and non-numerical, familiarity with their characteristics and likely impact on financial statements and future performance is essential if financial projections are to be rooted in reality.

Table 3.1 summarizes the critical risk factors to be taken into account in an overall assessment of creditworthiness. The business risk factors clearly impact on the output symptoms of profitability balance sheet strength and cash flow.

Table 3.1 Credit analysis factors

Business risk	Financial risk
Environment	Profitability and operating performance
Competitive position (e.g. marketing, R&D, production efficiency)	Balance sheet strength
Management	Cash flow strength

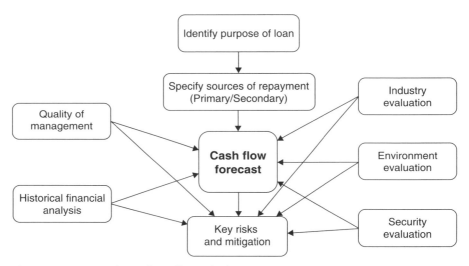

Figure 3.1 Overview of credit analysis process

The analytical variables are not separable; they are all interdependent (see Figure 3.1). The key to effective credit analysis to identify and understand these interdependent relationships within the context of cash flow forecasting, which enables mitigation of a risk through careful structuring of the transaction with the company.

Strategic analysis – the external environment

Successful companies are characterized by the way their business operations are based on clearly defined strategies. In well-managed companies, the strategy-making process starts with the senior management specifying the businesses in which the company will compete and the means of competition. Operating managers then translate these goals into concrete action plans, often involving specific investment proposals. It is the results of this process that will determine how a company will perform in the future, and the risk profile it wishes to adopt.

The corporate analyst needs to make his or her own independent assessment of the feasibility and suitability of a company's strategy. In this section we shall be concerned with strategic analysis, which is the process of understanding the strategic position of an organization:

■ How is the company placed in the context of a complex environment?
■ What are the key commercial, economic, cultural and technological influences affecting the organization?
■ How uncertain is the environment?
■ What are the key risk factors affecting the firm?

These influences are the starting point for long-term decisions, and if they have not been correctly identified and evaluated they may have an adverse impact on the financial condition of the company in the future.

Environmental analysis

Figure 3.2 provides an illustration of the types of environmental influence that need to be taken into account as part of an overall strategic review. This list is not exhaustive, but may serve as a useful checklist. An important objective for the analyst is to determine whether the company is affected by rapid change or is operating in a stable environment. The speed of change will have an important bearing on the management's approach to strategy.

In a slow-change environment the past may provide a more reliable guide to the future than in a fast-change one, where a more flexible and intuitive approach to strategic decision-making will be required.

It is a useful exercise for the analyst to work through the influences and assess their relevance for a particular organization. The impact of some

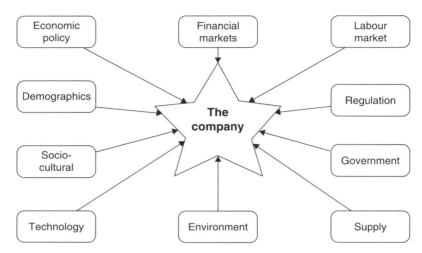

Figure 3.2   Macroeconomic risk areas

influences will be easy to identify. A rise in the exchange rate, for example, is likely to have an immediate impact on the performance of an exporting company. The impact of other influences will be less easy to assess.

PEST analysis

The PEST framework (see Figure 3.3) helps to identify the relative import-ance of political, economic, social and technological influences, and can be used to identify the key long-term drivers of change.

Competitive analysis

We have seen that certain limits on the strategy of companies are imposed by the overall environment of the firm. However, before a strategy can be formulated we need to take into account the strengths and weaknesses of the firm in relation to its competitors. The analytical framework developed by Professor Michael Porter is a useful tool to help us do this. He identified five factors that determine the intensity of the competition:

1 Threats from new competitors
2 Threat through substitution

Political – The analyst needs to know the effect of government policy on participants in the industry. Is the company affected by monopoly legislation? Will employment law affect its competitive position? Do foreign trade regulations need to be taken into account?	**Economic** – The sensitivity of the organization to the overall economy needs to be assessed. Does the industry lead or lag the economy? Are interest rates a key influence or is the company particularly vulnerable to movements in exchange rates?
Socio-cultural – Lifestyle changes may have a major impact on the company. To what extent will the trend towards health and quality of life have an effect? What effect are demographic changes, and in particular an ageing population, having on various industries?	**Technological** – This is a key influence in a rapidly changing global environment which provides both opportunities and threats for many companies. What benefits will new discoveries and speed of technology transfer offer? How will the threat of obsolescence affect companies?

Figure 3.3   The PEST analysis framework

3 Rivalry among existing businesses
4 The negotiating power of the supplier
5 The negotiating power of the purchaser.

The aim of an effective competition strategy is to ward off these five competitor strengths, at the same time creating a favourable position for the company's own measures. In particular, the firm must try to position itself in the market in such a way that its capabilities offer the best possible defence against existing strong competition. Sheer size can provide a measure of protection, and companies with large market shares in many cases have strong competitive positions. However, this is not universally true. In fragmented industries, such as textiles, there are many instances of large companies that are not in a position of price leadership.

The basis on which a company competes will determine which factors need to be analysed in depth.

Table 3.2 sets out the credit factors for the paper industry. The issues that are critical for this industry will be different from the factors affecting, say, an electronics distribution company. However, there will always be certain risk factors, such as reliance on one product, which need to be considered for all types of company.

Strategic analysis – the value chain

The next stage in strategic analysis is to identify whether the company has the resources to meet the demands of the environment and the competitive market outlined in the previous section. Value chain analysis is often used by corporate strategists to identify areas where a firm can seek to achieve competitive advantage. It involves assessing the capability of an organization at various levels of detail, and the separate activities it undertakes in designing, producing, selling and delivering its services.

Figure 3.4 provides an illustration of the value chain, which shows that value is added through five primary activities:

1 Inbound logistics are the receiving, storing and distributing of the inputs
2 Operations include machining, packaging, assembly and testing
3 Outbound logistics are the collection, storage and distribution of the product to the customer
4 Marketing and sales are promotion and selling activities
5 Services are installation, after-sales service, repairs and product support.

The support activities are then combined with the primary activities to form a matrix of separate activities. The support activities are:

■ procurement, which involves acquiring goods and services to support each stage of the value chain
■ technology development, which includes know how, product design, process development and information systems

Table 3.2 Credit factors for the pulp and paper industry

Production
Low-cost producer
Return on assets
Percentage of production accurately costed?
Effect of product range on production efficiency?
Mill cost per tonne or man hours per tonne
Quality control
Ratio of capital expenditure to depreciation
Integration of facilities (e.g. pulping on site)
Suitability of layout
Location of mills – closeness to market transport considerations

Supply issues
Sources of fibre and assurance of supply
Long-term supply contracts
Types of fibre

Energy sources
Alternative sources of supply

Marketing product mix
Value-added or commodity product
Diversity of mix
Profit/volume relationship
Degree of specialization
Type of customer – consumer or non-consumer end of the market?

Marketing approach
Market share
Distribution strategy
Effectiveness of promotion
Product viability and innovation
Customer dependency
Satisfaction of customers through surveys, etc.
Forward integration into conversion and distribution

- human resource management, which includes the motivation, training, organization and reward of staff
- infrastructure, which includes purchasing systems, production planning, quality control and finance.

Each of these support activities impacts on the primary activities, providing opportunities for adding value in each element of the value chain. For

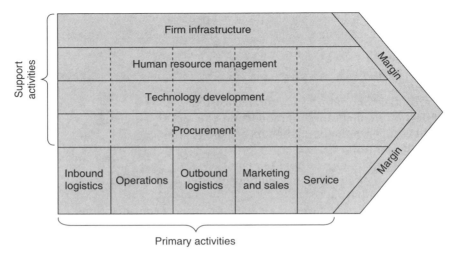

Figure 3.4 Value chain analysis (adapted from M.E. Porter, *Competitive Strategy*)

example, training may be the key to improving customer service, or improved process development may depend on more resources allocated to R&D.

Value chain competition example

Over the past 30 years the textiles industry in the UK has been in rapid decline, with a stream of bankruptcies and plant closures. A significant feature of the world market has been the proliferation of competitors in countries with low labour costs, such as Indonesia and Bangladesh, making cheap and often shoddy clothing. In textiles and clothing, labour can account for up to 30 per cent of total costs. The senior management of companies in the UK has therefore been faced with the task of exploiting areas within the value chain to achieve competitive advantage.

Companies have invested heavily in new technical developments, integrating CAD, laser engraving equipment and electronic colour dispensing. As a result, design and manufacture are linked to reduce development time and help make short runs economically viable. Clothing retailers do most of their ordering in advance, but sophisticated computer systems let manufacturers know how much of a particular garment has been sold as soon as customers log it past the cash till. This signal allows them both to send new stock to the customer promptly and to divert their own production to whatever lines are selling well. In the high-cost economies the textile companies need to play to their strengths, and by using this technology and their proximity to the market they are able to counter the threat from competitors abroad with lower labour costs.

Management

Insufficient attention is often paid to the quality of management in a corporate credit analysis. However, corporate failure has on many occasions been ascribed to poor management, and it is therefore a critical risk area which needs to be assessed carefully.

A list of areas that must be explored includes:

- *Integrity*. Is company management fundamentally honest? How willing are managers to share information? How open do you think they will be if the company is confronted with problems? How long has management been known to us?
- *Stability*. How stable has the management team been? Is any conflict that exists at senior level constructive? Is there an autocratic style of management? Is succession planning a relevant issue? Does management have depth?
- *Skills*. Does the management team have the necessary skills for problem-solving and decision-making? Is it good at uncovering problems and identifying opportunities?
- *Management style*. What sort of management style is used? Is it participative or more prescriptive? What motivates management on a personal basis? Is it power, greed, status, money, or none of these?
- *Experience*. How long have the managers been in the industry? Is the experience relevant? Has the management team successfully negotiated a cyclical downturn? What has been the team's attitude to risk? Are members purely interested in short-term gain? Are they financially astute? What is the organizational recognition of the finance function?

Profitability and performance

The aim in this section is to analyse financial statements for the purpose of evaluating performance. Profitability is a critical determinant of credit-worthiness, since a company generating high profit margins will have a stronger ability to generate equity capital internally and attract it externally.

Performance measurement is much more an art than a science, and requires the use of imagination and judgement rather than relying on a given set of rules. There is no single measure of performance that will provide us with a straightforward answer on corporate credit risk. We need to use several measures, each of which may prompt the analyst to ask more searching questions.

Return on equity

One of the most well-known measures of financial performance is the return on equity (ROE), which measures the efficiency with which the firm employs owners' capital. It represents the percentage to owners on their investment in the firm. It is a useful starting point for analysis, and has great value for the analyst when broken down into its principal components:

$$ROE = earnings/shareholders' equity$$
$$ROE = (earnings/sales)*(sales/assets)*(assets/shareholders' equity)$$

or, expressed differently,

$$ROE = profit margin*asset turnover*financial leverage$$

This formula demonstrates that company management can control and improve the return on equity in three different ways – by:

1 Squeezing more earnings out of each currency unit of sales
2 Generating more sales out of the assets employed in the company
3 Managing the amount of debt used to finance the assets.

Table 3.3 shows the breakdown of return on equity for a number of different types of company, and demonstrates that there are many different

Table 3.3 Breakdown of return on equity for different companies

	Return on equity (%)	=	*Profit margin (%)*	×	*Asset turnover*	×	*Financial leverage*
Bank	15.2	=	2.7	×	0.18	×	31.30
Manufacturer	14.6	=	10.7	×	0.88	×	1.55
Retailer	15.1	=	1.2	×	4.20	×	3.00
Utility	13.1	=	10.7	×	0.51	×	2.41

paths to achieving a high return on equity. In the remainder of this section we shall examine profitability in more detail, before continuing to the next two sections to look at asset turnover and leverage.

Net profit margin

The net profit margin shows the residual of revenues after operating costs, expenses, financial costs, taxes and exceptional items. Table 3.3 shows that profit margins differ widely among different industries, depending on the nature of the product and the company's competitive strategy.

Profitability and performance measurement

In order to obtain a more comprehensive analysis of performance, we need to extend our analysis of profitability to more than just the net profit figure. We need to examine each item of the profit and loss account, as well as trends over a period of time. Increases or decreases in turnover, the breakdown of sales from different products and geographic areas, and the detail of the cost structure all need to be analysed.

Two commonly used profit statistics are:

$$\text{Gross margin} = \text{gross profit/net sales}$$

and

$$\text{PBIT margin} = \text{profit before interest and tax (PBIT)/net sales}$$

The gross margin reflects the relationship of cost, volume and prices in the production or purchase of goods. It is often regarded as the 'raw profit', and highlights the basic operating efficiency of a company.

The PBIT margin is favoured by many analysts because it not only identifies operating efficiency but also takes into account administrative efficiency. It does not, however, take into consideration the level of debt or the tax liability that the company is carrying.

The profit margin and asset turnover relationship

The profit margin and asset turnover tend to vary inversely. A leading UK specialist plastics processing company, for example, has an asset turnover ratio of less than one. This is because it requires a heavy investment in assets, particularly plant and machinery, to add value to the raw materials. As a result, it is able to produce a specialized final product that commands high profit margins.

A food retailer, on the other hand, adds little to product value, and will consequently have low profit margins and high asset turnover.

It should be apparent, therefore, that a company with a high profit margin is not necessarily better than a low-margin company. It all depends on the combined effect of the profit margin and the asset turnover.

Reliability of financial information

We have looked at various techniques for analysing corporate performance, but we still have to establish the quality and reliability of the information on which we are basing our analysis. We have seen many examples internationally of companies that apparently were in good financial condition but then collapsed within a short period of reporting good results.

However, if the analyst had carried out a detailed examination of the company, it would have been possible in most cases to have detected signs of impending disaster. The majority of these signs would have needed ferreting out of the notes. In recent years the presentation of accounts has been improved, and they have now become more rigorous and robust than in the late 1980s.

We must nevertheless not lose sight of the fact that financial managers, particularly of quoted companies, are going to want to present their accounts in the best possible light, and will use the ingenuity of their advisers to do this.

The analyst needs to bear in mind, therefore, that any 'creative accounting' will dishonestly attempt to inflate reported profits, and in particular earnings per share, and also to report profits at the expense of the balance sheet. This may result in profits being reported without an equivalent amount of cash being generated. Cash is ultimately more important than profits, since it is cash that pays interest and dividends. The lack of it causes companies to fail.

Accounting quality is a critical issue in corporate analysis. It is important to know that ratios derived from financial statements can be used accurately to measure a company's performance, and that there is a common frame of reference to assist with comparative analysis. Accounting issues to be reviewed include:

■ *Valuation of assets*. Financial statements are prepared after judgements of valuation have been made by a company's auditors. This is most apparent with fixed assets and stock, so it is important that there is consistent valuation to avoid distortions to the profit and loss and balance sheets. The closing stock value is particularly important, because even small changes in the value can have a large impact on corporate profits.
■ *Capitalization of interest*. Some companies, particularly in the real estate and retail sector, will add the interest charges into the cost of assets when they are borrowing money to finance a major building project. This will protect the profit and loss in the short run, although profits will be affected by a higher depreciation charge in the future. The analyst should make adjustments for capitalized interest when calculating the company's interest cover, a key ratio for determining creditworthiness (see Asset management, below).

■ *Contingent liabilities*. Contingent liabilities are liabilities that may become concrete in the future. They are specified in a company's annual report, but are usually tucked away at the end of the notes. For some companies they have become potentially disastrous. Examples of contingent liabilities are guarantees of subsidiary borrowings, performance bonds and discounted bills.

■ *Depreciation*. Changes in depreciation methods have often been used as a way of manipulating profitability. These changes can be particularly hard to identify because they do not count as a change in accounting policy, and therefore do not have to be noted as a change in the accounting policy notes.

■ *Ratio analysis*. Despite the difficulties of interpretation referred to above, financial statements offer much valuable information to the analyst. Ratio analysis is widely used, and this technique can reveal much about a company and its operations. However, we should remember that the appropriate value for ratios is dependent on a company's specific circumstances, and that comparing ratios to rules of thumb has little value.

Comparing a company's ratios to industry ratios provides a useful indicator as to how the company is performing against its peer group. However, most companies have their own special differentiating factors, which results in some ratios deviating from industry norms.

Another useful method to evaluate ratios is trend analysis. Ratios should be calculated for a company over several years, and note taken of how they change over time. Trend analysis eliminates company and industry differences, enabling the analyst to make more accurate assessments of corporate creditworthiness and its change over time. Such pedestrian analytical methods in a volatile economic environment of hire and fire, merge and divest may, however, be limited in effectiveness.

Asset management

Asset turnover and liquidity

We saw in the previous section that the asset turnover of a company is to some extent determined by a company's products and industry sector.

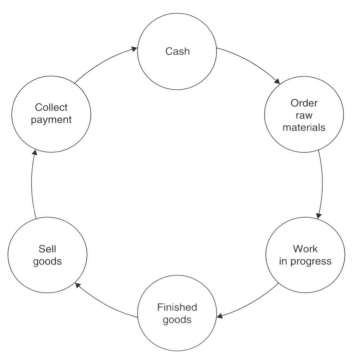

Figure 3.5 Asset conversion cycle

A low asset turnover signifies a capital-intensive business, and a high turnover the reverse. However, this is not the whole story. Management effectiveness in controlling all types of assets is vital.

Control of current assets is especially critical. The management team needs to make sure that there is sufficient liquidity in the company to turn operating assets into cash or another transferable asset (see Figure 3.5). It is therefore important for the analyst to pay particular attention to trade debtors and stock. Many companies have one-half or more of their money invested in current assets, and so it is easy to see that changes in the way these assets are managed can significantly affect the financial position of the company.

The current ratio compares the assets that will turn into cash within the year to the liabilities that need to be paid within the year. This ratio is still widely used by analysts as a measure of company liquidity, but in many respects it is a crude indicator. A low level of liquidity does not necessarily mean that the company is high risk, and may even be evidence of efficient financial management. Conversely, a high liquidity ratio tells us nothing about the quality of the assets and whether, for example, debtors are liquid within a month, or perhaps a year. It is therefore necessary to delve deeper and analyse each type of asset individually. This, in turn, will improve our understanding of how a company's operating decisions can have a favourable impact on the company's ROE.

When we are measuring working capital efficiency, we are often comparing the firm's investment in an asset to sales (or a closely related figure). If a company's stock has risen over time, this could be due to the fact that sales have risen and stock has risen in line with this increase. Alternatively, management may have been less efficient in its control of stock and allowed an undesirable build-up. The ratio distinguishes between changes triggered by sales increases and other, perhaps less favourable, causes. Several different measures of working capital efficiency are shown below.

Stock turnover

The stock turnover ratio, also known as inventory turnover is defined as:

$$\text{Inventory turnover} = \text{cost of goods sold/inventory}$$

A stock turn of, say, two times means that an average item of stock turns over twice per year – or, put differently, the average item sits in stock for six months. It should be noted that the number of days a firm holds stock varies between industries, and will also depend on the types of stock-management techniques (such as just-in-time) that are in place.

Several alternative definitions of the stock turnover ratio exist, including sales divided by stock. The analyst should ensure that a consistent approach is adopted at all times. If sales are used as the numerator, the stock turnover ratio will differ significantly, especially in the case of companies with high gross profit margins. Costs of goods sold is more appropriate than sales, because sales include a profit mark-up which does not apply to stock.

Collection period

The collection period provides information about a company's debtors' management, and is defined as:

Collection period = trade debtors/credit sales per day

If all sales are on credit, we can use net sales in place of credit sales. Credit sales per day is defined as credit sales for the accounting period divided by the number of days in the accounting period. This ratio reveals a great deal about a company's credit policy and the efficiency with which it can collect money from its customers. A long collection period may also indicate an inferior quality product that requires better credit terms than its competitors to increase its appeal. The collection periods for various industries in the UK are shown in Table 2.4.

Payment period

The payment period is simply the collection period applied to creditors:

Payment period = trade creditors/credit purchases per day

Average payment periods vary considerably from industry to industry, and it is often the case that industries with long stock-holding and debtor periods have longer payment periods. It is also useful to consider this ratio in the context of a Five Forces competitive analysis, and see what the result tells us about the relative bargaining power between company and supplier.

Net working assets to sales and overtrading

Once an analysis on an item-by-item basis has been carried out, it is very useful to have a picture of the size of a company's total investment in working capital. Net working assets to sales is calculated as:

Net working assets/sales = (stocks + debtors − creditors)/sales

This ratio is useful in determining how much cash will be required by a company during a growth phase, and is a useful ratio (as we shall see) for forecasting purposes. It may, in fact, underestimate the real need, because debtors and stock tend to grow faster than sales, especially at times of rapid growth.

Some companies will have high net working assets to sales ratios simply because this reflects the type of industry they are in. However, when this ratio is high compared to a peer group, it may provide a signal to creditors that the financial condition of the company is deteriorating. This is particularly common with small companies whose fast-growth strategies are over-ambitious. Many of these firms pursue risky financial policies as part of the overall strategic objectives of the firm.

An example from the electronics distribution industry shows why the analyst needs to give careful consideration to the issues facing rapidly growing sales-oriented companies. This company increased its sales from €10.6 million to €18.1 million in one year, with operating profits rising from €117,000 to €545,000. At the same time short-term debt rose from €450,000 to nearly €3 million. A detailed financial analysis showed that the company had a net working assets to sales ratio of 0.47. This was a clear case of a firm with working capital investment exceeding the ability to generate funds internally.

The next stage of analysis is to examine each working capital component on an item-by-item basis. Is stock being managed adequately? Are debtors at a satisfactory level?

There is a tendency for companies that experience rapid sales growth to enter a debt spiral in order to fund their operational capital requirements. In other words, the company is growing too fast and sales are too high for the financial resources of the company. This condition of over-trading represents a big risk to creditors, and immediate remedial action is required by management doing one or more of the following:

■ reducing the level of business activity
■ increasing the capital base
■ maintaining tight control over working capital.

Capital structure

Financial leverage

Financial leverage is the substitution of debt for equity in company financing. It is the third lever available to company management to improve the return on equity. However, this is not to say that the use of debt will always result in an improved return for shareholders. During the 1980s, debt and leverage were seen as an expression of management's efforts to boost shareholders' returns. Even hard-headed finance managers and executives were afflicted by the fashion for borrowing funds on a highly leveraged basis. However, the arrival of the recession at the end of the boom period led to the discrediting of leveraged financing and a need to shore up balance sheets through new equity issues.

So what is the optimal balance between debt and equity? Academics have been labouring over this question for many years, and this has resulted in the publication of many papers on the subject and in hours of deliberation at conferences.

One of the theories at the forefront is Professor Myers' static trade-off theory, which emphasizes the tax advantages for a company in borrowing. At a certain level, however, the costs of the risks inherent in indebtedness become so significant as to outweigh the tax gains, and further borrowing pushes the firm towards bankruptcy.

One of the problems of applying the theory is that, in practice, most companies are neither on the brink of collapse nor sitting on a cash mountain. There is a large intermediate range where there is very little evidence that finance managers make an effort to move along the curve to any given debt/equity mix.

In reality, capital adequacy is much more dependent upon the quality and reliability of cash flows than on any particular debt ratio. It may vary substantially according to the nature of the firm, its assets, the industry and the economic environment. Table 3.4 shows borrowing ratios across various sectors in the US and UK.

Apart from the differences in the levels of absolute gearing between the two countries, it is noticeable that construction and property – two of the industries that might be expected to be exposed to high levels of market risk – have gearing levels above those of the utility companies. The figures do not appear to support the commonsense viewpoint that

Table 3.4 Borrowing ratios by sector, US v. UK

Sector	UK (%)	US (%)
Extraction	0.55	0.83
Construction	0.47	1.16
Engineering	0.42	0.77
Chemicals	0.54	0.81
Utilities	0.36	0.92
General retail	0.32	0.77
Transport	1.10	1.13
Breweries	0.31	0.47
Property	0.89	2.21
Oil exploration	1.07	0.61

Source: Datastream.

companies in less risky sectors will take on more debt. The reality of operating a company subject to complex and often highly regulated business environments intervenes.

At the end of the day, we need to remember that financial leverage is a technique to substitute debt financing for owners' equity in the hope of increasing equity returns. The word 'hope' is important here, because leverage does not always have the intended effect. If operating profits are below a critical value, financial leverage will reduce rather than increase equity returns. We can therefore say that financial leverage increases the return to owners in most instances, but it also increases the risk. To see these effects more clearly, let's look at the impact of financial leverage on return on capital.

Let us take as an example a property investment company which wishes to purchase a property costing €1 million, let to tenants at €90,000 per annum (see Table 3.5). The company has no other assets. Operating costs are €10,000 per annum. Apart from the proposed loan to finance the property, there are no other liabilities. There are two alternative financing proposals. Under scenario A, the entrepreneurs will provide 40 per cent of the finance and 60 per cent will be made available from the bank. Under scenario B, 80 per cent will be debt finance and 20 per cent provided in the form of equity.

Table 3.5 The impact of financial leverage on return on capital – balance sheets for a property company (€ 000s)

	Scenario A		Scenario B	
	Interest rate 6%	Interest rate 12%	Interest rate 6%	Interest rate 12%
Assets				
Property	1000		1000	
Liabilities				
Bank loans	600		800	
Equity	400		200	
Total liabilities	1000		1000	
Profit & Loss				
Rental income	90	90	90	90
Less:				
interest to bank	(36)	(72)	(48)	(96)
running costs	(10)	(10)	(10)	(10)
Net profit	44	8	32	(16)
Return on assets (%)	4.4	0.8	3.2	(1.6)
Return on capital (%)	11	2	16	(8)

It can be seen that under the more aggressive financing structure (scenario B), the return on capital is higher to the shareholders at the lower rate of interest of 6 per cent per annum. However, if interest rates rise to 12 per cent, the company is making a loss under scenario B because of the high interest charges and the return on capital is negative. This is a demonstration of the fact that increased leverage increases the level of risk. Under the more conservative financing structure (scenario A), the return on capital is positive even with the higher interest rate of 12 per cent per annum.

Financial flexibility

A discussion of capital structure issues needs to take into consideration the fact that financing decisions are not a one-time event. In reality, the individual decision regarding an appropriate debt–equity mix is part of the long-term strategy of a firm. Moreover, the strategy is to some extent determined by the ease with which a company has access to the capital markets over time (remember that the financial markets were listed as a key environmental influence earlier in this chapter).

Financial flexibility is concerned with the ability of a company to refinance its debt through other financial institutions or the capital markets. For example, if a company has reached its debt capacity, its only external financing option may be the equity market. However, if for any reason the raising of funds through the equity market is unattractive, or not feasible, a company may find itself unable to raise funds to pursue the company's future strategy. There may be an argument, therefore, for raising funds from shareholders while the opportunity is available, so leaving the company with greater flexibility to refinance its obligations or raise new debt in the future.

Interest cover

The first test of earnings quality is the firm's ability to pay interest over time. Analysts are interested in the ability of the firm to service debt not just in the short term but also for the whole period that the risk is outstanding. Interest cover is calculated as profit before interest and tax, divided by interest payable. Analysts look for profits that are a consistently high multiple of interest as a sign of health. If the firm has an interest multiple of 10, it is able to pay its interest 10 times over – or see profits fall to one-tenth of the current level before interest servicing is at risk.

Table 3.6 sets out some of the key ratio medians for US industrial companies by rating category. These are among some of the key ratios used by Standard & Poor, a leading credit agency in analysing credit strength. The rating agencies are careful to point out that ratios are helpful in determining a company's position relative to rating categories. They are not intended to be hurdles. Furthermore, as ratings need to be valid over the whole business cycle, ratios of a particular firm at any point in the cycle may not appear to be in line with its assigned debt ratings.

The medians are constantly being affected by changing economic and environmental factors. However, Table 3.6 shows the importance of

Table 3.6 Standard and Poor's financial ratios, industrial long-term debt three-year (1992–1994) medians

	AAA	AA	A	BBB	BB	B
Interest pretax cov. (x)	21.39	10.02	5.67	2.90	2.25	0.74
EBITDA interest cov. (x)	31.68	14.78	8.25	5.02	3.46	1.56
Funds from operations/ total debt (%)	109.8	75.4	49.1	30.3	20.2	9.8
Long-term debt/ capital (%)	9.7	18.9	28.8	40.7	50.2	62.2
Total debt/capitalization inc. ST debt (%)	22.6	28.3	36.7	45.3	55.6	71.4

debt/equity and interest cover ratios in the credit decision. Analysts look for profits that are a consistently high multiple of interest as a sign of health. Table 3.6 demonstrates the large difference in interest cover between an AAA company and a typical B-rated company.

Cash flow

Cash flow analysis is probably the most useful tool available to the analyst in assessing company strength. Cash is the source of payment of dividends, interest and loan principal. Its broad principles are not difficult to grasp, but the detail can become complex, and there are times when a good knowledge of accounting is required.

Cash and profit

We saw in Chapter 2 that there is scope to manufacture profits through creative accounting. The 'creation' of cash, on the other hand, is almost impossible. The amount of cash in a bank account is not in any way reliant on a subjective opinion.

Creative accounting may partly explain why the cash generation of a company may differ from profitability, but this is by no means the full story.

There are many other reasons why cash and profit will differ, and these are examined below.

Let us start by considering a sale made by a company to one of its customers. If the sale is for cash, then cash realization and income realization happen at the same time. If it is a credit sale, then the sale is recognized as income when the invoice is raised and the corresponding contra-entry is a debit to debtors. When the customer pays after, say, 60 days, debtors are credited and the cash account is debited for the relevant amount. Over the course of the year a company is going to have many such transactions, and the net position may be as follows at the year end:

Debtors at beginning of year	€150,000
Debtors at end of year	€250,000
Profit and loss – sales	€1,000,000

Armed with this information we are able to determine the amount of cash inflow over the year in respect of sales, to take into account the timing differences that affect cash flow. We must first take the sales figure and adjust it by the change in debtors from the beginning to the end of the year.

$$\text{Cash inflow due to sales} = \text{sales} + \text{debtors at period beginning} - \text{debtors at period end}$$

The cash inflow due to sales is therefore €1,000,000 + (€150,000 − €250,000) = €900,000. In other words, if debtors increase, the change in debtors is subtracted from sales, and if debtors decrease, the change is added to sales.

We can see that items on the profit and loss statement have a corresponding category on the balance sheet to account for the timing differences between income/expense recognition and cash receipt/expenditure. We can therefore devise a more generic formula as a method of calculating cash flow from the profit and loss and differences in balance sheet items:

$$\text{Cash flow} = \text{(decrease in assets) OR (increase in assets) OR (increase in liabilities) OR (decrease in liabilities)} + \text{(credits to P/L) OR (debits to P/KL)}$$

If the resulting cash flow is positive, it is an inflow (i.e. a source). If the resultant cash flow is negative, it is an outflow.

It will now be clear that cash flow statements do not provide any new information, but are simply a reformulation of information provided elsewhere. However, it is still important for an analyst to be able to derive his or her own cash flow statement from a profit and loss and balance sheet. First, not all accounting standards bodies require a cash flow statement to be prepared and, even in countries where they are a requirement, exceptions do apply. Secondly, there is no better way for an analyst to get to grips with the financial fundamentals of a company than to draw up his or her own cash flow statements.

Operational cash flow

The operational cash flow is the cash flow associated with the company in its normal course of business. This represents the powerhouse of the company, and is the 'quality' cash flow to which the analyst needs to pay particular attention.

The activity format normally begins with the operating profit shown on the profit and loss for the relevant financial period. The Financial Reporting Standard requires a note (usually tucked away at the end of the annual report!) reconciling operating profit to the cash flow from operating activities. The most important components of this note are operating profit, depreciation and changes in working capital. Depreciation is a non-cash item, and therefore the annual charge needs to be added back in the cash flow statement. Also, because cash flow analysis is about cash realization, not income realization using accrual accounting, we need to make the adjustments for working capital explained earlier:

- *Returns on investments and servicing of finance.* These consist principally of priority outflows in respect of interest paid, dividends paid and the interest element of finance leases.
- *Taxation.* This shows the amount of tax actually paid, and often differs substantially from the amount shown on the profit and loss statement. This is because of the effect of advanced corporation tax, and because tax is normally charged in one year and paid in the next.
- *Investing activities.* This includes sales and disposals of fixed assets and acquisitions.

- *Financing activities.* This shows the cash flows from external sources of finance, including lenders and equity providers.
- *Net movement in cash and short-term investments.* This is the final calculation, and the analyst should ensure that the results reconcile from the balance sheet and cash flow.
- *Cash flow analysis.* It is an important principle of lending that each loan should have two independent sources of repayment (primary and secondary). The capacity to repay through cash generation (as opposed to a third-party guarantee) requires analysis in three different areas: (1) operational cash flow strength and the funds generated from the sale of goods and services in the day-to-day operations; (2) financial flexibility, which, as we have seen, is the ability of a company to refinance its debt through alternative sources of finance; and (3) operational flexibility, which is the ability of a company to raise cash through the liquidation of an asset or make operational changes to increase cash flow.

Our analysis can be strengthened by considering not only the overall amount of the cash flow but also the sources and uses of the cash. This can be done effectively by breaking down the cash inflows and outflows as depicted in Figure 3.6.

This will give a picture of the relative sources and uses of cash, and should be followed by a secondary phase of analysis which concentrates on issues such as the quality of the acquisitions and the effect on the underlying business of asset disposals.

It is also important to consider multi-period cash flows. A company that shows a steady and stable earnings stream in profit terms is likely to be a better credit than one where the aggregate earnings over a number of years are the same but which suffers volatility from year to year. The same is true for cash flow. We need to bear in mind that although cash flow analysis is the key tool for the creditor, the timing of cash flows is often irregular and they lack the smoothing effect of accruals.

Cash flow forecasting

To this point we have looked at past and present performance, evaluating existing financial statements. It is now time to look to the future.

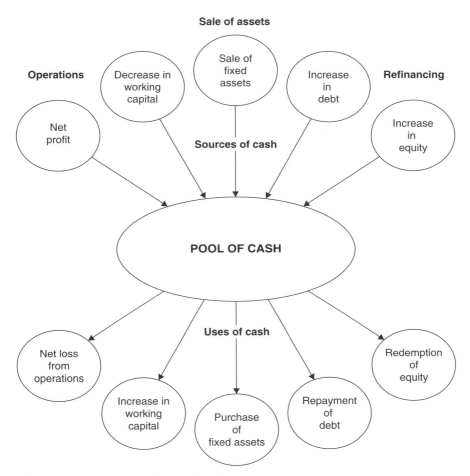

Figure 3.6 Sources and uses of cash

Every loan that has operating cash flow as its primary repayment source will be repaid by future cash flows.

Forecasting is notoriously difficult, but it is still an extremely valuable exercise to prepare a prediction of what a company's financial statements may look like in the future. An important use of pro forma forecasts is to estimate the company's future need for external financing.

Percent-of-sales forecasting

One simple yet effective way to project company financial performance is to tie as many of the profit and loss and balance sheet figures as possible to future sales. The rationale for this approach is the tendency (which we examined earlier) for P&L items and most current assets and current liabilities to vary directly with sales.

For example, if stock on the balance sheet has historically been about 24 per cent of sales and next year's sales are forecast to be €10 million, we would expect inventories to be approximately €2.4 million. This will not be true for all of the entries in a company's financial statements, and it will be necessary to make independent forecasts of items, such as capital expenditure, which are not directly linked to sales. Nonetheless, the percent-of-sales method does provide a powerful forecasting tool when combined with accurate sales forecasts and careful extrapolation of past trends. The input variables usually include:

- sales growth
- operating margin
- interest rates
- depreciation
- dividend payout rates
- capital expenditure
- working capital activity ratios
- increases in equity
- changes in long-term debt
- tax rates.

These are the cash drivers that will determine not only the shape of the balance sheet and profit and loss statement, but also the cash flow. By assigning a value to each one of these variables, an analyst can prepare an integrated financial forecast that will show the cash demands of the company in the future. Management may help either by providing the cash flow forecasts or by giving their views on operational issues, which will aid the analyst in making assumptions.

However, always remember that company forecasts are going to tend to paint an optimistic future and certainly will not be predicting failure. In most cases analysts should regard management forecasts as a best-case scenario, and significant changes in the assumptions for the cash drivers must be made to reflect a less favourable scenario.

Forecasting methodology

Many corporate analysts have PC-based spreadsheet software adapted for forecasting clients' financial performance. This saves a great deal of time and allows 'what if' analysis, permitting the analyst to adjust the variables to show different scenarios. Some lending situations are so complex and specific in nature (such as the building of the Eurotunnel, or a metro, a gold mine or an oil field project) that customized spreadsheets enabling the incorporation of key variable inputs will be required. We analyse such a spreadsheet in Chapter 5.

With a properly constructed forecasting model, the analyst will be able to prepare an integrated financial projection of this company by attaching values to the cash drivers for each year of the forecast period. The historical values and the ratio analysis will assist the analyst with this task.

PC-based systems have many advantages, but the analyst must use forecasting models with care:

■ It is important to identify the really critical variables. Is there one driver to which a company is particularly sensitive? Has there been correct identification of how a company will react to an increase in sales?
■ The interrelationship between the variables must be considered. Can, for example, an improvement in the stock to sales ratio be achieved without an investment in a stock control system, i.e. a capital expenditure item?
■ The forecasts should be consistent with company strategy the environment and historic performance.
■ Computer printouts tend to be 'believable', but it is important to remember that all forecasts are only as good as the assumptions. Furthermore, it is necessary to remember that uncertainty increases with time.

Sustainable growth

We have seen that when companies are growing, they consume cash. Debtors and stock consume cash at a faster rate than growth in creditors can support the growth of the company. The net working assets to sales ratio, which we referred to earlier, provides a useful indicator of how much cash a company will require to support a certain level of growth. A typical manufacturing company may require an investment of 30 pence in working capital to fund every extra pound of sales.

The sustainable growth rate is the rate at which a company can grow without increasing its leverage, provided that it maintains:

■ the dividend payout ratio
■ after tax profit margins
■ net working asset activity ratios
■ the sales/fixed asset ratio.

The sustainable growth rate is given by the following formula:

$$\text{Sustainable growth} = P(1 - d)/(1 - D)\,(NWA + FA) - P(1 - d)/(1 - D)$$

where

P = after tax profit margin/sales
d = dividend payout ratio
D = bank debt/bank debt plus equity
NWA = net working assets/sales
FA = fixed assets/sales.

The analyst needs to use his or her knowledge of the company to estimate whether sales growth in excess of the sustainable rate is going to be of concern. Sometimes this may be perfectly acceptable for a period of, say, two years, given the strategy of the company. At other times, it may be a sign that the company is heading for a debt spiral.

Corporate failure

We noted earlier that there have been a number of corporate failures in recent years which have happened soon after accounts have been prepared showing the company to be in an apparently sound financial condition. However, close scrutiny of the financial statements, particularly the notes, would have revealed weaknesses which would have served as a warning for creditors to protect any exposure that they may have had to the company.

This serves to emphasize the importance of early identification of problems. The earlier the difficulties are spotted, the greater the opportunities for remedial action.

Reasons for failure

Several ostensibly amusing checklists have been compiled regarding warning signals of poor management. The most common causes of corporate failure are:

1 Autocratic chief executive (Maxwell, Nadir, Conrad Black)
2 Weak board of directors (Maxwell, Nadir, Conrad Black)
3 Combined role of chairman and chief executive
4 Fraud and corruption in accounting practices (Maxwell, Nadir, Conrad Black, Parmalat)
5 Lack of senior management experience in the company's industry (RUMASA)
6 Management neglect of the core business activity
7 Cyclical decline in demand which expose company weaknesses with regard to the environment, management controls and capital structure.

The New York Times suggests a more up-to-date list of perks.[1]

---

[1] 'Haircuts. Shower curtains. Parking reimbursements. Country club memberships. Use of corporate jets ... James Follo, the chief financial officer of Martha Stewart Living Omnimedia, testified that Ms Stewart had asked the company to reimburse her $17,000 annually for her weekend driver as well as for trips to her hairdresser, coffee and other items. The trial of L. Dennis Kozlowski and Mark H. Swartz, two former top executives at Tyco International, a manufacturing conglomerate, has revealed that Tyco paid an array of their expenses including tuition to private schools for Mr Swartz's three children and $1 million for a birthday party in Sardinia for Mr Kozlowski's wife. And then there was the infamous $6,000 shower curtain and a $15,000 umbrella stand. In 2002, a filing in the divorce of John F. Welch Jr, the former chairman of General Electric, disclosed that G.E. was paying for a Manhattan apartment, New York Knicks tickets and other benefits for him even after he retired. He later agreed to give up many of the perks.' (Alex Berenson, 'From coffee to jets, perks for executives come out in court, *New York Times*, 22 February 2004.)

Most company problems allegedly arise due to the combination of the above. For example, Maxwell exhibited points (1) and (2); similarly, RUMASA showed (1), (2) and (5),[2] Crédit Lyonnais (1) and (5), etc.

It is unfortunate that this heirarchization of causes in classic business literature omits to mention the most recent cause of corporate failure – criminal fraud, as witnessed with the managements of BCCI, Enron, Worldcom, Parmalat, Barings, or the defunct auditor Andersen, who signed off on Enron's accounts (and shredded evidence to the same), to name a few.

None of these collapses are due to classic analytical explanations such as 'mature product cycle', 'poor working capital', 'entry of new competitors' or 'business cycle'. These collapses are due to greed and fraud perpetrated by two actors – management and auditors. Note that these are only the companies that have collapsed … what other surprises do top management and the auditors have waiting for us? When significant numbers of corporations are restating their profits downwards, this is suggestive of general rather than episodic breakdowns.

Recent research

Research was carried out by a leading firm of stockbrokers, County NatWest WoodMac (now NatWest Markets), into corporate failure during the early 1990s. The key conclusions were as follows:

- Fast, aggressive expansion, whether organic or by acquisition, is a likely precursor to problems. If also accompanied by a sharp rise in debt, particularly short-term borrowings, this should be viewed as very worrying.
- Dominant personalities are often connected with the companies that have foundered. Where there is a combined chairman/chief executive, often reinforced with a large shareholding, the extent of his or her influence is unchecked. Companies tend to be run like personal

---

[2]A summary of the RUMASA and Crédit Lyonnais collapses features in Andrew Fight's *Understanding International Bank Risk*, published by John Wiley & Sons (2004).

playthings, with the use of corporate jets to entertain friends (Kowalski of Tyco, Conrad Black of Hollinger International, Ladreit de Lacharriére of Fimalac/Fitch). Boardroom 'strife' should also be viewed as a leading indicator of trouble.
■ 'Hype' often comes before a fall.

Failure prediction models

Credit analysis should adopt a holistic approach which relies on a combination of ratio analysis, cash flow strength and non-financial variables. Some academics have conducted empirical research to see whether there is any one group of ratios that can be a more reliable guide to predicting corporate failure than others.

Edward Altman in the USA developed the 'Altman Bankruptcy Predictor'. Credit-scoring techniques such as the Altman Bankruptcy Predictor (also called solvency analysis) use an offshoot of classic ratio analysis known as multiple discriminant analysis (MDA). MDA simply takes two populations, failed and non-failed corporations, and compares (discriminates between) the two population groups. Altman takes five well-known ratios expressed as decimals, multiplies each one by a weighted coefficient, and then totals them up into a 'Z score'. Z scores are then assembled for industries and compiled into a database classified according to SIC industry codes schemes.

The five ratios look at liquidity, profitability, leverage, solvency and activity:

■ X1 = working capital/total assets
■ X2 = retained earnings/total assets
■ X3 = earnings before interest and taxes/total assets
■ X4 = market value equity/book value of total liabilities
■ XS = sales/total assets.

A company Z score is then referred to a bell curve (calculated from the totality of the sample universe depicting the overall parameters of corporate failure) to situate that particular company's probability of failure within the bell curve.

Table 3.7 The Altman solvency analysis model

XYZ Corporation, Industry SIC Code XXXX	2000	2001	2002	2003
Working capital/total assets*1.2	0.3343	0.2715	0.2397	0.3007
Retained earnings/total assets*1.4	0.3177	0.2662	0.2472	0.1231
EBITDA/total assets*3.3	0.0382	0.0044	(0.1055)	(0.2337)
Net worth/total debt*0.6	0.4946	0.3836	0.3545	0.1622
Sales/total assets	1.6599	1.5213	1.6768	1.7574
TOTAL Z SCORE	2.8447	2.4471	2.4126	1.9096

Range:
−4.000 to + 2.675 = 94% chance of bankruptcy in 1 year (average = 0.290)
+1.999 to + 2.999 = overlap area (grey area)
+3.000 to + 8.000 = solvent (average = 5.020).
Source: Edward I Altman, ZETA analysis, *Journal of Finance*, 1977.

We mention this technique in passing because analysts should be familiar with it; however, it is an idea whose time may have passed, since the mergers, realignments, and volatility of companies operating in an increasingly globalized market with cross-border electronic funds flows and different ratios across industries and borders renders such classic analytical techniques pedestrian. Moreover, the corruption of financial data does not help the accuracy of such statistically driven models.

The company Z score therefore gives an assessment of the element of risk inherent in a given company. As noted, each ratio is multiplied by a weighted coefficient as follows:

$$Z = 1.2X1 + 1.4X2 + 3.3X3 + 0.6X4 + X5$$

An example of the Altman solvency analysis model appears in Table 3.7:

When used to assess manufacturing firms in the USA, this analysis technique was 95 per cent accurate in predicting bankruptcy within one year and 72 per cent accurate within two years. The financial structure and ratios of various companies can obviously vary from one country or industry to another, and the use of such techniques must therefore take these factors into account when being interpreted. Although it is tempting to adjust the model in order to conform with conditions peculiar to a given country, this can affect the accuracy of the model's forecasting.

A variation on the Altman model, called the Syspas system, has been developed in the UK by Professor Richard Taffler from City University. As with the Altman system, Syspas looks at companies' financial ratios and scores them on a weighted combination. The approach is founded on multiple discriminant analysis: company performance needs to be assessed on a combination of ratios. The model has achieved country-specific effectiveness in predicting some of the recent corporate casualties in the UK. As with the Altman model, however, applying this model in an international context is somewhat more problematical.

The difficulty in adopting purely quantitative methods is that they rely on accounting data, which recent financial scandals have indicated are often corrupted and therefore unreliable for basing a financial analysis on. Therefore, whilst more subjective, a holistic approach can be a more likely assessment of failure provided financial analysts undertaking the analysis are proactive in their thinking and well structured in their argumentation, rather than seeking easy pre-digested formulae that will absolve them of engaging in assuming personal responsibility for their financial analysis.

Chapter 4

Cash flow forecasting of financial statements

Why cash flow analysis?

Banks lend cash to their clients, collect interest in cash, and require debt repayment in cash. Nothing else, just cash.

Term lending is typically to finance a company's medium- to long-term needs (five to seven years). Very often the loan is to purchase an asset which is expected to generate future cash flow and contribute towards the repayment of the loan. The assets being financed by the facility, such as plant or equipment, are usually expected to produce other assets, which, via manufacturing and sale, will generate sufficient cash to repay the loan. The fixed asset being financed is therefore not expected to be converted to cash to repay the loan. Rather, profits produced by the new equipment are the source of cash used to repay the loan. This is a long-term (multi-year) process.

Traditional bank credit analysis, however, typically resides in a balance sheet ratio analysis based on the borrower's historic financial statements. Classic balance sheet ratio analysis is useful in assessing the borrower's 'cushion' available to bank creditors in a bankruptcy scenario. However, no responsible banker is going to justify a credit proposal with the rationale that there is an adequate cushion of assets available in a bankruptcy. For one thing, there are too many legal and other variables which will make the likelihood of repayment in such a scenario uncertain – assets may be located in juridically unenforceable countries, or the attendant legal costs may be high.

The source of repayment in any term lending situation is cash, and a proper analysis should reside on an assessment of the borrower's ability to service future debt commitments by generating cash from future business operations, not from a liquidation. Furthermore, the purpose of analysis is to estimate the likelihood of liquidation scenarios occurring in order to avoid them in the first place.

Cash flow does not mean profits. For example, poor or declining profitability will not necessarily result in weak cash flows. A company's sales may fall, but it may still generate significant amounts of cash by selling off plant and equipment. If it uses up finished inventories and does not invest in more raw materials, then it will conserve cash.

This ability to post losses but generate a positive cash flow is illustrated in Figures 4.1 and 4.2. These screencaps are extracted Vodafone's accounts, and we can see that while the company has posted three years

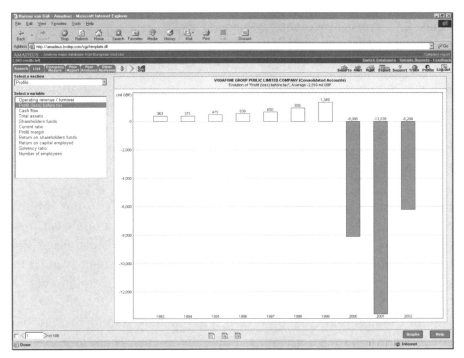

Figure 4.1 Vodafone accounts – profit (loss) before tax
Source: Bureau Van Dijk, AMADEUS 2004

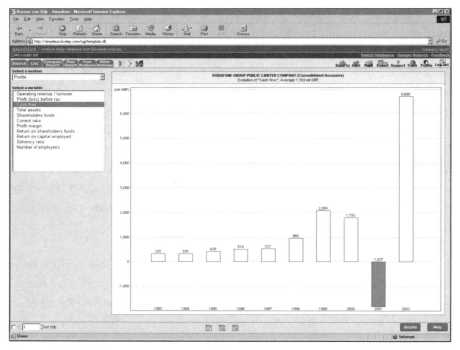

Figure 4.2   Vodafone accounts: cash flow
Source: Bureau Van Dijk, AMADEUS 2004

of losses, it only generated one year's negative cash flow. This distinction between profits and cash flow is graphically depicted in Figures 4.1 and 4.2. Bankers should therefore be more interested in cash flow than profit. Published profits can be manipulated, whereas cash generated by a company cannot.

In other words, to assess a potential borrower's ability to pay interest and service debt, we must focus on the ability to generate cash from future operations. This requires working through the distortions arising from accrual accounting on historical financial statements, and constructing projected financial and subsequently cash flow statements.

This will require the creation of projected income statements and balance sheets, and then deriving cash flow statements. These forecasts can later be adjusted or 'sensitized' to gain an understanding of the range of possible future operations.

To be able to pay all its debts as they become due, a company must be continually generating cash. This can only be done through:

- cash flow from operations
- sale of assets
- refinancing.

To assess the company's ability to generate cash in any of the above three areas, the company's capacity must be reviewed in three different areas:

1 NOCF – the ability to service debt through cash flows
2 Financial flexibility – the ability to raise new debt or equity
3 Operational flexibility – the ability to raise cash through asset disposals.

For financial projections, we shall be concerned with constructing operational cash flow models in order to better assess the company's operational characteristics in these areas. This chapter shall therefore explore how to use already analysed historical financial statements to construct financial and cash flow projections.

Finally, we will show how to use the results of such an analysis to produce a concise, logical, and effective credit assessment to evaluate the servicing of existing debt as well as structure future debt commitments.

Purpose of projections

Financial projection techniques are intended to enhance the understanding of a company and its lending situation. They are not intended to replace common sense or provide quick and ready answers. In addition to using the techniques outlined in this book, any good analyst will be alert to any other 'warning signals', which may or may not be quantifiable but may be useful signposts in the path of inquiry.

The objective of projections is to make a reasonable forecast of a firm's future performance and probable financial condition that will allow you, as the analyst, to answer questions such as:

■ Will the firm be able to pay back its current debt obligations out of future cash flow?

■ How much additional financing will the firm need to finance its future growth?

■ What is the firm's future debt capacity? What is the maximum amount of debt that can be serviced out of cash flow, given the firm's other needs, such as working capital, plant expenditures, etc.?

■ What are the available shrinkage margins in the projected cash flow? How much can sales revenues, profit margins, and cash flow shrink before payback is in jeopardy?

■ Will the firm be too highly leveraged as a result of increased debt resulting from growth?

■ Given the above, how should the loan be structured? What kind of repayment schedule should be set up for the new debt?

■ What forms of protection and control need to be included in the loan agreement in order to afford maximum safety for the bank's money?

Financial projections will enable you to assess factors such as the true purpose of a facility – whether it is appropriate for the purpose being considered (project finance, expansion, acquisition, debt refinancing) or whether it is for non-specific purposes (a warning signal) – to identify the term lending risks, and gauge the likelihood of repayment.

Financial projections can also have other uses: often companies need to restructure their debt profile for a variety of valid reasons. Financial projections will enable an assessment of the problems being considered, and identify the most appropriate repayment schedule in terms of the company's future cash flow (i.e. bullet, repayment, or interest servicing only).

Finally, in order to protect the bank's loans, projections can give an idea of sensitive areas in which the company may be vulnerable. In such cases, you may wish to include certain financial covenants in order to ensure the borrower operates within a certain set of constraints, in order to protect the facility.

After you have spread (ideally) three years of historical financial statements and stepped back to think about them, the first step in setting the groundwork for the tedious process of constructing projected cash flows is to construct projected financial statements: profit and loss, and then balance sheet statements.

In this chapter we will be looking at the financial statements of a fictitious company – AmaOS (Automated Management Operating Systems), a manufacturer of computer components and networking solutions. We will be working off accounts that have been cast into a standardized format known as a spreadsheet, and using those spreadsheets to build financial and cash flow projections.

Historical performance and variable input analysis

Historical analysis is the starting point for projecting a firm's future performance and financial condition. Analysing a firm's past performance and operations provides a basis for projecting a firm's performance under future conditions. The most important element for you to bear in mind when undertaking an historical financial analysis for building projections is to identify the key variables influencing the company, since it is this 'variable input analysis' that is your main tool in building the financial projections.

If, in historical analysis, you have been able to determine what has probably caused the demonstrated results, and if you have some information about future conditions provided by statistical organizations, industry projections or company plans, you can begin to make assumptions as to what future events may occur and how these events will affect the firm's future performance.

Financial statements over a minimum of three (and preferably five) years provide an opportunity to examine a variety of causes and effects in a firm's historical performance. The analysis of the firm's historical operations, performance and financial condition will help you to form reasonable assumptions about what is likely to happen in the future.

Before beginning projections, you should summarize your analysis of the company's performance in the following areas:

- Is the company operationally healthy?
- Is the company financially strong, or too highly leveraged?
- Are markets growing, stable or shrinking?
- How is the company situated amongst its competitors?
- A summary of present financial condition and existing cash flow
- Strength and weaknesses in management, industry position, nature of products and attendant risks, economic cyclicality
- Management performance as an influencing variable
- Operating risks
- Historical spreadsheets.

This book assumes that you are familiar with the mechanics of spreading historical financial statements (such as the historical figures for AmaOS), and that you already have a set to use for projections. Understanding spreadsheets is essential if you are to use them in preparing projections.

Defining the initial assumptions

The value of any set of projections revolves around the reasonableness of the underlying assumptions used in preparing them, and their whole credibility resides on this plain fact. Consequently, it is useful to remember a few golden rules on projected cash flows:

- *Projections are sales driven*. It is crucial to qualify the projection assumptions. Regardless of whether the projections are prepared by the customer or the analyst, without qualifying the assumptions on which they are based, they next to worthless.
- *Customers may produce certain scenarios* – for example, best case, most likely and worst case. Taking the customers' most likely scenario, you should play devil's advocate to their reasonableness and, where necessary, make adjustments. (If you want empirical evidence of customer optimism, ask any experienced banker if a customer has ever projected failure!)

■ *The bank must protect itself against a downside*. Once projections have been prepared, adjustments (also known as 'sensitivity analysis') must be made to reflect a reasonable worst-case scenario. The bank must then ensure that it will be adequately protected in such a scenario.

■ *Don't get lost in the numbers*; projections are not reality. Rather, step back and see if the projections make sense. Are the company's forecasts of 12 per cent annual growth in a mature industry characterized by over capacity realistic?

Often, in a term lending situation the borrower and/or agent bank may provide forecasted rates of sales growth. These may be perfectly adequate to construct forecasts on, but you, as analyst, will at least want to examine the assumptions underlying the growth rates in order to be satisfied that these assumptions are realistic. You can also make your own assumptions and then check them out with the customer in a marketing call.

Procedure for constructing projections

Projections are sales driven – in other words, company performance is linked to the inflow of money into the company. The projection of other income statement and balance sheet accounts is related, directly or indirectly, to the projected sales level. Sales level is, for example, a main determinant of asset growth – the higher the sales, the higher the working investment needed to support the sales.

There are two sources of financing:

1 Profits earned and retained in the business
2 Outside financing, either through increased equity (such as through the issuance of stock) or increased debt.

The process of creating a pro forma income statement and balance sheet can be broadly summarized as determining:

■ probable sales revenue and related income statement expense items
■ probable total asset growth and corresponding liability growth

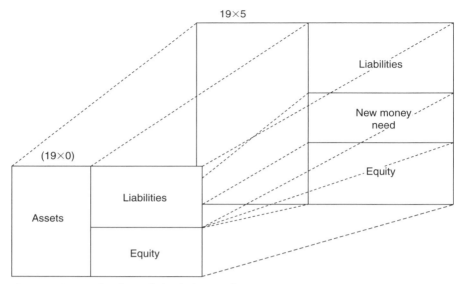

Figure 4.3 Projection of the balance sheet

■ a bottom line profit figure and how much additional financing the company will need to support asset growth.

Figure 4.3 illustrates the projection of the balance sheet.

One approach to constructing projections

■ Summarize conclusions from historical analysis
■ Define assumptions underlying your variable input analysis for the future performance and conditions in the industry and economy
■ Define the objectives of the projections
■ Project income statement and balance sheet accounts.

The typical outline for projecting profit/loss and balance sheet statements (which we will treat section by section) can be summarized as in Table 4.1.

In projecting the various items in Table 4.1, you will see that some are driven by a number of variables related to net sales, which are known as 'cash drivers'. These drivers are listed in Table 4.2.

Table 4.1 Typical outline for projecting profit/loss and balance sheet statements

---

Project income statement items
■ Sales
■ CGS
■ SGA
■ Other sundry items as per historical averages

Project assets
■ Determine CAPEX + new depreciation
■ Determine working capital components
■ Bring forward sundry items
■ Approximate cash (or leave open to later adjustments)
■ Total assets side of balance sheet

Project known liabilities
■ Determine working capital components
■ Determine existing LTD runoff
■ Determine proposed facility debt runoff
■ Bring forward sundry liabilities
■ Estimate tax account
■ Bring forward previous year's net worth
■ Total liabilities side of balance sheet

NOTE: At this point, we have not yet determined the firm's profits for the year (retained earnings) or the amount of new debt it will need to take on to balance the gap between its sources and uses of funds. Therefore, the figure calculated at this point is not equal to total liabilities. The amount needed to balance the total known liabilities to projected total assets is a plug figure, 'new money need'. New money need consists of some amount of retained earnings and/or some amount of new debt.

Determine new debt need
■ Plug new money
■ Determine composition of new money need
■ retained earnings + new debt/equity
■ calculate interest expense
■ complete income statement
■ fine-tune balance sheet (cash/debt)
■ Evaluate reasonableness of projections and adjust assumptions as necessary

Draw conclusions and make recommendations
■ Sensitize cash flow
■ Recommend allocation of new debt, as well as form, tenor and amount of the banks participation
■ Recommend amortization schedule for new debt

Table 4.2 Cash drivers

Profit and loss drivers include:	*Balance sheet drivers include:*
■ Sales growth ■ Cost of goods sold (% of sales) ■ Gross profit (% of sales) ■ Selling, general and admin expenses: SGA (% of sales) ■ Plant expenditure/capital expenditure (% of sales) ■ Interest rates ■ Tax rates ■ Dividend payout ratio ■ Access to capital markets	■ Inventory turnover ■ Accounts receivable turnover ■ Accounts payable turnover

You will be closely concerned with these drivers, and should understand their casual relationships. You should also understand how sensitive the company is to each cash driver, and how variable each driver is when subjected to either management or external influences. The first group of drivers concerns the bulk of the preparation of the profit and loss projections, while the second group concerns preparation of the balance sheet projections.

We now turn our attention to the first category: projecting the income statement.

Table 4.3 shows four years of historical figures for AmaOS in spreadsheet form, with ratios already calculated. The projection method will be illustrated with reference to these figures, which should be studied. AmaOS is seeking to borrow €100 m from your bank, to be repaid in three equal instalments starting in the second year.

Profit and loss statement projections

In setting the groundwork for preparing projections, it is useful to examine your historical spreadsheets and think carefully about the company's

Table 4.3   AmaOS historical spreadsheet

NAME:	AmaOS		
LOCATION:	UK		
BUSINESS:	Manufacturing		
AUDITOR:	Andersen	FYE	31 DEC
CONSOLIDATED:	Yes	GBP 000	

ASSETS	2000	2001	2002	2003
Cash	124,019	194,212	69,323	131,680
Marketable Securities				
Accounts Receivable – Trade	54,809	130,629	100,432	88,628
Accounts Receivable – Other				
Sundry Current Assets				
Inventory	105,625	132,650	334,541	207,424
Raw Materials	16,360	25,367	47,099	26,162
Work in Progress	491	1,478	1,227	
Finished Goods	75,664	92,354	255,644	159,880
Other	13,110	13,451	30,571	21,382
CURRENT ASSETS	**284,453**	**457,491**	**504,296**	**427,732**
Land, Buildings, Equipment	15,393	29,122	53,607	53,803
Leased Assets				
Plant in Construction				
Accumulated Depreciation	−2,018	−3,835	−7,754	−7,621
TOTAL OTHER GENERAL ASSETS	**13,375**	**25,287**	**45,853**	**46,182**
Quoted Investments				
Unquoted Investments	1,058	1,242	44,699	28,537
Invest in Associated Companies				
Loans to Associated Companies				
Prepaid Expenses				
Sundry Assets	229	553	452	
Goodwill				
Other				
TOTAL ASSETS	**299,115**	**484,573**	**595,300**	**502,451**

(*continued*)

LIABILITIES

Bank Loans and O/Ds				
Other ST Debt	27,552	111,137	148,407	99,450
CPLTD				
CPLO				
Customer Prepayment				
Accounts Payable	8,451	10,336	37,475	41,063
Accrued Expenses	5,569	9,950	27,636	5,877
Income Tax Payable	48,076	64,654	40,455	9,059
Dividends Payable	2,726	5,678	5,684	5,643
Due to Affiliates				
Sundry CL 1				
Sundry CL 2				
CURRENT LIABILITIES	**92,374**	**201,755**	**259,657**	**161,092**
Long Term Debt	24,848	24,848	24,848	24,848
New Debt				
Subordinated Debt				
Total Long Term Debt	24,848	24,848	24,848	24,848
Other Creditors				
TOTAL LIABILITIES	**117,222**	**226,603**	**284,505**	**185,940**
Deferred Taxes				
Minority Interest				
Common Stock	52,500	52,500	52,500	52,500
Preferred Stock				
Capital Surplus				
Revaluation Reserve				
Legal Reserve				
FX – Translation Reserve				
Retained Earnings	129,393	205,470	258,295	264,011
NET WORTH	**181,893**	**257,970**	**310,795**	**316,511**
TOTAL LIABILITIES & NET WORTH	**299,115**	**484,573**	**595,300**	**502,451**
Cross-check (TA-TL)	0	0	0	0
Contingent Liabilities:				

NAME: AmaOS
LOCATION: UK
BUSINESS: Manufacturing
AUDITOR: Andersen   FYE   31 DEC
CONSOLIDATED: Yes   GBP 000

PROFIT & LOSS	2000	2001	2002	2003
NET SALES	525,684	645,174	638,756	614,538
Cost of Sales	349,786	397,865	429,845	438,745
Depreciation				
Amortization of Goodwill				
Capital Grants				
GROSS PROFIT	**175,898**	**247,309**	**208,911**	**175,793**
SGA	**50,644**	**192,622**	**144,302**	**230,791**
NET OPERATING PROFIT	**125,254**	**54,687**	**64,609**	**−54,998**
Net Interest Expense	1,491	1,491	1,491	1,491
Interest Income				
Prov Dbt Recv				
Equity Income				
NPBT	**123,763**	**53,196**	**63,118**	**−56,489**
Provision for Income Tax				
Deferred Tax Provision				
NPAT	**123,763**	**53,196**	**63,118**	**−56,489**
Unusual Items:				
FX Gains/Losses	17,916	−9,518	30,045	−59,865
Unrealized F/X Gain/Loss				
Realiz Profits of Rel Co		−13,363	−19,752	−2,340
Reval Reserve				
Sundry Res				
Goodwill on Consol				
Unexplained Adjustment				
NPAUI	**105,847**	**76,077**	**52,825**	**5,716**
Dividends − Common				
− Preferred				
Min Int Expense				
RETAINED EARNINGS	**105,847**	**76,077**	**52,825**	**5,716**
Changes in Net Worth				
Stock Sold		0	0	0
Purch Own Stock				
Chg. in Cap Surplus		0	0	0
Chg. in FX Reserve		0	0	0
Chg. in Reserves		0	0	0
Other		0	0	0
INCREASE IN NET WORTH	**105,847**	**76,077**	**52,825**	**5,716**
Cross Check RE:	−	0	0	0
Cross Check NW:	−	0	0	0

(continued)

NAME:	AmaOS		
LOCATION:	UK		
BUSINESS:	Manufacturing		
AUDITOR:	Andersen	FYE	31 DEC
CONSOLIDATED:	Yes	GBP 000	

FACT SHEET	2000	2001	2002	2003
ROE (%)	68.04%	20.62%	20.31%	−17.85%
ROS (%)	23.54%	8.25%	9.88%	−9.19%
ATO	1.76	1.33	1.07	1.22
ALEV	1.64	1.88	1.92	1.59
Sales (M/MM)	525684	645174	638756	614538
Chg. in Sales (%)	#N/A	22.7%	−1.0%	−3.8%
CoGS/S (%)	66.5%	61.7%	67.3%	71.4%
GPM (%)	33.5%	38.3%	32.7%	28.6%
SGA/S (%)	9.6%	29.9%	22.6%	37.6%
NOP/S (%)	23.8%	8.5%	10.1%	−8.9%
TIE	84.0	36.7	43.3	#N/A
IE/Av. FD (%)	2.85%	1.58%	0.96%	1.00%
NPBT/S (%)	23.5%	8.2%	9.9%	−9.2%
Inc. Taxes/NPBT (%)	0.0%	0.0%	0.0%	#N/A
NPAT/S (%)	23.5%	8.2%	9.9%	−9.2%
NPAUI/S (%)	20.1%	11.8%	8.3%	0.9%
Div./NPAT (%)	0.0%	0.0%	0.0%	0.0%
Work. Investment	146414	242993	369862	249112
Chg. in WI (%)	#N/A	66.0%	52.2%	−32.6%
WI/S (%)	27.9%	37.7%	57.9%	40.5%
AR DOH	38	74	57	53
INV DOH	110	122	284	173
RM DOH	17	23	40	22
WIP DOH	1	1	1	0
FG DOH	79	85	217	133
AP DOH	9	9	32	34
AE DOH	5	6	18	3
Av. GP T/O	#N/A	#N/A	#N/A	#N/A
Av. NP T/O	#N/A	#N/A	#N/A	#N/A
Av. GP/DepExp.	#N/A	#N/A	#N/A	#N/A
Av. AccDep./DepExp.	#DIV/0!	#DIV/0!	#DIV/0!	#DIV/0!
Av. NP/DepExp.	#N/A	#N/A	#N/A	#N/A
Current Ratio	3.08	2.27	1.94	2.66
Quick Ratio	1.94	1.61	0.65	1.37
Coverage Ratio	2.43	2.02	1.77	2.30
CMB Leverage	0.64	0.88	0.92	0.59
% of Total Footings:				
STD(+CPLTD + CPLO)	9.2%	22.9%	24.9%	19.8%
Spont. Fin.	4.7%	4.2%	10.9%	9.3%
LTD	8.3%	5.1%	4.2%	4.9%
Grey Area	0.0%	0.0%	0.0%	0.0%
Equity	60.8%	53.2%	52.2%	63.0%
CA	95.1%	94.4%	84.7%	85.1%
Net Plant	4.5%	5.2%	7.7%	9.2%
Other	0.4%	0.4%	7.6%	5.7%
Asset Cover (TA − TSL/TA)	60.8%	53.2%	52.2%	63.0%
WC Adequacy (WC/CA)	67.5%	55.9%	48.5%	62.3%
Reliance on Inventory	−81.8%	−92.8%	26.9%	−28.5%
Change in WC (%)	#N/A	33.1%	−4.3%	9.0%

NAME:	AmaOS		
LOCATION:	UK		
BUSINESS:	Manufacturing		
AUDITOR:	Andersen	FYE	31 DEC
CONSOLIDATED:	Yes	GBP 000	

CASHFLOW	2001	2002	2003
NPAUI: NET PROFIT AFTER UNUSUAL ITEMS	**76,077**	**52,825**	**5,716**
+ Interest Expense	1,491	1,491	1,491
Unusual: Plant	−9,518	30,045	−59,865
Investment	0	0	0
FX − Adj.	−13,363	−19,752	−2,340
Other (1 + 2)	0	0	0
Other (3 + 4 + 5)	0	0	0
− Interest Income	0	0	0
− Dividend Income	0	0	0
− Equity Income	0	0	0
− Commission Income	0	0	0
Sundry Inc./Exp.	0	0	0
+ Prov. f. Income Tax	0	0	0
− Income Tax Paid	16,578	−24,199	−31,396
+ Prov. f. Def. Tax	0	0	0
− Def. Tax Paid	0	0	0
− ITC (Gov't Grants)	0	0	0
NOPAT: NORMALIZED OP PROFIT AFTER TAX	**71,265**	**40,410**	**−86,394**
+ Depreciation	0	0	0
+ Amort. of Goodwill	0	0	0
+ Prov. f. Dbtf. Rec.	0	0	0
COPAT: CASH OPERATING PROFIT AFTER TAX	**71,265**	**40,410**	**−86,394**
Gross (Net) A/Rec.	−75,820	30,197	11,804
− A/Rec. charged off	0	0	0
Inventory	−27,025	−201,891	127,117
Cust. Prepayments	0	0	0
Acc./Payable	1,885	27,139	3,588
Accrued Expenses	4,381	17,686	−21,759
Chg. Work. Inv.	−96,579	−126,869	120,750
Prepaid Expenses	0	0	0
Due to Affiliates	0	0	0
Sundry C.A.	0	0	0
Sundry C.L. (1 + 2)	0	0	0

(*continued*)

CACO: CASH AFTER CURRENT OPERATIONS	−25,314	−86,459	34,356
− Interest Expense	−1,491	−1,491	−1,491
− CPLTD (incl. CPLO)	0	0	0
− Finan. Payments	−1,491	−1,491	−1,491
CBLTU: CASH BEFORE LONG TERM USES	−26,805	−87,950	32,865
− Net Pl. Expend.	−2,394	−50,611	59,536
Investments	−184	−43,457	16,162
+ Interest Income	0	0	0
+ Dividend Income	0	0	0
Sundry Inc./Exp.	0	0	0
Market. Secur. + Dep.	0	0	0
Due from Affiliates	0	0	0
Sundry NCA	−324	101	452
Sundry NCL	0	0	0
Unusual: all other	13,363	19,752	2,340
+ ITC (Gov't Grants)	0	0	0
CBF: CASH BEFORE FINANCING	−16,344	−162,165	111,355
Short Term Debt	83,585	37,270	−48,957
Long Term Debt	0	0	0
Minority Interest	0	0	0
Grey Area	0	0	0
FX − Translation G/L	0	0	0
− Dividends paid	2,952	6	−41
Chg. in Net Worth	0	0	0
Change in Cash	**70,193**	**−124,889**	**62,357**
Cash Account	**−70,193**	**124,889**	**−62,357**

history and performance. This will help you to form the forecast assumptions you will be working with. This can be done with the aid of a score sheet (see forecast assumptions sheet below), listing your projection assumptions and then working down each item

Net sales projections

The starting point in building projections is to analyse the anticipated growth in net sales. Pro forma sales projections can be prepared using the most basic assumptions (e.g. 'flat 8.5 per cent growth in net sales per annum') ranging up to more detailed variants such as subdividing the company's various operations into either geographic or product lines and forecasting each division's performance (including acquisition/ disposal/capital expenditures) to arrive at an overall total.

Likewise, other models may factor in several variables such as fluctuating prices of the goods delivered plus the operating capacity of the production stream. For example, production may be at 90 per cent of capacity and the price at €70 per unit, or production may fall to 75 per cent of capacity but the market price rise to €110 per unit.

These assumptions may be further refined by factoring in expected inflation rates and economic growth or recession rates. Such economic data are available from sources such as the Central Statistical Office in the UK, or publications produced by banks or industry groups covering the economy in their home countries. Sales forecasts may also be provided by the company in its annual report or facility information memorandum.

It is important to break down the identifiable variables affecting the net sales figure over time accurately, so that key or vulnerable elements can be identified and individually manipulated. This is why often the net sales projections may be calculated in a stand-alone matrix specifically designed for this purpose. A detailed process of reflection is necessary to arrive at a reasonable estimate of net sales, since all other items will be derived (directly or indirectly) from this figure. Such a matrix for a manufacturing company with several product lines is depicted in Table 4.4.

Sales projections present the greatest analytical challenge, since this account encompasses the greatest number of variables and unknowns. The company's own forecast of sales, sometimes included in the annual report, can provide a starting point for projecting sales, but the company's projections should always be tested against the analyst's own assumptions and understanding of the problems that confront the company and that may affect its success in meeting its goals.

Table 4.4 Stand-alone matrix from net sales projections

COMPANY: SALES FORECAST	HISTORIC 2000 SALES	2001 %GR	2001 SALES	2002 %GR	2002 SALES
HOUSEHOLD FABRICS					
SEGMENT #1	0.0	0.00%	0.0	0.00%	0.0
SEGMENT #2	0.0	0.00%	0.0	0.00%	0.0
SEGMENT #3	0.0	0.00%	0.0	0.00%	0.0
TOT DIVISION 1	0		0		0
ECON INDICATORS 1					
DIVISION 1					
SEGMENT #1					
SEGMENT #2					
SEGMENT #3					
INDUSTRIAL FABRICS					
SEGMENT #1	0.0	0.00%	0.0	0.00%	0.0
SEGMENT #2	0.0	0.00%	0.0	0.00%	0.0
SEGMENT #3	0.0	0.00%	0.0	0.00%	0.0
TOT DIVISION 3	0		0		0
ECON INDICATORS 3					
DIVISION 3					
SEGMENT #1					
SEGMENT #2					
SEGMENT #3					
APPAREL FABRICS					
SEGMENT #1	0.0	0.00%	0.0	0.00%	0.0
SEGMENT #2	0.0	0.00%	0.0	0.00%	0.0
SEGMENT #3	0.0	0.00%	0.0	0.00%	0.0
TOT DIVISION 4	0		0		0
ECON INDICATORS 4					
DIVISION 4					
SEGMENT #1					
SEGMENT #2					
SEGMENT #3					
OTHER					
SEGMENT #1	0.0	0.00%	0.0	0.00%	0.0
SEGMENT #2	0.0	0.00%	0.0	0.00%	0.0
SEGMENT #3	0.0	0.00%	0.0	0.00%	0.0
TOT DIVISION 5	0		0		0
ECON INDICATORS 5					
DIVISION 5					
SEGMENT #1					
SEGMENT #2					
SEGMENT #3					
TOTAL SALES	0		0		0

There is no one way to approach sales projections; however, these broad areas should be considered for each product line:

- What are the future economic conditions affecting the company likely to be?
- What is the industry outlook, and what are the demand factors in the company's line of business? Are there problems with sources of supply, competition, over- or under-capacity, consumer demand, etc.?
- How has the company historically performed under various economic conditions? What have been the major influences on sales?
- What are the company's identifiable strategies with respect to its product lines?

The problem in making sales projections is seldom too few data, but rather too many. This means the analyst needs to understand the underlying fundamentals of the company's past sales performance and outlook for the industry and economy, be able to make reasonable assumptions about the variables most likely to impact future performance, and eliminate extraneous variables.

Determining the probable future level of sales is ultimately a matter of judgement, estimate and approximation.

There are two broad methods of projecting net sales:

1 Evaluating the volume and price components of sales revenue for each separate product line, determining those factors that are likely to influence future volume and price levels, and estimating a total probable dollar sales figure
2 Relating the firm's past sales performance to overall conditions in the industry or economy, obtaining forecasts of future industry or economic conditions, and deriving a figure for projected sales.

We will look more closely at these two approaches.

Evaluating volume and pricing components

The dollar sales figure is a function of the volume of goods sold or services rendered and the price the company is able to obtain for these goods or services.

Factors to consider when determining the probable future volume of sales for each product line include the following:

- *Health of the market.* Is the company's product one that will be in demand in the future, or is it a product for which demand is decreasing? Is the product subject to unforeseen changes in consumer taste?
- *Production capacity.* At what percentage of total capacity is the firm now operating, and how much additional volume can it generate with its current capacity? If increased volume depends on increased capacity, how quickly can new capacity be put on?
- *Competitive conditions.* What is the company's position with regard to its competitors? Does the company have a competitive edge, and can it maintain its market share? Can its markets be expanded? Are there substitute products that will inhibit volume growth or trigger volume declines?
- *General economy.* Who are the consumers of the company's product? Is the product sold to distributors, wholesalers, retailers, or company-owned stores or outlets? Which factors can affect their demand for the product – economic, fashion, geographic, cyclicality?
- *Cost flexibility.* Can the company pass off increased costs to the consumer? Does the company's product enjoy brand-name identification advantages that make it possible to increase prices without diminishing demand, or does the company have a reputation for quality or service that makes price relatively unimportant – is the company's product one that is in short supply but high demand?

The number of factors that could affect a company's sales volume and product price is almost limitless, but a knowledge of the economic, market and industry conditions, the nature of the business and the characteristics of the company's asset conversion cycle will assist you in limiting the number of factors that will have a major impact on the company being analysed.

Relating a firm's performance to industry and economic conditions

Historical analysis may sometimes indicate a relationship between a firm's sales level and conditions in the industry and economy.

Specifically, a relationship might be found to exist between sales and some other variable, such as total industry sales or certain economic indicators. When a forecast of the other variable is available, the projected sales figure can be derived. Some examples will illustrate:

- *Sales projections by market share.* In some cases it may be appropriate to project sales by market share. The first step in this method is to analyse the company's historic market share. Has it been growing, stable, shrinking?
- *Sales projections in relation to economic indicators.* Historical analysis may sometimes indicate a relationship between sales and certain economic indicators. For example, we may observe for a particular company:

	Sales	Index of industrial production
20X1	4.3	100
20X2	4.6	200
20X3	4.9	300
20X4	5.2	400
20X5	5.5	500

When such a relationship has been observed to exist historically, it may sometimes be used as a basis to determine a projected sales figure, provided we have an estimate for the future value of the other variable – in this case, the index of industrial production.

This technique uses a method of calculation known as linear regression. It is important, however, to realize that linear regression is effective typically when dealing with large population samples – for example, of several hundred data points (e.g. voter registration patterns linked to income). Using linear regression techniques to project corporate data where the variables are relatively limited in number (five years) can often lead to misleading results, since individual extraneous events can skew the linear regression model more than in cases where the population size is in the hundreds if not thousands. Small population samples thus are inherently vulnerable to larger margins of error. It is therefore useful to temper this methodology with subjective observations based upon your knowledge of the industry or company in question.

Example

The following example shows how to calculate forecasted growth rates using the sample historical spreadsheet for AmaOS.

AmaOS's historical performance for the past four years yielded the following growth rates:

2000	2001	2002	2003
na	+22.7%	−1.0%	−3.8%

Average annual sales growth = 5.98 per cent.

AmaOS's historical financials indicate that sales have slackened. This could be due to a variety of causes. It is your responsibility to identify and quantify the factors underlying such a decline, because they will be important in helping you estimate future sales growth rates.

Let's assume that AmaOS's chairman states in the annual report that the drop in sales is due to an ageing product line and economic recession. However, AmaOS's annual report informs you that the company has been developing a new product line which is scheduled to enter the market next year. Furthermore, let's assume that your independent research will have compiled data from government statistical sources which estimates that economic growth (GDP) is expected to grow by 5 per cent annually for the next five years. You may therefore feel that a projected sales growth rate of 4 per cent for 2004 (year 1), and 6 per cent for 2005, 2006, 2007 and 2008 (years 2, 3, 4, and 5) is a more realistic scenario than the straight-line average figure of 5.98 (which moreover factored in the exceptional 22.7 per cent increase in net sales for 2001).

The sales forecast assumptions worksheet figures should therefore read as follows:

	2004	2005	2006	2007	2008
Net sales:					
€614,538	**€639,120**	**€677,467**	**€718,115**	**€761,202**	**€806,874**
Last actual year	4% growth	6% growth	6% growth	6% growth	6% growth

You will have worked out these figures from a combination of historical data plus factors that you have estimated. In preparing forecasts, it is important to summarize the assumptions used and include them with the forecasts in order to enable the reader to understand the underlying assumptions.

Next, select and check the factors that you think are relevant to the industry in which the company being analysed operates. The essential issue is to arrive at a forecasted rate of growth that you feel is realistic.

Completing the profit and loss projections

Once you have established pro forma net sales growth forecasts and projected them over the number of years being considered (usually five, although this can be longer), then constructing projected profit and loss statements, at least to the net operating profit level, is a relatively straightforward operation.

The usual starting point is to take an historical average of the various cash drivers from the historical profit and loss statement, namely:

- cost of goods sold
- gross profit
- SGA, and
- operating profit

and calculate them as an average percentage of net sales in the historical income statement spread. These percentages are then used in conjunction with the pro forma net sales forecasts to calculate their expected value in the projected income statements.

This technique should be applied to *operational items* which arise as a consequence of the activity generated by sales in the company's income statements.

Some factors, however, may not necessarily be linked to the company's historical sales activity, and will require specialized treatment. Cost of goods sold may require adjustments for anticipated changes, such as the availability of a key raw material used in the operational process. Another example is if the proposed facility is to acquire a company or operation that is operating with higher than average costs, or will generate additional costs following absorption into the company; these should also be factored in. It is the task of you, as the analyst, to identify such pertinent factors and understand how they can affect the drivers.

Cost of goods sold/gross margin projections

Cost of goods sold (CGS) is a function of sales. One logical technique used to project cost of goods sold is therefore to calculate a CGS/sales ratio, based on the historical relationship of cost of goods sold to sales (+ any other assumptions or factors that may affect the ratio in the future). The historical average ratio of CGS/sales can be then applied to the projected sales figure to yield a projected cost of goods sold figure:

Projected CGS = projected sales*(historical CGS/sales ratio)

To further refine the projected CGS/sales ratio, the analyst looks at the major components of cost of goods sold (such as raw materials, labour, overhead) and can then consider factors that have determined the cost level of each of these in the past and that may affect them in the future. Reasonable assumptions about what may happen in the future can then be made.

Data that may be employed in the determination of probable cost levels in the future include:

- projected rate of inflation and the company's ability to pass on increased costs to its customers
- industry and economic data, such as projected price increases for raw materials or energy sources
- information on labour contracts coming due in the future, and settlements reached by similar companies
- the operating leverage – that is, the relationship of fixed costs to total costs in the firm's cost structure.

If a company has a high operating leverage (high fixed costs to total costs), then as sales increase, the cost per unit – and consequently the CGS/sales ratio – will tend to decrease.

Conversely, if a firm has low operating leverage (high variable costs to total costs), then as sales increase, total costs will tend to increase proportionately and, other things being equal, the CGS/sales ratio will tend to remain relatively constant.

This is why you should carefully consider the nature of the CGS breakdown in the company you are analysing.

Example

In AmaOS's historical PL, the historical gross profit/sales margin has fluctuated as follows:

FACT SHEET	2000	2001	2002	2003	2004
GPM (%)	33.5%	38.3%	32.7%	28.6%	#N/A

Average GPM = 33.3 per cent.

Since no particular trends are evident in this index, you may want to use the average gross profit margin of 33.3 per cent for your five-year forecasts. If this is the case, then your gross profit will evolve as follows:

	2004	2005	2006	2007	2008
Net sales: €614,538	€639,120	€677,467	€718,115	€761,202	€806,874
Last actual year	4% growth	6% growth	6% growth	6% growth	6% growth
33.3% GPM historical average	33.3% GPM	33.3% GPM	33.3% GPM	33.3% GPM	33.3% GPM
GPM	€212,827	€225,596	€239,132	€253,480	€268,689

Having worked out AmaOS's gross profit using historical GPM averages in conjunction with projected sales growth, you can now work out AmaOS's cost of goods sold figure by calculating the difference between net sales and gross profit and inserting the amount in AmaOS's cost of goods category (above gross profit and below net sales).

Working out AmaOS's CGS is important because it's one of the elements used in calculating balance sheet amounts linked to turnover ratios (inventory, accounts payable and accounts receivable ratios). Hence, by difference, AmaOS's projected CGS works out as follows:

	2004	2005	2006	2007	2008
Net sales: €614,538	€639,120	€677,467	€718,115	€761,202	€806,874
Last actual year	4% growth	6% growth	6% growth	6% growth	6% growth
CGS	€426,293	€451,870	€478,983	€507,721	€538,185
33.3% GPM historical average	33.3% GPM	33.3% GPM	33.3% GPM	33.3% GPM	33.3% GPM
GPM	€212,827	€225,596	€239,132	€253,480	€268,689

Selling, general and administrative expense (SGA)

The technique for projecting the SGA account is similar to that for other sales-driven expense items in the P&L statement. This involves examining historic trends in the SGA/sales ratio and selecting a projected ratio that can then be applied to the projected sales figure to determine projected SGA expenses in cash terms. Alternatively, you can establish SGA by projecting operating profit (as with gross profit) and then work backwards to establish SGA.

The former approach is, however, preferable, as a number of factors can affect SGA, and analysis should include conditions that may cause a rise or fall in this account. For example, if AmaOS intends to achieve sales growth by expanding into new markets, it is likely that there will be an increase in selling expenses typically associated with 'start-up costs' (salaries, commissions, advertising, legal, and consulting fees).

Depending on the type of company, SGA may or may not be critical. SGA will be more important for retail stores than for a manufacturer. Other companies may spend on advertising or R&D (which will probably be cut back in a recession, since they fall under management control). You should understand the nature of the company you are analysing, and adjust these figures accordingly.

Operating profit

As with net sales and gross margin, forecasting expense items from gross profit on down to operating profit (SGA, depreciation, other expenses) follows a similar process. To determine operating profit, you can either:

- calculate SGA as in the preceding paragraph and subsequently derive operating profit, or
- calculate the historical operating profit average and then work out the various expense items above operating profit and below gross profit by calculating the difference between the two.

At this stage, you should begin to get a feel of the company's projected sales performance.

Example

Using the historical AmaOS spreadsheets, we see that operating expenses, SGA, is also accompanied by depreciation and other costs. For the sake of simplicity, we can estimate these items as a group by working out the average percentage of operating profit to historical sales:

FACT SHEET	2000	2001	2002	2003	2004
OP/sales (%)	23.8	8.5	10.1	−8.9	#N/A

Average OP/Sales = 8.37 per cent.

This average percentage can then be used to estimate future operating profits based on future net sales.

Projecting AmaOS's operating income at a historical average figure of 20.1 per cent of net sales (OPM: operating profit margin), the resulting projected operating income is:

	2004	2005	2006	2007	2008
Net sales: €614,538	€639,120	€677,467	€718,115	€761,202	€806,874
Last actual year	4% growth	6% growth	6% growth	6% growth	6% growth
CGS	€426,293	€451,870	€478,983	€507,721	€538,185
33.3% GPM historical average	33.3% GPM	33.3% GPM	33.3% GPM	33.3% GPM	33.3% GPM
GPM	€212,827	€225,596	€239,132	€253,480	€268,689
8.37% OP/sales historical average	8.37% OPM	8.37% OPM	8.37% OPM	8.37% OPM	8.37% OPM
Operating profit	53,494	56,703	60,106	63,712	76,535

You can now insert the difference between gross profit and operating profit as a plug representing all expenses grouped together in the operating expenses category (depreciation, SGA, other).

Alternatively, if required, you can (as previously mentioned) break down the projected operating expenses into their individual categories based on their historical average of operating expenses.

Since the purpose of projections is often to establish overall parameters for structuring loan facilities and constructing financial covenants, it may not be necessary to forecast sub-category items individually.

Profit before tax

After deriving operating income, you will find that the subsequent income statement categories are not directly linked to the company's sales activity. In our model, given the absence of intermediary items, we have assumed that AmaOS's PBT follows the historical average of 7.57 per cent as follows:

Year	2000	2001	2002	2003	Avg
Net sales	525,684	645,174	638,756	614,538	606,038
NPBT	123,763	53,196	63,118	−56,489	45,897
NPBT/sales	23.54%	8.25%	9.88%	−9.19%	7.57%

The main categories which are deducted from operating profit to arrive at profit before tax are described below:

■ *Interest expense/interest income.* In order to calculate these items, you will have to arrange the company's existing as well as proposed debt into a debt runoff schedule (this will be treated in the balance sheet section). Realistic interest rate forecasts should then be used in order to calculate what the company's projected interest expenses will be. Preparing existing/projected debt into a debt runoff schedule is important because this will be used to construct the debt portion of the liabilities section of the balance sheet. You should therefore leave this area blank until you have completed the new debt calculations for the balance sheet, and then return to the profit and loss statement to complete the interest expense section.

■ *Extraordinary items.* While by definition 'extraordinary and unpredictable', extraordinary items should be included when required. These items are not linked to sales driven activity; however, they can have a significant impact on the company's cash flow and you should therefore attempt to identify and quantify them. For example, is the company expecting to sell (asset strip?) or buy any operating units as part of the organization plan which your term lending facility is destined to finance, and are losses or gains expected to arise as a consequence? You should try to gain an understanding of the company's future plans if possible, in order to factor such variables into your forecasts.

Once you have determined profit before tax, most likely based on historical averages and then accordingly adjusting back for interest expense and extraordinaries, you will want to arrive at your *profit after tax* figure. This will require projecting taxes and dividends, which are treated as follows:

■ *Taxation.* Taxation rates should be forecasted; you can use the standard rates in effect in the country in which the company is operating. For companies with operations in several countries, it may be preferable to calculate a flat historical average of taxation as a function of profit before tax (as in the example PL statement), and apply this average percentage against the projected profit before tax figure to arrive as a projected tax figure.

■ *Dividends.* Dividends will impact the level of retained earnings, which will follow through to net worth and affect the company's requirement for new financing. Therefore, you should attempt to estimate the expected level of dividends and funds available to be ploughed back into retained earnings in order to arrive at an estimated retained earnings figure for each of the projected periods. To arrive at this estimate, work out the average historical ratio of dividends to profit after tax (known as the dividend payout ratio), and, as in the case of taxation above, deduct it from profit before tax in order to obtain your projected net profits.

As these categories are not sales driven, you may have to account for them individually, and provide some sort of justification of the figures in your projection assumptions summary sheet.

In the abbreviated PL example, for sake of simplicity, the PBT and PAT have been calculated using historical averages against net sales of 7.57 per cent (in this case identical, since there are no intermediary items).

Once you have completed the above, you will have a preliminary set of projected income statements which you should study in order to see whether the company's future performance looks hopeful, and as optimistic as the company's pronouncements in the information memorandum – which, albeit informative, is designed to sell the financing package.

However, your task is far from complete at this stage! Many of these accounts may be impacted by balance sheet developments. This is why the next logical step is to use your initial P/L projections (see Table 4.5)

Table 4.5 Completed AmaOS forecasted P/L statement

NAME:	AmaOS
LOCATION:	UK
BUSINESS:	Manufacturing
AUDITOR:	31 DEC Andersen
CONSOLIDATED:	Yes

PROFIT & LOSS	2003	2004	2005	2006	2007	2008
NET SALES	614,538	639,120	677,467	718,115	761,202	806,874
Cost of Sales	438,745	426,293	451,871	478,983	507,722	538,185
Depreciation						
Amortization of Goodwill						
Capital Grants						
GROSS PROFIT	175,793	212,827	225,596	239,132	253,480	268,689
SGA	230,791	159,333	168,893	179,026	189,768	192,154
NET OPERATING PROFIT	−54,998	53,494	56,703	60,106	63,712	76,535
Net Interest Expense	1,491					
Interest Income						
Prov Dbt Recv						
Equity Income						

(continued)

NPBT	**+56,489**	**53,494**	**56,703**	**60,106**	**63,712**	**76,535**
Provision for Income Tax Deferred Tax Provision						
NPAT	**−56,489**	**53,494**	**56,703**	**60,106**	**63,712**	**76,535**
Unusual Items:						
FX Gains/Losses Unrealized F/X Gain/Loss	−59,865					
Realiz Profits of Rel. Co.	−2,340	5,000	6,000	7,000	8,000	9,000
Reval Reserve Sundry Res Goodwill on Consol Unexplained Adjustment						
NPAUI	**5,716**	**48,494**	**50,703**	**53,106**	**55,712**	**67,535**
Dividends – Common Dividends – Preferred Min. Int. Expense						
RETAINED EARNINGS	**5,716**	**48,494**	**50,703**	**53,106**	**55,712**	**67,535**
Changes in Net Worth						
Stock Sold Purch. Own Stock	0	0	0	0	0	0
Chg. in Cap Surplus	0	0	0	0	0	0
Chg. in FX Reserve	0	0	0	0	0	0
Chg. in Reserves	0	0	0	0	0	0
Other	0	0	0	0	0	0
INCREASE IN NET WORTH	**5,716**	**48,494**	**50,703**	**53,106**	**55,712**	**67,535**
Cross Check RE:	0	0	0	0	0	0
Cross Check NW:	−0	0	0	0	0	0

and cash drivers to work out key elements in your balance sheet projection. Once the balance sheet projections have been completed, you may then, for good measure, have to return to the profit and loss to 'fine tune' certain items (such as interest expenses/income) before undertaking the cash flow construction.

Balance sheet projections

Making balance sheet projections differs from the approach adopted in the income statement projections. There are several different techniques used for the different accounts in the balance sheet.

The starting point is to project items in the balance sheet directly related to sales and income activity, known as 'working investment'.

Key activity ratios (see Table 4.6) are used in conjunction with the projected figures derived in the income statement to calculate these items.

Table 4.6 Completed AmaOS forecasted ratio sheet

NAME:	AmaOS
LOCATION:	UK
BUSINESS:	Manufacturing
AUDITOR:	Andersen
CONSOLIDATED:	Yes

FACT SHEET	2003	2004	2005	2006	2007	2008
ROE (%)	−17.85%	14.66%	13.64%	12.82%	12.15%	12.93%
ROS (%)	−9.19%	8.37%	8.37%	8.37%	8.37%	9.49%
ATO	1.22	1.23	1.20	1.24	1.26	1.26
ALEV	1.59	1.42	1.36	1.23	1.15	1.08
Sales (M/MM)	614538	639120	677467	718115	761202	806874
Chg. in Sales (%)	−3.8%	4.0%	6.0%	6.0%	6.0%	6.0%
CoGS/S (%)	71.4%	66.7%	66.7%	66.7%	66.7%	66.7%
GPM (%)	28.6%	33.3%	33.3%	33.3%	33.3%	33.3%
SGA/S (%)	37.6%	24.9%	24.9%	24.9%	24.9%	23.8%
NOP/S (%)	−8.9%	8.4%	8.4%	8.4%	8.4%	9.5%
TIE	#N/A	#DIV/0!	#DIV/0!	#DIV/0!	#DIV/0!	#DIV/0!
IE/Av. FD (%)	1.00%	#REF!	0.00%	0.00%	0.00%	0.00%
NPBT/S (%)	−9.2%	8.4%	8.4%	8.4%	8.4%	9.5%
Inc. Taxes/ NPBT (%)	#N/A	0.0%	0.0%	0.0%	0.0%	0.0%

(continued)

NPAT/S (%)	−9.2%	8.4%	8.4%	8.4%	8.4%	9.5%
NPAUI/S (%)	0.9%	7.6%	7.5%	7.4%	7.3%	8.4%
Div./NPAT (%)	0.0%	0.0%	0.0%	0.0%	0.0%	0.0%
Work Investment	249112	260773.17	276419.69	293004.78	310585.08	329417.3
Chg. in WI (%)	−32.6%	4.7%	6.0%	6.0%	6.0%	6.1%
WI/S (%)	40.5%	40.8%	40.8%	40.8%	40.8%	40.8%
AR DOH	53	55	55	55	55	55
INV DOH	173	172	172	172	172	172
RM DOH	22	0	0	0	0	0
WIP DOH	0	0	0	0	0	0
FG DOH	133	0	0	0	0	0
AP DOH	34	21	21	21	21	21
AE DOH	3	8	8	8	8	8
Av. GP T/O	#N/A	#REF!	#N/A	#N/A	#N/A	#N/A
Av. NP T/O	#N/A	#REF!	#N/A	#N/A	#N/A	#N/A
Av. GP/ DepExp.	#N/A	#REF!	#N/A	#N/A	#N/A	#N/A
Av. AccDep./ DepExp.	#DIV/0!	#REF!	#N/A	#N/A	#N/A	#N/A
Av. NP/DepExp.	#N/A	#REF!	#N/A	#N/A	#N/A	#N/A
Current Ratio	2.66	11.81	12.20	11.77	11.59	11.68
Quick Ratio	1.37	6.45	6.83	6.40	6.22	6.29
Coverage Ratio	2.30	2.87	3.27	4.55	6.63	11.68
CMB Leverage	0.59	0.42	0.36	0.23	0.15	0.08
% of Total Footings:						
STD (+CPLTD+ CPLO)	19.8%	0.0%	0.0%	0.0%	0.0%	0.0%
Spont. Fin.	9.3%	7.2%	7.0%	7.3%	7.4%	7.4%
LTD	4.9%	22.4%	19.2%	11.5%	5.5%	0.0%
Grey Area	0.0%	0.0%	0.0%	0.0%	0.0%	0.0%
Equity	63.0%	70.3%	73.8%	81.2%	87.1%	92.6%
CA	85.1%	85.2%	85.9%	85.7%	85.8%	86.0%
Net Plant	9.2%	9.3%	9.0%	9.3%	9.5%	9.5%
Other	5.7%	5.5%	5.1%	4.9%	4.7%	4.5%
Asset Cover (TA − TSL/TA)	63.0%	70.3%	73.8%	81.2%	87.1%	92.6%
WC Adequacy (WC/CA)	62.3%	91.5%	91.8%	91.5%	91.4%	91.4%
Reliance on Inventory	−28.5%	−101.4%	−108.6%	−100.5%	−97.2%	−98.1%
Change in WC (%)	9.0%	51.9%	9.8%	1.9%	4.2%	6.5%

For items such as cash and marketable securities, an average percentage approach of total assets or a 'plug' figure in conjunction with 'new money need' (calculated using debt runoff schedules and projected assets after all other balance sheet calculations are completed) can be used.

For the liabilities side of the balance sheet, you should first determine the known quantities. This will include items linked to sales (accounts payable). For items such as debt, debt runoff schedules incorporating the company's existing debt runoff schedules (provided in the company's accounts), and the debt runoff schedule of the proposed term lending facility should be prepared. Other items can be brought forward on a historical average basis (e.g. tax accounts).

For net worth projections, you will rely on a combination of projected retained earnings and expected equity injections. Finally, you will have to balance assets with liabilities: this will require calculating the company's 'new money need': a 'plug' figure which can be used in conjunction with the cash/marketable securities caption (after all other balance sheet calculations are completed).

You should note that a substantial number of the accounts that you will be projecting are sales driven, and will be calculated using sales driven ratios. Hence, in addition to using projection assumptions and the projected profit and loss statement you will be making extensive use of the ratio sheet, which is based on your historical spreadsheets. You should be familiar with the ratio sheet and aware of how the various ratios are calculated, since you will be manipulating them in order to construct your projections.

We shall examine each of these areas on a case-by-case basis in further detail below.

A depiction of a balance sheet exhibiting a typical growth scenario can be seen in Figure 4.4.

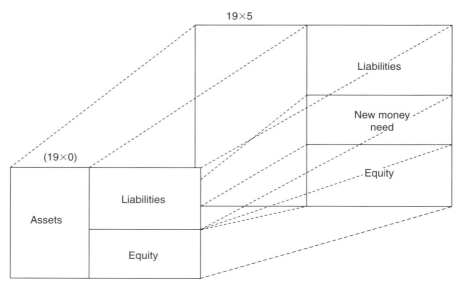

Figure 4.4 Projection of the balance sheet

Assets

The usual method of projecting the balance sheet is first to determine the primary asset categories which are linked to sales activities, and then adjust sundry items and cash to arrive at a preliminary total.

The working investment segment is the logical starting point in balance sheet projections, since the accounts are a direct function of sales. Working investment levels can have a significant effect on a firm's overall cash flow, since they are primarily composed of current assets and current liabilities. In addition, working investment levels are subject to a wide variety of rapidly changing conditions, and are largely a function of management discretion.

Working investment needs frequently increase proportionately with sales. However, there are many factors that can affect each component discretely, and that can alter the overall relationship of working investment to sales. To achieve the greatest accuracy in projections, therefore, working investment components are projected separately.

The technique usually applied in forecasting the working investment components is as follows.

1 Examine the historical turnover ratios on the ratio sheet of the spreadsheet, the relationship of the working investment components to sales (or cost of goods sold), and determine the causes for these historical ratios:
   ■ Sales/accounts receivable = Accounts receivable turnover
   ■ CGS/inventory = inventory turnover
   ■ CGS/accounts payable = accounts payable turnover
   ■ CGS/accrued expenses = accrued expenses turnover.
2 Decide on a turnover ratio that reflects your reasonable assumptions about what is likely to happen in the future to alter these ratios. Overall factors to consider include the following:
   ■ Historical trends – have the turnover ratios been relatively stable, or have they Fluctuated?
   ■ Projected economic conditions – what stage in the economic cycle do the projections represent, and how will the firm likely react to the economic conditions? (For example, in a recession a firm may liquidate inventory in anticipation of continued slowdown.)
   ■ Sales assumptions – working investment projections should reflect the assumptions on which sales have been projected. For example, sales increases resulting from the anticipated introduction of a new product line will usually be accompanied by an increase in the working investment accounts.
   ■ Factors affecting individual working investment components – factors to consider when evaluating the individual working investment components include accounts receivable (changes in selling terms as a means of meeting competition or extending markets); inventory (accounting methods – LIFO, FIFO – purchase commitments, availability of supply, price of raw materials); accounts payable (changes in term of trade, ability to ride trade, purchase commitments); and accrued expenses (ability to cut back on workforce or overhead, changes in the cost structure for labour or overhead).
3 Calculate the dollar value of each working investment account by applying the projected turnover rate for the account to the projected sales (or cost of goods sold) figure.

4 Check the reasonableness of the projected figures: (this means that the accuracy of the aforementioned is not certain and may need subjectively to be overridden).

Fixed assets, capital expenditure and depreciation

Depending on the type of company (capital intensive aircraft manufacturer), this forms one of the most important asset categories. Projections of the level of plant expenditures are based on three considerations:

1 *Management's plans for plant expenditure.* A company will often provide information on anticipated capital expenditures and operating capacities in its annual report. The amount and purpose of plant expenditures must be consistent with the assumptions on which sales projections have been made, and with the conclusions from historical analysis of the plant account.
2 *Historical analysis of plant.* Historical analysis of the plant account can provide information on the age, adequacy, capacity, utilization and efficiency of existing plant, and can assist the analyst in assessing the reasonableness of management's plans for plant expenditures.
3 *Sales assumptions.* The levels of sales and plant are inter-related. Although plant does not usually vary directly with sales, for a variety of reasons (accounting conventions, management decisions as to useful life, over- or under-capacity utilization, construction start-up time, and the fact that sales are in relatively current dollars and plant in older dollars), plant projections must be consistent with assumptions used to project sales. Important here is the aforementioned distinction between price and volume increases in sales. A sales increase attributable wholly to price requires no additional capacity. If there is a historical relationship between the level of sales and plant/machinery, the fixed asset turnover ratio may be helpful.

Example

Let us consider sales/net fixed assets (for simplicity's sake, net fixed assets excludes depreciation).

In our model, the last year's historical Sales/NFA ratio is:

$$614{,}538/46{,}182 = 13.30687281 \times$$

(meaning that 1 net fixed asset unit generates 13.3 units of sales).

Accordingly, for 2004, NFA is obtained by inverting the Sales/NFA ratio or:

$$639{,}120/13.30687281 = 48{,}029.$$

To derive net fixed assets for future years, that year's net sales figure is used in conjunction with the Sales/NFA ratio, as follows:

Historical	2004	2005	2006	2007	2008
Net sales: €614,538	€639,120	€677,467	€718,115	€761,202	€806,874
Sales/NFA ratio: 13.30687281	13.30	13.30	13.30	13.30	13.30
46,182	48,029	50,911	53,966	57,204	60,636

Inventory turnover

Again, depending on the type of company (e.g. supermarket or trading intermediary vs mobile telephone manufacturer), one of the most important categories of assets in a company's balance sheet is the level of inventories held. This account is directly related to the company's sales activity, and is the one most likely to reflect any changes in this activity.

The level of inventory held by a company varies from industry to industry, and is typically expressed as a function of sales; for example, a supermarket will perhaps hold 25 days inventory while a shipbuilder or aircraft manufacturer may approach 280 days. There are various statistical publications that provide data and averages regarding these ratios.

The objective therefore is to use the company's projected level of sales and historical average of DOH ratios to 'generate' an estimate of the levels or days of inventory that will be held by the company on the basis that if you know two elements of a formulae, you can calculate the third.

Example

From our historical spreadsheets, you will have seen that the historical ratio sheet contains four years of inventory DOH ratios. Since this performance will have varied over time, you can approximate the company's historical performance by taking an average of previous years' inventory DOH ratios.

FACT SHEET	2000	2001	2002	2003	2004
INV DOH	110	122	284	173	#N/A

Average inventory DOH = 172.14 days.

Once you have the average figure, you may see that there has been a 'trend' where the period has been gradually increasing. You may wish to override the DOH figure yourself in light of your current knowledge of the company.

In any case, once you have agreed on a inventory days-on-hand figure, you will want to derive a balance sheet pro forma inventory figure for each of the years you are projecting.

Adapting the inventory days on hand ratio:

$$(Inventory/CGS)*365 = inventory\ DOH$$

The formula to calculate the projected level of receivables is:

$$(CGS*inventory\ DOH)/365 = projected\ inventory$$

For example, using our sample spreadsheet CGS data,

	2004	2005	2006	2007	2008
CGS	€426,293	€451,870	€478,983	€507,721	€538,185

to project inventory for 2004, the calculation would be:

	2004	*2005*	*2006*	*2007*	*2008*
DOH	*172.14/365	*172.14/365	*172.14/365	*172.14/365	*172.14/365
Inventory DOH	201,042				

Try working out the inventory for years 2005 onwards.

Accounts receivable turnover

You can use the same approach outlined in the inventory example above to project accounts receivable. Once you have taken an average or agreed on a days receivable figure, you will want to derive a pro forma figure for each of the years you are projecting.

Example

Once again, adapting the accounts receivable in days ratio, the formula to calculate the projected level of receivables is:

(Net sales*receivables DOH)/365 = projected receivables

FACT SHEET	*2000*	*2001*	*2002*	*2003*	*2004*
AR DOH	38	74	57	53	#N/A

Average AR DOH = 55.50 days.

Using our spreadsheet data,

	2004	*2005*	*2006*	*2007*	*2008*
Net sales	€639,120	€677,467	€718,115	€761,202	€806,874

to project accounts receivable for 2004, the calculation would be:

	2004	2005	2006	2007	2008
DOH	*55.50/365	*55.50/365	*55.50/365	*55.50/365	*55.50/365
Accounts receivable DOH	97,175				

Try working out the accounts receivable for years 2005 onwards.

Cash and marketable securities

Cash and marketable securities are the accounts that are least related to sales and the company's ongoing operations:

- Cash arises from temporary liquid excesses due to seasonal variations, the sale of assets, or can be accumulated for special purposes such as potential acquisitions
- Marketable securities typically represent a temporary surplus of unused liquid assets which have been 'parked' into investment vehicles that provide a return on the assets.

In any case, it will be up to you to decide what levels of cash you believe will be appropriate for the company's future requirements, and qualify that level in your projection assumptions. You have considerable latitude with this heading, and can adjust it as you deem appropriate, within reason.

The cash accounts are also useful in the 'sensitizing' scenarios, where all the variables will have been calculated and the assets side of the balance sheet does not equal the liabilities. The 'cash' figure in the balance sheet can be adjusted to bring them into reconciliation (within reason!). You should also not forget to account for the fact that interest income is expected to be generated from these funds, and insert an estimated interest income figure in the projected profit and loss statement.

Example

In our sample worksheet, the company's sales growth is rather low. As we discussed, companies in a low sales growth scenario typically have strong liquidity. This, coupled with the new €100 million facility, means that the company's new money need is non-existent. In fact the company uses the facility to reduce its current liabilities, thereby strengthening its working capital position generates a cash surplus. Accordingly, after having worked out all the asset categories whose amounts are linked to the PL statement, a plug figure will eventually be inserted in the cash figure to balance the accounts.

As you sensitize for various scenarios (prepayment of debt, purchase of fixed assets), you will find that the relevant adjustments will occur in this category.

Liabilities

Once you have completed projecting the main asset categories, you must turn to the liabilities side to determine how this activity is going to be funded.

As with some of the asset categories, some of the liability accounts can be determined from net sales and the profit and loss account. This would include accounts payable and taxes. Other items such as debt can be worked out from historical data, as well as the facility you may be assessing in your credit proposal. Future injections of net worth may be disclosed or included.

Other accounts, however, will require some assessment: retained earnings and new money need. We discuss each of these categories in further detail below.

Current liabilities

Current liabilities typically include short-term funding facilities (overdrafts) and accounts payable. To project future overdrafts is not really feasible, since they are not sales driven: you may therefore want to keep this category at a historical average or 'plug' since, as with the 'cash' accounts, overdrafts are not directly linked to any of the drivers we mentioned earlier.

In the example AmaOS forecasts, we have assumed that the new €100 million facility has been used to pay down the short-term debt portion of current liabilities and therefore current liabilities have been substantially reduced.

Accounts payable

The case for projecting accounts payable is identical to those other sales-driven asset categories outlined previously.

Once you have taken an average of historical days payables, or agreed on a days payable figure, you will want to derive a pro forma figure for each of the years you are projecting. Once again, adapting the accounts receivable DOH ratio, the formula to calculate the projected level of accounts payable is:

$$(CGS*payables\ DOH)/365 = projected\ payables$$

Example

From the spreadsheet:

FACT SHEET	2000	2001	2002	2003	2004
AP DOH	9	9	32	34	#N/A

Average AP DOH = 21.07 days.

	2004	2005	2006	2007	2008
CGS	€426,293	€451,870	€478,983	€507,721	€538,185

To project accounts payable for 2004, the calculation would be:

	2004	2005	2006	2007	2008
DOH	*21.07/365	*21.07/365	*21.07/365	*21.07/365	*21.07/365
Accounts payable DOH	24,609				

Try working out the accounts payable for years 2005 onwards.

Accrued expenses payable

The case for projecting accrued expenses payable is identical to that of accounts payable outlined above. Once you have taken an average of historical accrued expenses DOH, or agreed on an accrued expenses DOH figure, you will want to derive a pro forma figure for each of the years you are projecting.

Once again, adapting the accrued expenses payable DOH ratio, the formula to calculate the projected level of accrued expenses is:

((CGS + SGA)*accrued expenses DOH)/365 = projected accrued expenses

From the spreadsheet:

FACT SHEET	2000	2001	2002	2003	2004
AE DOH	5	6	18	3	#N/A

Average AE DOH = 8.00 days.

	2004	2005	2006	2007	2008
CGS	€426,293	€451,870	€478,983	€507,721	€538,185
SGA	€159,333	€168,893	€179,026	€189,768	€192,154
TOT	€585,626	€620,763	€658,009	€697,489	€730,339

To project accrued expenses for 2004, the calculation would be:

	2004	*2005*	*2006*	*2007*	*2008*
AE DOH	*8.00/365	*8.00/365	*8.00/365	*8.00/365	*8.00/365
Accrued expenses payable DOH	12,835				

Try working out the accrued expenses figure for years 2005 onwards.

Debt runoff schedule + future facility

Figure 4.5 illustrates debt runoff and debt capacity.

Building a debt runoff schedule is important because:

- it will enable you to see what sort of debt levels the company will be operating with, and the level of interest expense that will arise (to be inserted in the profit and loss projections)
- it will help you to estimate the company's 'new debt need' and complete the projected balance sheet
- it will help you in building an appropriate debt amortization schedule for new credit facilities your bank may be underwriting or participating in.

The company's latest annual report usually provides a breakdown of the company's debt according to various criteria (including current lease obligations, which are regarded as financing costs) in the notes to the financial accounts. Indeed, EC directives now require financial accounts to include debt amortization breakdowns in years. The breakdown you should be most interested in is the repayment schedule in years.

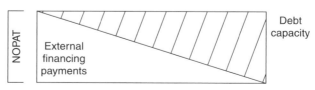

Figure 4.5 Debt runoff and debt capacity

Example

Let's assume that AmaOS's debt repayment schedule in the notes to the financial statements in its 2003 annual report shows that existing long-term debt (€24.848 million) is fully repaid in three years, with one-third being repaid each year. You can therefore include this in the debt runoff table under 'existing debt' and reduce it by one-third in 2004 (to €16.494 million), by one third in 2005 (to €8.247 million) and by one-third in 2006 (to €0), the final year. The debt runoff table at this stage should show how the company's debt is reduced (see Table 4.7).

Since you are most likely building these forecasts in order to gauge the appropriateness of a term lending facility whose terms and conditions you will have been provided with, you will also want to include the new facility in the table. Let's assume AmaOS's 2004 €100 million loan facility is repayable one-third in 2005, one-third in 2006 and one-third in 2007. This means that if the loan is granted in 2004, your new facility will show €100 million for 2004 and 2005, €66 million in 2006, €33 million in 2007, and €0 million in 2008.

You should arrange AmaOS's debt runoff in a format such as Table 4.7. The table should include the company's existing debt as well as proposed term debt facility (which forms the subject of the credit analysis). The runoff schedule should cover the life of the projections, and should then be totalled up to show the company's projected outstanding levels of debt. The total should then be inserted in the long-term debt portion of the forecasted balance sheet, and shown to run off accordingly. This can either be included as a single category or kept as two separate debt items for additional clarity when you insert them in the projected balance sheet: existing debt runoff and new debt runoff.

You will also want to estimate the interest expense the company will incur on this total debt (using a forecasted interest rate, 9 per cent in Table 4.7) at the bottom of the debt maturity table, since this figure will be later be inserted in the company's PL statement under the 'interest expense' category.

Table 4.7   Long-term debt and capital lease runoff schedule for AmaOS

AmaOS
LONG-TERM DEBT AND CAPITAL LEASE RUNOFF SCHEDULE
Interest Rate 9%

		2003	*2004*	*2005*	*2006*	*2007*	*2008*
1	Curr Port LTD	24,848	16,494	8,247	0	0	0
	LTD	0	0	0	0	0	0
	Int Expense	2,227	1,484	742	0	0	0
2	Curr Port LTD	0	0	0	0	0	0
	LTD	0	0	0	0	0	0
	Int Expense	0	0	0	0	0	0
3	Curr Port LTD	0	0	0	0	0	0
	LTD	0	0	0	0	0	0
	Int Expense	0	0	0	0	0	0
4	Curr Port LTD	0	0	0	0	0	0
	LTD	0	0	0	0	0	0
	Int Expense	0	0	0	0	0	0
5	NEW LT DEBT		100,000	100,000	66,667	33,333	0
	LTD	0	0	0	0	0	0
	Int Expense	0	9,000	9,000	6,000	3,000	0
6	Curr Port LTD						
	LTD	0	0	0	0	0	0
	Int Expense	0	0	0	0	0	0
7	CPLO	0	0	0	0	0	–
	LT O/S	0	0	0	0	0	0
	Int Expense	–	0	0	0	0	0
	TOT CPLTD	*0*	*0*	*0*	*0*	*0*	*0*
	TOTAL LTD	*24,741*	*116,494*	*108,247*	*66,667*	*33,333*	*0*
	TOT Int Exp 9%	*2,227*	*10,484*	*9,742*	*6,000*	*3,000*	*0*

Finally, it is very important to note that the debt runoff schedule is not a forecast of future levels of debt, but only that debt which already exists or is to be committed. Depending on the preliminary income statement, balance sheet and new equity projections, you may find that the company will generate a need for additional debt over and above that included in the debt runoff schedule. This separate future category is accordingly entitled 'new money need' (which can be either debt or equity), and is inserted under that heading in the projections.

Net worth

Forecasting net worth is relatively straightforward. The first step is to project expected levels of shares, factoring in any share issues that may or may not happen. Unless you have specific information concerning share issues, it is best to err on the side of conservatism and assume that any new money will consist of debt as opposed to new share issues (unless this is a specific requirement in the facility documentation).

You will also want to add the projected retained earnings from the income statement to the retained earnings brought forward in the balance sheet as outlined above, although this may be adjusted slightly subsequent to the 'fine tuning' of income statement items such as interest expenses, which will follow your initial set of rough projections.

Example

In our sample projections, we have assumed that AmaOS's equity remains unchanged at €52.5 million and that net worth growth is provided by net profit after dividend payments (retained earnings) as follows:

	2004	2005	2006	2007	2008
Share Cap Historical	52,500	52,500	52,500	52,500	52,500
Ret Earnings 264,011	312,505	363,208	416,314	472,026	539,561
Year's result	48,494	50,703	53,106	55,712	67,535
Net Worth	365,005	415,708	468,814	524,526	592,061

New money need

It is most likely that, after adding up the projected balance sheet, with all the categories you've projected, you'll find assets will not correspond to liabilities on the first attempt. This gap is represented in Figure 4.6 as 'new money need'. The reason for this is simply that each item was derived independently using heterogeneous criteria.

You may also find that your initial interest expense projections in the profit and loss will require an adjustment following your projected 'new

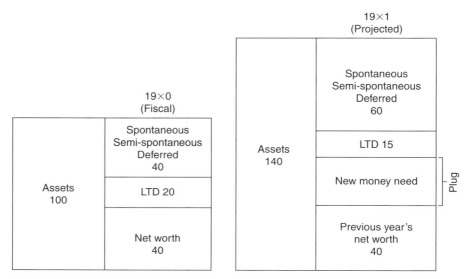

Figure 4.6 New money need

money need' figure. This will require a corresponding adjustment of your projected retained earnings figure to carry to the net worth account. This will then require a further incremental increase in 'new money need'. On computer programs this series of two or three cycles of adjustments is automatically calculated and is known as 'iterations'.

'New money need' is where this fine tuning comes in. After all these adjustments have been made, the balancing element can now be the cash account (surplus) or, if a desired balance has been established there, the new money need account (need).

A typical methodology is sequentially to:

■ extrapolate on a straight-line basis retained earnings
■ add the provisional P/L retained earnings account to the projected B/S retained earnings account
■ carry forward cash at the last year's historical (or average) levels
■ see where potential needs will arise.

New money need (NMN) is a 'plug' figure determined by Projected total assets – Projected known liabilities, as depicted in Figure 4.6.

Note that new money need, which is the gap between projected total assets and projected liabilities, will also include the amounts by which the original debt will have been amortized (see Figure 4.6).

(In our example spreadsheet, there is no new money need since the €100 million new money facility is being used to pay down current liabilities and thereby strengthen the company's working capital position.)

The picture is thus completed by inserting the new money need plug figure, which will equalize the assets and liabilities. This figure can be positive or negative, depending on the funds flows assumed. A 'positive cash balance' (or a 'negative new money need') will represent an excess of funds over the forecast needs, while a negative cash balance or positive accounts payable balance will indicate the need for obtaining additional funds.

Various sources of cash to service debt

The cash flow diagram in Chapter 3, Figure 3.6, illustrates that new money need can be obtained from various sources.

If operating profit is not sufficient to meet financing payments, alternative sources of cash may be available. However, if insufficient profitability is the major problem with the cash flow, these alternative sources of cash will be merely short-term palliatives.

- *Sources of equity and intercompany debt.* If the firm is closely held, or is a parent or subsidiary of a stronger firm with a vested interest in the firm's financial well-being, equity or debt injections may be available in times of cash flow difficulties.
- *Refinancing and restructuring.* As interest rates have increased over the years, many companies have committed to short-term debt, betting that rates would drop. Firms are often willing to refinance to stretch out loan amortization schedules over a longer term, thus reducing financing payments. The company may also have unused lines of credit that could be drawn down to pay current portions of long-term debt on a temporary basis. The tenor of the debt, however, may be due to other factors, such as high leverage that has prevented access to long-term markets.

(continued)

■ *Cash and marketable securities.* Some firms hold cash and/or marketable securities above what might be needed to meet seasonal needs, and these may sometimes be liquidated as an alternate source of cash. Companies frequently build up these accounts in periods of high earnings in anticipation of poor periods or periods of heavy expenditures, such as for the building of a plant.

■ *Working investment.* Permanent working investment can often be reduced by tightening inventory controls or receivables collections, thus releasing cash to be used for other purposes. Must a base stock of inventory, for example, be maintained at existing levels? Can sales terms be accelerated, or can the firm obtain better terms from its suppliers? In addition, a one-time infusion of cash can sometimes be obtained by selling a group of receivables to a factor.

■ *Fixed asset investments.* Another option sometimes available to a firm is the sale and leaseback of fixed assets providing a one-time source of cash. The firm may have other assets or investments of value that can be sold without restricting the firm's operating capacity.

■ *Dividends.* Although firms may be unwilling to cut off entirely the payment of dividends, they may be willing to pay them out at a lower level. Other methods of 'tightening the belt' include delaying plant expenditures or discontinuing unprofitable operations. Knowledge of the firm's operations is essential in order to identify such sources.

Fine tuning the ultimate amount of new money need is done by a process of estimation. There are four steps:

1 Estimate retained earnings and new debt
2 Calculate interest expense on new debt
3 Complete income statement based on interest expense estimates
4 Fine tune initial estimate of retained earnings and repeat above three steps.

Finally, you should step back a while and think about your 'new debt need' figure. While you may have a 'plug' figure which balances your projections and appears reasonable, you will want to consider what this actually represents.

Obviously, it represents new debt obtained from other banks. Is this in itself a reasonable assumption? Will the company be able to fund itself via the capital markets without any difficulties? Does this tally with say the company's credit rating? Although your projections may indicate that the company can operate in a state of equilibrium, perhaps the indicators will be negative and the company will not be able to obtain new debt for a variety of reasons. You should therefore think carefully about what this 'new debt need' figure represents, and the likelihood of obtaining it without any undue difficulties.

Amortization schedule for new debt

Once the pro forma accounts and cash flow have been completed and new money need estimated for five projected years, the analyst can use 'sensitivity analysis' to test the upper and lower boundaries of the firm's probable future debt capacity.

This basically means playing with input variables such as sales, expenses, interest rates, currency rates, debt amortization schedules, etc. The idea is to see which of these variables can have the most adverse impact on the company's financial condition, so that appropriate measures or control mechanisms can be structured.

This will also require defining the composition of new money need, as the manner in which this is broken down will have an impact on the company's balance sheet structure, funding costs and risk profile. It does not make sense, for example, to allocate the entirety of a company's new money need to debt if this weakens the company's capital structure to the point that it cannot service its debt, violates its financial covenants or net worth covenants, or weakens its credit rating.

This is why sensitivity analysis and the breakdown of new money need may result in the bank imposing certain conditions on the borrower, such as minimum net worth covenants, or commitments for future capital increases via various vehicles such as long-term debt, private placements, mezzanine finance, etc.

The allocation of new debt thus requires an analysis of the firm's projected cash flow. The technique usually employed is first to review the major projected sources and uses of cash on a cumulative basis. For example, if the new debt is being used to finance plant, the need is long term.

The tenor of the need is, in fact, probably longer than the bank would be willing to finance. In such a case, a revolving credit with takeout from a private placement would be one possible financing package.

In general, the issues that should be considered in structuring new money need can be summarized as follows:

- Debt servicing ability must be considered. The analyst must judge whether the additional financing payments, particularly CPLTD, that would result from the particular financing vehicle can be covered by the firm's cash flow and dividends.
- Tenor matching may indicate an appropriate allocation of new debt need. In general, the tenor of the asset being financed should match the tenor of the financing vehicle.
- The timing of the financing need is another consideration. For example, a revolving credit may be appropriate for a financing need that fluctuates throughout the year or the five-year period, while a standby term loan may be suited to finance construction that will be completed in stages.
- Flexibility in repayment is also important. If, for example, the firm's projected cash flow indicates flexibility in its ability to repay a loan, a revolving credit may be more appropriate than a term loan.
- The firm's historical preference in choosing financing vehicles should be reviewed, and may indicate the type of financing that should be recommended (e.g. a company may prefer debt in order to avoid share issues and the spectre of hostile takeovers).
- The financial leverage resulting from the new debt taken on should be considered. An increase in debt may result in a capital structure that

is too highly leveraged to provide the bank sufficient protection against loss.

■ Previous loan covenants should also be considered – it would be counterproductive to impose conditions that would cause the borrower to default on previous loan commitments.

Along with determining the composition of new debt there is the need to determine an appropriate amortization schedule which is reasonable in relation to the firm's projected cash flow. This is to ensure that the recommended amortization schedule:

■ is consistent with other requirements such as liquidity
■ does not cause the company to violate existing financial covenants
■ provides a comfortable margin of free cash flow or unused debt capacity to absorb unforeseen adverse circumstances.

As new debt amortizes, several things can happen to the company's projected financial statements:

■ The CPLTD from the runoff of the new debt will increase the total CPLTD shown in the financing payments section of the cash flow. The new debt should be structured so as to start amortizing only when the firm can pay it back, and not before.
■ Total liabilities will not change (other things remaining equal), but current liabilities will increase by the amount of the CPLTD associated with new debt running off.
■ Ratios and other measures linked to current liabilities will change whilst ratios that vary with total liabilities (such as the leverage ratio) will remain the same.

The implication of these changes is that a firm's liquidity will be affected as new debt runs off. This is why it is important to consider these effects when structuring lending facilities.

Completed AmaOS forecasted balance sheet

Table 4.8 is the completed AmaOS forecasted balance sheet.

Table 4.8   Completed AmaOS forecasted balance sheet

NAME:	13.306873	AmaOS
LOCATION:		UK
BUSINESS:		Manufacturing
AUDITOR:	31 DEC	Andersen
CONSOLIDATED:		Yes

ASSETS	2003	2004	2005	2006	2007	2008
Cash	131,680	144,160	168,087	159,973	161,533	173,471
Marketable Securities						
Accounts Receivable – Trade	88,628	97,175	103,006	109,186	115,737	122,682
Accounts Receivable – Other						
Sundry Current Assets						
Inventory	207,424	201,042	213,105	225,891	239,445	253,811
Raw Materials	26,162					
Work in Progress						
Finished Goods	159,880					
Other	21,382					
CURRENT ASSETS	**427,732**	**442,378**	**484,198**	**495,051**	**516,715**	**549,964**
Land, Buildings, Equipment	53,803	48,029	50,911	53,966	57,204	60,636
Leased Assets						
Plant in Construction						
Accumulated Depreciation	−7,621					
TOTAL OTH GENERAL ASSETS	**46,182**	**48,029**	**50,911**	**53,966**	**57,204**	**60,636**
Quoted Investments						
Unquoted Investments	28,537	28,537	28,537	28,537	28,537	28,537
Invest in Associated Companies						
Loans to Associated Companies						
Prepaid Expenses						
Sundry Assets						
Goodwill						
Other						
TOTAL ASSETS	**502,451**	**518,944**	**563,646**	**577,554**	**602,456**	**639,137**

LIABILITIES						
Bank Loans and O/Ds						
Other ST Debt	99,450					
CPLTD						
CPLO						
Customer Prepayment						
Accounts Payable	41,063	24,609	26,086	27,651	29,310	31,069
Accrued Expenses	5,877	12,835	13,606	14,422	15,287	16,007
Income Tax Payable	9,059					
Dividends Payable	5,643					
Due to Affiliates						
Sundry CL 1						
Sundry CL 2						
CURRENT LIABILITIES	**161,092**	**37,445**	**39,691**	**42,073**	**44,597**	**47,076**
Long Term Debt	24,848	16,494	8,247			
New Debt		100,000	100,000	66,667	33,333	
Subordinated Debt						
Total Long Term Debt	24,848	116,494	108,247	66,667	33,333	0
Other Creditors						
TOTAL LIABILITIES	**185,940**	**153,939**	**147,938**	**108,740**	**77,930**	**47,076**
Deferred Taxes						
Minority Interest						
Common Stock	52,500	52,500	52,500	52,500	52,500	52,500
Preferred Stock						
Capital Surplus Revaluation Reserve						
Legal Reserve						
FX – Translation Reserve						
Retained Earnings	264,011	312,505	363,208	416,314	472,026	539,561
NET WORTH	**316,511**	**365,005**	**415,708**	**468,814**	**524,526**	**592,061**
TOTAL LIABILITIES & NET WORTH	**502,451**	**518,944**	**563,646**	**577,554**	**602,456**	**639,137**
Cross-check (TA – TL)	0	0	−0	−0	0	0
Contingent Liabilities:						

Cash flow projections

Now that we've completed our balance sheet and income statement forecasts, we can turn to analysing the spreadsheet generated cash flow forecasts to gain an understanding of how the anticipated scenario will impact on the company's expected performance, see whether the company will have sufficient cash flow to service and amortize new and existing debt, and establish whether the proposed repayment schedule is appropriate.

There are several formats that can be devised for cash flow projections. The cash flow statement for AmaOS (see Table 4.9) is a typical sample. It should be noted that there is no standardized method of calculating cash flows, and that analysts can use differing models.

Construction and evaluation of future cash flow model

Cash flows can be constructed in several ways, from the simple to the more time consuming. We will consider a relatively time-consuming model which appears in the AmaOS spreadsheets in order to gain a clear understanding of the underlying principles of the typical computer-generated cash flow model.

Once these principles are understood, producing various sensitized scenarios by changing some of the underlying assumptions will have the advantages of the speed of the computer model coupled with an understanding of the underlying principles.

The first step in constructing a cash flow is to identify sources and uses of funds, as these phrases are commonly used by companies.

Remember that an increase in assets represents a USE of cash and will therefore be a cash outflow (i.e. NEGATIVE), while an increase in liabilities represents a SOURCE of cash or funding and will therefore be a cash inflow (i.e. POSITIVE). For clarity, negative figures in the cash flow should be in <parenthesis>.

Examples of sources and uses appear in Table 4.10.

These inflows and outflows are depicted in Chapter 3, Figure 3.6.

Table 4.9 Completed cash flow projections sheet

NAME: AmaOS
LOCATION: UK
BUSINESS: Manufacturing
AUDITOR: 31 DEC   Andersen
CONSOLIDATED: Yes

CASHFLOW	2003	2004	2005	2006	2007	2008
NPAUI: NET PROFIT AFTER UNUSUALS	**5,716**	**48,494**	**50,703**	**53,106**	**55,712**	**67,535**
Bloc 1						
+ Interest Expense	1,491	0	0	0	0	0
Unusual:	−59,865	0	0	0	0	0
Plant						
Investment	0	0	0	0	0	0
FX-Adj.	−2,340	5,000	6,000	7,000	8,000	9,000
Other (1 + 2)	0	0	0	0	0	0
Other (3 + 4 + 5)	0	0	0	0	0	0
− Interest Income	0	0	0	0	0	0
− Dividend Income	0	0	0	0	0	0
− Equity Income	0	0	0	0	0	0
− Commission Income	0	0	0	0	0	0
Sundry Inc./Exp.	0	0	0	0	0	0
+ Prov. f. Income Tax	0	0	0	0	0	0
− Income Tax Paid	−31,396	−9,059	0	0	0	0
+ Prov. f. Def. Tax	0	0	0	0	0	0
− Def. Tax Paid	0	0	0	0	0	0
− ITC (Gov't Grants)	0	0	0	0	0	0

(continued)

NOPAT: NORM OP PROFIT AFTER TAX	−86,394	44,435	56,703	60,106	63,712	**76,535**
Bloc 2						
+Depreciation	0	0	0	0	0	0
+Amort. of Goodwill	0	0	0	0	0	0
+Prov. f. Dbtf. Rec.	0	0	0	0	0	0
COPAT: CASH OP PROFIT AFTER TAX	−86,394	44,435	56,703	60,106	63,712	**76,535**
Bloc 3						
Gross (Net) A/Rec.	11,804	−8,547	−5,830	−6,180	−6,551	−6,944
−A/Rec. charged off	0	0	0	0	0	0
Inventory	127,117	6,382	−12,063	−12,786	−13,553	−14,367
Cust. Prepayments	0	0	0	0	0	0
Acc./Payable	3,588	−16,454	1,477	1,565	1,659	1,759
Accrued Expenses	−21,759	6,958	770	816	865	720
Chg. Work. Inv.	120,750	−11,661	−15,647	−16,585	−17,580	−18,832
Prepaid Expenses	0	0	0	0	0	0
Due to Affiliates	0	0	0	0	0	0
Sundry C.A.	0	0	0	0	0	0
Sundry C.L. (1+2)	0	0	0	0	0	0
CACO: CASH AFTER CURRENT OPS	34,356	32,774	41,056	43,521	46,132	**57,703**
Bloc 4						
−Interest Expense	−1,491	0	0	0	0	0
−CPLTD (incl. CPLO)	0	0	0	0	0	0
= Finan. Payments	−1,491	0	0	0	0	0

CBLTU: CASH BEFORE L/T USES	32,865	32,774	41,056	43,521	46,132	57,703
Bloc 5						
− Net Pl. Expend.	59,536	−1,847	−2,882	−3,055	−3,238	−3,432
Investments	16,162	0	0	0	0	0
+ Interest Income	0	0	0	0	0	0
+ Dividend Income	0	0	0	0	0	0
Sundry Inc./Exp.	0	0	0	0	0	0
Market. Secur. + Dep.	0	0	0	0	0	0
Due from Affiliates	0	0	0	0	0	0
Sundry NCA	452	0	0	0	0	0
Sundry NCL	0	0	0	0	0	0
Unusual: all other	2,340	−5,000	−6,000	−7,000	−8,000	−9,000
+ ITC (Gov't Grants)	0	0	0	0	0	0
CBF: CASH BEFORE FINANCING	111,355	25,927	32,174	33,466	34,894	45,271
Bloc 6						
Short Term Debt	−48,957	−99,450	0	0	0	0
Long Term Debt	0	91,646	−8,247	−41,580	−33,334	−33,333
Minority Interest	0	0	0	0	0	0
Grey Area	0	0	0	0	0	0
FX − Translation G/L	0	0	0	0	0	0
− Dividends paid	−41	−5,643	0	0	0	0
Chg. in Net Worth	0	0	0	0	0	0
Change in Cash	62,357	12,480	23,927	−8,114	1,560	11,938
Cash Account	−62,357	−12,480	−23,927	8,114	−1,560	−11,938

Table 4.10 Sources and uses of assets

SOURCES (inflow)	USES (outflow)
Cash generated from operations	Cash absorbed by operations
Equity issues	Dividends
Sale of fixed assets	Purchase of asset/investment
Additional short/long term debt	Repayment of debt
Dividends from associates	Payments to minority interests
Government grants	Closure/redundancy costs
Increase accounts payable	Decrease accounts payable
Decrease inventories	Increase inventories
Decrease accounts receivable	Increase accounts receivable

Preparing the cash flow is the most purely mechanical aspect of our task, since all the underlying variable assumptions and guesswork and estimates will already have been factored into our profit and loss/balance sheet statements. There is no new information to consider, but there is analysis to be done so that we can better understand what the figures mean.

We will consider the cash flow statement (Table 4.9) bloc by bloc.

The first bloc of the cash flow matrix starts with the bottom figure of the income statement, net profit after unusual items, and adjusts this figure accordingly (see Table 4.11).

The idea is to remove all the distortions arising from extraordinary items and dividend payments and arrive at a normalized operating profit after tax figure. For example, the losses attributed to subsidiaries and FX movements in the company's P/L are added back since these funds were actually generated (but deducted in the P/L) by the company during the year.

The second bloc (see Table 4.12) in the cash flow statement in turn is adjusted for depreciation and other non-cash items such as goodwill. This translates into a rough estimate of cash flow, which some banks use as their definition of cash flow.

On our matrix, we refer to this as cash operating profit after tax.

Table 4.11 The first bloc of the cash flow matrix

NPAUI: NET PROFIT AFTER UNUSUALS	5,716	48,494	50,703	53,106	55,712	67,535
Bloc 1 +Interest Expense	1,491	0	0	0	0	0
Unusual: Plant	−59,865	0	0	0	0	0
Investment	0	0	0	0	0	0
FX-Adj.	−2,340	5,000	6,000	7,000	8,000	9,000
Other (1 + 2)	0	0	0	0	0	0
Other (3 + 4 + 5)	0	0	0	0	0	0
−Interest Income	0	0	0	0	0	0
−Dividend Income	0	0	0	0	0	0
−Equity Income	0	0	0	0	0	0
−Commission Income	0	0	0	0	0	0
Sundry Inc./Exp.	0	0	0	0	0	0
+Prov. f. Income Tax	0	0	0	0	0	0
−Income Tax Paid	−31,396	−9,059	0	0	0	0
+Prov. f. Def. Tax	0	0	0	0	0	0
−Def. Tax Paid	0	0	0	0	0	0
−ITC (Gov't Grants)	0	0	0	0	0	0
NOPAT: NORM OP PROFIT AFTER TAX	−86,394	44,435	56,703	60,106	63,712	76,535

COPAT basically adjusts NOPAT by adding back these items because they represent non-cash expenses which have been deducted from the income statement. The company's actual cash expenses during the year were less (by the amount of the items) than was recorded on the income statement, so we adjust accordingly. The idea is to arrive at a net operating cash figure through these adjustments.

To work towards a true estimate of the company's cash flow, however, you must adjust for more than just depreciation. This is where the third bloc of the cash flow statement comes in (see Table 4.13). This bloc adjusts our gross operating cash flow figure by the variations witnessed

Table 4.12 The second bloc of the cash flow matrix

CASH FLOW	2003	2004	2005	2006	2007	2008
NOPAT: NORM OP PROFIT AFTER TAX *Bloc 2*	−86,394	44,435	56,703	60,106	63,712	76,535
+Depreciation	0	0	0	0	0	0
+Amort. of Goodwill	0	0	0	0	0	0
+Prov. f. Dbtf. Rec.	0	0	0	0	0	0
COPAT: CASH OP PROFIT AFTER TAX	−86,394	44,435	56,703	60,106	63,712	76,535

in the current assets and current liabilities categories, also referred to as 'cash after current operations' (changes in working investment).

Here, we are eliminating the distorting effects of the various working investment balance sheet movements in order to arrive at a view of the actual cash generated by the company's operations. For example, in 2005 we see that inventory increased by €12 million, and the gross accounts receivable account by €5.8 million (negative). Conversely, accounts payable increased by €1.4 million (positive). Remember, an increase in assets represents an outflow of funds while an increase in liabilities represents an inflow of funds.

Moving through the various current asset/current liability items in the balance sheet items, this tracks the changes between the previous year's and current year's accounts, as shown above. Hence, this third bloc of the cash flow statement adjusts COPAT for the various changes in working investment, to yield a cash after current operations figure.

In this bloc, we are basically adjusting for the change from one year to the next that has occurred in both current assets and current liabilities in order to establish whether the net movement represented an inflow or outflow of funds in the company's accounts. To place this in perspective, if the company had high levels of inventory in the previous year and ran them down without purchasing large quantities of raw materials to

Table 4.13 The third bloc of the cash flow matrix

CASH FLOW	2003	2004	2005	2006	2007	2008
COPAT: CASH OP PROFIT AFTER TAX	−86,394	44,435	56,703	60,106	63,712	76,535
Bloc 3						
Gross (Net) A/Rec.	11,804	−8,547	−5,830	−6,180	−6,551	−6,944
−A/Rec. charged off	0	0	0	0	0	0
Inventory	127,117	6,382	−12,063	−12,786	−13,553	−14,367
Cust. Prepayments	0	0	0	0	0	0
Acc./Payable	3,588	−16,454	1,477	1,565	1,659	1,759
Accrued Expenses	−21,759	6,958	770	816	865	720
Chg. Work. Inv.	120,750	−11,661	−15,647	−16,585	−17,580	−18,832
Prepaid Expenses	0	0	0	0	0	0
Due to Affiliates	0	0	0	0	0	0
Sundry C.A.	0	0	0	0	0	0
Sundry C.L. (1 + 2)	0	0	0	0	0	0
CACO: CASH AFTER CURRENT OPS	34,356	32,774	41,056	43,521	46,132	57,703

replace them, this development represents a contribution to the company's cash flow.

The fourth bloc adjusts CACO for financing payments and interest expenses to arrive at a cash flow before long term uses (financing) uses (see Table 4.14).

Basically, the company's financial commitments can be divided into two areas:

1 Interest expenses on the company's current debt obligations
2 Repayments of principal on its debt which is due in the current year (called current portion of long term debt, or CPLTD).

Table 4.14   The fourth bloc of the cash flow matrix

CASH FLOW	2003	2004	2005	2006	2007	2008
CACO: CASH AFTER CURRENT OPS	34,356	32,774	41,056	43,521	46,132	57,703
Bloc 4 −Interest Expense	−1,491	0	0	0	0	0
−CPLTD (incl. CPLO)	0	0	0	0	0	0
=Finan. Payments	−1,491	0	0	0	0	0
CBLTU: CASH BEFORE L/T USES	32,865	32,774	41,056	43,521	46,132	57,703

Adjusting CACO to obtain CBLTU is one of our most accurate indicators of the cash generated by the company. CBLTU is our most important measure because it not only indicates what amount of cash was actually generated by the company during its year of operations, it also shows us how much cushion or interest coverage the company has available to service debt commitments. However, we aren't through yet!

The fifth bloc (cash before financing) indicates where the company's internal funding came from – plant expenditures, investments, interest income, purchase or sale of securities, or unusual items (see Table 4.15).

CBF leads us in turn to the sixth and final bloc of the statement – where the company's external financing is coming from (see Table 4.16).

For AmaOS, we can see that the company's long-term debt reduced by €8.247 million and that this (decrease in liabilities) represented an out-flow of funds (hence negative in the cash flow statement).

The final line of the cash statement, after tracking all the changes in the balance sheet except the cash account, leaves a residual figure which corresponds to the actual movement in the cash account (in this case, an increase of €23.9 million).

Table 4.15 The fifth bloc of the cash flow matrix

CASH FLOW	2003	2004	2005	2006	2007	2008
CBLTU: CASH BEFORE L/T USES	32,865	32,774	41,056	43,521	46,132	57,703
Bloc 5	59,536	−1,847	−2,882	−3,055	−3,238	−3,432
−Net Pl. Expend.						
Investments	16,162	0	0	0	0	0
+Interest Income	0	0	0	0	0	0
+Dividend Income	0	0	0	0	0	0
Sundry Inc./Exp.	0	0	0	0	0	0
Market. Secur. +Dep.	0	0	0	0	0	0
Due from Affiliates	0	0	0	0	0	0
Sundry NCA	452	0	0	0	0	0
Sundry NCL	0	0	0	0	0	0
Unusual: all other	2,340	−5,000	−6,000	−7,000	−8,000	−9,000
+ITC (Gov't Grants)	0	0	0	0	0	0
CBF: CASH BEFORE FINANCING	111,355	25,927	32,174	33,466	34,894	45,271

Needless to say, if the end result of the cash flow statement does not balance, this means that an error has occurred – typically:

■ the balance sheet does not balance
■ the income statement does not properly reconcile the difference between net profit and its various allocations, leaving the year's retained earnings to reconcile with the change in retained earnings in the company's balance sheet
■ there is an error in the programming of the cash flow spreadsheet (check your positives and negatives: assets: Y1 – Y2, liabilities: Y2 – Y1!).

Table 4.16 The sixth bloc of the cash flow matrix

CASH FLOW	2003	2004	2005	2006	2007	2008
CBF: CASH BEFORE FINANCING	111,355	25,927	32,174	33,466	34,894	45,271
Bloc 6						
Short Term Debt	−48,957	−99,450	0	0	0	0
Long Term Debt	0	91,646	−8,247	−41,580	−33,334	−33,333
Minority Interest	0	0	0	0	0	0
Grey Area	0	0	0	0	0	0
FX – Translation G/L	0	0	0	0	0	0
−Dividends paid	−41	−5,643	0	0	0	0
Chg. in Net Worth	0	0	0	0	0	0
Change in Cash	62,357	12,480	23,927	−8,114	1,560	11,938
Cash Account	−62,357	−12,480	−23,927	8,114	−1,560	−11,938

Cash flow ratio analysis

Having completed our financial projections, we can now step back and try to see what it all means. Usually, the computer models will calculate a series of ratios based on the projected cash flow statements. While the thrust of this book has been on the mechanics involved in preparing projected financial statements as opposed to the subject of ratio analysis, it is worth briefly touching on the specialized ratios that relate to cash flow statements (see Table 4.17).

Interest cover ratio

$$\text{Interest times cover} = \text{NOCF/interest expense}$$

Table 4.17 Ratios relating to cash flow statements

ADDITIONAL FIGURES:	2003	2004
NOPAT/FP	−57.95	#N/A
NOPAT/(FP + DIV.)	−56.40	7.87
FREE CASH FLOW	−87884.88	44435
FREE CF (after Div.)	−87925.88	38792
GROWTH FUNDED INTERNALLY	0.0%	328.9%
G.F.I. (after Div.)	0.0%	287.2%
YEARS TO SERVICE RATIO	#N/A	2.6
Y.T.S. (after Div.)	#N/A	2.6

This ratio basically measures how many times the company's cash flow can cover its interest expense (i.e. service but not repay existing debt commitments). A cover greater than 1 is essential, and bankers typically look for a factor of 3 or greater. This is dependent on the volatility of operating profits and interest rates. If you have a ratio of 1.5 or lower, you should find out what the company is doing now or in the future in order to correct this position, or else re-analyse the credit to see if there are other viable sources of repayment (e.g. asset sales).

Financing payments cover ratio

Finance PMT times cover = NOCF/(interest expense + CPLTD + dividends)

This ratio examines what portion of operational cash flow is used to service debt and pay dividends. Again, the higher the ratio, the better the credit. This ratio is perhaps of more use than most debt cover ratios for those larger corporate customers whose dividends are cut by management only in the last resort.

Total debt payout

Total debt payout years = total interest bearing debt/NOCF

This ratio helps to give a feel for the company's ability to repay debt on current (historic) cash flow performance. It is particularly useful when compared to a company's debt repayment schedule. (European Community companies must note in their accounts how much debt matures in one year, two years, and three to five years.)

Long term debt payout

LT debt payout years = total interest bearing LTD/NOCF

This ratio is similar to the previous one. It assumes, however, that the short-term debt in current liabilities, although only committed one year at a time, is evergreen in nature. The banks making the commitments might view the situation differently!

When looking at the number of years, it is important to relate it to the expected life of the assets that are generating the cash flow: if the payout is within five years, this would be conservative for a property investment company but not for a service company with minimal fixed assets.

Debt service ratio

DSR = NOCF/(ST debt + CPLTD + interest expense)

This is the real test of whether a company can service its debt assuming the bankers call in all short-term borrowings, as well as measuring whether cash flow covers interest expense and the amortizing portion of long-term debt.

The bank's control over such types of lending will reside on establishing financial covenants and conditions on the borrower to ensure that the lender retains some element of control on the borrower should the financial condition deteriorate. This topic will be treated in a subsequent section.

Sensitivity analysis

We are now ready to put into use the concepts we have been exploring. Some words of caution should, however, be expressed at this point. All of the forecasting methods described up to here are based on the initial assumptions we have made. The assumptions necessary to make fore-casts are often made, with substantial uncertainty, on the basis of:

■ historical relationships (to the extent that it is reasonable to expect the future to be the same as the past)
■ management forecasts (to the extent that there are not obvious forces biasing management)
■ industry data (not overly useful, as there typically exists a wide range of diverse companies within an industry)
■ common sense.

Although you may not know which variables the results are most sensi-tive to, you may have an idea. If these variables can be isolated, not only can the area of concern be isolated but also, and just as importantly, the extent to which the expected results would be affected by changes in these variables can be established.

This can be accomplished by running a series of new forecasts in which all the original assumptions except one are held constant. This is known as a 'sensitivity analysis'. In such an analysis, each of the variables can be changed individually to determine which are of crucial importance.

For example, you may not be convinced by the company's sales projec-tions and may want to change them, or you may decide that cost of goods sold will rise, as will debt or interest expenses, and want to 'sen-sitize' the forecasts accordingly.

You may also want to see how much of a sales downturn and for how long would be required before a company started to violate its financial covenants and erode its net worth, position in order to assess what sort of worst-case scenario the company could survive.

With computer forecasting models you can test these changes within a matter of minutes, and generate infinite variations such as 'base line' (neutral), 'downside', 'expensive debt', 'equity injection', 'Rasta Dub Mix', 'Party House Mix' or which ever mix your credit committee prefers.

Figures 4.7–4.11 obviously depict the linear nature of the extrapolated statements. Reality, of course, is anything but linear.

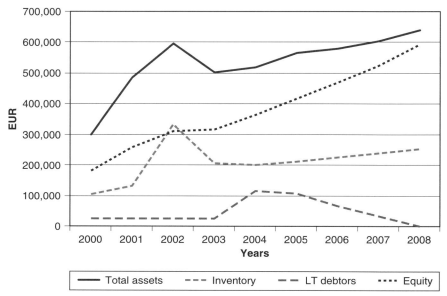

Figure 4.7 AmaOS financial highlights

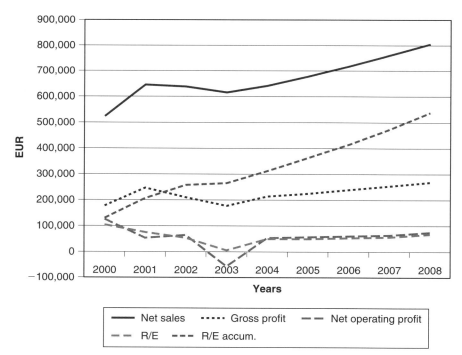

Figure 4.8 AmaOS P/L

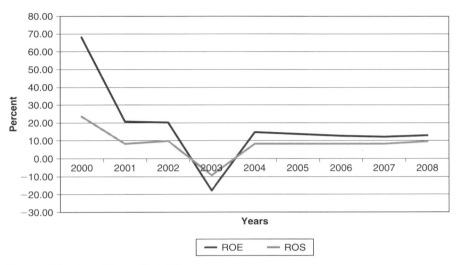

Figure 4.9 AmaOS profitability

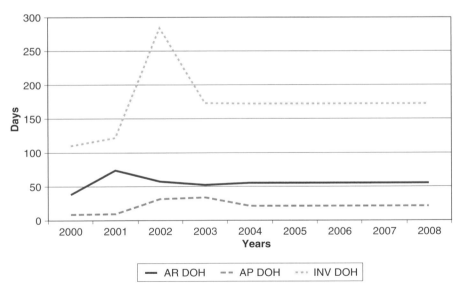

Figure 4.10 AmaOS activity ratios

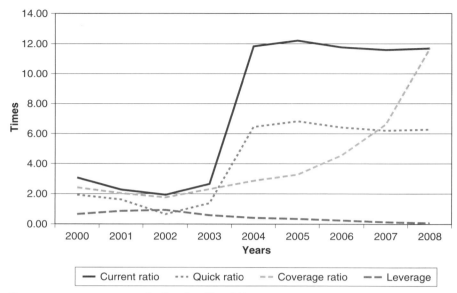

Figure 4.11 AmaOS capitalization/liquidity

Protection and control in term lending

Covenants, events of default, and their relationship to projections

Cash flow forecasting is a tool, and obviously should be linked to the issues of protection and control. In term lending, the bank expects to be repaid from cash flow – primarily from a level of future profits. From our analysis of financial projections, we can see that the bank's protection against loss in term lending has two aspects:

1. The future prospects of the firm – that is, its ability to generate a high and stable level of profits in the future (i.e. future sources of cash)
2. The future financial strength of the firm, as measured by its liquidity (working capital position) and leverage (i.e. future uses of cash, primarily debt obligations).

Analysis of problem credits in the past has shown the key financial and other indicators that accompany trouble in a firm's ability to generate sufficient cash flow (either internally or externally) to meet its needs and ensure its solvency include the following:

- inadequate working capital
- a sharp fall in the market value of a company's stock, reflecting the market's perception of the company's future cash flow
- low or negative retained earnings in relation to assets
- an unexpected change in 'corporate objectives' or 'business profile', such as in introducing new products or divisions
- vulnerability to economic cycles from debt heavy balance sheets or high fixed cost operations
- debt repayment schedules inappropriate in relation to cash flow.

In order to protect against loss and to control the source of repayment, loan agreements are drawn up in order to define and govern the conditions surrounding and affecting the proposed loan. Loan documentation in itself could form the subject of an entire book. We shall however, touch briefly on aspects that relate specifically to the company's financial condition and ability to generate cash flow sufficient to service debt commitments.

The first requirement is to ensure that the debt amortization schedules which have been set up in the loan agreement are appropriate in terms of the firm's projected cash flow. The second is to verify that financial covenants, which are designed to preserve and control the firm's cash flow and its financial strength, have been included in the loan documentation.

Financial covenants are conditions which define the framework of the financial plan agreed upon by the company and the bank. Drafting this framework is typically a process of negotiation, and the degree of protection which is obtained through such negotiations can vary and is often imperfect. Indeed, some companies may vigorously resist the inclusion of such covenants. We briefly cover the main types below:

- *Primary covenants* include factors that have a direct impact on the company's financial statements. These include limitation of future debt (including contingent liabilities), prohibition of new secured debt or obligations which will rank ahead of the proposed term loan ('negative pledge'), provision for a minimum level of working capital, and provision for a minimum level of net worth. Such limits can either be defined in absolute ($/*) or ratio terms. Requirements for the company to provide audited financial statements on a regular basis in order to verify the above should also be included in the loan agreement.

- *Secondary covenants* include aspects related to the company's management and ongoing operations. These can include prohibition on the sale of subsidiaries or assets, limitations in the prepayment of other debt, prohibitions on mergers or consolidations without consent of the lenders, limitations in investments or capital expenditures, and limitations in dividends. Conversely, rather than limiting dividend payments, 'ratcheting' clauses requiring minimal annual increases in net worth may be included.

In assessing the future loan facility, it will be necessary to test the covenants that have been included in the loan agreement and see how they hold up against the projections you will have prepared. You may want to sensitize your forecasts for a downside scenario to see whether the proposed covenants will enable the banks to take action to protect their loan before it becomes too late to arrest the company's financial deterioration.

Finally, there are 'events of default'. These establish conditions under which the lending bank has the right to accelerate repayment of the loan. This right to accelerate is rarely used, but typically gives the lenders the control to renegotiate lending terms or take other steps in order to protect the loan before it is too late. The events of default that we are concerned with refer specifically to breaching (failing to meet) financial covenants. Often, lenders may temporarily breach covenants; in these cases, waivers are typically requested from (and granted by) the banks.

While loan covenant issues are not directly related to the mechanics of cash flow projections and analysis, the final projections you will have prepared will naturally be held up against those covenants to see how effective they are. It is therefore a good idea to have addressed these issues in the event you are questioned on them.

Conclusion

What confidence can you have in forecasts? A frank answer is 'not very much', although there are a number of factors that could qualify that answer. That, however, is partially beside the point. The main value of forecasts to the analyst is not necessarily diminished by the fact that they may be perceived not to be completely airtight. It is easy for critics to look at a given forecast and shoot holes in it on the basis that there are bound to be certain assumptions that will not hold true. Furthermore, the greater the number of assumptions and the further into the future they go, the more sceptical the observer becomes – for the possible scenarios are literally limitless.

Too often, bankers ascribe too much meaning to such forecasts. To recap, projections are useful:

■ to evaluate appropriateness of proposed term lending
■ in constructing covenants/facility structure
■ as a tool in ultimate credit decision
■ as tools in problem loan restructuring.

They are not meant to predict the future, but can be useful in helping to reach an informed decision.

It should also be noted that the exponential effect on straight-line scenarios means that a small variation in Year 1 assumptions, extrapolated through to Year 5, may result in completely ridiculous balance sheet structures necessitating manual 'nip and tuck' overrides, thus making a mockery of the exercise of carefully selecting input variables. If this is the case, you should backtrack and ensure that you are making the proper assumptions, or at least develop convincing answers to the probing questions your credit committee will no doubt relish subjecting you to.

Analysts and rating analysts traditionally harp on about the 'quality of cash flow', which basically considers that a company which can report a 'steady and consistent earnings stream' is a 'better credit' than one whose aggregate earnings over a number of years is the same but which suffers volatility from year to year.

While this sounds wonderful in theory, in an era of mergers, acquisitions, divestitures, and permanent restructurings, as well as layoffs and outsourcing, harping on the virtues of stable cash flow today seems as pedestrian as advocates of historical ratio analysis were considered to be by aficionados of cash flow analysis in the 1980s. A look at the Vodafone cash flow provides ample evidence of this.

Moreover, the plethora of accounting scandals in 2003 and acknowledgement by industry gurus that the accounting profession has regressed to exercises of profit inflation, obfuscation, legerdemain, dysfunction and fraud means that the foundation of your analytical work – published accounts – may in themselves be unreliable.

To adopt a well known maxim of computer programming: 'GIGO' (Garbage In, Garbage Out) means that it is absolutely essential that you, the analyst, be able to understand the underlying quality of the information you are incorporating into your financial projections model and accordingly understand the inherent shortcomings of the data as well as the projection model.

Indeed, the main value of projections may not be as a forecasting tool but as a due diligence tool to ensure, in the event your bank is sued for negligence, that 'prudent lending principles' using 'established financial analysis techniques' were 'diligently adhered to', and that the finger of blame can thus move on, during the witch hunt, to the auditors of the company's financial statements!

Finally, while the use of sophisticated software packages which produce forecasts save time, you should understand how they work. You don't have to be a computer programmer, but you should at least know whether, for example, if you lower or raise debt in a company's balance sheet, will the changes arising in interest expenses be calculated by the model and accordingly inserted in the profit and loss statement or not? Another example is a case where you base the level of accounts receivable on sales. If you decide to change the sales growth assumption, do you have to adjust accounts receivable accordingly on the balance sheet, or does the computer model do so automatically?

While computer models are accurate and save time, you should at least understand how the model works so that you are able to answer any trick questions your enemies in the credit committee may throw at you.

Chapter self-test

1. Projections are useful for:
   (a) Predicting future company performance
   (b) Identifying a company's sensitive financial areas
   (c) Predicting bankruptcy
   (d) Identifying potential financial problems
   (e) Giving clues to a company's ability to repay debt

2. A company is expected to repay a large loan in semi annual instalments over a period of five years. The expected source of repayment would normally be:
   (a) The company's levels of cash
   (b) The company's finished goods in inventory
   (c) Accounts payable
   (d) Interest income
   (e) Cash flow from operations

3. What is the importance of net worth in cash flow analysis?
   (a) It indicates the company's ability to repay a loan
   (b) It indicates financial strength
   (c) It is used in calculating gearing
   (d) It indicates management effectiveness
   (e) None of the above

4. CF analysis differs from profit analysis in that:
   (a) It is harder to predict
   (b) Profit can be positive while CF can be negative, meaning the company may experience debt repayment problems
   (c) It is more precise than profit analysis
   (d) It can be used to predict gearing
   (e) It accounts for funds flows other than profit

5. What is cash flow lending?
   (a) Lending where repayment is from ongoing operations
   (b) Lending where repayment is secured by collateral
   (c) Lending where repayment is guaranteed by a parent

6. Building projections starts with forecasting:
   (a) Profits
   (b) Profitability
   (c) Sales
   (d) Gearing
   (e) Debt

7. What are cash drivers?
   (a) Items that contribute to profits
   (b) Items that generate cash
   (c) Profit and loss items that are linked to certain balance sheet items
   (d) Items that repay debt
   (e) Items that are used to project balance sheet accounts

8. Forecast assumptions are important because they
   (a) Predict future activity
   (b) Inform the reader of what underlies the projections
   (c) Define what variables are being used
   (d) Predict failure
   (e) Are used in calculating activity ratios

9. Historical profit margins are useful because they
   (a) Give clues to past performance
   (b) Can predict failure
   (c) Indicate profitability
   (d) Are used in calculating projected profit and loss accounts
   (e) Can indicate upwards or downwards trends

10. What can be wrong with using historical averages in projections?
    (a) They give a broad idea of the company's performance
    (b) They are useful in comparing subject with competitors
    (c) They do not accounts for trends which may have occurred

(d) They can give a good basis for projections

(e) They can even out the effects of one-off occurrences

11. In the balance sheet example, we have assumed that AmaOS's surplus funds arising from the €100 million debt facility and retained earnings stream are balanced on the assets side of the balance sheet by cash holdings. Which criticisms of this scenario are valid?

(a) Cash should be linked to sales

(b) It is unlikely that AmaOS would borrow debt just to hold it as cash and not invest it in fixed assets

(c) Cash should be used to repay debt

12. Why might AmaOS hold the surplus funds as cash?

(a) To generate interest income

(b) To increase working capital

(c) To use for unforeseen major acquisitions

13. If AmaOS shifted its surplus holdings from cash to fixed assets, what would happen?

(a) Sales would increase

(b) Cash flow would increase

(c) Working capital would decrease

14. Using the information below, fill in the blanks:

Sales 450,000

Gross profit margin 35%

Operating profit margin 17%

Inventory DOH 95

Accounts payable DOH 68

Accounts receivable DOH 37

Cost of goods sold

Gross profit

Operating profit

Inventory

Accounts payable

Accounts receivable

15. Why is new money need usually assumed to be debt?
    (a) To obtain conservative gearing ratios
    (b) Companies rarely indicate equity issues over a five-year timeframe
    (c) It results in a higher interest expense yielding a conservative interest cover ratio

16. If you adjust CGS upwards to account for increased future expenditures, what will happen to accounts payable?
    (a) Accounts payable will increase
    (b) Accounts payable will decrease
    (c) There will be no change

17. If trends indicate that inventory turnover is going to slow down, which element in the projections calculation (CGS*Inv DOH/365) would you change, and how, to account for this?
    (a) Cost of goods sold up
    (b) Inventory DOH up
    (c) Inventory DOH down
    (d) a, b
    (e) a, c

18. If AmaOS uses its €100 million facility to reduce current liabilities, which of the following statements would be true?
    (a) Working capital would rise
    (b) Interest expenses would fall
    (c) Interest expenses would be more predictable

Chapter self-test answers

Q1: (b), (d), (e)

Q2: (e)

Q3: (e) (although all are true, only (e) relates to CF analysis)

Q4: (b), (e)

Q5: (a)

Q6: (c)

Q7: (c), (e)

Q8: (b), (c)

Q9: (a), (d), (e)

Q10: (c)

Q11: (b)

Q12: (c)

Q13: (e)

Q14: Cost of goods sold   292,500

Gross profit   157,500

Operating profit   76,500

Inventory (CGS)   76,130

Accounts payable (CGS)   54,493

Accounts receivable (CGS)   9,650

Q15: (a), (b), (c)

Q16: (a)

Q17: (b)

Q18: (a), (c). Current liabilities would fall, improving the working capital position. The long-term funding profile would be not only more predictable but more stable. (b) might be true, but you can't answer (b) because it is unlikely that you could establish the true interest cost of fluctuating current liabilities.

Chapter 5

Cash flow forecasting of project finance

Introduction

In the previous section we looked at how to build projected financial statements based on historical financial statements, and in turn use the cash flow statement generated by the spreadsheet to undertake an analysis about the borrower's future ability to repay credit facilities. This exercise in turn entailed mastering various supporting component techniques such as net sales projections, historical averages of ratios, manipulating ratios, constructing debt runoff schedules, and making assumptions about allocation of new money needs. All this is useful when looking at a company with a historical track record.

There are other scenarios, however, that require cash flow projection techniques – for example, a merger of two companies, or the case of creating a special purpose vehicle to build a large-scale construction project such as a metro system, airport, road or dam. Here we are also interested in the use of projections, for example in understanding the future condition of an entity that a lender may be presently considering extending finance to. In this case, the key importance in preparing projections is not only to assess the inherent credit risk but also how to enhance that risk due to judicious structuring of the financing facility and identification of negotiating points to enhance that security further.

The underlying data and focus of this analysis will therefore be quite unlike that in the preceding chapter, and the analytical and construction techniques will be significantly different.

In this chapter we will look at the case of a special purpose vehicle designed to build a housing subdivision for expatriates in a foreign country, as this injects an element of juridical uncertainty into the equation and necessitates building financial projections without the use of a balance sheet or historical data. In effect, you, as an analyst, are forming a set of financial projections without any underlying historical financial data.

In this example, your bank is being approached to participate in a syndicated loan facility whose terms and conditions are summarized as follows.

Details of project and borrower

Borrower	OASIS RESIDENCES (Durakistan) Ltd
Amount	€2,000,000 participation in a €8,000,000 loan (it is proposed that the bank should act as Agent Bank)
Purpose	To finance the construction of 40 executive houses in Durakistan, a small country in the Middle East, together with associated engineering and site works
Period of drawdown	Eighteen months from date of loan
Repayment	Five equal annual instalments of €1,600,000 commencing 12 months from date of loan agreement
Security offered by customer	Charge over the project plus the possibility of a guarantee from Oasis Residences (International) Ltd
Interest rate	Tentatively 8%

Oasis Residences (International) Ltd., the international arm of the Oasis Residences Group PLC, has formed a new company – Oasis Residences (Durakistan) Ltd – for the purpose of the above project. Oasis Residences (International) Ltd does not, however, have any equity interest in this new company. Local interests wholly own it under the law of the land.

The borrower has entered into a form of agreement with the Emir of Durakistan to lease a plot of land in Durakistan, and will enter into further contracts with Oasis Residences (Homes) Ltd UK for the supply and erection of 40 prefabricated houses.

The engineering, ancillary site works etc. will be carried out by local subcontractors. The company advises that the demand for houses of this nature from international companies operating in Durakistan for their expatriate staff is strong. In view of the serious shortage of accommodation in the area, no difficulty is foreseen in letting the houses; in fact, a number of Letters of Intent to lease the houses are already being negotiated.

Repayment of the loan will come from the rental income, after deduction of overheads, payments under the Head Lease, etc.

The Oasis Residences Group is a good customer of the bank, but the bank's General Management Committee has recommended that further exposure should be on a secured basis only. The legal opinion and cash flow have been obtained, and extracts are reproduced here.

The following legal opinion has been received from the bank's lawyer:

> The 'Head Lease' of the land constitutes an agreement whereby the use of the land, and all proceeds there from, are granted by the lessor to Oasis Residences (Durakistan) Ltd for a period of ten years. Oasis Residences (Durakistan) Ltd have an obligation under the agreement to complete the housing project up to local building standards within period of two years at a cost of not less than €8 million. This is to ensure sufficient expenditure in Durakistan and on the project. If it does not comply with this obligation within the specified two years, the lessor has the right to terminate the agreement and reclaim the land. At the end of the ten-year lease period, ownership of the land, the housing and all proceeds there from revert to the lessor.

> This is necessarily a rather artificial agreement when considered in the light of the whole transaction, and we feel that we should add the following general comments. The Law of the State of Durakistan relating to the business of contracts of works requires that all companies must either be wholly owned by a Durakistani national or be granted a Durakistani decree of exemption before it can operate in this field. At the present the authorities are not issuing such decrees, and so the majority of construction companies are operating by supplying a Durakistani company with management and expert construction advice. In practice, this means that their position is exactly the same as set out in the agreement. This fact is fully

accepted by the authorities, who have never interfered with or questioned this practice as it is appreciated that such expertise is necessary, but at the same time the ultimate responsibility or the works remain with a Durakistani as required by the relevant legislation. In this case, the authorities are less likely to investigate this work as it is not their practice to interfere in an individual Durakistani's affairs.

In conclusion, therefore, we would comment that, although some vestige of doubt must remain as such practice has never been brought before the commercial court and has not been directly approved in all the circumstances, we consider that in practice this is a satisfactory arrangement.

The agent bank has provided summary financial statements for the project.

Cash flow forecasting

Step one

Before committing to financing, you are asked to identify the major risks of the project. In particular:

■ what questions would you ask about the assumed cash flow figures (see Table 5.1)?
■ what relevant general points can be made?

Observations

■ No rental increases or variable testing have been factored into the model
■ No occupancy rates or variable testing have been factored into the model
■ There is no segregation of operational and financial expenses
■ There is no variable testing of interest expenses
■ There is no ability to calculate financial rations
■ First indications indicate a weak (negative) cash flow, but it is difficult to see this in terms of total cash inflows
■ This is basically a rudimentary and poorly designed set of projections, although there is enough information present to undertake a more thorough analysis.

Table 5.1   Oasis Residences Project Finance Case Study No. 1

YEAR	1	2	3	4	5	6	7	8	9	10
Cash Inflows										
Equity Capital	1000									
Loan	7300	700								
Rental Income	240	2340	2340	2340	2340	2340	2340	2340	2340	2340
Net Elec Receipts	2	144	144	144	144	144	144	144	144	144
Total Inflows	**8542**	**3184**	**2484**	**2484**	**2484**	**2484**	**2484**	**2484**	**2484**	**2484**
Cash Outflows										
Construction Costs	6657	952								
Legal Fees	200									
Ground Rent	500	500	500	500	500	500	500	500	500	500
Loan Interest	255	534	448	320	192	64				
Loan Repayment		1600	1600	1600	1600	1600				
Total Outflows	**7612**	**3586**	**2548**	**2420**	**2292**	**2164**	**500**	**500**	**500**	**500**
Cash Surplus/ Deficit	**930**	**−402**	**−64**	**64**	**192**	**320**	**1984**	**1984**	**1984**	**1984**
Cumulative Surplus/Deficit	**930**	**528**	**464**	**528**	**720**	**1040**	**3024**	**5008**	**6992**	**8976**

Step two

You are asked to check whether the cash flow cover for interest payable and debt repayment each year is acceptable.

Rearrange the cash flow table to arrive at new lines for:

■ net cash flow before finance payments
■ interest and debt repayment
■ total interest and debt payments.

Calculate the debt service ratio for each year. What comments would you make about it?

(See Table 5.2.)

Observations

- The model has been redesigned to include cash flow *before* and *after* financing payments
- This enables debt service ratios in function of pre-finance available cash flows to be calculated

Table 5.2 Oasis Residences Project Finance Case Study No. 2

YEAR	1	2	3	4	5	6	7	8	9	10
Cash Inflows										
Equity Capital	1000									
Loan	7300	700								
Rental Income	240	2340	2340	2340	2340	2340	2340	2340	2340	2340
Net Elec Receipts	2	144	144	144	144	144	144	144	144	144
Total Inflows	8542	3184	2484	2484	2484	2484	2484	2484	2484	2484
Cash Outflows										
Construction Costs	6657	952								
Legal Fees	200									
Ground Rent	500	500	500	500	500	500	500	500	500	500
Operating Outflows	7357	1452	500	500	500	500	500	500	500	500
Net CF Before Finance Pmts	1185	1732	1984	1984	1984	1984	1984	1984	1984	1984
Loan Interest	255	534	448	320	192	64				
Loan Repayment		1600	1600	1600	1600	1600				
Total Debt + Interest Pmts	255	2134	2048	1920	1792	1664	0	0	0	0
Total Outflows	7612	3586	2548	2420	2292	2164	500	500	500	500
Cash Surplus/Deficit	930	−402	−64	64	192	320	1984	1984	1984	1984
Cumulative Surplus/Deficit	930	528	464	528	720	1040	3024	5008	6992	8976
Debt Service Ratio	4.65	0.81	0.97	1.03	1.11	1.19	NA	NA	NA	NA

- We can therefore see that the DS ratio is consistently weak and that the facility is ill-adapted to the project cash flows (as they stand)
- The model still does not enable variable input analysis to be made, however, and is still a poorly designed spreadsheet.

Step three

For the purposes of analysis, and to assist in restructuring the finance package, the bank decides that a minimum figure of 1.40 should be set for the debt service ratio. Considering the riskiness of the project, this should be sufficient to maintain acceptable cover in the event of adverse variations in constructing costs and rental income.

Working within this new constraint, it comes up with a revised cash flow (see Table 5.3).

Table 5.3 Oasis Residences Project Finance Case Study No. 3

YEAR	1	2	3	4	5	6	7	8	9	10
Construction Costs	−6657	−952								
Legal Fees	−200									
Ground Rent	−500	−500	−500	−500	−500	−500	−500	−500	−500	−500
Rental Income	240	2340	2340	2340	2340	2340	2340	2340	2340	2340
Net Elec Receipts	2	144	144	144	144	144	144	144	144	144
NOCF	**−7115**	**1032**	**1984**	**1984**	**1984**	**1984**	**1984**	**1984**	**1984**	**1984**
Equity Capital	2000									
Loan	5500	1000	500							
NC Before Finance	**385**	**2032**	**2484**	**1984**	**1984**	**1984**	**1984**	**1984**	**1984**	**1984**
Loan Interest		451	395	306	204	202	275			
Loan		1005	1385	1111	1213	1215	1075			
Total Fin Outflows	0	1456	1780	1417	1417	1417	1350	0	0	0
NCF	385	576	704	567	567	567	634	1984	1984	1984
DS Ratio		1.40	1.40	1.40	1.40	1.40	1.47	NA	NA	NA

Calculate the debt service ratio for each year. What comments would you make about it?

Observations

The spreadsheet has been redesigned to separate cash inflows from operations, and from debt. We also see that the project financing has been restructured with:

- a €1 million reduction in the loan outstanding
- a €1 million capital injection varying (lowered) annual repayments
- a longer repayment period stretching over six years as opposed to five.

This shows the ability to inject capital and adjust the size/tenor of the facility to yield a more acceptable DS ratio (as a potential negotiating point). However, this is not ideal, since the repayment period is a non-standard six years. Moreover, none of the key underlying net sales assumptions have been identified or tested.

The new spreadsheet enables the company forecasts and DS rations to be graphically depicted as in Figures 5.1 and 5.2.

Step four

The bank tests the new package by flexing:

- construction costs
- rental prices
- occupancy rates
- electricity receipts
- equity injections
- debt injections
- amortization schedules
- interest expenses.

This necessitates a complete redesign of the spreadsheet to enable the manipulation of variable inputs. The resulting effect on the cash flow is shown in Table 5.4.

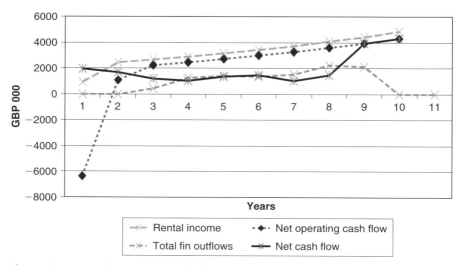

Figure 5.1 Housing project cash flow model, base case

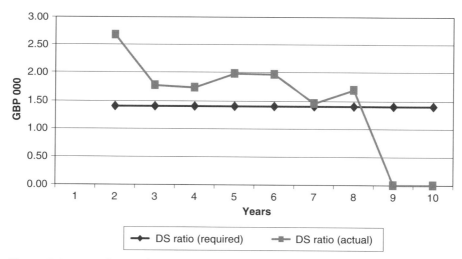

Figure 5.2 Housing project cash flow model, debt service ration – base case

Table 5.4   Oasis Residences Project Finance Case Study No. 4

VARIABLE INPUT ZONE										
Increase in house rent	9.0%		DSR	130%		Int Rate	6%		Equity	1500
Increase in land rent	3.0%	Y1	FULL rent	2340		Y1 elec	144			
Occupancy	40%	95%	95%	95%	95%	95%	95%	95%	95%	95%
FULL occupancy	2340	2551	2780	3030	3303	3600	3924	4278	4663	5082

YEAR	1	2	3	4	5	6	7	8	9	10
Construction Costs	−6657	−952								
Legal Fees	−200									
Ground Rent	−500	−515	−530	−546	−563	−580	−597	−615	−633	−652
Rental Income	936	2423	2641	2879	3138	3420	3728	4064	4429	4828
Net Elec Receipts	58	137	137	137	137	137	137	137	137	137
Net Operating Cash Flow	−6363	1093	2247	2469	2712	2978	3268	3586	3933	4313
Equity Capital	1500									
Loan	6800	1000	200							
NCF Before Finance	1937	2093	2447	2469	2712	2978	3268	3586	3933	4313
Loan outstanding	6800	7800	7200	6200	5200	4000	2000	0	0	0
Loan Interest		408	468	432	372	312	240	120	0	0
Loan			800	1000	1000	1200	2000	2000		0
Total Fin Outflows	0	408	1268	1432	1372	1512	2240	2120	0	0
Net Cash Flow	1937	1685	1179	1037	1340	1466	1028	1466	3933	4313
Carry forward Net	1937	3621	4801	5838	7178	8644	9672	11137	15070	19383
DS Ratio Actual		268%	177%	172%	198%	197%	146%	169%	NA	NA
DS Ratio Required		140%	140%	140%	140%	140%	140%	140%	140%	140%

Comment on the impact on the bank and on shareholders. Are any further measures needed?

Observation

It is obvious that the earlier three spreadsheets were poorly designed and did not enable a proper sensitivity analysis to be made. Accordingly, the final spreadsheet has been completely redesigned with the following innovations:

- All input variables are colour-coded to the appropriate area of the spreadsheet.
- All input variables are grouped at the top of the spreadsheet in a 'dashboard format' so that individual variables can be changed and the net effect seen in the spreadsheet.
- Key financial indicators are linked to graphs that provide a clear view of the project cash flow dynamics.
- Rental income in the previous models exhibited no increases for ten years! The new spreadsheet sensitizes the rental income stream to two key elements – rental increases and occupancy rates.
- The occupancy rates can therefore build up more slowly and rental increases be phased in over time. This has a dramatic effect on project cash flow and the profits accumulated during the ten-year timeframe.
- Electricity receipts are linked the occupancy rates.
- Land rent is subject to an annual increase.
- Equity can be adjusted.
- Outstanding debt is subject to variable interest rate changes.

Such a model enables the identification of all key variables and adoption of measures to improve the security of the facility, such as:

- negotiating rent increases in the tenancy contracts
- obtaining bloc commitments from company rentals
- planning and identifying potential vacancies
- understanding how much discount can be offered without excessively adverse impact on project cash flows

■ the advantages in setting up an escrow account in order to monitor cash flows and hold portions of the accumulated surplus as security to compensate for the legal ambiguity of property rights in Durakistan.

The end result is that it is possible to construct a cash flow model where the FP ratio is entirely adequate. The next step of course is negotiating a facility which is accepted by the borrower and is sufficiently well structured to meet with interest in the syndication marketplace.

Conclusion

This project finance forecasting model illustrates several key points:

1 The need to be able to construct projections when no financial statements are available
2 The need to identify key project variables
3 The need to select the appropriate indices to measure performance
4 The need to consider carefully the above two points in designing a spreadsheet that incorporates all relevant elements of the project and enables the manipulation and testing of key variables.

Chapter 6

Pro forma forecasts using AMADEUS electronic databases

Subscription services via the Internet provide information on nearly anything anybody might need. Such information can be particularly useful to see what a company has been doing since its last published annual report. For example, a company could have changed its corporate structure, dismissed certain members of management, sold or acquired a subsidiary, entered into an alliance or cooperative agreement with a competitor to market or distribute a product, or availed itself of the services of a rival bank in closing a transaction.

One such on-line database is AMADEUS. AMADEUS (Analyse MAjor Database from EUropean Sources) is a comprehensive, pan-European database containing financial information on 7 million public and private companies in 38 European countries. It combines data from over 30 information providers (IPs). AMADEUS is a modular product; you can choose the level of coverage that you require – the top 250,000 companies, the top 1.5 million, or all companies. AMADEUS is available on CD/DVD-ROM, as an intranet feed and on the Internet.

AMADEUS is exclusive to BvDEP and its information providers, and is not available via any other platform. BvDEP identifies the best source of information in each country and applies strict inclusion criteria to prevent any bias in coverage.

A standard company report includes:

- twenty-two balance sheet items
- twenty-five profit and loss account items
- twenty-six ratios
- descriptive information, including trade description and activity codes (NACE 1, NAICS or US SIC can be used across the database)
- ownership information, which is researched by BvD's own team of consultants
- Reuters' news, security and price information
- links to an executive report with integral graphs
- a report comparing the financials of the company's default peer group.

In addition to the existing ratios you can also create your own, which you can display in the reports and also use in your searches and analyses.

Each company is part of a default peer group based on its activity codes, and integral graphs illustrate its position in this peer group. A company tree diagram instantly illustrates the structure of the group.

The advantage of AMADEUS is that it provides the ability to undertake peer group analysis. Typically it comes to the fore when there is a wealth of data to work with. The financial ratios calculated on the spreadsheet can be compared with published data, such as lists of industry standard ratios.

The problem here is that you do not know how the spreadsheets and resulting calculations from the published sources have been arrived at, which would render comparison between the published work and the analysts' spreadsheet meaningful.

The screencap in Figure 6.1 illustrates the company search mechanism.

Such on-line databases are rapidly supplanting traditional paper-based annual reports and idiosyncratic and heterogeneous spreadsheet models.

The on-line database can be accessed by web browser, and reports converted into exportable RTF or XL format for subsequent manipulation.

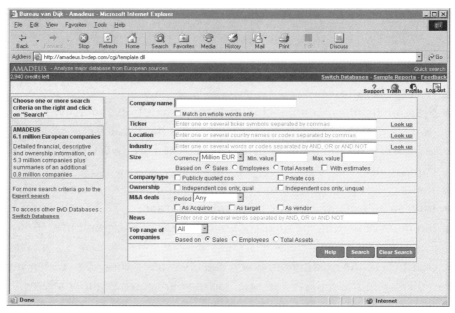

Figure 6.1 The company search mechanism
Source: Bureau Van Dijk, AMADEUS 2004

Forecasts can therefore be prepared quickly by extracting the financial statements for, say, two companies, and combining them into a spreadsheet model (see Chapter 4) to effect hypothetical merger projections.

It should be remembered, however, that you become completely dependent on the accuracy of the accounts classified by BVD into its database.

Here, we provide the full spreadsheet for a major EU corporate, Vodafone, the mobile telephone operator (see Table 6.1).

Table 6.1   Spreadsheet for Vodafone

VODAFONE GROUP PUBLIC LIMITED COMPANY

Vodafone House/The Connection
RG14 2FN NEWBURY

UNITED KINGDOM

Phone: +44 1635 33251

Web site: www.vodafone.co.uk

Reporting basis	**Consolidated data**
BVD ID number:	GB01833679
BVD account number:	GB01833679C
ISIN number:	GB0007192106
SEDOL number:	0719210
VALOR number:	000416029
Date of incorporation:	17/07/1984
Legal form:	Public, quoted
Latest account date:	31/03/2003
Account published in:	GBP
Type of account avail.:	Consolidated

Status: Active
Publicly quoted: Yes

Main exchange: London Stock Exchange SETS

Ticker symbol: VOD

Operating revenue/Turnover:	30,375 mil	**P/L for period:**	−9,164 mil
Market Cap: (9/01/2004):	100,893,417 th	**Employees:**	66,667
Primary Nace Rev 1.1 code:	6420 – Tele-communications		

Peer Group: 6420 VL – (very large companies)

No. of recorded shareholders: 6   **No. of rec. subsidiaries:**   77

BvD Independence Indicator: A−

FINANCIAL PROFILE

Consolidated data	31/03/2003 12 months milGBP	31/03/2002 12 months milGBP	31/03/2001 12 months milGBP	31/03/2000 12 months milGBP	31/03/1999 12 months milGBP
Operating revenue/turnover	30,375	22,845	15,004	7,873	3,360
Profit (loss) before tax	−6,208	−13,539	−8,095	1,349	935
Cash flow	6,690	−1,837	1,793	2,084	965
Total assets	163,280	162,900	172,065	153,368	3,644
Shareholders funds	131,534	133,428	147,782	142,360	815
Current ratio	0.60	0.70	1.43	0.57	0.52
Profit margin (%)	−20.44	−59.26	−53.95	17.13	27.83
Return on shareholders funds (%)	−4.72	−10.15	−5.48	0.95	114.80
Return on capital employed (%)	−3.41	−8.49	−4.35	1.17	48.70
Solvency ratio (%)	80.56	81.91	85.89	92.82	22.36
Number of employees	66,667	67,178	53,325	29,465	12,642

(continued)

VODAFONE GROUP PUBLIC LIMITED COMPANY
INDUSTRY/ACTIVITIES

Trade Description
Group is principally engaged in the provision of mobile telecommunications, providing mobile voice, messaging, business, information and entertainment services to its global customer base.

UK SIC (2003) code(s)
Primary code:
6420 – Telecommunications

Secondary code(s):
7415 – Holding companies including head offices

NACE Rev. 1.1 code(s)
Primary code:
6420 – Telecommunications

Secondary code(s):
7415 – Management activities of holding companies

US SIC code(s) [derived from NACE Rev. 1.1 code(s)]
Core code:
489 – Communications services, not elsewhere specified

Primary code(s):
4899 – Communications services, not elsewhere specified

Secondary code(s):
6712 – Offices of bank holding companies
6719 – Offices of holding companies, not elsewhere classified
6722 – Management investment offices, open-end

NAICS 2002 code(s) [derived from NACE Rev. 1.1 code(s)]
Core code:
5179 – Other Telecommunications

Primary code(s):
517910 – Other Telecommunications

Secondary code(s):
551111 – Offices of bank holding companies
551112 – Offices of other holding companies

VODAFONE GROUP PUBLIC LIMITED COMPANY

BALANCE SHEET Consolidated data	31/03/2003 12 months milGBP	31/03/2002 12 months milGBP	31/03/2001 12 months milGBP	31/03/2000 12 months milGBP	31/03/1999 12 months milGBP
Fixed assets	154,689	153,462	154,375	150,851	2,852
Intangible fixed assets	108,085	105,944	108,839	22,206	329
Tangible fixed assets	19,574	18,541	10,586	6,307	2,150
Other fixed assets	27,030	28,977	34,950	122,338	372
Current assets	8,591	9,438	17,690	2,517	792
Stocks	365	513	316	190	45
Debtors	2,858	3,397	1,863	977	385
Other current assets	5,368	5,528	15,511	1,350	362
Cash & cash equivalent	475	80	68	159	6
Total assets	163,280	162,900	172,065	153,368	3,644
Shareholders funds	131,534	133,428	147,782	142,360	815
Capital	4,275	4,273	4,054	3,797	155
Other shareholders funds	127,259	129,155	143,728	138,563	660
Non-current liabilities	17,453	16,017	11,906	6,567	1,299
Long term debt	13,175	12,584	10,772	6,038	1,137
Other non-current liabilities	4,278	3,433	1,134	529	162
Current liabilities	14,293	13,455	12,377	4,441	1,530
Loans	1,443	1,329	3,618	796	174
Creditors	2,497	3,335	1,899	706	216
Other current liabilities	10,353	8,791	6,860	2,939	1,141
Total shareh. funds & liab.	163,280	162,900	172,065	153,368	3,644
Working capital	726	575	280	461	214
Enterprise value	91,142	102,376	108,872	177,159	36,820
Number of employees	66,667	67,178	53,325	29,465	12,642

(*continued*)

PROFIT AND LOSS ACCOUNT Consolidated data	31/03/2003 12 months milGBP	31/03/2002 12 months milGBP	31/03/2001 12 months milGBP	31/03/2000 12 months milGBP	31/03/1999 12 months milGBP
Operating revenue/ turnover	30,375	22,845	15,004	7,873	3,360
Sales	n.a.	n.a.	n.a.	n.a.	n.a.
Costs of goods sold	17,896	n.a.	8,702	4,359	1,809
Gross profit	12,479	n.a.	6,302	3,514	1,551
Other operating expenses	17,774	n.a.	12,741	2,533	704
Operating P/L	−5,295	−11,834	−6,439	981	847
Financial revenue	210	−860	−500	756	183
Financial expenses	1,123	845	1,156	388	94
Financial P/L	−913	−1,705	−1,656	368	89
P/L before tax	−6,208	−13,539	−8,095	1,349	935
Taxation	2,956	2,140	1,290	685	252
P/L after tax	−9,164	−15,679	−9,385	664	683
Extr. and other revenue	n.a.	n.a.	n.a.	n.a.	n.a.
Extr. and other expenses	n.a.	n.a.	n.a.	n.a.	n.a.
Extr. and other P/L	0	0	0	0	0
P/L for period	−9,164	−15,679	−9,385	664	683
Export turnover	n.a.	n.a.	11,560	4,972	1,273
Material costs	n.a.	n.a.	n.a.	n.a.	n.a.
Costs of employees	2,266	1,987	1,540	874	349
Depreciation	15,854	13,842	11,178	1,420	282
Interest paid	1,123	845	1,156	388	94
Cash flow	6,690	−1,837	1,793	2,084	965
Added value	13,035	3,135	5,779	4,031	1,661
EBIT	−5,295	−11,834	−6,439	981	847
EBITDA	10,559	2,008	4,739	2,401	1,129

VODAFONE GROUP PUBLIC LIMITED COMPANY
RATIOS

Consolidated data	31/03/2003 12 months	31/03/2002 12 months	31/03/2001 12 months	31/03/2000 12 months	31/03/1999 12 months
Current ratio	0.60	0.70	1.43	0.57	0.52
Liquidity ratio (%)	0.58	0.66	1.40	0.52	0.49
Shareholders liquidity ratio (%)	7.54	8.33	12.41	21.68	0.63
Solvency ratio (%)	80.56	81.91	85.89	92.82	22.36
Gearing (%)	14.37	13.00	10.50	5.17	180.80
Share funds per employee (Ths.)	1,973	1,986	2,771	4,831	64
Work. capital per employee (Ths.)	11	9	5	16	17
Total assets per employee (Ths.)	2,449	2,425	3,227	5,205	288
Profit margin (%)	−20.44	−59.26	−53.95	17.13	27.83
Return on shareholders funds (%)	−4.72	−10.15	−5.48	0.95	114.80
Return on capital employed (%)	−3.41	−8.49	−4.35	1.17	48.70
Return on total assets (%)	−3.80	−8.31	−4.70	0.88	25.67
Interest cover	−4.72	−14.00	−5.57	2.53	9.00
Stock turnover	83.22	44.53	47.48	41.44	75.17
Collection period (days)	34	54	45	45	41
Credit period (days)	30	53	46	32	23
Net assets turnover	0.20	0.15	0.09	0.05	1.59
Costs of employees/oper. rev. (%)	7.46	8.70	10.26	11.10	10.39
Operat. rev. per employee (Ths.)	456	340	281	267	266
Aver. cost of empl./year (Ths.)	34	30	29	30	28
Profit per employee (Ths.)	n.a.	n.a.	n.a.	46	74
Cash flow/turnover (%)	22.02	−8.04	11.95	26.47	28.73
Gross margin (%)	41.08	n.a.	42.00	44.63	46.15
EBIT margin (%)	−17.43	−51.80	−42.92	12.46	25.20
EBITDA margin (%)	34.76	8.79	31.58	30.50	33.60
Export turnover/total turnover (%)	n.a.	n.a.	77.05	63.15	37.87

(*continued*)

VODAFONE GROUP PUBLIC LIMITED COMPANY
BOARD MEMBERS AND OFFICERS

Name	Function
Peter Bamford	Director
Michael Boskin	Director
Alec Broers	Director
John Buchanan	Director
Vittorio Colao	Director
Thomas Geitner	Director
Paul Hazen	Director
Julian Horn-Smith	Director
Penny Hughes	Director
Kenneth Hydon	Director
Ian Maclaurin	Director
Arun Sarin	Director
David Scholey	Director
Jurgen Schrempp	Director
Luc Vandevelde	Director
Stephen Scott	Company Secretary

Auditors
Deloitte & Touche

VODAFONE GROUP PUBLIC LIMITED COMPANY
SHAREHOLDERS

Company name	Country	Type	Ownership		Source		Company inform.		
			Direct (%)	Total (%)	Source ident.	Date of inform.	Closing date	Op. revenue (mil USD)*	Total assets (mil USD)
Shareholders									
1. Bank of New York	n.a.	B	13.40	n.a.	RS	05/2002	n.a.	n.a.	n.a.
2. UNICAJA – Montes de Piedad y Caja de Ahorros de Ronda, Cadiz, Almeria, Malaga Y Antequera	ES	B	0.13	n.a.	WW	05/2003	><	510	15,440
3. Gent C.C.	n.a.	I	–	n.a.	RS	03/2002	–	–	–
4. Horn-Smith J.M.	n.a.	I	–	n.a.	RS	03/2002	–	–	–
5. Hutchison Whampoa Ltd	HK	C	–	n.a.	OS	05/2003	><	9,647	63,302
6. Hydon K.J.	n.a.	I	–	n.a.	RS	03/2002	–	–	–

* For an insurance company the corresponding value is the Gross Premium Written, and for a bank it is the Operating Income (memo).

This is a quoted company.

VODAFONE GROUP PUBLIC LIMITED COMPANY SUBSIDIARIES (Roll-up structure)*

Company name	Country	Ownership Direct (%)	Total (%)	Level of own.	Status	Source ident.	Date of inform.	Company inform. Closing date	Op. revenue (mil USD)*	Total Assets (mil USD)
1. Project Telecom PLC	GB	100.00	100.00	1	UO+	OS	10/2003	><	508	123
2. Vodafone Finance Limited	GB	100.00	100.00	1	UO+	RM	03/2002	><	n.a.	6,404
3. Vodafone Americas INC	US	–	100.00	n.a.	UO+	RM	03/2002	n.a.	n.a.	n.a.
4. Vodafone Deutschland Gmbh	DE	–	100.00	n.a.	UO+	RM	03/2002	><	3,579	n.a.
5. Vodafone Europe B.V.	NL	–	100.00	n.a.	UO+	RM	03/2002	=	n.a.	6,820
6. Vodafone International B.V.	NL	–	100.00	n.a.	UO+	RM	03/2002	=	1,325	7,901
7. Vodafone International INC.	US	–	100.00	n.a.	UO+	RM	03/2002	n.a.	n.a.	n.a.
8. Vodafone Ireland Limited	IE	–	100.00	n.a.	UO+	RM	03/2002	n.a.	n.a.	n.a.
9. Vodafone Limited	GB	–	100.00	n.a.	UO+	RM	03/2002	=	6,238	15,665
10. Vodafone New Zealand Limited	NZ	–	100.00	n.a.	UO+	RM	03/2002	n.a.	n.a.	n.a.
11. Vodafone UK Limited	GB	–	100.00	n.a.	UO+	RM	03/2002	><	0	32,523
12. General Mobile Corporation Limited	GB	WO	WO	1	UO+	JO	05/2002	=	n.a.	159
13. Mobile Telecom Group Limited	GB	WO	WO	1	UO+	JO	05/2002	=	35	6
14. Voda Limited	GB	WO	WO	1	UO+	JO	05/2002	=	n.a.	934
15. Vodacall Limited	GB	WO	WO	1	UO+	JO	05/2002	=	n.a.	n.a.
16. Vodafone (New Zealand) Hedging Limited	GB	WO	WO	1	UO+	JO	05/2002	><	n.a.	253
17. Vodafone Asia Pacific Limited	GB	WO	WO	1	UO+	JO	05/2002	=	n.a.	0
18. Vodafone Cellular Limited	GB	WO	WO	1	UO+	JO	05/2002	=	n.a.	1,828
19. Vodafone Corporate Secretaries Limited	GB	WO	WO	1	UO+	JO	05/2002	=	n.a.	0
20. Vodafone Euro Hedging Limited	GB	WO	WO	1	UO+	JO	05/2002	><	n.a.	44,723
21. Vodafone Euro Hedging Two	GB	WO	WO	1	UO+	JO	05/2002	><	n.a.	30,778
22. Vodafone European Investments	GB	WO	WO	1	UO+	JO	05/2002	=	n.a.	143,766
23. Vodafone European Portal Limited	GB	WO	WO	1	UO+	JO	05/2002	=	n.a.	0
24. Vodafone Global Products and Services Limited	GB	WO	WO	1	UO+	JO	05/2002	><	284	267
25. Vodafone Group (Directors) Trustee Limited	GB	WO	WO	1	UO+	JO	05/2002	=	n.a.	0
26. Vodafone Group Pension Trustee Limited	GB	WO	WO	1	UO+	JO	05/2002	=	n.a.	0
27. Vodafone Group Services Limited	GB	WO	WO	1	UO+	JO	05/2002	><	113	164

No.	Company										
28.	Vodafone Group Share Schemes Trustee Limited	GB	WO	WO	1	UO+	JO	05/2002	=	n.a.	0
29.	Vodafone Group Share Trustee Limited	GB	WO	WO	1	UO+	JO	05/2002	=	n.a.	0
30.	Vodafone International Holdings BV	NL	WO	WO	1	UO+	JO	03/2003	=	n.a.	20,433
31.	Vodafone International Operations Limited	GB	WO	WO	1	UO+	JO	05/2002	=	n.a.	260,557
32.	Vodafone Investments Limited	GB	WO	WO	1	UO+	JO	05/2002	=	n.a.	1,063
33.	Vodafone Mobile Communications Limited	GB	WO	WO	1	UO+	JO	05/2002	=	n.a.	5,172
34.	Vodafone Mobile Enterprises Limited	GB	WO	WO	1	UO+	JO	05/2002	=	n.a.	46,052
35.	Vodafone Nominees Limited	GB	WO	WO	1	UO+	JO	05/2002	=	n.a.	0
36.	Vodafone Overseas Finance Limited	GB	WO	WO	1	UO+	JO	05/2002	><	n.a.	4,598
37.	Vodafone PTY Limited	AU	WO	WO	1	UO+	JO	03/2003	n.a.	n.a.	n.a.
38.	Vodafone Satellite Services Limited	GB	WO	WO	1	UO+	JO	05/2002	><	0	117
39.	Vodafone Ventures Limited	GB	WO	WO	1	UO+	JO	05/2002	=	n.a.	3
40.	Vodafone Yen Finance Limited	GB	WO	WO	1	UO+	JO	05/2002	=	n.a.	3,788
41.	Vodafone Americas INC	US	WO	n.a.	1	UO+	WW	01/2003	><	5,181	17,553
42.	Vodafone D2 GMBH	DE	–	99.70	n.a.	UO+	RM	03/2002	><	1,533	10,363
43.	Vodafone Holding GMBH	DE	–	99.60	n.a.	UO+	RM	03/2002	><	12,478	70,881
44.	Vodafone Information Systems GMBH	DE	–	99.60	n.a.	UO+	RM	03/2002	=	283	201
45.	Vodafone Network PTY Ltd	AU	–	95.50	n.a.	UO	RM	03/2002	n.a.	n.a.	n.a.
46.	Vodafone Pacific Limited	AU	–	95.50	n.a.	UO	RM	03/2002	n.a.	n.a.	n.a.
47.	Vodafone Espana SA	ES	–	91.60	n.a.	–	RM	03/2002	><	2,617	2,597
48.	Vodafone Magyarország Mobil Távközlési RT.	HU	–	83.90	n.a.	UO	OS	10/2002	><	74	406
49.	Vodafone Malta Limited	MT	–	80.00	n.a.	UO	RM	03/2002	n.a.	n.a.	n.a.
50.	Vodafone Libertel N.V.	NL	77.56	n.a.	1	UO	OS	11/2002	=	1,626	1,834
51.	Omnitel Pronto Italia	IT	–	76.59	n.a.	UO	RM	03/2002	><	5,096	7,256
52.	Arcor Ag & Co. KG	DE	–	73.59	n.a.	UO	RM	03/2002	=	1,425	2,013
53.	Europolitan Vodafone AB	SE	–	71.09	n.a.	UO	RM	03/2002	=	742	1,096
54.	J-Phone Co Ltd	JP	–	69.70	n.a.	UO	RM	03/2002	n.a.	n.a.	n.a.
55.	Japan Telecom Holdings Co., Ltd.	JP	–	66.70	n.a.	UO	RM	03/2002	=	15,002	15,312
56.	Vodafone Egypt Telecommunications Co SAE	EG	–	60.00	n.a.	UO	RM	03/2002	n.a.	n.a.	n.a.
57.	Panafon Hellenic Telecommunications Company SA	GR	–	51.90	n.a.	UO	RM	03/2002	n.a.	n.a.	n.a.
58.	Vodafone Telecel-Comunicações Pessoais, S.A.	PT	–	50.90	n.a.	–	RM	03/2002	><	838	878

(continued)

Company name	Country	Ownership				Source		Company inform.		
		Direct (%)	Total (%)	Level of own.	Status	Source ident.	Date of inform.	Closing date	Op. revenue (mil USD)*	Total Assets (mil USD)
59. **Mannesmann Italiana**	IT	–	MO	n.a.	UO	WW	05/2003	><	6	3
60. Vodafone Ag & Co. OHG	DE	–	MO	n.a.	UO	WW	04/2003	n.a.	12,200	n.a.
61. Vodafone Americas INC	US	–	MO	n.a.	UO	WW	06/2003	n.a.	21	n.a.
62. Vodafone Fiji Limited	FJ	–	49.00	n.a.	UO–	RM	03/2002	n.a.	n.a.	n.a.
63. Cellco Partnership	US	–	45.00	n.a.	UO–	RM	03/2002	n.a.	19	n.a.
64. Verizon Wireless INC.	US	45.00	n.a.	1	–	WW	10/2002	><	7,659	15,843
65. Grupo Lusacell SA DE CV	MX	–	34.50	n.a.	UO–	RM	03/2002	n.a.	n.a.	n.a.
66. Vodacom Group (PTY) Limited	ZA	–	31.50	n.a.	UO–	RM	03/2002	n.a.	n.a.	n.a.
67. **Cie Transatlantique Telecommunication (Transtel)**	FR	30.00	n.a.	1	–	SC	08/2003	><	0	1,264
68. Safaricom Limited	KE	–	30.00	n.a.	UO–	RM	03/2002	n.a.	n.a.	n.a.
69. **Belgacom Mobile**	BE	–	25.00	n.a.	–	RM	03/2002	><	2,157	1,787
70. **Swisscom Mobile AG**	CH	–	25.00	n.a.	–	RM	03/2002	><	2,965	2,711
71. RPG Cellular Services Limited	IN	–	20.80	n.a.	–	RM	03/2002	n.a.	n.a.	n.a.
72. **Mobifon SA**	RO	–	20.10	n.a.	–	RM	03/2002	><	437	495
73. **Societe Francaise DU Radiotele Phone (SFR)**	FR	20.00	n.a.	1	–	SC	08/2003	><	6,658	5,587
74. **Polkomtel S.A.**	PL	–	19.60	n.a.	–	RM	03/2002	><	1,283	1,853
75. **Cegetel Groupe**	FR	15.00	n.a.	1	–	WW	02/2003	><	5,633	7,556
76. China Mobile (Hong Kong) Limited	HK	3.27	n.a.	1	–	PC	12/2002	><	15,804	34,419
77. **Vodafone Group (Senior Managers) Trustee Limited**	GB	–	n.a.	n.a.	–	RT	04/2001	><	n.a.	0

* For an insurance company the corresponding value is the Gross Premium Written, and for a bank it is the Operating Income (memo).

Appendices

Appendix 1: Credit rating agency rating scales

Moody's Issuer Rating Symbols

Aaa   Issuers rated Aaa offer exceptional financial security. While the creditworthiness of these entities is likely to change, such changes as can be visualized are most unlikely to impair their fundamentally strong position.

Aa   Issuers rated Aa offer excellent financial security. Together with the Aaa group, they constitute what are generally known as high-grade entities. They are rated lower than Aaa-rated entities because long-term risks appear somewhat larger.

A   Issuers rated A offer good financial security. However elements may be present which suggest a susceptibility to impairment sometime in the future.

Baa   Issuers rated Baa offer adequate financial security. However, certain protective elements may be lacking or may be unreliable over any great period of time.

Ba   Issuers rated Ba offer questionable financial security. Often the ability of these entities to meet obligations may be moderate and not well safe-guarded in the future.

B   Issuers rated B offer poor financial security. Assurance of payment of obligations over any long period of time is small.

Caa   Issuers rated Caa offer very poor financial security. They may be in default on their obligations or there may be present elements of danger with respect to punctual payment of obligations.

Ca   Issuers rated Ca offer extremely poor financial security. Such entities are often in default on their obligations or have other marked shortcomings.

C   Issuers rated C are the lowest-rated class of entity, are usually in default on their obligations, and potential recovery values are low.

Note: Moody's applies numerical modifiers 1, 2, and 3 in each generic rating category from Aa to Caa. The modifier 1 indicates that the issuer is in the higher end of its letter rating category; the modifier 2 indicates a mid-range ranking; the modifier 3 indicates that the issuer is in the lower end of the letter ranking category.

Source: Moody's Investor Service.

Standard & Poor's Long Term Debt Ratings

AAA The highest rating assigned by Standard & Poor's. Capacity to pay interest and repay principal is extremely strong.

AA A very strong capacity to pay interest and repay principal and differs from the highest rated issues only to a small degree.

A Debt rated A has a strong capacity to pay interest and repay principal although it is somewhat more susceptible to the adverse effects of changes in circumstances and economic conditions than debt in higher rated categories.

BBB An adequate capacity to pay interest and repay principal. However, adverse economic conditions or changing circumstances are more likely to lead to a weakened capacity to pay interest and repay principal than in higher rated categories.

BB Debt rated BB and below is regarded as having predominantly speculative characteristics. The BB rating indicates less near-term vulnerability to default than other speculative issues. However, the issuer faces major ongoing uncertainties or exposure to adverse economic conditions which could lead to inadequate capacity to meet timely interest and principal payments.

B Indicates a greater vulnerability to default than BB but currently issuer has the capacity to meet interest payments and principal repayments. Adverse business, financial or economic conditions will impair capacity or willingness to pay interest and repay principal.

CCC Denotes a currently identifiable vulnerability to default and dependence upon favourable business, financial and economic conditions to meet timely payment of interest and repayment of principal. In the event of adverse business, financial or economic conditions, it is not likely to have the capacity to pay interest and repay principal.

CC The rating CC is typically applied to debt subordinated to senior debt that is assigned an actual or implied CC rating.

C Typically applied to debt subordinated to senior debt which is assigned an actual or implied CC rating.

C1 The rating C1 is reserved for income bonds on which no interest is being paid.

D Borrower is in default. The UDU rating is also used when interest payments or principal repayments are expected to be in default at the payment date, and payment of interest and/or repayment or principal is in arrears.

From AA to B, a plus (+) or minus (−) may be added to give two further gradations of risk for each letter.

Source: Standard & Poor's International Creditweek.

Standard & Poor's Short Term Commercial Paper Debt Ratings

A1	The degree of safety regarding timely payment is either overwhelming or very strong. Those issues determined to possess overwhelming safety characteristics are denoted with a plus (+) designation.
A2	Capacity for timely payment is strong. However, the relative degree of safety is not as high as for issues rated A1.
A3	A satisfactory capacity for timely payment, though somewhat more vulnerable to the adverse effects of changes in circumstances than obligations carrying the higher designations.
B	Only an adequate capacity for timely payment. However, such capacity may be damaged by changing conditions or short-term adversities.
C	Doubtful capacity for payment.
D	Issue is either in default or is expected to be in default upon maturity.

Source: Standard & Poor's International Creditweek.

Appendix 2: Country risk criteria

Political risk profile

1. **Characteristics of political system**
   (a) Type of government
   (b) Process and frequency of political succession
   (c) Degree of public participation
   (d) Degree of centralization in decision-making process

2. **Executive leadership**
   (a) Relationship with supporting government institutions
   (b) Relationship with supporting political coalitions

3. **Government institutions**
   (a) Responsiveness and access to executive leadership
   (b) Effectiveness and efficiency
   (c) Policy responsibilities

4. **Social coalitions**
   (a) Major socio-economic and cultural groups (i.e. church, military, landowners, management, labour, ethnic groups, etc.)
   (b) Political parties and their constituencies

5. **Social indicators**
   (a) Level and growth of per capita income, and other measures of the standard of living
   (b) Distribution of wealth and income
   (c) Regional disparities
   (d) Homogeneity of the populace

6. **External relations**
   (a) Relationship with major trading partners
   (b) Relationship with neighbouring countries
   (c) Participation in international organizations

Economic risk profile

1. **Demographic characteristics**
    (a) Level and growth of population
    (b) Age distribution
    (c) Urbanization trends

2. **Structure of the economy**
    (a) Extent and quality of infrastructure
        (i) Transportation and communications
        (ii) Utilities
        (iii) Housing
        (iv) Education
        (v) Health services
    (b) Natural resource endowment
        (i) Agriculture, forestry, fishing
        (ii) Non-energy minerals
        (iii) Energy resources
    (c) Distribution of productive activities
        (i) Agriculture and livestock
            (1) Land tenure system
            (2) Degree of mechanization
            (3) Principal crops
            (4) Markets
        (ii) Forestry and fishing
        (iii) Mining
        (iv) Construction
            (1) Residential
            (2) Non-residential
        (v) Manufacturing
            (1) Concentration and size of manufacturers
            (2) Product types (i.e. consumer, intermediate and capital goods)
            (3) Markets
        (vi) Services-financial/non-financial, public/private
    (d) Public sector participation in productive activities

3. **Recent economic trends**
    (a) Composition and growth of aggregate demand (nominal and real terms)
        (i) Consumption
            (1) Private sector
            (2) Public sector
        (ii) Investment
            (1) Private sector
            (2) Public sector
        (iii) External savings (i.e. exports/imports)
    (b) Domestic economy
        (i) Total production (i.e.: GDP)
        (ii) Production by sector
            (1) Agriculture, forestry and fishing
            (2) Mining
            (3) Construction
            (4) Manufacturing
            (5) Utilities
            (6) Services
        (iii) Price movements and major determinants
            (1) External factors
            (2) Wages
            (3) Public sector deficit financing
            (4) Private sector credit expansion
            (5) Supply bottlenecks
        (iv) Employment trends
            (1) Level of growth of employment and labour force
            (2) Labour participation rates
            (3) Unemployment rate and structure
            (4) Sectorial trends
            (5) Regional trends
            (6) Composition of employment: public vs. private
    (c) External sector
        (i) Current account balance
            (1) Export growth and composition
                (a) Agricultural commodities
                (b) Minerals
                (c) Manufactured goods

    (2) Destination of exports (i.e. markets)

    (3) Price and income elasticity of exports

    (4) Import growth and composition

        (a) Food

        (b) Other consumer goods

        (c) Energy

        (d) Other intermediate goods

        (e) Capital goods

    (5) Price and income elasticity of imports

    (6) Geographic origin of imports

    (7) Terms of trade

    (8) Services account

        (a) Interest payments and receipts

        (b) Transportation

        (c) Other

    (9) Transfers

  (ii) Capital account balance

    (1) Direct investment

    (2) Long-term capital flows

        (a) Private sector

        (b) Public sector

    (3) Short-term capital flows

    (4) Access to capital markets

        (a) Types of instruments used

        (b) Types of borrowers and lenders

 (iii) International reserves

    (1) Level

    (2) Composition (i.e.: gold, foreign exchange)

    (3) Secondary reserves

 (iv) External debt

    (1) Amount outstanding

    (2) Composition by borrower

        (a) Central government

        (b) Other public sector

        (c) Publicly guaranteed

        (d) Private

    (3) Composition by lender
       (a) Bilateral
       (b) Multilateral
       (c) Private financial institutions
       (d) Suppliers' credits
    (4) Maturity structure
    (5) Currency composition
    (6) Growth rate
    (7) Comparison with export earnings and GDP
    (8) Debt service payments
       (a) Amortization
       (b) Interest
       (c) Comparison with export earnings
       (d) Future debt service schedule

4. Economic policy
  (a) Price and wage policies
    (i) Wage settlement process
       (1) Trade union activity
       (2) Management groups
       (3) Role and influence of government
    (ii) Degree of wage indexation
    (iii) Productivity trends
    (iv) Non-wage benefits and unemployment insurance
    (v) Direct price controls
       (1) Public sector tariffs
       (2) Private sector pricing
    (vi) Price subsidies (agricultural, industrial, etc.)
  (b) Monetary policy
    (i) Level of development of financial system
       (1) Types of financial institutions
       (2) Types of financial instruments
       (3) Role of government in credit allocation
       (4) Foreign participation
    (ii) Trends for monetary aggregates
       (1) Money supply growth targets and actual experience
       (2) Domestic credit expansion

        (a) Public sector

        (b) Private sector

    (3) Velocity (national income/money supply)

    (4) Changes in international reserves

  (iii) Monetary policy instruments

    (1) Reserve requirements

    (2) Open market operations

    (3) Credit controls

    (4) Interest rate regulations

    (5) Ability to sterilize international reserve flows

    (6) Controls on foreign borrowing and

    (7) Rediscount facilities

(c) Fiscal policy

  (i) Structure of the public sector

    (1) Central government

    (2) Social security system

    (3) State agencies and enterprises

    (4) Regional and local governments

  (ii) Budgetary process

    (1) Executive branch

    (2) Legislative branch

    (3) Major constituencies (business, labour, etc.)

  (iii) Revenues

    (1) Composition

        (a) Direct taxes-personal income, corporate income, property, others

        (b) Indirect taxes-valued added, sales, export & import duties, others

        (c) Service charges and public sector tariffs

    (2) Income elasticity of revenues

    (3) Distribution of tax burden by income groups

    (4) Overall tax burden (% of GDP)

    (5) Tax collection and evasion

    (6) Tax incentives (i.e. investment, export, employment)

  (iv) Expenditures

    (1) Current expenditures

        (a) Distribution by expenditure category

        (b) Transfers to households

        (c) Transfers to other levels of government

     (2) Capital expenditures

  (v) Current operating balance (absolute level and relative to GDP)

 (vi) Gross financing requirements (operating balance plus net capital expenditures)

     (1) Trend relative to GDP

     (2) Means of financing

        (a) Domestic money creation

        (b) Domestic borrowing

        (c) External borrowing

(vii) Public sector debt: domestic and external

     (1) Size (direct and guaranteed)

     (2) Debt service requirement

     (3) Debt management

(d) External policies

  (i) Exchange rate policy

 (ii) International reserve management

(iii) Export promotion measures

(iv) Import substitution/trade protectionist measures

(e) Long-term planning and special programs

  (i) Energy

 (ii) Industrial development/restructuring

(iii) Employment creation

(iv) Others

S&P's sovereign rating profile

In order to evaluate the elements in the preceding political and economic risk profile, the most recent five years of the following information should be incorporated.

1. Demographic characteristics

  (a) Total population (millions)

  (b) Age structure (% of total)

     (i) 0–14

  (ii) 15–64
  (iii) 66 and over
(c) Urban population (% of total)
(d) Total labour force (millions)
      (i) % Employment agriculture
     (ii) % Employment industry

2. Economic structure & growth
(a) GDP, current prices
(b) GDP, constant prices
(c) GDP per capita, current prices
(d) Composition of real GDP (%)
      (i) Agriculture
     (ii) Mining
    (iii) Manufacturing
    (iv) Construction
     (v) Electricity, gas & water
    (vi) Transportation & communication
   (vii) Trade & finance
  (viii) Public administration
    (ix) Other services
(e) Investment, constant prices
(f) Investment, current prices
(g) Investment/GDP
(h) Net energy imports/total energy consumption (%)

3. Economic management
(a) Consumer price index
(b) Money supply-M1
(c) Money supply-M2
(d) Domestic credit
(e) Wage index
(f) Unemployment rate
(g) Budget deficit/GDP (%)
(h) Public expenditures/GDP (%)

4. Government finance
(a) Current revenues

(b) Current expenditures

(c) Operating balance

(d) Net capital expenditures

(e) Budgetary balance

(f) Non-budgetary balance

(g) Domestic financing

(h) Foreign financing

5. **External payments**

(a) Exchange rate

    (i) Local currency/USUSD

    (ii) Local currency/SDR

(b) Imports/GDP (%)

(c) Composition of imports (%)

    (i) Food

    (ii) Non-food agricultural

    (iii) Non-fuel mining & metals

    (iv) Fuels

    (v) Machinery & equipment

    (vi) Other manufactured goods

(d) Composition of exports (%)

    (i) Food

    (ii) Non-food agricultural

    (iii) Non-fuel mining & metals

    (iv) Fuels

    (v) Machinery & equipment

    (vi) Other manufactured goods

(e) Balance of payments

    (i) Exports

    (ii) Imports

    (iii) Trade balance

    (iv) Net factor services (interest payments)

    (v) Net transfers

    (vi) Current account balance

    (vii) Long-term capital flows

        (1) Public

        (2) Private

    (viii) Short-term capital flows
- (1) Public
- (2) Private

    (ix) Errors and omissions

    (x) Reserves movements

    (xi) Current account balance/GDP (%)

    (xii) Current account balance/exports (%)

(f) International reserves
- (i) Central bank reserves, minus gold
- (ii) Central bank gold reserves (millions of troy ounces)
- (iii) Reserves, rest of banking system
- (iv) Reserves/imports (%)
- (v) Net foreign assets of banking system
- (vi) Imports (%)

(g) External debt
- (i) Long-term debt
  - (1) Public
  - (2) Private
- (ii) Short-term debt
  - (1) Public
  - (2) Private
- (iii) External debt/GDP (%)
- (iv) Debt service payments a. Public b. Private
- (v) Debt service payments/exports (%)
- (vi) Debt service schedule

Appendix 3: Summary of lending types

Summary of lending types

	Purpose	Source of repayment	Risks	Protection against loss	Form of control
Temporary or seasonal finance	Financing the short-term seasonal build-up of current/working assets	Cash received from the successful conversion of the raw material asset into completed goods which have been sold, and the payment received	Inability to recover costs through company's unsuccessful completion of the asset conversion process	Asset marketability/liquidity; management's ability to complete asset conversion cycle; short time factor	Structure facility to enable lender to review situation frequently before renewal of facility or disbursement of funds
Working investment lending	Evergreen (permanent) financing of a permanent level of circulating working assets	Successful completion of successive transactions of turnover and cash flow; liquidation of (easily marketable) assets in default situation	Inability to generate sufficient cash flow; decline in market value of assets below amount needed to satisfy senior creditors in the event of liquidation	Management's ability to keep the flow of transactions moving and to generate a satisfactory level of profits over a number of years; liquidity of the assets being financed, and low shrinkage of value in a forced sale	Demand/short-term notes; security and proper documentation; debt limitations and covenants where appropriate
Cash flow lending	Financing of long-term fixed or plant assets; financing of corporate acquisitions	Cash from profits generated by the asset being financed, by the company's operations, and by the profits retained in the business over time	Inability of the company or management to generate a sufficient level of profits to cover operating costs and debt servicing costs	Management's ability to generate profits; adequate equity cushion; unused debt capacity	Include covenants in the loan agreement which ensure that the company's financial structure remains within certain parameters

Appendix 4: Complete AmaOS spreadsheet

NAME: AmaOS
LOCATION: UK
BUSINESS: Manufacturing
AUDITOR: Andersen
CONSOLIDATED: Yes

FYE EUR 000   31 DEC

ASSETS	2000	2001	2002	2003	2004	2005	2006	2007	2008
Cash	124,019	194,212	69,323	131,680	144,160	168,087	159,973	161,533	173,471
Marketable Securities									
Accounts Receivable – Trade	54,809	130,629	100,432	88,628	97,175	103,006	109,186	115,737	122,682
Accounts Receivable – Other									
Sundry Current Assets									
Inventory	105,625	132,650	334,541	207,424	201,042	213,105	225,891	239,445	253,811
Raw Materials	16,360	25,367	47,099	26,162					
Work in Progress	491	1,478	1,227						
Finished Goods	75,664	92,354	255,644	159,880					
Other	13,110	13,451	30,571	21,382					
CURRENT ASSETS	284,453	457,491	504,296	427,732	442,378	484,198	495,051	516,715	549,964
Land, Buildings, Equipment	15,393	29,122	53,607	53,803	48,029	50,911	53,966	57,204	60,636
Leased Assets									
Plant in Construction									
Accumulated Depreciation	−2,018	−3,835	−7,754	−7,621					
TOTAL OTHER GENERAL ASSETS	13,375	25,287	45,853	46,182	48,029	50,911	53,966	57,204	60,636
Quoted Investments									
Unquoted Investments	1,058	1,242	44,699	28,537	28,537	28,537	28,537	28,537	28,537
Invest in Associated Co's									
Loans to Associated Co's									
Prepaid Expenses									
Sundry Assets	229	553	452						
Goodwill									
Other									
TOTAL ASSETS	299,115	484,573	595,300	502,451	518,944	563,646	577,554	602,456	639,137

LIABILITIES

Bank Loans and O/D's									
Other ST Debt	27,552	111,137	148,407	99,450					
CPLTD									
CPLO									
Customer Prepayment									
Accounts Payable	8,451	10,336	37,475	41,063	24,609	26,086	27,651	29,310	31,069
Accrued Expenses	5,569	9,950	27,636	5,877	12,835	13,606	14,422	15,287	16,007
Income Tax Payable	48,076	64,654	40,455	9,059					
Dividends Payable	2,726	5,678	5,684	5,643					
Due to Affiliates									
Sundry CL 1									
Sundry CL 2									
CURRENT LIABILITIES	92,374	201,755	259,657	161,092	37,445	39,691	42,073	44,597	47,076
Long Term Debt	24,848	24,848	24,848	24,848	16,494	8,247			
New Debt					100,000	100,000	66,667	33,333	
Subordinated Debt									
Total Long Term Debt	24,848	24,848	24,848	24,848	116,494	108,247	66,667	33,333	0
Other Creditors									
TOTAL LIABILITIES	117,222	226,603	284,505	185,940	153,939	147,938	108,740	77,930	47,076
Deferred Taxes									
Minority Interest									
Common Stock	52,500	52,500	52,500	52,500	52,500	52,500	52,500	52,500	52,500
Preferred Stock									
Capital Surplus									
Revaluation Reserve									
Legal Reserve									
FX – Translation Reserve									
Retained Earnings	129,393	205,470	258,295	264,011	312,505	363,208	416,314	472,026	539,561
NET WORTH	181,893	257,970	310,795	316,511	365,005	415,708	468,814	524,526	592,061
TOTAL LIABILITIES & NET WORTH	299,115	484,573	595,300	502,451	518,944	563,646	577,554	602,456	639,137
Cross-check (TA-TL)	0	0	0	0	0	–0	–0	0	0
Contingent Liabilities:									

(continued)

Appendix 4: (continued)

NAME: AmaOS   AmaOS
LOCATION: UK   UK
BUSINESS: Manufacturing   Manufacturing
AUDITOR: Andersen   Andersen
CONSOLIDATED: Yes   Yes

FYE 31 DEC
GBP 000

PROFIT & LOSS	2000	2001	2002	2003	2004	2005	2006	2007	2008	AVERAGE	AVERAGE (%)
NET SALES	525,684	645,174	638,756	614,538	639,120	677,467	718,115	761,202	806,874	606,038	100.00
Cost of Sales	349,786	397,865	429,845	438,745	426,293	451,871	478,983	507,722	538,185	404,060	66.67
Depreciation											
Amortisation of Goodwill											
Capital Grants											
GROSS PROFIT	175,898	247,309	208,911	175,793	212,827	225,596	239,132	253,480	268,689	201,978	33.33
SGA	50,644	192,622	144,302	230,791	159,333	168,893	179,026	189,768	192,154	154,590	25.51
NET OPERATING PROFIT	125,254	54,687	64,609	−54,998	53,494	56,703	60,106	63,712	76,535	47,388	7.82
Net Interest Expense	1,491	1,491	1,491	1,491						1,491	0.25
Interest Income											
Prov Dbt Recv											
Equity Income											
NPBT	123,763	53,196	63,118	−56,489	53,494	56,703	60,106	63,712	76,535	45,897	7.57
Provision for Income Tax											
Deferred Tax Provision											
NPAT	123,763	53,196	63,118	−56,489	53,494	56,703	60,106	63,712	76,535	45,897	7.57
Unusual Items:											
FX Gains/Losses	17,916	−9,518	30,045	−59,865						−5,356	−0.88
Unrealised F/X Gain/Loss											

Realis Profits of Rel Co	−13,363	−19,752	−2,340		5,000	6,000	7,000	8,000	9,000	−11,818	−1.95
Reval Reserve											
Sundry Res											
Goodwill on Consol											
Unexplained Adjustment											
NPAUT	105,847	76,077	52,825	5,716	48,494	50,703	53,106	55,712	67,535	60,116	9.92
Dividends – Common –											
Preferred											
Min Int Expense											
RETAINED EARNINGS	105,847	76,077	52,825	5,716	48,494	50,703	53,106	55,712	67,535	60,116	9.92
Changes in Net Worth											
Stock Sold	0	0	0	0	0	0	0	0	0	0	0.00
Purch Own Stock	0	0	0	0	0	0	0	0	0	0	
Chg in Cap Surplus	0	0	0	0	0	0	0	0	0	0	0.00
Chg in FX Reserve	0	0	0	0	0	0	0	0	0	0	0.00
Chg in Reserves	0	0	0	0	0	0	0	0	0	0	0.00
Other	0	0	0	0	0	0	0	0	0	0	0.00
INCREASE IN NET WORTH	105,847	76,077	52,825	5,716	48,494	50,703	53,106	55,712	67,535	60,116	9.92
Cross Check RE:	—	—	−0	−0	0	0	0	0	0	0	
Cross Check NW:	—	—	−0	−0	0	0	0	0	0	0	

(continued)

Appendix 4: (continued)

NAME:	AmaOS				AmaOS				
LOCATION:	UK				UK				
BUSINESS:	Manufacturing				Manufacturing				
AUDITOR:	Andersen				Andersen				
CONSOLIDATED:	Yes	FYE	31 DEC		Yes				
		GBP 000							

FACT SHEET	2000	2001	2002	2003	2004	2005	2006	2007	2008	AVERAGE (%)
ROE (%)	68.04	20.62	20.31	−17.85	14.66	13.64	12.82	12.15	12.93	22.78
ROS (%)	23.54	8.25	9.88	−9.19	8.37	8.37	8.37	8.37	9.49	8.12
ATO	1.76	1.33	1.07	1.22	1.23	1.20	1.24	1.26	1.26	1.35
ALEV	1.64	1.88	1.92	1.59	1.42	1.36	1.23	1.15	1.08	1.76
Sales (M/MM)	525684	645174	638756	614538	639120	677467	718115	761202	806874	
Chg. in Sales (%)	#N/A	22.7	−1.0	−3.8	4.0	6.0	6.0	6.0	6.0	5.98
CoGS/S (%)	66.5	61.7	67.3	71.4	66.7	66.7	66.7	66.7	66.7	66.72
GPM (%)	33.5	38.3	32.7	28.6	33.3	33.3	33.3	33.3	33.3	33.28
SGA/S (%)	9.6	29.9	22.6	37.6	24.9	24.9	24.9	24.9	23.8	24.91
NOP/S (%)	23.8	8.5	10.1	−8.9	8.4	8.4	8.4	8.4	9.5	8.37
TIE	84.0	36.7	43.3	#N/A	#DIV/0!	#DIV/0!	#DIV/0!	#DIV/0!	#DIV/0!	
IE/Av. FD (%)	2.85	1.58	0.96	1.00	#REF!	0.00	0.00	0.00	0.00	1.60
NPBT/S (%)	23.5	8.2	9.9	−9.2	8.4	8.4	8.4	8.4	9.5	8.12
Inc. Taxes/NPBT (%)	0.0	0.0	0.0	#N/A	0.0	0.0	0.0	0.0	0.0	
NPAT/S (%)	23.5	8.2	9.9	−9.2	8.4	8.4	8.4	8.4	9.5	8.12
NPAUI/S (%)	20.1	11.8	8.3	0.9	7.6	7.5	7.4	7.3	8.4	10.28
Div./NPAT (%)	0.0	0.0	0.0	0.0	0.0	0.0	0.0	0.0	0.0	0.00
Work. Investment	146414	242993	369862	249112	260773.1705	276419.6945	293004.7839	310585.0843	329417.3045	
Chg. in WI (%)	#N/A	66.0	52.2	−32.6	4.7	6.0	6.0	6.0	6.1	
WI/S (%)	27.9	37.7	57.9	40.5	40.8	40.8	40.8	40.8	40.8	
AR DOH	38	74	57	53	55	55	55	55	55	55.50
INV DOH	110	122	284	173	172	172	172	172	172	172.14
RM DOH	17	23	40	22	0	0	0	0	0	25.53
WIP DOH	1	1	1	0	0	0	0	0	0	0.73
FG DOH	79	85	217	133	0	0	0	0	0	128.44

AP DOH	9	9	32	34	21	21	21	21	21	21.07
AE DOH	5	6	18	3	8	8	8	8	8	8.00
Av. GP T/O	#N/A	#N/A	#N/A	#N/A	#REF!	#N/A	#N/A	#N/A	#N/A	
Av. NP T/O	#N/A	#N/A	#N/A	#N/A	#REF!	#N/A	#N/A	#N/A	#N/A	
Av. GP/DepExp.	#N/A	#N/A	#N/A	#N/A	#REF!	#N/A	#N/A	#N/A	#N/A	
Av. AccDep./DepExp.	#DIV/0!	#DIV/0!	#DIV/0!	#DIV/0!	#REF!	#N/A	#N/A	#N/A	#N/A	
Av. NP/DepExp.	#N/A	#N/A	#N/A	#N/A	#REF!	#N/A	#N/A	#N/A	#N/A	
Current Ratio	3.08	2.27	1.94	2.66	11.81	12.20	11.77	11.59	11.68	2.49
Quick Ratio	1.94	1.61	0.65	1.37	6.45	6.83	6.40	6.22	6.29	1.39
Coverage Ratio	2.43	2.02	1.77	2.30	2.87	3.27	4.55	6.63	11.68	2.13
CMB Leverage	0.64	0.88	0.92	0.59	0.42	0.36	0.23	0.15	0.08	0.76
% of Total Footings:										
STD (+CPLTD + CPLO) (%)	9.2	22.9	24.9	19.8	0.0	0.0	0.0	0.0	0.0	19.22
Spont. Fin. (%)	4.7	4.2	10.9	9.3	7.2	7.0	7.3	7.4	7.4	7.29
LTD (%)	8.3	5.1	4.2	4.9	22.4	19.2	11.5	5.5	0.0	5.64
Grey Area (%)	0.0	0.0	0.0	0.0	0.0	0.0	0.0	0.0	0.0	0.00
Equity (%)	60.8	53.2	52.2	63.0	70.3	73.8	81.2	87.1	92.6	57.31
CA (%)	95.1	94.4	84.7	85.1	85.2	85.9	85.7	85.8	86.0	89.84
Net Plant (%)	4.5	5.2	7.7	9.2	9.3	9.0	9.3	9.5	9.5	6.65
Other (%)	0.4	0.4	7.6	5.7	5.5	5.1	4.9	4.7	4.5	3.52
Asset Cover (TA-TSL/TA) (%)	60.8	53.2	52.2	63.0	70.3	73.8	81.2	87.1	92.6	57.31
WC Adequacy (WC/CA) (%)	67.5	55.9	48.5	62.3	91.5	91.8	91.5	91.4	91.4	58.57
Reliance on Inventory (%)	−81.8	−92.8	26.9	−28.5	−101.4	−108.6	−100.5	−97.2	−98.1	−44.08
Change in WC (%)	#N/A	33.1	−4.3	9.0	51.9	9.8	1.9	4.2	6.5	#N/A

(continued)

Appendix 4: (continued)

NAME:	AmaOS		
LOCATION:	UK		
BUSINESS:	Manufacturing		
AUDITOR:	Andersen		
CONSOLIDATED:	Yes		

FYE 31 DEC
GBP 000

CASH FLOW	2001	2002	2003	2004	2005	2006	2007	2008
NPAUI: NET PROFIT AFTER	76,077	52,825	5,716	48,494	50,703	53,106	55,712	67,535
UNUSUAL ITEMS								
+Interest Expense	1,491	1,491	1,491	0	0	0	0	0
Unusual: Plant	−9,518	30,045	−59,865	0	0	0	0	0
Investment	0	0	0	0	0	0	0	0
FX-Adj.	−13,363	−19,752	−2,340	5,000	6,000	7,000	8,000	9,000
Other (1 + 2)	0	0	0	0	0	0	0	0
Other (3 + 4 + 5)	0	0	0	0	0	0	0	0
−Interest Income	0	0	0	0	0	0	0	0
−Dividend Income	0	0	0	0	0	0	0	0
−Equity Income	0	0	0	0	0	0	0	0
−Commission Income	0	0	0	0	0	0	0	0
Sundry Inc./Exp.	0	0	0	0	0	0	0	0
+Prov. f. Income Tax	0	0	0	0	0	0	0	0
−Income Tax Paid	16,578	−24,199	−31,396	−9,059	0	0	0	0
+Prov. f. Def. Tax	0	0	0	0	0	0	0	0
−Def. Tax Paid	0	0	0	0	0	0	0	0
−ITC (Gov't Grants)	0	0	0	0	0	0	0	0
NOPAT: NORMALISED OPERATING PROFIT AFTER TAX	71,265	40,410	−86,394	44,435	56,703	60,106	63,712	76,535

+Depreciation	0	0	0	0	0	0	0
+Amort. of Goodwill	0	0	0	0	0	0	0
+Prov. f. Dbtf. Rec.	0	0	0	0	0	0	0
COPAT: CASH OPERATING PROFIT AFTER TAX	71,265	40,410	−86,394	44,435	56,703	60,106	63,712	76,535
Gross (Net) A/Rec.	−75,820	30,197	11,804	−8,547	−5,830	−6,180	−6,551	−6,944
−A/Rec. charged off	0	0	0	0	0	0	0	0
Inventory	−27,025	−201,891	127,117	6,382	−12,063	−12,786	−13,553	−14,367
Cust. Prepayments	0	0	0	0	0	0	0	0
Acc./Payable	1,885	27,139	3,588	−16,454	1,477	1,565	1,659	1,759
Accrued Expenses	4,381	17,686	−21,759	6,958	770	816	865	720
Chg. Work. Inv.	−96,579	−126,869	120,750	−11,661	−15,647	−16,585	−17,580	−18,832
Prepaid Expenses	0	0	0	0	0	0	0	0
Due to Affiliates	0	0	0	0	0	0	0	0
Sundry C.A.	0	0	0	0	0	0	0	0
Sundry C.L. (1+2)	0	0	0	0	0	0	0	0
CACO: CASH AFTER CURRENT OPERATIONS	−25,314	−86,459	34,356	32,774	41,056	43,521	46,132	57,703
−Interest Expense	−1,491	−1,491	−1,491	0	0	0	0	0
−CPLTD (incl. CPLO)	0	0	0	0	0	0	0	0
=Finan. Payments	−1,491	−1,491	−1,491	0	0	0	0	0
CBLTU: CASH BEFORE LONG TERM USES	−26,805	−87,950	32,865	32,774	41,056	43,521	46,132	57,703
−Net Pl. Expend.	−2,394	−50,611	59,536	−1,847	−2,882	−3,055	−3,238	−3,432
Investments	−184	−43,457	16,162	0	0	0	0	0
+Interest Income	0	0	0	0	0	0	0	0
+Dividend Income	0	0	0	0	0	0	0	0
Sundry Inc./Exp.	0	0	0	0	0	0	0	0

(continued)

Appendix 4: (continued)

	2001	2002	2003	2004	2005	2006	2007	2008
Market. Secur. + Dep.	0	0	0	0	0	0	0	0
Due from Affiliates	0	0	0	0	0	0	0	0
Sundry NCA	-324	101	452	0	0	0	0	0
Sundry NCL	0	0	0	0	0	0	0	0
Unusual: all other	13,363	19,752	2,340	-5,000	-6,000	-7,000	-8,000	-9,000
+ITC (Gov't Grants)	0	0	0	0	0	0	0	0
CBF: CASH BEFORE FINANCING	-16,344	-162,165	111,355	25,927	32,174	33,466	34,894	45,271
Short Term Debt	83,585	37,270	-48,957	-99,450	0	0	0	0
Long Term Debt	0	0	0	91,646	-8,247	-41,580	-33,334	-33,333
Minority Interest	0	0	0	0	0	0	0	0
Grey Area	0	0	0	0	0	0	0	0
FX-Translation G/L-	0	0	0	0	0	0	0	0
Dividends paid	2,952	0	-41	-5,643	0	0	0	0
Change in Net Worth	0	0	0	0	0	0	0	0
Change in Cash	70,193	-124,889	62,357	12,480	23,927	-8,114	1,560	11,938
Cash Account	-70,193	124,889	-62,357	-12,480	-23,927	8,114	-1,560	-11,938
ADDITIONAL FIGURES:	2001	2002	2003	2004	2005	2006	2007	2008
NOPAT/FP	47.80	27.10	-57.95	#N/A	#N/A	#N/A	#N/A	#N/A
NOPAT/(FP + DIV.)	-48.77	27.21	-56.40	7.87	#DIV/0!	#DIV/0!	#DIV/0!	#DIV/0!
FREE CASH FLOW	69774.12	38919.12	-87884.88	44435	56703	60106	63712	76535
FREE CF (after Div.)	72726.12	38925.12	-87925.88	38792	56703	60106	63712	76535
GROWTH FUNDED INTERNALLY (%)	70.5	21.9	0.0	328.9	306.0	306.0	306.0	343.8
G.F.I. (after Div.) (%)	73.5	21.9	0.0	287.2	306.0	306.0	306.0	343.8
YEARS TO SERVICE RATIO	1.9	4.5	#N/A	2.6	1.9	1.1	0.5	0.0
Y.T.S. (after Div.)	1.9	4.5	#N/A	2.6	1.9	1.1	0.5	#N/A

Suggested reading

Brett, M. (2003) *How to Read the Financial Pages*. Century Business Books.

Fight, A. (2004). *Credit Risk Management*. Elsevier.

Fight, A. (2004). *Project Finance*. Elsevier.

Fight, A. (2004). *Syndicated Lending*. Elsevier.

Fight, A. (2004). *Understanding International Bank Risk*. Elsevier.

Fridson, M. (1995). *Financial Statement Analysis*, 2nd edn. Wiley.

Griffiths, I. (1995). *New Creative Accounting*. Macmillan.

Holmes, G. and Dunham, R. (1994). *Beyond The Balance Sheet*. Woodhead-Faulkner.

Holmes, G. and Sugden, A. (1996). *Interpreting Company Reports and Accounts*, 5th edn. Prentice Hall.

Hussey, R. (1999). *A Dictionary of Accounting*. Oxford University Press.

McKenzie, W. (1994). *Understanding and Interpreting Company Accounts*. FT Pitman Publishing.

Nobes, C. (2001). *Pocket Accounting*. Penguin Group.

Partnoy, F. (1999). The Siskel and Ebert of financial markets: two thumbs down for the credit rating agencies. *Washington University Law Quarterly*, 77, 619–712.

Plewa, F. and Friedlob, G. (1994). *Understanding Cash Flow*. John Wiley.

Smith, T. (1996). *Accounting for Growth*. Century Business.

Stott, J. R. (2003). *Teach Yourself Basic Accounting*. Hodder and Stoughton.

Whitehead, G. (1998). *Book-keeping and Accounting*. Pitman Publishing.

Glossary

Acceleration   After a default, the loan is fully due and payable. Repayments are accelerated to the present.

Account party   In a commercial letter of credit, the party instructing the bank to open a letter of credit and on whose behalf the bank agrees to make payment.

Accounting period   The period of activity which the accounts reflect (e.g. a year, six months, etc.).

Accounts payable (Payables or Creditors)   Amounts owed to suppliers for goods or services received.

Accounts receivable (Receivables or Debtors)   Amounts owed by customers or buyers as a result of a sale of goods, or the performance of a service.

Accruals   Allowing for income or costs when they are incurred and not when they are either received or paid out.

Accrued interest   Interest earned but not collected.

Acid test (Quick ratio)   The relationship between the current assets which may be quickly converted into cash (excluding stock) and current liabilities – i.e. current assets, less inventories divided by current liabilities.

ADB   Asian Development Bank.

Ad valorem   Off the gross or stated value, usually a percentage.

Advance agent   A loan drawdown is advanced by the funder.

After tax cash flow   Total cash generated by the project annually, defined as profit after-tax plus depreciation.

Aged analysis   A form of reporting based on the time a financial item has been outstanding, commonly used for receivables and payables.

Agent   The bank charged with administering the project financing. Generic: a party appointed to act on behalf of a principal entity/person.

Agent banks   The banks that arrange the financing on behalf of a corporate borrower. Usually, the banks commit to underwrite the whole amount if they are unable to fully place the deal. Typically, however, the place the bulk of the facility, and retain a portion on their books for themselves.

All-in rate   Interest rate which includes margin, commitment Fees, up-front fees.

Amortization   The technique of writing-off an asset over a period of time.

Amortization   Reduction of capital or up-front expenses (capitalized) over time, often an equal amount p.a. Sometimes describes Repayments.

Amortization   The process of paying off an amount gradually by spreading the payments over several years.

Amortization (depreciation)   A process of establishing an expense in respect of assets (normally fixed assets) over a number of accounting periods to reflect the value of an asset over its economic life.

Annual report   The company's annual accounts, audit statement, and narrative account of the year at hand. Presentations vary considerably.

Annuity   The sum of principal and interest is equal for each period.

Arbitrage   Take advantage of discrepancies in price or yields in different markets.

Arrangement fees   For their efforts in arranging the deal, agent banks collect arrangement fees. These fees are attractive because they represent revenues that do not have to be generated by the balance sheet, which is subject to capital adequacy ratios.

Arranger   The senior tier of a syndication. This implies the entity that agreed and negotiated the cash flow forecasting structure. Also refers to the bank/underwriter entitled to syndicate the loan/bond issue.

Articles of association   This document is drawn up by the company when it is formed and lays down the internal rules by which the directors will run the company.

Asset   Something a company or person owns or has use of, and which is expected to be of economic benefit.

Asset   The physical project and its associated contracts, rights, and interests of every kind, in the present or future, which can be valued or used to repay debt.

Asset-backed securities   Securities collateralized by a pool of assets. The process of creating securities backed by assets is referred to as asset securitization.

Assets   Resources or legal rights owned by the business. These may be physical (e.g. a building) or contractual (e.g. a receivable).

Assets   Any item owned by a company or individual that can be given a monetary value and used if necessary to pay debts. There are many kinds of assets, described by terms like current assets and fixed assets.

Asset turnover ratio   A broad measure of asset efficiency, defined as net sales divided by total assets.

Assignment   Grant of the right to step in to the position of a party to a contract or legal agreement.

Associate company   A company which is more than 20 per cent owned by another company. A company will take onto its own profit and loss account its share of the associate's profits or losses.

Audit   A process of examination of financial statements and the underlying accounting. An independent audit will provide a systematic investigation of the accounting systems and controls to ensure compliance with prescribed accounting and auditing standards.

Audit   An official examination and checking of a company's accounts by an independent accountant called an auditor, to certify that the accounts (as presented by the directors) comply with the law, and in their opinion give a true and fair view of the company's affairs.

Auditors   Accountants who certify that the company's accounts have been reviewed in accordance with FRS (Financial Reporting Standards for the UK – see below) and note the findings of their inquiry.

Authorized signatories   Persons authorized to sign on behalf of the company borrowing the money. Specimen signatures are usually in a booklet provided by the company. It is the bank's (i.e. analyst's) responsibility to verify this: if the signatory is not authorized, the company does not have to pay the money back.

Availability   The project financing is available for drawdown. A period prior to financial close may also be included.

Available cash flow   Total cash sources less total cash uses before payment of debt service.

Average life   Average for all repayments, usually weighted by amounts outstanding.

Avoided cost   The capital and expense that would otherwise have to be spent if the project did not proceed.

Balance sheet   A statement reflecting the financial position at a specific moment in time.

Balance sheet   The accounts which show assets, liabilities, net worth/ shareholders' equity.

Balloon payment   A large single repayment.

BAR   Builders' All Risk, a standard construction insurance.

Barter   The physical form of countertrade.

Basis point (bp)   One hundred bp equals 1 percentage point.

Bearer Bond   The Bond certificate is itself. Negotiable. (It is not recorded as being owned by any particular Investor.)

Best efforts   A very high standard of undertaking, nevertheless excusable in the event of *force majeure* or failure to execute the matter in question after trying to do so on a sustained, dedicated basis.

BI   Business interruption insurance available once the project is in business.

Bid bond   A small percentage (1–3 per cent) of the tender contract price is established as a bid 'performance' bond. Once the contract is awarded, bid bonds are refunded to the losers.

Blocked currency   Due to inconvertibility, or transfer risk, a currency cannot be moved out of the country.

Bond   The paper evidence of a legal promise by the issuer to pay the investor on the declared terms. Bond are usually negotiable. Bonds are customarily longer term, say 5–25 years. Short-term bonds are usually referred to as notes.

BOO   Build Own Operate (and Maintain).

Book runner   The arranger or bank extending the invitations for a syndication and tallying final take.

Borrower risk   Risks pertaining to the company, including management, profitability, non-performance, and bankruptcy: all factors relating to the borrower.

BOT   Build Own Transfer, where the project is transferred back to the party granting the concession. The transfer may be for value or at no cost.

Break even   The reduction of a cash flow forecasting net cash flow to zero by changing an input variable such as price or costs.

Broker   A party which brings together sponsors, finance, or insurances but is not acting as a principal.

Builders-All Risk   The standard insurance package during construction.

Bullet   A one-time repayment, often after no/little amortization of the loan. A balloon.

Bullet repayment   A loan whose interest is payable at intervals agreed in the loan agreement, and whose principal is repayable in a lump sum at final maturity. The source of repayment is usually a new facility that is put into place.

Buy-back   A promise to repurchase unsold production. Alternatively, a promise to repay a financial obligation.

Buydown   A once-off payment out of LDs to reflect cash flow losses from sustained underperformance. Often used to 'buy' down the cash flow forecasting loan.

Buyer credit   Financing provided to a buyer to pay for the supply of goods or services usually by an exporting country or the supplier company.

Call   An option to buy a security or commodity for a set price at a given time in the future.

Call option   A contract sold for a price that gives the holder the right to buy from the writer of the option, over a specified period, a specified property or amount of securities at a specified price.

Cap   A ceiling on an interest or FX rate through a swap, options, or by agreement.

Capex   Capital expenditures usually by way of direct investment.

Capital   Money invested in the business by its owners.

Capital & reserves (Shareholders' funds/net worth)   The value the owners have invested in the business. This is represented by share capital and reserves.

Capitalized interest   Prior to completion, the convention is to capitalize interest into the project financing – i.e. to borrow to pay interest. See IDC.

Capital markets   A broad term to include tradable debt, securities and equity as distinct from private markets or banks.

Cash flow   The inflow and outflow of cash through a company. It is used to describe the cash needed to finance operating expenses and other obligations.

Cash flow   The generation of cash by a project.

Cash flow forecast   Estimation of expected cash flow used to alert management to future cash shortages and surpluses.

CDC   Commonwealth Development Corp – a British development finance institute.

Certificates of registration   These certify that the company has registered with the state authorities. Photocopies are usually available from the company on request.

Charge   Under Crown Law, the document evidencing mortgage security. A fixed charge refers to a defined set of assets, and is usually registered. A floating charge refers to other assets which change from time to time, e.g. cash at bank, inventory, etc., which become a fixed charge after a default.

Claw back   The ability to recover prior project cash flow that may have been distributed/paid away as dividends to the sponsors.

Close company   A company which is under the control of five persons or less, or is under the control of its directors.

Club   A group of underwriters who do not need to proceed to syndication.

Coface   The French ECA.

Co-financing   Where the different lenders agree to fund under the same documentation and security packages, yet may have different interest rates, repayment profiles and term, perhaps via A and B tranches.

Co-generation   Besides electricity, another energy is produced and sold from the waste heat from a power plant, e.g. steam, hot air, refrigeration.

Collar   A ceiling and floor to an interest or FX rate structured through swaps, options, hedging, or by agreement.

Collateral   Additional security pledged to support a project financing.

Co-manager   A second-tier participant, ranked by size of participation.

Combined cycle   The waste heat from an electric generation unit is recovered as steam, which is used to generate more electricity through a steam turbine.

Commitment fee   A per annum fee applied to the portion of the unused project financing (the amount not yet drawn down) until the end of the availability period.

Company (Corporation)   A legal entity with perpetual succession.

Compensation trade   The form of countertrade where an incoming investment is repaid from the units/revenues generated by that investment.

Complementary financing   Where different lenders agree to fund under similar yet parallel documentation and a pro-rata security package.

Completion   In a project financing, when the project's cash flows become the primary method of repayment. It occurs after a completion test. Prior to completion, the primary source of repayment is usually from the sponsors or from the turnkey contractor.

Completion risk   Construction, development, or cost overrun risk. The risk that a project will not be able to pass its completion test.

Completion test   A test of the project's ability to perform as planned and generate the expected cash flows. The time when the project can move from recourse to a project financing.

Compound   Interest is reinvested to earn additional interest in the following period.

Consortium   All of the participants or developers. For the early stages of a project it may be a loose association, not a legal or contractual entity/JV.

Constant dollar   Inflation or escalation is not applicable. Prices and costs are de-escalated/re-escalated to a single point in time.

Contingency   An additional amount/percentage to any cash flow item, e.g. Capex. Care is needed to ensure it is either 'to-be-spent' or a cushion.

Contingent   For liabilities, those that do not yet appear on the balance sheet – guarantees, supports, lawsuit settlements. For support or recourse, the trigger may occur at any time in the future.

Contingent liabilities   Items that do not represent a liability on the balance sheet at the time of statement date but which could do so in the future. Such items include guarantees issued in favour of third parties, and lawsuits currently in progress whose outcome is uncertain.

Convertible   A financial instrument that can be exchanged for another security or equity interest at a pre-agreed time and exchange ratio.

Cost of goods sold   The direct cost of acquiring or producing goods which have been sold.

Counterparty   The other participant, usually in a swap or contract, and includes intermediaries.

Countertrade   One party supplies a unit/funding in return for other material/funding See Barter.

Country risk   Includes sovereign risk, but usually an estimate of the likelihood of a country debt rescheduling which will prompt currency inconvertibility. Sometimes referred to as sovereign risk.

Coupon   The interest amount or rate payable on a bond. A coupon may be physically attached to the bond certificate.

Covenant An agreed action to be undertaken (Positive) or not done (Negative). A breach of a covenant is a default.

Covenants Conditions in the loan agreement signed by the bank and the borrower, which the borrower must respect. Covenants can cover conditions on management performance, disposal of subsidiaries, negative pledges, amounts of debt incurred, and adherence to financial ratios. Non-compliance is known as an event of default.

Cover The amount above unity of a debt service ratio.

CPI Consumer Price Index, a measure of inflation at the consumer level.

Credit The process of taking a risk for the settlement of an obligation in the future.

Credit enhancement The issuance of a guarantee, L/Q or additional collateral to reinforce the credit strength of a project financing.

Credit scoring Technique used to evaluate a potential borrower according to a pre-defined matrix procedure. Usually used in retail banking and credit card processing; may be used in evaluating corporates.

Creditworthy The risk of default on a debt obligation by that entity is deemed low.

Cross-collateral Project participants agree to pool collateral, i.e. allow recourse to each other's collateral.

Cross default A default by another project participant or by the sponsor (other than the project financing) triggers a default.

Crown Law Law derived from English law, e.g. as in England, Ireland, Canada, PNG, Australia, Hong Kong, Singapore, India, Malaysia.

Cure Make good a default.

Current assets Assets owned which by their nature are likely to be transformed (sold, used in production, increased or decreased) within one year. These include stocks, cash, debtors and prepayments.

Current dollar Actual or real prices and costs. Escalation/inflation effects are included.

Current liabilities Liabilities which will have to be met by the business within the next year. These include short-term bank debt, creditors, taxes due.

Current ratio Current assets divided by current liabilities (a liquidity ratio).

Cushion The extra amount of net cash flow remaining after expected debt service.

D:E ratio   The amount of debt as a ratio of equity, often expressed as a percentage.

D:E swap   Debt in a blocked currency is swapped for equity in a local company project, usually at a discount.

DCF   Discounted cash flow, where net cash flow is brought to a present value using a given percentage discount rate.

Debenture   Long-term loan secured on specific assets or through a floating charge on the business as a whole; a legal security over the issuer's general credit/balance sheet.

Debottle-necking   Each transition of a project's flowsheet or sequence is optimized to increase output. This may require minimal Capex.

Debt   The obligation to repay an agreed amount of money.

Debt service   Principal repayments plus interest payable; usually expressed as the annual dollar/currency amount per calendar or financial year.

Deductible   An amount or period which must be deducted before an insurance payout or settlement is calculated.

Default   A covenant has been broken or an adverse event has occurred. A money default means a repayment was not made on time. A technical default means a project parameter is outside defined/agreed limits, or a legal matter is not yet resolved.

Default interest   A higher interest rate payable after default.

Defeasance   Some or all of the debt is cash collateralised, usually indirectly or via Zero-coupon structures.

Deficiency   The amount by which project cash flow is not adequate for debt service.

Deficiency agreement   Where cash flow, working capital or revenues are below agreed levels or are insufficient to meet debt service, then a deficiency or make-up agreement provides the shortfall to be provided by the sponsor or another party, sometimes to a cumulative limit.

Defined event   The definition applicable to the trigger of a loss in an insurance policy, particularly PRI.

Depreciation   The amount by which a fixed asset is diminished in value in a particular year through its use in the business. This amount is charged directly against profits.

Depreciation   Amortization for accounting (book), tax calculations or income calculations. A regular reduction in asset value over time.

Derivative A financial instrument based on an underlying contract or funding, such as a swap, option or hedge.

Devaluation Either a formal reduction in the FX rate or one gradually occurring according to FX market forces.

DIS Delay-in-start-up insurances which can cover all non-site *force majeures*, change in a law and contingent contractor liability (efficacy). Sometimes called advanced loss-of-profits insurances or advanced business interruption insurance.

Discount rate The annual percentage applied to NPV or PV calculations (and is often the all-in interest rate or the interest rate plus margin for project financing). The discount rate may be the WACC.

Dividend The payment or distribution by a business to its shareholders; the amount paid out per share, usually once or twice a year, by a company from its profits as decided by the board of directors.

Documentation Anything (such as certificates of registration, loan agreements, guarantees, etc.) relating to the legal agreements and guarantees governing the facility extended to the borrower.

Documentation risk The risk of non-repayment due to a defect in the loan agreement or security arrangements. This can arise due to faulty drafting, mitigating circumstances, juridically non-enforceable and faulty collateral, or guarantees which have expired and not been renewed. The analyst is not expected to assess legal issues, but is expected to obtain legal opinions when necessary and note them in the credit analysis.

Double dip Tax depreciation is accessed in two countries concurrently.

Drawdown The borrower obtains some of the project financing, usually progressively according to construction expenditures plus IDC.

Drop-dead A fee payable when the underlying transaction does not proceed.

DSCR Debt service cover ratio; usually annual.

DTI Department of Trade and Industry. It is a valuable source of information on companies and many business matters in the UK and abroad.

Earnings Net income, net profit.

EBIT Earnings before interest and taxes.

EBIT DA Earnings before interest and tax, depreciation and amortization.

EBRD European Bank for Reconstruction and Development targeted at Eastern Europe and the former Soviet Union, an MIA.

ECA Export credit agency established by a country to finance its national's goods, investment and services. They often offer PRI.

ECGD Export Credit Guarantee Dept., the UK ECA.

EDC Export Development Corp., Canada's ECA.

EFIC Export Finance Insurance Corp., Australia's ECA.

EIS Environmental impact statement, which may have been subject to public comment.

Engineering risk Design risk. The impact on project cash flow from deficiencies in design or engineering.

Environmental risk Economic or administrative consequence of slow or catastrophic environmental pollution.

Equity The owners equity in the company is a residual interest, a claim on the assets not required to meet the claims of lenders and creditors. Equity will comprise the amounts originally contributed by the owners, along with profits from previous years which have not been distributed by way of dividend.

Equity In a project financing, the cash or assets contributed by the sponsors. For accounting, it is the net worth (or total assets) minus liabilities.

Equity In the context of credit analysis, this refers to the net value of all assets after deduction of all charges. Also known as share capital or shareholder's funds.

Equity kicker A share of ownership interest in a company, project or property, or a potential ownership in them. The kicker may take the form of stock, warrants, purchase options, percentage of profits, or percentage of ownership.

Escrow Where documents or money accounts are put beyond the reach of the parties.

Eurobonds Bonds issued in any currency and commonly listed in Luxembourg. They cannot be traded in the USA. Eurobonds are often Bearer Bonds.

Eurodollar € deposited with banks outside the USA.

Events of default A covenant in the loan agreement which the borrower failed to meet, enabling the bank to call the loan in for prepayment. Such events can range from the Channel tunnel boring failing to reach mile 12.75 on 25 October, to mailing an annual report to the lending bank three days late.

Evergreen facility A facility that automatically renews itself unless the borrower or lender gives notice to cancel.

Execute Formal signing of documentation. To implement an action required under the documentation.

Expropriation The state has taken over a company or project, implying compensation will be paid. Nationalization. Creeping expropriation occurs when a government squeezes a project by taxes, regulation, access or changes in law.

Factoring Selling of invoices to raise cash. Debts of various kinds are put together and sold to banks or corporate treasurers. A term used in international trade.

Fee A fixed amount or a percentage of an underwriting or principal.

Final take The final participation.

Finance lease The lessor receives lease payments to cover its ownership costs. The lessee is responsible for maintenance, insurance, and taxes. Some finance leases are conditional sales or hire purchase agreements.

Financial close When the documentation has been executed and conditions precedent have been satisfied or waived. Drawdowns are now permissible.

Financial year end The close of the year accounts (FYE).

Financing agreements The documents which provide the project financing and sponsor support for the project as defined in the project contracts.

Fiscal year-end The end of the tax year as defined by the tax authorities.

Fixed assets Assets owned which by their nature are not likely to be transformed (sold, used in production, increased or decreased) within one year. These include land and buildings, plant and machinery fixtures and fittings.

Fixed cost Operating cost which does not vary per unit of output.

Fixed rate Interest rate that is fixed for a defined period.

Float See IPO.

Floating charge Security, in the form of a range of assets, which is given by the company for a loan.

Floating rate Interest rate that is reset periodically, usually every couple of months or sometimes daily.

Floor A level which an interest rate or currency is structured not to go below.

Force majeure Events outside the control of the parties. These events are acts of man, nature, governments/regulators, or impersonal events. Contract performance is forgiven or extended by the period of *force majeure*.

Foreign exchange The conversion of one currency into another.

Forex FX, Foreign exchange.

Forward contract Forwards. An agreement to exchange currency or interest obligations in the future. For tradable commodities or securities, an agreement to buy or sell at a future date.

FRNs Floating rate notes, where the interest is reset by a panel or by reference to a market floating rate.

FRS/SSAP Financial Reporting Standard/Statement of Standard Accounting Practices. A set of standardized guidelines and procedures which have become mandatory for directors in the UK for all company accounts.

Full recourse No matter what risk event occurs, the borrower or its guarantors guarantee to repay the debt. By definition, this is not a project financing unless the borrower's sole asset is the project.

Funding risk he impact on project cash flow from higher funding costs or lack of availability of funds. Interest risk.

Funds Value used in a business (includes cash, credit, capital).

Futures These are formal agreements to purchase a given item in the future at a price agreed today. The practice began in Chicago in the nineteenth century and centred around the agricultural market, but records show that it was common in Holland and Japan in the sixteenth century. The purpose is to hedge against price changes.

Futures market A market where forward contracts can be traded before their maturity.

FX Foreign exchange.

FX rate One currency unit expressed in terms of another. Foreign exchange rate.

FX risk The effect on project cash flow or debt service from a movement in the FX rate for revenue, costs, or debt service.

Gas turbine Electricity generation by way of a turbine from burning natural gas or liquid fuels.

Gearing This is a ratio that sums up the financial standing of a company. It is obtained by dividing the total interest bearing debt by the shareholders' funds. The higher the number, the greater the risk. A company that has a large proportion of its permanent capital from debt is referred to as being highly geared.

General partner The partner with unlimited liability.

Goodwill The amount paid in excess of book value on the balance sheet, usually for intangible assets such as trademarks or licences.

Grace After a default, days of grace may be stated within which the cure is effected. A period when interest or principal is not yet payable, usually a period after start-up/commissioning/completion in a project financing.

Gross margin Sales revenue minus cost of goods sold.

GSM Global System for Mobiles, a mobile phone standard.

Guarantee Usually an undertaking by a third party to assume the debts of the borrower in the event of default. A common situation with parent/affiliate lending arrangements. Guarantees can and do expire, and the analyst should ensure in the credit review that they are either still valid, or have been renewed.

Guarantor A party who will guarantee repayment or performance of a covenant.

Heat rate The amount of fuel required to generate a kilowatt hr (kwh) of electricity, usually expressed as an energy value such as kilojoules (kJ).

Hedge To take a forward contract or option to effect an anticipated change in a currency, commodity, interest rate or security, so that gains or losses are offset.

Hell-or-high-water An absolute commitment, with no contractual defence.

Hermes The trade finance agency for Germany.

Hire purchase The user of the asset is entitled to purchase the asset according to a pre-agreed method. The user may be the owner for tax purposes.

Holding company Company which holds, directly or indirectly, more than 50 per cent of a subsidiary company, or controls the composition of the board of directors.

Hurdle rate A minimum IRR.

IFC International Finance Corporation, the private enterprise arm of the World Bank.

Illiquid Not easily traded or not readily converted to cash.

Incipient default   Potential default.

Income   Operating cash flows less overheads and depreciation, either before tax (BT) or after tax (AT). Earnings.

Inconvertibility   Where a local currency cannot be exchanged for another currency. Often includes transfer risk.

Indemnity   A legal obligation to cover a liability, however arising.

Indexed rate   An interest rate linked to an index, usually the CPI.

Information memorandum   An information circular which the borrowing company and agent banks will prepare providing information relating to the company and its borrowing requirements, and which is circulated to interested parties during a loan syndication.

Infrastructure risk   The impact on project cash flows from infrastructure problems. Sometimes labelled transportation risk.

Institutions   Insurance companies, pension funds, trusts, foundations, mutual funds, funds managers, bank investment departments.

Instrument   A financial tool. Sometimes a discrete type of funding or a security.

Intangible assets   Assets which are neither physical nor financial (e.g. goodwill, licences, trademarks).

Interest rate   The percentage payable to the lender calculated at an annual rate on the principal. May be all-in.

Interest risk   The impact on project cash flow from higher interest costs or lack of availability of funds. Funding risk.

Intermediary   An entity standing between parties to funding or a swap. An intermediary may be at risk.

Inventory   Finished goods, raw materials or work in process.

Inverse order   Applied to the periodic repayment schedule, and means from the end, expected maturity. 'Current order' means the next periodic principal repayment.

Investment bank   The US term for a merchant bank.

Investment grade   For a rating, the rating level above which institutional investors have been authorized to invest.

Investor/creditor community   Entities which provide funds to companies. Investors buy shares in the company (equity), while creditors lend money to companies (debt).

IPO   An initial public offering of shares. A float.

IPP   Independent power plant, a BOO development.

IRR The discount rate to make the NPV zero. Multiple IRRs occur mathematically if the periodic cash flows change sign more than once.

Islamic loan Interest cannot be charged. Rather, the loan is structured using discounts, sale/lease, profit participation, or repurchase agreements.

Iterations The number of times circular references in a spreadsheet are recalculated before the calculation reaches an (approximated) acceptable degree of accuracy (interest expenses calculated on projected debt, projected debt based on the final P + L result which depends on interest expense, etc. ...). Computers perform such laborious calculations instantly.

Joint venture (JV) The legal means of dividing the project's equity either by shareholdings in a company (incorporated JV) or by way of a contract (unincorporated JV).

Junk A high-yield bond of speculative grade.

L/C Letter of credit, a guarantee to pay limited to an amount and time triggered by defined events or exchange of agreed documents. Used for credit enhancement.

Latent default A potential default that may have always been present but unidentified.

Lawsuits Items which do not appear on the balance sheet but can have a financial impact on the company. Also considered as 'contingent liabilities', these should be explained in the notes to the financial statements.

LDs Liquidated damages. The amount payable for delays and substandard performance under a construction, equipment supply, or 0 & M contract.

Lead arranger The senior tier of arranger.

Lead bank A senior bank involved in the negotiations for a project financing. Subordinate to an arranger.

Lead manager Senior tier of lender in a loan syndication.

League tables A ranking of lenders and advisers according to the underwriting, final take, or number of cash flow forecasting loans or advisory mandates.

Lease The owner of an asset (lessor) agrees to receive lease payments/ rentals from the user (lessee), usually at a fixed rental level. The lessor/owner takes the benefit of depreciation as a tax deduction. Its primary security is the asset.

Lease rate   The equivalent interest rate calculated from a stream of lease payments.

Lease term   The life of a lease including any renewal options.

Legal risk   A risk that a defect in the documentation will affect cash flow or debt service.

Lending risk   Risks relating to lender, including legal enforceability, documentation, interest rates, etc. The risks the bank is getting into by putting the loan into place.

Lessee   The user who pays lease rentals to the owner/lessor.

Lessor   The owner of a leased asset.

Leverage   1. This is the American term for gearing. 2. In the UK this is the same as gearing, with the addition of non-interest bearing external debt.

Leveraged lease   A lessor borrows to finance a leased asset. Recourse may be limited to the lease rentals or the asset.

Liability   Obligation of a company to make payment for goods or services already received.

Liability   The obligation to repay a defined amount or to perform a service.

LIBOR   London Interbank Offered Rate, often quoted as a 1-, 3-, 6-month rate for €.

Lien   A legal security interest in an asset.

Limited recourse   Under certain conditions (legal or financial), there is access to the sponsor's credit or other legal security for repayment (besides the project's cash flows). There is usually recourse in the event of fraud or misrepresentation/non-disclosure. Thus non-recourse is better described as 'limited-recourse'.

Liquid   Easily traded or converted to cash.

Liquidation   The process of disposal or sale of the project or project assets with the proceeds used to repay the project financing.

Liquidation   Selling off the company's assets to satisfy creditors during a winding up. The main risk in a liquidation is asset shrinkage – whether the assets being liquidated can fetch a market value sufficient to satisfy all the creditors.

Liquidity   The pool of accessible funds, either in cash or in assets that may be converted rapidly into cash to meet immediate debts.

Liquidity   The ability to convert current assets into cash to meet current liabilities when they fall due.

Liquidity ratios   The acid test and current ratios used to measure changes in liquidity between various accounting periods.

Listed company   A public company whose shares are listed on the Stock Exchange so that a 'market' can be made in its shares.

Loan agreement   Every loan should have one. These define the rules and obligations binding on the lenders, borrowers guarantors and related parties.

Loan officers   The persons who look after client relations and new business opportunities. The analyst's work is to evaluate objectively the companies and businesses that loan officers are proposing to lend to, and submit their evaluations in the credit review process.

Loans, short-term   Loans under one year in duration.

Loans, term   Loans of between three and seven years' duration.

Long term   Three years or more; in accounting, more than one year.

Long-term liabilities   Liabilities of the business which will fall due in a period more than 12 months from the balance sheet date.

Loss payee   A party to whom an insurance loss payment or settlement may be paid directly.

LP   Limited partner who is not liable for the debts of the partnership beyond the funds contributed.

Make-up   Where a cash flow or capital item is deficient, the amount of such deficiency – e.g. an interest make-up relates to the interest amount above a ceiling percentage.

Management accounting   Part of the accounting system used to provide information for managing the business in a form required for internal use, compared to financial accounting, which is for external use and must reflect prescribed formats and content.

Manager   A medium-level participant established according to final take.

Mandate   The formal appointment to advise on or arrange a project financing.

Margin   The amount expressed in percentage p.a. above the interest rate basis or cost of funds. For hedging and futures contracts, the cash collateral deposited with a trader or exchange as insurance against default.

Market risk   Changes to the amounts sold or the price received, which impacts on gross revenue. Sometimes called sales risk.

Market value   The price at which an asset may be bought or sold.

Maturity   The final date a cash flow forecasting loan is repayable. The end of the term.

Maturity schedules   The repayments on the loan. A good set of company financial statements will break out all the various debts which they have, the interest rates, and periods of repayment. The analyst should pay particular attention to bullet repayments on future cash flow. Debt maturity schedules in years in financial statements are now required by EC directives.

Medium term   Two to six years.

Memorandum of Association   This is a document drawn up by each newly formed company, which lays down the rules that govern the company's dealings with the outside world. It includes company name, the activities of the company, details of share capital, list of shareholders.

Merchant bank   A bank which, besides lending and deposit-taking (usually not from the public), engages in trading and advisory services, and acts as an underwriter and funds manager of securities.

MIGA   Multilateral Investment Guaranty Agency, the PRI arm of the World Bank.

MILA   Multilateral agency such as IFC, ADB.

Mine-mouth   Where the coal mine is beside the power station. A dedicated coal mine.

Minority interests   Where a company does not own 100 per cent of the shares of a subsidiary company, the percentage of shares which are held by outside investors is called a minority interest. The appropriate procedure is to include the full amount of the subsidiary's assets and liabilities in the consolidated balance sheet, with the proportion financed by outside investors represented by a credit balance described as 'minority interest'.

MITI   Ministry of International Trade and Industry of Japan.

Monetization   Securitization of the gross revenues of a contract.

Monte Carlo   Simulations using random numbers.

MW   Megawatts – one thousand kW, or one million watts.

Negative pledge   The borrower agrees not to pledge any of its assets as security and/or not to incur further indebtedness.

Negotiable   A financial instrument can be bought or sold by another investor, privately or via a stock exchange/computer trading.

Net realizable value   When relating to a company's products, this is the actual or estimated selling price less all costs of manufacturing and costs to be incurred in marketing, selling and distributing.

Net worth (Owners' equity)   The value owed by a business to its owners reflecting the difference between the total value of all assets and total of all liabilities. It is the value attributable to the owners in respect of the net financial position of the business.

Nominal value   The face value of a share.

Non-recourse   The financiers rely on the project's cash flows and collateral security over the project as the only means to repay debt service. This usually occurs after completion.

NPV   The periodic net cash flows are each discounted by the discount rate to a present date, and the appropriate cash outflows/investment for construction or acquisition are deducted from the total.

O&M   Operations and maintenance.

Offtake(r)   The purchase(r) of the project's output.

Open-cycle   The waste energy/exhaust from a power plant is not captured.

Operating cash flow   Project revenues less (cash) Opex.

Operating risk   Cost, technology and management components which impact Opex and project output/throughput. Costs includes inflation.

Opex   Operating expenses, always expressed as cash. Therefore, depletion and depreciation are excluded.

Option   A contract in which the writer of the option grants the buyer of the option the right, but not the obligation, to purchase from or sell to the writer something at a specified price within a specified period of time (or a specified date).

Ordinary shares   These give the holder the right to vote on major decisions and to participate in the profits of the company by way of dividend payments.

Oversubscription   Underwriting commitments from a syndication exceeds the amount sought by the amount of over subscription.

Overrun   The amount of Capex or funding above the original estimate to complete the project.

p.a.   per annum, yearly.

Parent company   Company that owns a majority of shares in another company.

Pari passu   Equal ranking of security pro-rata to the amount owed.

Participant   A party to a funding. It usually refers to the lowest rank/ smallest level of funding. Alternatively, it is one of the parties to the project financial/project documents.

Participant risk   The credit of the participants and the risk of non-performance under the project contracts or financing agreements.

Participation   The amount of loan/bond issue taken directly or from another direct lender/underwriter.

Partnership   The partners agree to a proportional share of profits and losses and thus have the same tax treatment.

Payback   The period in years to recover the investment or loan. It may be calculated on a discounted, non-discounted, leveraged or unleveraged basis.

Payment   The amount that is required to repay a loan with interest and fees.

Performance bond   A bond of 5–10 per cent of a contract payable if a project is not completed as specified. Usually part of a construction contract or supply agreement.

Physical completion   The project is physically functioning, but not yet (fully) generating cash flow.

Placement   Securities are placed with a small group of investors.

Point   One percentage point on a note or a bond.

Political risk   Eight risks, usually comprising currency inconvertibility, expropriation, war and insurrection, terrorism, environmental activities, landowner actions, non-government activists, legal, and bureaucratic/ approvals. The first three are insurable. It overlaps with the political component of *force majeure* risk.

Potential default   A condition where a default would occur in time, or where a notice or default event has not yet been formalized.

PPA   Power purchase agreement, a long-term power supply contract.

Preference shares   Non-voting shares which carry the preferential right to receive a dividend out of profits of a fixed percentage of the share capital before the ordinary shareholders get any dividend.

Premium   The cost of an insurance policy. The price of an option. An extra margin payable with prepayment of principal.

Prepayment   Repayment of greater than the scheduled amount. If forced, it is referred to as a mandatory prepayment.

PRI   Political risk insurance.

Price earnings ratio   The relationship between a company's profits and the publicly quoted value of its shares. This is usually expressed as market value of shares/earnings per share.

Prime rate   A (US) bank interest rate charged to prime customers for loans in excess of $100,000.

Principal   The quantity of the outstanding project financing due to be paid. Generic: a principal is a party bearing an obligation or responsibility directly (as distinct from an agent).

Private company   This is a company which is not a public company; all companies with the word 'limited' at the end of their name are private companies.

Private placement   The placement of debt or equity investment is not publicized and may not be tradable.

Production   A defined portion of the proceeds of production up to a dollar amount.

Production loan   A project financing where the repayment is linked to the production, often on a $/unit basis.

Profit & loss account   A record of income and expenses in the business in a specific period of time.

Pro forma   A financial projection based on assumptions.

Project   The asset constructed with or owned via a project financing which is expected to produce cash flow at a debt service cover ratio sufficient to repay the project financing.

Project contracts   The suite of a agreements underlying the project.

Project financing   A loan structure which relies for its repayment primarily on the project's cash flow, with the project's assets, rights and interests held as secondary security or collateral.

Pro rata   Shared or divided according to a ratio or in proportion to participations.

Prospectus   A formally approved document describing the business and affairs of the issuer and the terms and conditions of the security. An Offering Circular in the US filed with the SEC, e.g. for an IPO or a Rule 144a Bond Issue.

Public company   Defined by the Companies Act 1985 as a company limited by shares or by guarantee (shareholders' liability is limited to the amount of share capital or to the amount of guarantee given), which has a minimum share capital of €50,000, whose Memorandum states that it is a Public company. All public companies will have the words Public Limited Company (or PLC) at the end of their name, but note that a Public company is not necessarily a listed company.

Purchasing power parity   A view that differential escalation rates (in different countries) determines the systematic change in FX rates.

Put   An option to sell (back) a security or commodity at a set price at a given time.

Rating   The ranking, usually grades of A to E, of the creditworthiness/ability to repay. The ranking of bonds is related to the estimated percentage default rate. Countries are similarly ranked, and ranking may include an estimation of political risk.

Ratio analysis   Calculation of financial ratios as an aid to interpretation.

Ratio analysis   The technique of analysing company performance by calculating financial ratios for historical and comparative purposes.

Receiver   A person/entity appointed under the legal security documents to administer the security on behalf of the project financiers.

Recourse   In the event that the project (and its associated escrows, sinking funds or cash reserves/standby facilities) cannot service the financing or completion cannot be achieved, then the financiers have recourse to either cash from other sponsor/corporate sources, or other non-project security.

Refinancing   Repaying existing debt and entering into a new loan, typically to meet some corporate objective such as the lengthening of maturity or lowering the interest rate.

Regulatory actions   Legal requirements on a company. If the government passes a law forcing chemical companies to process carcinogenic waste instead of dumping it in our drinking water, this is known as a regulatory action. Regulatory issues can adversely impact a company's profitability and viability.

Representations   A series of statements about a project, a sponsor, or the obligations under the project contracts or the financing agreements.

Reserve account   A separate amount of cash or L/C to service a payment requirement such as debt service or maintenance.

Residual   The assumed value of an asset at the end of a loan, lease or pro forma cash flow. It is sometimes insured.

Residual cover   The cash flow remaining after a project financing has been repaid expressed as a percentage of the original loan.

Residual cushion   The amount of net cash flow from the project after the project financing has been repaid. If it is expressed as a percentage of the original loan amount, it is the 'residual cover'.

Retention   An amount held back from construction contract payments to ensure the contractor completes the construction, when the retention (5–15 per cent of the contract price) is returned to the contractor.

Return on assets (ROA)   Net profits after taxed divided by assets. This ratio helps a firm determine how effectively it generates profits from available assets.

Return on equity (ROE)   Net profits after taxes divided by stockholders' equity.

Revenues   Sales or royalty proceeds. Quantity multiplied by price realized.

Rights issue   The opportunity for a company's shareholders to invest more money in the company by subscribing for new shares at a cost less than the current market price.

Risk   The event which can change the expected cash flow forecast for the project financing. 'At risk' means the cash or loan. For insurance, it means the total amount or type of event insured.

ROCE   Return on capital employed.

Royalty   A share of revenue or cash flow to the government or grantor of the concession or licence.

Rule 144a   Under US SEC regulations, a Rule 144a security (usually bonds but can be equity/shares) can be placed with professional investors who are prequalified/registered and take minimum €100,000 amounts. Less strict document/disclosure/due diligence is permitted than for a full prospectus.

SACE   The Italian ECA.

Sales (Sales turnover)   The value of goods sold or services provided in a specific accounting period. Sometimes described as 'revenues'.

Sales completion   The project has reached physical completion and has delivered product or generated revenues in satisfaction of a sales completion test.

Salvage value   The estimated selling price of an asset once it has been fully depreciated.

SEC   Securities & Exchange Commission, which regulates disclosure and practices for companies and public issues of debt and equity in the USA.

Securitization   Packaging up a stream of receivables or assets to fund via a capital markets, tradable funding.

Security   A legal right of access to value through mortgages, contracts, cash accounts, guarantees, insurances, pledges or cash flow, including licences, concessions and other assets. A negotiable certificate evidencing a debt or equity obligation/shareholding.

Security   The assets or guarantees you claim when the loan is in default. Forms of security can vary from high-grade government bonds to partially completed stock, and are defined in the loan agreement.

Security agreement   An agreement in which title to property is held as collateral under a financing agreement, usually by a trustee.

Senior   Ranking for repayment, security or action. Most project financings are senior debt obligations with first, senior security.

Sensitivity   A change to a cash flow input to determine the change to DSCR.

Setoff   Money held on behalf of a borrower may be applied to repay the loan. It usually implies without the permission of the borrower.

Share premium   Money received by the company for a share issue which is in excess of its nominal value.

Shareholders' equity   Net worth. Book value of total assets less total liabilities.

Short-term   Up to 12 months.

Sinking fund   A regular payment is set aside in anticipation of a future payment.

SOE   State-owned enterprise.

Sovereign risk   The government's part of political risk.

Sponsor   A party wishing to develop a project. A developer. A party providing financial support.

Spreadsheet   The analyst's main tool in unscrambling a typical set of company accounts.

Statement of cash flow   A statement which reconciles movements in cash between two accounting periods.

Steam turbine   Electricity generation from steam pressure.

Structure   How a project financing is drawn down, repaid, and collateralized secured.

Subordinated   The subordinated party accepts a lower priority of repayment and/or security than senior debt.

Subsidiary company   A company in which all of its share capital is owned by another company.

Sunk costs   Capital already spent.

Supplier credit   The supplier of goods or services agrees to deferred repayment terms.

Supply risk   The raw materials or input to a project change from those assumed/projected. For a resources production project, this is called reserves risk.

Swap   An exchange of the basis of obligations to repay principal, interest or currency. For interest-rate swaps (floating to fixed), the underlying principal may not be exchanged.

Sweep   All available cash flow is used for debt service.

Syndication   The selling of a cash flow forecasting to a group of prospective participants, the syndicate.

Tail   The remaining reserves after the project financing has been repaid. Sometimes means the residual.

Take-and-pay   If the project's output is deliverable and can be taken, it will be paid for.

Take-or-pay   In the event the project's output is not taken, payment must be made whether or not the output is deliverable.

Takeout   A financing to refinance or take out another e.g. construction loan.

Tangible assets   Assets which have a tangible, real or ascertainable value.

Tangible net worth   The value attributable to shareholders when realistic (tangible) values are applied to the calculation of net worth.

Tenor   The number of years a loan is outstanding. The term.

Term   The loan life or tenor; the period to a loan's maturity. Generic: A condition attached.

Throughput   A throughput agreement is a hell-or-high-water contract to put and pay for material through a facility. *Force majeure* gives no relief.

TNW   Total net worth.

Tolling   A contract to process or convert a raw material into a saleable or finished product. The tolling contract does not require the purchase of the raw material or the sale of the output.

Tombstone   An advertisement listing the sponsor, amount funded, participants, and key roles.

Tranche   A separate portion of a project financing, perhaps with different financiers, margins and term.

Transfer risk   Currency cannot be sent out of the country, usually due to Central Bank restrictions or a national debt rescheduling.

Trustee   An independent or nominated third party who administers corporate or financial arrangements.

Turnkey   The construction of a project to meet a standard or the completion test where it is ready to produce cash flow. Turnkey contracts usually have LDs and retentions.

Turnover   The gross revenue net of VAT which the company has earned from providing goods/services to customers.

Underwriting   The commitment to fund is not contingent on syndication.

Unsecured   The financier has no security, merely the obligation/undertaking to repay.

Unwind   To reverse a swap or hedge.

WACC   Weighted Average Cost of Capital calculated from the returns on interest rates payable on the different components of a company's or a project's deemed capital structure.

Well   A drill hole in the petroleum industry.

Withholding   A tax on interest, royalty, or dividend payments, usually those paid overseas. It may be deducted at source.

Working capital   The amount of short-term funds available to a business to perform its normal trading operations. Usually defined as the difference between current assets and current liabilities.

Working capital   Cash required to fund inventories and accounts receivable. Accounting definition is current assets less current liabilities. It is recovered entirely when the project ceases.

Workout   The project financiers are responding to work out a potential problem or have arranged to take over the operation after a default to attempt to rehabilitate the cash flow generating capacity of the project.

World Bank   An MILA based in Washington DC. The international bank for reconstruction and development. Usually involved in government-related deals.

Yield   The financial return, usually expressed as a percentage p.a.

Zero coupon   No interest is paid. A bond or note is issued at a discount, which is calculated to yield a compound interest equivalent return.

Profitability indicators

Cost of goods sold (CGS)   The cost of the raw materials and resources used in the manufacturing process, both in their composition (wood for paper manufacturing) as well as in other manufacturing related resources (chemicals, electricity).

Dividend payout ratio   The ratio of dividends paid out as a percentage of net profits, useful in calculating the level of retained earnings.

Gross profit (GP)   Net sales revenue minus cost of goods sold = gross profit.

Gross profit margin (GPM)   This is the company's gross profit expressed as a percentage of net sales. This index is useful to see whether the company's sales activity is generating more or less profits. Historical average gross profit margins, in conjunction with projected future sales, are also useful in projecting future cost of goods sold and gross profits.

Net margins   Percentage of each sales pound remaining after all operating expenses and taxes have paid: net income divided by net sales.

Profit   The amount of funds available after satisfying preceding expenses. In descending order in the profit and loss statement, we are concerned with several types of profit: gross profit, operating profit, profit before interest and taxes, and net profit.

Profitability   Measures the amount of profit generated in relation to net sales. If your sales double and profits rise by only 20 per cent, you will have increased your profits but your profitability will have taken a sharp downturn.

Retained earnings (R/E)   The amount of a company's profits which are transferred to net worth after payment of dividends to the company's shareholders. From our projections viewpoint this item is important, as it contributes to growth in net worth and maintaining adequate leverage.

Return on assets (ROA)   Percentage return on each pound of assets employed: net income divided by total assets.

Return on equity (ROE)   Percentage return on each pound of equity employed: net income divided by net worth adjusted for intangibles.

Selling, general and administrative expenses (SGA) These are expenses arising from the company's ongoing operations in completing the manufacturing process.

SGA as a percent of sales Percent of each sales pound used for selling, general and administrative expense: SGA divided by net sales.

Turnover and efficiency indicators

Accounts payable in days Accounts payable/sales*365. This is another index linked to sales activity. Also known as supplier credit, this ratio measures the extent to which the company avails itself of credit from its suppliers. While modest levels are to be expected, undue variations can be indicative of liquidity problems in the company.

Accounts receivable in days Total accounts receivable/sales*365. Also known as the collection period, this ratio measures how long it takes the company to collect payments from its clients. This activity is linked to sales activity, but can vary for other reasons such as inadequate collection procedures.

Asset to sales (ATO) The ratio of assets to net sales, also known as asset turnover (ATO). This ratio basically measures how many units of sales a company is able to generate in terms of its balance sheet size. A company which is able to generate more sales then a competitor with a similar-sized balance sheet is more 'asset efficient'. Asset efficiency should not be confused with profitability, however: an asset-efficient company may generate a loss, unlike its less asset-efficient competitor, due to other variables (rising operating costs, loss on sale of sub, etc.).

Inventory in days Total inventory/sales*365. Inventory levels are directly linked to sales: if the company is keeping inventory longer than in previous years, this can be an indication of inadequate inventory controls (raw materials) or slow sales (finished goods). From the Land of The Rising Sun comes the vogue concept of 'just-in-time' inventory, which attempts to minimize levels of inventory held to the bare minimum (hours), as inventory represents financial resources lying idle. Easier said than done, though, if your business is located in a country prone to transport strikes.

Net plant to sales (NP/S) Net plant/sales. This ratio measures the amount of net plant needed to support each unit of sales. NP/S is a useful indicator in determining the level of capital expenditures which will be required to support projected sales growth. If sales rise, you will want to multiply sales by the historical average of the NP/S ratio to determine the level of future net plant.

Financial position indicators

Current ratio   The working capital relationship expressed as a ratio (current assets divided by current liabilities). A company with a current ratio of 1 or above is said to be liquid, and a company with a current ratio of below 1 to be illiquid.

Debt to equity ratio   This ratio, also known as 'leverage', measures the amount of debt relative to equity in the company's balance sheet: total liabilities divided by net worth. A company with a high debt to equity ratio is said to be highly leveraged or geared.

New money need (NMN/NDN)   A 'plug' figure required to reconcile projected liabilities with projected assets in order to finance the projected balance sheet growth. New money need (NMN) can be funded by debt or equity, or by a combination of the two. Without equity, this caption is known as 'new debt need' (NDN).

Quick ratio   A variant on the current ratio: the relative amount by which current assets which can be readily converted to cash (i.e. cash, marketable securities, and receivables but not inventories) exceed (or fall short of) current liabilities – in other words, current assets less inventories divided by current liabilities. This measures the amount available to creditors in a liquidation scenario after excluding the unsellable and half-completed bric-a-brac stored in its warehouses (e.g. used oil-drilling equipment that will fetch 10 cents on the dollar in a fire sale).

Working capital (W/C)   The difference between current assets and current liabilities. This represents the cushion available to cover current liabilities in the event they are all called in (if short-term uncommitted financing facilities are withdrawn). If a company's working capital is negative (i.e. current liabilities exceed current assets), the company is said to be 'technically insolvent'.

Working investment   Working investment is the amount of accounts receivable and inventory (current assets less cash/marketable securities) that must be financed by sources other than accounts payable and accrued expenses – in other words, the difference between current assets less current liabilities, excluding cash, marketable securities, overdrafts and other non-cash-driven 'working' elements. Working investment therefore is a net asset investment used in completing the manufacturing (sales) cycle that must be supported by either equity or borrowed money. In other words: $WI = (A/R + Inv.)(A/P + /E's)$.

Cash flow terms

Actual change in cash Amount by which the cash account on a balance sheet changes from the previous year. If calculated cash flow is properly constructed, cash after external financing will equal the actual change in cash.

Cash after debt amortization Cash position of the company after all operating expenses, financing costs and scheduled debt amortization is paid. If positive, the firm generates sufficient cash to pay interest and repay scheduled debt. If not, the company has to meet its financing requirements from external sources.

Cash after external financing Amount by which cash raised from external sources (i.e. debt or equity) exceeds/falls short of the financing requirements.

Cash from sales Cash collected in one year from sales made in that and previous years.

Financing requirements Amount of financing required to meet the combination of an operating cash deficit, debt amortization and capital spending. Calculated by deducting capital spending and long-term investment from cash after debt amortization.

Net operating cash flow The most important item in your cash flow statement, this is the amount of cash generated from sales after cost of goods sold and other operating costs are deducted and after movements in working capital (debtors, stocks, and creditors being the principle elements). This figure is referred to as net operating cash flow, or NOCF.

Cash ratios

Cash flow interest cover ratio NOCF/interest expense. This ratio indicates whether the company is generating sufficient cash flow to service (not repay) its debt commitments. If the ratio is below 1, the company is unable to service the interest, let alone repayment on its debt, and may be in serious difficulties.

Financing payments cover ratio NOCF/(interest expenses, dividends (or withdrawals), scheduled debt amortization and lease payments). This ratio indicates if the firm generates sufficient cash from operations to meet financing costs and amortize scheduled debt. If this ratio is greater than 1, the firm is able to pay financing costs and repay debt as scheduled. If the ratio is less than 1, the firm is not able to do so.

Total debt payout ratio (years) Total interest-bearing debt/NOCF. This ratio basically tells you how many years it will take the company to repay its current levels of debt.

Index

Acceleration, 210
Acceptance Credit facility, 30
Account party, 210
Accounting period, 210
Accounting Standards Board, 11
Accounting Standards Committee, 11
Accounts payable, 23, 26–7, 111,
    120–1, 210
  in days, 238
Accounts receivable, 24–6, 210
  in days, 238
  turnover, 117–18
Accruals, 12, 27, 210
Accrued expenses payable, 121–2
Accrued income, 25
Accrued interest, 210
Acid test (Quick ratio), 210
Actual change in cash, 240
Ad valorem, 210
Advance agent, 210
Adverse opinion, 15
After tax cash flow, 210
Aged analysis, 210
Agent, 210
Agent banks, 211

Agreed overdraft facility, 29–30
All-in rate, 211
Altman Bankruptcy Predictor, 73, 74
AMADEUS electronic databases,
    172–84
  company search mechanism, 174
Amortization, 129–31, 211
Andersen, Arthur, 37–8
Annual report, 10–33, 211
Annuity, 211
Arbitrage, 211
Arrangement fees, 211
Arranger, 211
Articles of Association, 11, 29, 211
Asset conversion cycle, 65
Asset management, 54–8
Asset to sales, 238
Asset turnover, 52
  and liquidity, 54–6
Asset turnover ratio, 212
Asset-backed securities, 211
Assets, 16–22, 112–19, 211, 212
  fixed, 23–4, 30–1, 114–15
  sources and uses, 138
Assignment, 212

Associate company, 212
Audit, 212
Auditors, 212
    problems with, 35–8
Auditors' report, 10, 14–15
Authorized share capital, 32
Authorized signatories, 212
Availability, 212
Available cash flow, 212
Average life, 212
Average price, 28
Avoided cost, 212

Balance sheet, 10, 15–16, 17–22,
    132–3, 212, 213
    date, 15
    projections, 109–12
    ratio analysis, 76
Balloon payment, 213
Bank loans, 27, 40
Banking facilities, 29–30
Barings, 72
Barter, 213
Basis point, 213
Bearer Bond, 213
Best efforts, 213
Bid bond, 213
Bills of exchange, 27, 30
Blocked currency, 213
Bond, 213
Book runner, 213
Book value, 31
Borrower risk, 213
Borrowing, 29–30
Borrowing ratios, 60
Break even, 213
Broker, 213
Build Own Operate, 213
Build Own Transfer, 213

Builders' All Risk, 213
Bullet, 213
Bullet repayment, 214
Business profile, 151
Business risk, 42
Buy-back, 214
Buydown, 214
Buyer credit, 214

Call, 214
Call option, 214
Called up share capital, 24
Cap, 214
Capital, 214
Capital & reserves, 214
Capital expenditure, 114–15
Capital markets, 214
Capital redemption reserve, 33
Capital structure, 58–63
Capitalized expenditure, 13
Capitalized interest, 53, 214
Cash after current operations, 140
Cash after debt amortization, 240
Cash after external financing, 240
Cash drivers, 74, 76
Cash flow, 63–6, 78, 214
Cash flow analysis, 66
    reasons for, 76–9
Cash flow forecasting, 66–70, 214
    definition, 1
    methodology, 69
    percent-of-sales forecasting,
        67–8
    sustainable growth, 69–70
    uses of, 6–7
Cash flow interest cover ratio,
    240–1
Cash flow lending, 199
Cash flow matrix, 139–44

Cash flow projections, 134–44
Cash flow ratio analysis, 144–6
Cash from sales, 240
Cash and marketable securities,
    118–19, 128
Cash and profit, 63–5
Certificates of registration, 215
Charge, 215
Claw back, 215
Close company, 215
Club, 215
Co-financing, 215
Co-generation, 215
Co-manager, 215
Coface, 215
Collar, 215
Collateral, 215
Collection period, 57
Combined cycle, 215
Commitment fee, 215
Companies Acts (1985, 1989), 10,
    12, 14
Compensation trade, 215
Competitive analysis, 44–6
Competitive conditions, 96
Complementary financing, 215
Completion, 215
Completion risk, 216
Completion test, 216
Compound, 216
Conrad Black, 71
Consistency, 12
Consortium, 216
Constant dollar, 216
Consumer Price Index, 217
Contingency, 216
Contingent liabilities, 54, 216
Convertible shares, 32, 216
Corporate credit analysis, 41

Corporate failure, 70–5
    failure prediction models,
        73–5
    reasons for failure, 71–2
Corporate objectives, 151
Cost flexibility, 96
Cost of goods sold, 100–2, 216, 237
Counterparty, 216
Countertrade, 216
Country risk, 189–98, 216
    economic risk profile, 190–5
    political risk profile, 189
    S&P's sovereign rating profile,
        195–8
Coupon, 216
Covenant, 217
Cover, 217
Creative accounting, 13–14
Credit, 217
Credit analysis, 42
Credit enhancement, 217
Credit factors, 47
Credit period, 26
Credit rating agency rating scales,
    186–8
Credit scoring, 217
Credit worthiness, 6
Creditors *see* Accounts payable
Creditworthy, 217
Cross default, 217
Cross-collateral, 217
Crown Law, 217
Cure, 217
Current assets, 24, 217
Current dollar, 217
Current liabilities, 24, 119–20,
    217
Current ratio, 217, 239
Cushion, 217

D:E ratio, 218
D:E swap, 218
Debenture (secured) loans, 27, 218
Debentures, 29, 218
Debottle-necking, 218
Debt, 111, 218
    capacity, 122
    intercompany, 127
Debt runoff schedule, 111, 122–4
Debt service cover ratio, 146, 219
Debt servicing, 6, 130, 218
Debt to equity ratio, 239
Debtors *see* Accounts receivable
Deductible, 218
Default, 218
Default interest, 218
Defeasance, 218
Deferred income, 27
Deferred shares, 32
Deficiency, 218
Deficiency agreement, 218
Defined event, 218
Delay-in-start-up insurances, 219
Department of Trade and Industry, 219
Depreciation, 3, 13, 31, 54, 114–15, 218
Derivative, 219
Devaluation, 219
Directors' report, 10
Disclaimer of opinion, 15
Discount rate, 219
Discounted cash flow, 218
Dividend payout ratio, 237
Dividends, 27, 106, 128, 219
Documentation, 219
Documentation risk, 219
Double dip, 219
Drawdown, 219
Drop-dead, 219

Earnings, 219
Earnings before interest and taxes, 219
Economic risk profile, 190–5
Engineering risk, 220
Enron, 36–8, 72
Environmental analysis, 43–4
Environmental impact statement, 220
Environmental risk, 220
Equity, 220
Equity investors, 9
Equity kicker, 220
Escrow, 220
Eurobonds, 220
Eurodollar, 220
European accounting systems, 9
European Bank for Reconstruction and Development, 219
Events of default, 152, 220
Evergreen facility, 221
Execute, 221
Exercise period, 32
Exercise price, 32
Experience, 49
Export credit agency, 220
Export Credit Guarantee Department, 220
Export Development Corporation, 220
Export Finance Insurance Corporation, 220
Expropriation, 221
External environment, 42–6
Extraordinary items, 106

Factoring, 221
Failure prediction models, 73–5
Fee, 221

Final take, 221
Finance lease, 221
Financial close, 221
Financial covenants, 8, 151–2
Financial flexibility, 61–2
Financial information, 52–4
Financial leverage, 58–61, 62
Financial performance, 41–75
Financial position indicators, 239–40
Financial projections, 79–81, 83–6
Financial reporting standards,
    11–14, 222
Financial risk, 41, 42
Financial statements, 8–40, 76–159
    annual report and accounts, 10–33
    problems with, 35–8
    profit and loss account, 10, 33–5
Financial year end, 221
Financing activities, 66
Financing agreements, 221
Financing payments cover ratio, 145,
    241
Financing requirements, 240
Finished goods, 28
First-in-first-out (FIFO), 28, 35
Fiscal year-end, 221
Fixed asset investments, 128
Fixed assets, 23–4, 30–1, 114–15, 221
Fixed cost, 101, 151, 221
Fixed rate, 32, 221
Floating charge, 215, 218, 221
Floating rate, 221
Floating rate notes, 222
Floor, 221
Force majeure, 222
Foreign exchange, 222
Forward contract, 222
Fraudulent manipulation of
    accounts, 13–14

Full recourse, 222
Fundamental uncertainty, 15
Funding risk, 222
Funds, 222
Future cash flow model, 134–44
Futures, 222
Futures market, 222

Gas turbine, 222
Gearing, 222
General partner, 223
Going concern, 12
Goodwill, 223
Grace, 223
Gross margin, 51, 52, 100–2, 223
Gross profit, 237
Gross profit margin, 237
GSM, 223
Guarantee, 223
Guarantor, 223

Healthy cash flow, 3–6
Heat rate, 223
Hedge, 223
Hell-or-high-water, 223
Hermes, 223
Hire purchase, 223
Historical analysis, 81–6
Holding company, 223
Hurdle rate, 223

Illiquidity, 223
Inbound logistics, 55
Incipient default, 224
Income, 224
Inconvertibility, 224
Indemnity, 224
Indexed rate, 224
Information memorandum, 224

Infrastructure risk, 224
Institutions, 224
Instrument, 224
Intangible assets, 30, 224
Integrity, 49
Intercompany debt, 127
Interest cover, 62–3, 144–5
Interest expense, 105–6
Interest income, 105–6
Interest rate, 224
Interest risk, 224
Intermediary, 224
International Finance Corporation,
    223
Inventory, 27, 224
    in days, 238
    turnover, 56, 115–17
Inverse order, 224
Investing activities, 65
Investment, 31
Investment bank, 224
Investment grade, 224
Investor/creditor community, 224
Islamic loan, 225
Issue share capital, 32
Iterations, 126, 225

Joint venture, 225
Junk, 225

Key activity ratios, 109–10

Last-in-first-out (LIFO), 35
Latent default, 225
Lawsuits, 225
Lay, Kenneth, 38
Lead arranger, 225
Lead manager, 225
League tables, 225

Lease, 225
Lease rate, 226
Lease term, 226
Legal risk, 226
Lending risk, 226
Lending types, 199
Lessee, 226
Lessor, 226
Letter of credit, 225
Leverage, 226
Leveraged lease, 226
Liability, 23, 119–31, 226
Lien, 226
Limited partner, 227
Limited recourse, 226
Liquidated damages, 225
Liquidation, 226
Liquidity, 64–6, 226
Liquidity ratios, 227
Listed company, 227
Loan agreement, 227
Loan creditors, 9
Loan document drafting, 8
Loan officers, 227
Loan repayment, 2
Loan structuring, 8
Loans, 227
London Interbank Offered Rate,
    226
Long-term debt payout, 146
Long-term liabilities, 24, 227
Loss payee, 227

Macroeconomic risk areas, 44
Make-up, 227
Management accounting, 227
Management style, 49
Mandate, 227
Margin, 227

Market health, 96
Market risk, 227
Market value, 227
Marketing and sales, 55
Maturity, 228
Maturity schedules, 228
Maxwell, 71
Memorandum of Association, 11, 228
Merchant bank, 228
Mine-mouth, 228
Ministry of International Trade and
    Industry of Japan, 228
Minority interests, 228
Monetization, 228
Monte Carlo simulation, 228
Multilateral Investment Guaranty
    Agency, 228

Nadir, Asil, 39, 71
Negative pledge, 152, 228
Negotiable, 228
Net margins, 237
Net movement in cash and short-
    term investments, 66
Net operating cash flow, 240
Net plant to sales, 238–9
Net profit margin, 51–2
Net realizable value, 229
Net sales projections, 92–9
    industry and economic conditions,
        96–8
    volume and pricing components,
        95–6
Net working assets, 57–8
Net worth (owners' equity),
    125, 229
New money need, 126–9, 239
Nominal value, 229
Non-recourse, 229

Obsolescence, 31
Offtake, 229
Open-cycle, 229
Operating cash flow, 65–6, 229
Operating leverage, 101
Operating profit, 103–5
Operating risk, 229
Operational items, 100
Operations and maintenance, 229
Option, 229
Ordinary shares, 32, 229
Outbound logistics, 55
Overdrafts, 27, 29
Overrun, 229
Oversubscription, 229

Parent company, 229
Pari passu, 230
Parmalat, 36, 71, 72
Participant, 230
Participant risk, 230
Participation, 230
Partnership, 230
Payables *see* Accounts payable
Payback, 230
Payment, 230
Payment period, 57
Payments on account, 27
PBIT margin, 51, 52
Percent-of-sales forecasting, 67–8
Performance bond, 230
PEST analysis, 44, 45
Physical completion, 230
Placement, 230
Point, 230
Political risk, 230
Political risk insurance, 231
Political risk profile, 189
Potential default, 230

Power purchase agreement, 230
Powers Report, 37–8
Preference shares, 32, 230
Premium, 230
Prepayment, 25, 230
Price earnings ratio, 231
Prime rate, 231
Principal, 231
Private company, 231
Private placement, 231
Pro forma, 231
Pro rata, 231
Procurement, 55
Production, 231
Production capacity, 96
Production loan, 231
Profit, 237
Profit (loss) before tax, 77, 105–9
Profit and loss account, 10, 24, 33–5,
   231
Profit and loss projections,
   86–109
Profit margin, 52
Profitability, 237
   indicators, 237–8
   and performance, 50–4
Project contracts, 231
Project feasibility, 8
Project finance, 160–71
Projected asset structure, 2
Projected earnings stream, 2
Prospectus, 231
Prudency, 12
Public company, 231
Purchasing power parity, 232
Put, 232

Qualified opinion, 14–15
Quick ratio, 210, 239

Ratcheting, 152
Rating, 232
Ratio analysis, 54, 232
Raw materials, 28
Receivables see Accounts receivable
Receiver, 232
Recourse, 232
Refinancing, 127, 232
Regulatory actions, 232
Representations, 232
Reserve account, 232
Reserves, 33
Residual, 232
   cover, 233
   cushion, 233
Restructuring, 127
Retained earnings, 237
Retention, 233
Return on assets, 233, 237
Return on capital employed, 233
Return on equity, 50–1, 233, 237
Returns on investments and
   servicing of finance, 65
Revaluation reserve, 24, 33
Revenues, 233
Rights issue, 233
Risk, 233
Royalty, 233
Rule 144a, 233
RUMASA, 71, 72

S&P's sovereign rating profile, 195–8
Sales, 233
Sales completion, 233
Sales projections, 97
Salvage value, 233
Securities & Exchange Commission,
   234
Securitization, 234

Security, 234
Security agreement, 234
Security perfection, 8
Selling, general and administrative
    expenses, 103, 238
Senior, 234
Sensitivity analysis, 83, 129, 146–50,
    234
Setoff, 234
Share capital, 23
Share premium, 24, 33, 234
Shareholders' equity, 234
Shareholders' funds, 24
Shares, 23
Short-term, 234
Sinking fund, 234
Skilling, Jeffrey, 38
Skills, 49
Sovereign risk, 234
Special purpose vehicles, 36
Sponsor, 234
Spreadsheets, 15, 17–22, 87–92,
    200–9, 234
SSAP 25, 34
Stability, 49
Standard accounting practice, 11–14
Standard and Poor's financial ratios,
    63
Standard price, 28
State-owned enterprise, 234
Statement of cash flow, 234
Statement of Standard Accounting
    Practices, 11, 222
Static trade-off theory, 59
Steam turbine, 234
Stock, 24, 27–8
Stock Exchange, 10
Stock turnover, 56
Stock valuation, 13

Stocks and work in progress, 27–8
Strategic analysis
    external environment, 42–6
    value chain, 46–9
Structure, 234
Subordinated, 235
Subsidiary company, 235
Sunk costs, 235
Supplier credit, 235
Supply risk, 235
Sustainable growth, 69–70
Swap, 235
Sweep, 235
Syndication, 235
Syspas system, 75

Tail, 235
Take-and-pay, 235
Take-or-pay, 235
Takeout, 235
Tangible assets, 235
Tangible fixed assets, 30–1
Tangible net worth, 235
Taxation, 65, 106
Technology development, 55
Temporary/seasonal finance, 199
Tenor, 130, 235
Term lending, 2, 3, 76, 235
    protection and control, 150–2
Term loans, 227
Terms of trade, 26
Throughput, 235
Tolling, 235
Tombstone, 236
Total debt payout ratio, 145–6, 241
Total net worth, 235
Trade creditors, 26–7
Trade debtors, 25
Tranche, 236

Transfer risk, 236
Trend analysis, 54
Trustee, 236
Turnkey, 236
Turnover, 34–5, 236
Turnover and efficiency indicators, 238–9

UK accounting systems, 9
Underwriting, 236
Unsecured, 236
Unwind, 236

Valuation of assets, 53
Value chain analysis, 46–9
Variable input analysis, 81–6
Vodafone, 175–84

Warrants, 32
Weighted Average Cost of Capital, 236
Weighted average price, 28
Withholding, 236
Work in progress, 28
Working capital, 236, 239
Working investment, 109, 112–13, 128, 239–40
Working investment lending, 199
Workout, 236
World Bank, 236

Yield, 236

Z score, 73
Zero coupon, 237

The Train of Ice and Fire

Ramón Chao

Translated by Ann Wright

First published in English by Route in 2009
PO Box 167, Pontefract, WF8 4WW
info@route-online.com
www.route-online.com

ISBN (13): 978-1-901927-37-5
ISBN (10): 1-901927-37-7

First published in French by Éditions de la Différence in 1994
as *Un train de glace et de feu*

The Train of Ice and Fire © Ramón Chao

English language translation © Ann Wright 2008

Support and special thanks to:
Claudia Antonia Arcila, Rob Brearley, Ian Daley,
Isabel Galán, Susana Galán, Pedro González Velasco,
Manuel Lafuente Angel, Benoît Le Mauff,
Kelly Pizarro, Reini Schühle, Emma Smith

Photography:
Youri Lenquette

Cover Design, Art Direction and Photography
made in The Designers Republic
www.thedesignersrepublic.com

A catalogue for this book is available from the British Library

Typeset in Bembo by Route

Printed by Mackays of Chatham

Route is supported by Arts Council England

Ramón Chao (Villalba, Lugo 1935) is a distinguished writer and journalist. He was chief editor for the Latin American service of Radio France Internationale, and worked for *Le Monde* and *Le Monde Diplomatique*. He is the French correspondent for Radio Colifata in Buenos Aires. In 1984 he created the prestigious Juan Rulfo Prize, an award for new Spanish language writers. He has written numerous essays and novels in French, Spanish and Galician. Amongst his works are *Las Travesías de Luis Gontán*, *Las Andaduras del Che*, *El Lago de Como* and *Porque Cuba Eres Tú*. He lives in Paris.

Ann Wright has translated fourteen books from Spanish and French including *Motorcycle Diaries*, *The Fragrance of Guava* and *I, Rigoberta Menchu*. She is a human rights activist and lectures on the theory and practice of civilian protection. She lives in London.

Foreword

Reading Ramón Chao's book envelops you in a world of smells and aromas, you see landscapes and faces, feel heat and cold so real you either want to shed your clothes or pile on extra layers, you hear the sound of an accordion, a guitar, a drum. You can follow the extraordinary Train of Ice and Fire through the regions of Colombia without leaving your armchair. Ramón shares with us this magical journey of scenery, music and smells that he made with the young musicians of Mano Negra.

Even if you don't travel on the roof of the train or look out of its grubby windows, you can still travel the same track. Or you can choose to do it the other way round and begin the journey where this serpent of iron and wood has reached its destination. The sequence doesn't matter. The surprises will remain the same on each route.

In the fifteen years which have passed since this train journey was made, a lot has changed. Sadly, mainly for the worse. These vagabonds wanted, among other things, to attract the attention of the Colombian government to regenerate the ailing railways. However, while the government promised this in public, it was already busily throwing soil into the grave of the railway. The bus owners' mafia was mightier.

These trains aren't as modern as those in Europe. The government didn't want to bother to find out why all these simple *campesinos* needed a train. Even less did they want to find out what they looked like from inside. They didn't want to waste time travelling past tiny, insignificant settlements or, worse still, actually stop there to look into the pleading eyes of the local children. They didn't even do it at election time when it might have looked like a semblance of closeness to the people. But it costs too much to bring back to life this wonderful and vital form of transport, and it wouldn't fill the pockets of the ruling class and their cronies with the millions that would make it worth their while.

In Colombia you can still hear the Vallenato and the Cumbia, but with angst-ridden undertones. Terror has taken possession of these breathtakingly beautiful regions in the north of the country, which change shape and colour with every kilometre. The paramilitaries, these gangs of murderers and drug traffickers organised by the army, have destroyed all normal forms of joyful expression under the pretext of fighting the guerrillas. In this conflict, which is in reality a civil war, the guerrilla has also done wrong to the people. Maybe the sugar-cane worker with his calloused hands who greeted Ramón, Manu and the other dreamers on the train with such warmth, has long since fallen victim to this war. His only sin was to own a piece of land that the *gamonal* (local *cacique*, big landowner and political boss rolled into one) or his military sidekick claimed for himself.

The music, however, the rich tones of which harmonised with the incomparable clatter of the train, was intended to inject these sun-bronzed people with joy and manifest itself in the swinging hips of a mulatto girl, or the white skin of the snack vendor in the streets of the Altiplano.

These joyful people, who the Train of Ice and Fire met along its journey, are still dreaming. It's a beautiful and necessary way to exorcise the ugliness of poverty. The people may well have less and less to live on, but from somewhere a bottle of rum or *aguardiente* materialises without fail, because the firewater stokes the longing for laughter and dance.

From the Caribbean to Bogotá, it is one single country, and the train's slow journey takes you through all the landscapes of the world. While you drink fruit juice that only the gods of pleasure could have conjured up, you can scale mountains, walk beside bountiful rivers and lagoons, cross plains or conquer mysterious wild places. Colombia is still that same country. It is struggling to escape the nightmare into which it was hurtled by those who have everything and yet still want more. Some day this jolting rattling train will return to witness the dawn of a new day.

Ignacio Ramonet

7

Prologue

I went to Colombia because I was scared. My two sons were involved in a journey on an as yet non-existent train, on rusty tracks, through dodgy guerrilla country. They would be crossing the Bajo Magdalena – the lower reaches of the Magdalena river – one of the most dangerous places on earth, an insurgent stronghold, fought over by paramilitaries, drug traffickers, criminals, kidnappers, murderers, or possibly all of them rolled into one. I was scared for them. Antoine went to Colombia first, to prepare the infrastructure for the trip, and stayed several months. He returned to Paris to attend to more pressing projects, and Manu left for Colombia with most of his rock group Mano Negra.

The previous year, on the group's Latin America tour (part of the Cargo '92 enterprise), Manu had noticed there weren't any railways in Colombia. True, there were grass and moss covered tracks and deserted railway stations, but the omnipotent air and road monopolies had gradually seen off the more democratic railways. Manu, who is very stubborn, was determined to reactivate a form of transport that is so crucial to a country's social and geographic fabric. Their train would go from Bogotá to Santa Marta and back, stopping at ten stations to give rock concerts, circus and theatre performances, and an exhibition of ice sculptures. I repeat, I was scared. There was talk of kidnapping, hostage-taking, murders. Manu was over there in the thick of it and I was in Paris calmly (so to speak) going to exhibitions, plays and libraries. I caught the train literally as it was moving off, under the illusion that with me beside him nothing could happen to Manu. But lots of things did happen. Firstly, the resurgence of our family's Hispano-American past. Watching my son dancing salsa convinced me that something from over there was in our genes. At home I'm considered a bit of fantasist, but my sons' attachment to the people and music of Latin America confirms my suspicions: my paternal grandfather is not the one that figures in our family tree, but Mario García Kohly, minister in the government of Cuba's first president Tomás Estrada Palma, and later Cuban ambassador to Spain. My grandmother left Galicia for Cuba, fleeing her quarrelsome drunken husband. She worked as a maid in García Kohly's house and got involved with him.

García Kohly's house was a meeting place for musicians and writers. The host himself wrote poems that didn't make much of a mark, except for the words of the *habanera* 'Tú' that he wrote under the pseudonym Ferrán Sánchez. The composer Sánchez de Fuentes was a regular visitor to the house, and it was he who put the *habanera* to music. I deduce from all this that the 'Tú' in question, symbol of Cuban sensuality, was that beautiful warm Galician lady with blue eyes and rosy cheeks; my sons' great-grandmother.

'In Cuba, beautiful island of burning sun,
under its sky of blue,
adorable brunette,
of all the flowers,
the queen is you.'

The drunken husband who had stayed in Galicia, arrived in Havana one unfortunate day looking for his wife. And since the droit de seigneur (the right to a legover) brings with it the duty of protection, the man was found with a bullet in his head at the corner of Escobar and Galiano, in Old Havana. I imagine that in Cuba it wasn't difficult for anyone with influence to order whatever he wanted. My father was born shortly afterwards. His strong likeness to García Kohly, according to a photo of the former ambassador in the Spanish encyclopaedia, leaves my detective thesis in no doubt. I don't want to cast aspersions, but astral calculations indicate that my father was conceived after my grandmother fled Spain and before the arrival of her wretched husband.

García Lorca said that to be a good Spaniard you have to have a Latin American dimension. My sons had discovered that in Paris. Apart from the fact that my professional activities involved Latin America, at home we always played the music of Beny Moré, Violeta Parra,

Atahualpa Yupanqui and many others. Bola de Nieve's song 'Ay Mama Inés' that Manu included in his repertoire, was one that he heard and sang all the time as a child. Manu reminded me not long ago that as teenagers, he and Antoine got into all sorts of mischief, but when they came home they'd meet someone like García Márquez, and that redressed the balance. I remember one of the first things Manu played on the guitar was a piece by the Cuban musician Leo Brouwer, and the first percussion instruments he and Antoine had were brought from Havana by Alejo Carpentier. For his part, Antoine was musical director of Radio Latina in Paris for a time and now produces Cuban music records, keeping close ties with the island.

In this book, I recount the vicissitudes of the journey made by the Train of Ice and Fire. They called it that because it was pulling a flaming wagon full of huge blocks of ice to Aracataca, Gabriel García Márquez' home town. Remember the opening chapter of *One Hundred Years of Solitude* when the gypsy Melquíades brings ice to the children of Macondo for the first time? But I think the most important thing, the thing that affected me most emotionally (apart from the wish lists the Colombian kids wrote) was the break-up of Mano Negra, that mythical group created by Manu, and including Antoine and my nephew Santi, that began rehearsing in the basement of my house.

Manu saw the train through till the end, but was totally burnt out. In another book, I recount how he recharged his batteries on a pioneering journey by motorbike from

Paris to Compostela, passing through places where the martyred bishop Prisciliano (executed in Tréveris and buried in Compostela in a tomb arbitrarily attributed to Santiago) had preached. To face a new life as a solo artist, without his band, Manu gathered strength from the land and sea of Cape Finisterre, where Old Europe ends and you look out towards the New World. In the bars of Camelle and Muxía, he began to write 'Bixo', 'La Vaca Loca', 'La Despedida'…and the rest is history.

Ramón Chao

Sunday 14 November, 1993
A New World

El Dorado airport, Bogotá. The plane lands on the dot. Ten past five. On the plane are Mano Negra's Santi and Kropol, drummer and trombonist respectively, trapezists Germain and Fabou, and my neighbours in Sèvres, Puce and Anouck. Puce has come on holiday, Anouck to make a video clip with Manu.

'Are you the train people? Go straight through.'

Formalities are waived.

A policeman asks me for a cassette for his daughter. What about? Who by? 'You should know,' he says. Right. An autograph, then. It's the first time it's happened to me. I've signed more than a few books in my time, but stopped in the street, never.

During the flight, Avianca had given out Colombian newspapers. There's a full-colour spread about us in the liberal paper *El Espectador*, the same in black and white in the conservative *El Tiempo*; television, radio...all the media is announcing the departure of the Train of Ice and Fire.

What else is in the paper? Senator Darío Londoño Cardona has just been assassinated; he's just the latest in an inexhaustible list. The Sports Minister, Miguel Angel

Bermúdez, is accused of sexual harassment by his secretary (it's becoming a pleonasm). He defends himself like a man:

'That's ridiculous, she's thirty-five years old!'

For a Colombian macho, or any other macho for that matter, a woman of thirty-five is over the hill. They should all be forced to read Ovid, to learn the art of love.

The election of Miss Colombia is the only other event capable of stealing our thunder. It's being held in Cartagena, in the square formerly used for the Inquisition. In those days, the monks of the fearsome Torquemada judged heretics and Jews; tortured as a matter of course, mostly roasted. Today it's the succulence of the flesh that is being judged. Doña Tera, a tropical Samaranch, is president of the concupiscence tribunal. She accepts candidates remodelled by surgery; it keeps doctors of her social class in work. At over eighty, Doña Tera is one of the most influential people in Colombia. Before Escobar appeared on the scene, there was only her and the President. But presidents, Conservative or Liberal, come and go. She and the Escobars remain.

Doña Tera has just embarked on a crusade against the trade in beauties. From now on, towns have to choose home-grown girls, not import them from elsewhere like Maradonas. To be elected Miss Colombia, the girl has to be centrist in politics and in love, like Doña Tera. They don't need to be bright. 'My idol is the painter García Márquez,' declared one famous queen. But in time they'll become veritable clairvoyants, unashamedly opining on the most diverse topics of public life.

Bogotá welcomes us with rain. It's normal. It rains all the time on the Altiplano. But when Gonzalo de Quesada and his men founded the city in 1538, they knew what they were doing. They rashly left the coast, penetrated forests, fought starvation, indigenous tribes, tigers and alligators, crossed deserts, climbed snowy peaks, ploughed through burning plains, leaving death in their wake, before reaching this *cordillera* and scaling its 10,000-foot-high mountains, where water turned to ice on their beards. They finally reached the Altiplano and achieved their ultimate goal. To be rid of mosquitoes.

Philippe comes to fetch us. This gentle dynamo has run the Fahrenheit Club in Issy-les-Moulineaux since 1984. He has also done logistics for Mano Negra since the group started. Philippe warns us:

'There's nothing to eat tonight, ditto for breakfast. In fact, we've had a few problems.'

He's taking us to the workshops in El Corzo, north of Bogotá, to see the train. Then he'll get us fixed up for the night.

Fine. We pile into two minibuses. Philippe agrees to stop at a bar. Watery coffee. Are we really in Colombia? The best beans go for export, we're told. After another half hour messing about, we reach the workshops of Ferrovías, the Colombian state railways.

Inside this huge hangar, about fifty Colombian and French idealists have built the Train of Ice and Fire out of a heap of scrap iron provided by Ferrovías: a locomotive in good shape and the carcasses of several decommissioned carriages, all rusty and dilapidated. If I may make a personal and literary reference, I'd say the workshop looks like Juan Carlos Onetti's shipyard.

'We could have brought a pre-packaged show, presented it, slept in a hotel, got back on the plane and gone home, but that's not what we want. We want to mix with Colombians, be involved in their lives, work with them on a daily basis. We don't want to barge in with our ice train, and only bring a dream,' says Cati, the woman running the production side of things.

Two days earlier, Cati had been summoned to the French embassy. A meeting with the 'Security Council'.

'So I arrive,' she tells me, 'in a leather jacket, under the disapproving eye of all those gentlemen. They remind me we will be travelling through a high-risk zone which makes the front pages every day because of the large number of deaths and kidnappings.

'They ask politely what security measures are in place, given that seventy French citizens, including a certain number of journalists, plus equipment for satellite transmission, will be aboard my little train. "Have I advised the Colombian Ministry of Defence? Will we have an escort? Will we have armed bodyguards on the train? Are the journalists aware of the risks they'll be running? What are the phone numbers of the stations we're stopping at? Have the local police and army been alerted? Am I not being a bit reckless?"

'I force myself to appear calm, and explain that I've been studying the security problem for a long time with Denis Vène, a former first secretary at the embassy. The fact that we're artists and politically neutral, and are offering free shows to the people, will be the best way of guaranteeing our safety. In any case, what would happen if there were a guerrilla attack? Retaliation from the army would catch us in the crossfire, and that would be an even bigger risk. The best thing for us to do would be to put out the white flag and try to talk. It's unlikely the guerrillas would kill us all, but they might want to use the media to put out a message and that's a risk we take. The journalists are aware of it, and even see the chance of a scoop! As for Radio Caracol, they're Colombians and know the situation in that area perfectly well.

'I could still see that worried look on the increasingly sceptical faces of my exam board. I heard them whispering about "discreet" contacts with the Ministry of Defence. But my arguments did convince them a bit. In any case, as the Colonel said, "What can we do? It's too late. I never thought this train would actually leave. I even thought the project had been abandoned."'

Yet here it is, the dream come true, utopia become reality. It takes our breath away.

The train is not the TGV or the Orient Express. On the contrary, it's a load of bric-a-brac put together by inexpert but passionate hands.

It has twenty-one carriages and freight cars, each one more outlandish than the next:

The fire-wagon with its sheet metal lining and asbestos insulation will travel enveloped in flames, and inside, the biggest diamond ever seen – a five-cubic-metre six-ton block of ice, pure and translucent like crystal.

The cage-wagon, like a metal cathedral, is home to

Roberto the flame-thrower, an enormous iguana metamorphosed into a dragon.

The Yeti-wagon will keep the tons of ice cold, and house...we still don't know what.

The ice-wagon, aka the grotto of a child-friendly sleepy polar bear who unleashes a snowstorm when he wakes up.

The museum-wagon reconciles fire and ice in its frozen sculptures.

The fairground wagons combine the magical and the daring.

The stage-wagon is the scenario for Colombian musicians and the French groups Mano Negra and French Lovers.

And finally the crane-wagon, created and built by our boys as a structure for the trapeze and tightrope acts.

There is also a wagon for the acrobats' equipment; a tattoo-wagon where Tom and Dani will tattoo intrepid souls for a couple of pesos; wagons for others props; and even a studio-wagon for broadcasting via parabolic dish for Radio Caracol and Radio France Internationale.

We eventually get a bite to eat. Plastic bread with processed cheese, thin little sausages, and Colombian-style pizza reminiscent of the ones Cubans used to eat.

Didier Jaconelli – Coco from now on – comes to greet the newcomers. Coco used to be with the Royal de Luxe theatre company. In 1992, the AFAA (French Association for Action in the Arts), whose mission it is to disseminate French culture abroad, organised the four-month tour of the cargo ship *Melquíades-Ville de Nantes* round seventeen Latin American countries. On board were Royal de Luxe, Mano Negra, Philippe Genty and Philippe Decouflé. Coco was in charge of Royal's pyrotechnics. He also played about fifteen roles in 'The True History of France', notably that of Napoleon. A little genius is Coco. More of that later. He has been forced to see an ophthalmologist because he seriously damaged his eye while he was welding. The doctor has forbidden him to make the train journey and wants to hospitalise him for twenty-four hours. It will be one of life's great injustices if Coco can't realise his dream.

Philippe has good news.

'For tonight, you can bunk down in the train, or go to the house. I don't recommend the train. It's leaving for Bogotá at six for the weigh-in.'

Not much choice there, then.

This is the moment I feared ever since Cati asked me to chronicle the journey. I had accepted on condition Manu Chao had no problem with it. I saw Manu at a Mano Negra rehearsal at Ornano Studios.

'So, I hear you're coming with us?'

'Yes, Manu, if it's okay with you.'

'I'm not the organiser, but you're welcome.'

A few days later, however, Manu set a few conditions.

'What you write must be accessible to everyone. You mustn't use too many literary references. Your last novel was too ornate. I couldn't finish it.'

Wow!

'We can always give it a go, Manu. I'll do my best.'

21

On top of that, I had two or three other sources of anxiety. First, my dreams were populated by guerrillas, bandits, soldiers, paramilitaries, drug traffickers; that charming mix that makes Colombia the world's most violent country. 800 political assassinations a year, 25,000 murders altogether last year (1992). In my nightmares, all sorts of disasters befall us: bombs exploding on the track, attacks by armed gangs, gun battles, knives stuck in hearts.

Once I'd got over those particular anxieties, another fear crept into their place. Looking for things to worry about must come naturally to me. How could I spend a month and a half in a train with people whose culture was alien to me and who, to cap it all, were young enough to be my kids? And, above all, how would I survive without my daily shower?

Philippe takes us to 'the house' in a bumpy pick-up truck. The more intrepid stay behind on site. Work is well behind schedule, so they'll help the technical people through the night.

The house looks fine from the outside. An Andalusian-style hacienda with an octagonal ground and first floor. It's one of two pads rented by the 'Prod' (production side of things), the other being in an area of Bogotá called La Candelaria.

'Armed with 550,000 francs,' says Cati, 'Coco and I packed our bags and arrived here fourteen months ago, mainly to get to know the country and try and figure out how everything works. It's very important to know who is who, and who does what.'

That half a million francs had been advanced to Cati by the AFAA. Its director, Jean Digne, had already taken serious risks when he took on that lunatic project Cargo '92. For him, culture isn't only about the *Comédie Française*, it's in the provinces, in the suburbs, in the street. The success of Cargo '92 obviously encouraged him to try again, despite a frankly unfavourable political context.

The inside of the house is like a gypsy encampment. When I was young I dreamed of running off with some bohemians who turned up in my village with a mangy goat. I'll never forget how they made it mount a stool to a drum roll. But now the opportunity presents itself, I'm not so keen.

Rather ugly blokes and girls come and go, there's a quick round of first-name introductions. Outside it's pouring with rain but the fairground stalls have to be loaded into the wagons, Roberto has to be put to bed, the Ice Museum and the flame-throwers need finishing. Jaquot, Carine, Régis, Anne-Marie, Isa, Manu and thirty others, in mud up to their knees, load the equipment. All is not well. The train isn't ready, the block of ice hasn't formed. The truck bringing the machine to make ten-ton ice cubes was stolen by guerrillas a few days ago. Not knowing what to do with a machine like that, they abandoned it in a ditch. But we have to leave. Tomorrow or never, orders Cati. The Yeti will await its glacial niche with its secular patience.

So, we leave tomorrow, come what may. The more intrepid among us go on working in the downpour, the less courageous go discreetly home.

Each room has three or four mattresses on the floor. I throw my sleeping bag (that I've brought from Paris) on the least disgusting-looking one. Thankfully, out of discretion, or respect for my incipient grey hairs, I get a corner to myself.

I fall into a deep sleep.

Monday 15 November
Leave Facatativá

I begin the day without a shower. There are two in the house but they're so ghastly I'd rather wait and see what else turns up. Some faces are familiar. Tomasín and Garbancito from Mano Negra; Chino formerly of Négresses Vertes, Cati, Manu. All good people. But how did they stomach those toilets?

The train returns from the weigh-in, ready for off. Jean-Pierre Linger, the 'ice man', has had a bit of a shock.

'Yes, I was blown away. It was the first time the train had actually been on the track so I wanted to go to Bogotá for the weigh-in. I wanted to be on top of the train, so I was sitting on the cistern. On the way back from Bogotá, we stopped for a few minutes at La Mosquera for some kind of technical reasons, and three ragged kids climbed onto a wagon. I saw it all from up on the cistern and said to myself, "They have to get off because we're leaving." So I went down to make them get off. Two of them were scared because I was a bit too rough, and they got off. But the third one stayed on the wagon. I said, "Hop it, you have to get off." He was about to jump but the train had picked up speed by then. He could have hurt himself, so I grabbed hold of his shirt and said, "Look, it's okay, the train isn't going very far, it'll stop at El Corzo and I'll pay for you to take the bus back." He said, "D'you know how much the bus ticket costs?" "It won't be that much," I replied, "we'll have a bite to eat when we get there." And we kept talking. He was filthy. I realised when I put my hand on his head, his hair stuck to me, it was hard, really hard. We were standing on the cistern, holding on to the rail. I asked him where he was from, if he was from La Mosquera, and he said, "I live on the street, I don't have any parents." "Got any friends?" "Yes, I've got two." "The two that jumped off the train?" There was a long silence. He looked very sad. Then he turned to me and said, "Do you have children?" I said no. He said, "Ever thought of adopting one?" I felt a lump in my throat. There was another long silence and then, well, we sort of changed the subject. I don't think he was fooled.

'Anyway, the end of the story is that when we got to El Corzo, I said, "We won't be seeing each other at Christmas," and I give him a 5,000-peso note, which isn't nothing. He took the money and his first reaction was to hold it up to the light to see if it was a fake. I burst out laughing and said I wasn't about to slip him a bum note. And when he saw everybody laughing, it was the only time I saw him give a real belly laugh.

'I didn't see the kid again, but I tell you it really hit home, it was hard. I've always worked in workshops, it's the first time I've ever come across a street kid. When a kid looks you in the eye and asks if you want to adopt him, and you know you don't have kids…and pushing forty-five, I wouldn't mind some…'

This sentimental Basque has been working on the train since July. Some of the other technicians arrived a year ago. They're all showbiz specialists, masters of their craft, from fields as different as film, theatre, circus and music. These gentle dreamers, with earrings, Iroquois haircuts and leather jackets, bought blankets and mattresses, slept five or six to a room, and began work in October 1992. Most of them have left their families in France and aren't earning any money with this project, more like they're spending their own to keep the troupe afloat. You have to be ready to turn your hand to anything: you may be a film director at home but here you're welding.

As far as the technicalities go, they've not only had to fit out the train and organise the show, but also reconnoitre the journey, look for water sources to refill the cistern, and make sure security measures are up to scratch.

'Given the state of the track, we'll be travelling at fifteen kilometres an hour. We can't avoid derailments, but at this speed we can easily get the wagons back on the track with a jack,' explains Diablito, a Ferrovías railwayman.

It's looking good.

Departure is set for two in the afternoon. 'Hurry up,' says Iván Almeida, a rather macho-looking latino whose exact function I'm not sure about. Not the latino function, of course, I've been known to exercise it myself from time to time, but his professional function. We're already two hours late!

Jokes abound. The team says Ferrovías will never

respect our schedule. Iván protests. The two locomotives that will make the descent have been carefully selected, goods train traffic has taken a back seat; we have priority all along the line.

Still to bring aboard the stage-wagon are the huge machines and Dédé's crane. It's chaos: I see bedding and straw mats thrown in through the windows, the sponsors are there, astonished, Zouzoute has driven a nail through his calf, he has to be taken to hospital, hurry, we're up and off. Ricardo Alarcón, president of Radio Caracol arrives with his children. Cati disappears, leaving me to look after him.

The road to Bogotá that runs alongside the track is blocked with cars. Cati gives our train places out.

Cati shares the production side with Fernando. She's a great girl. She'd been living in Brazil for several years when she was hired to do the administration for the *Melquíades* tour. I've seen Cati talk to presidents, press people and publishing people. She's irresistible, Cati Benainous.

She promises me a couchette in a carriage that in a previous life transported silver.

'Here's your bedroom.'

No couchette. Just a bench for sorting mail. Hang on, didn't trains have couchettes a half century ago? The windows of our coach are pretty basic (like Wild West convoys), rectangular, with bars, and a fine grill designed to stop even the tiniest mosquito in its tracks. In fact, it is an old postal car, one of those that always got robbed.

What am I complaining about? They haven't stuck me

with those punks in French Lovers, or with the abominable tattooists, but with the crème of the passengers. Cramped, yes, but good company. I take a lower berth. The others are occupied by François Bergeron, Fred the sound technician, and Patrick, his assistant.

Bergeron is Mano Negra's official film-maker. He has done the group's best video clips ('Out of Time Man'), the Pigalle tour, and one of the films about Cargo '92.

Next to them, are Carlos Rojas, a Colombian film director who helped to make Roberto, Iván Almeida and Juan Manuel Roca. As well as being an excellent poet, Juan Manuel is a journalist on *El Espectador*, a Bogotá daily that Escobar's hit men have in their sights. They have already killed the editor, Guillermo Cano, a journalist called Giraldo, and bombs have damaged the paper's premises on several occasions.

It is half past four. Most of the show's equipment has been battened down. There are still, however, a few bills to pay. 'We will honour them, we want to be meticulous to the end.' The grants we were promised are late arriving, especially the one from the Ministry of Culture. 'The problem is,' sighs Cati, 'seen from Paris, Colombia is a long way away.'

About a hundred people have come to see us off. Local people, and even some from Bogotá. A few soldiers are controlling the traffic. The locomotive, a Spanish-built U 10 B diesel, gives three whistles. It squeaks, it moves, it teeters like a toddler not sure on its pins. But the miracle is happening, the crazy dream in Coco's imagination is becoming reality. He says:

'After the Cargo '92 South America tour last year, I spent a lot of time travelling in Colombia. I saw train tracks everywhere but never trains. I asked about it at Bogotá central station. The engines still worked. But none left the marshalling yards. Hundreds of towns that had been served by trains in the past had been cut off, leaving them hostage to the army, drug traffickers and the guerrillas. I told myself something needed to be done. But what? So, to make people talk about something other than terror in Colombia, I conjured up this idea of a train with a show reconciling the two hereditary enemies, fire and ice.'

But there was another difficulty. In Colombia, trains are ghosts. You see a few goods trains, between derailments, but passenger trains haven't existed since 1979. They used to exist although the development of the railways was much slower in Colombia than in Mexico and especially Argentina, which in 1910 had 28,000 kilometres of track. Building tracks that could cross Colombia's three huge mountain ranges was an impossible dream. Nonetheless, several lines were opened, notably the Sun Express that connected Bogotá with the port of Santa Marta on the Atlantic coast. This gave rise to one of the continent's most famous songs:

Santa Marta tiene trén	Santa Marta has a train
Pero no tiene tranvía	But it hasn't got a tram
Si no fuera por la zona, ay caramba	If it wasn't for the zone, ay caramba
Santa Marta moriría, ay caramba	Santa Marta would die, ay caramba

There was a train in Santa Marta but it lacked the good local infrastructure, symbolised by the tramway. The port survived thanks to the banana region. Until about 1920, the railways were used primarily to link the coffee-growing areas to the seas and rivers. As late as 1922, 90% of trains transported coffee. These lines were viable, but did not form a rail network. Each responded to a different agenda, some of them reserved for one particular product, like the private railway of the United Fruit Company. You couldn't travel from one region to another, only come into the country and go out. They were accused of disrupting the Colombian economy by favouring links with abroad to the detriment of interregional development. Aware of this problem, in the 1920s the government launched a vast programme aimed at creating an integrated railway network, centred on Bogotá; the number of kilometres of track in use doubled from 1922 to 1934.

In 1903, the United States occupied Panama, until then an integral part of Colombia. Was it secession, or daylight robbery as most Colombians still claim today? That was certainly the view at the time. Besides, President Theodore Roosevelt, who dubbed the Colombian government 'a band of Sicilian and Calabrian bandits', had no qualms in announcing in public that he had 'taken' Panama. Of the twenty-five million dollars in compensation paid by the United States, fifteen million were invested in the railways; when this money ran out, the government resorted to public loans on the North American market.

Soon the train in Santa Marta was no more. Following the assassination of Jorge Eliécer Gaitán, and especially during the dictatorship of Rojas Pinilla, an offensive against the labour movement lead to the dismantling of large State enterprises. The railways in particular, but also the ports, faced savage competition from the private sector – bus and truck monopolies in collusion with successive governments. The development of domestic air transport by Avianca, one of the world's oldest airlines, sealed the fate of the railways.

Today, the Colombian rail network covers 3,200 kilometres, of which only 1,600 are in use. The powers that be have let the tracks deteriorate by blocking investment over the last fifteen years or so. As a result, trains derail all the time.

'In 1990,' says Luis Bernardo Villegas, president of Ferrovías, 'there was a derailment every half hour and the trains went no faster than twelve kilometres an hour. This year, the average speed has risen to twenty-three kilometres an hour and we've had 1,000 derailments, two of which were really dangerous.'

That's not going to stop Coco. In Colombia, he discovers the existence of a National Plan for the Rehabilitation of the Colombian Rail Network.

'When I saw that little Frenchman come in my office, I thought the Virgin Mary was giving me a sign,' Luis Bernardo Villegas goes on. 'The government had just decided to rehabilitate 2,500 kilometres of track, initially for goods traffic. The problem was that most Colombians were against dismantling the old Colombian National

Rail Company and sacking its workforce. A serious dose of PR was needed.'

We imagine the sponsor's face when a proposal for a cultural operation like this lands on his desk, with the particular frisson of journeying through zones controlled by guerrillas, drug traffickers, and diverse paramilitary groups.

Coco is not put off. When he gets back to Paris, he goes straight to Manu Chao, lead singer of Mano Negra, various members of Royal de Luxe and Cati Benainous. They all decide to jump aboard and start preparing the project: to reactivate the disused Sun Express line and take a passenger train along it. The team baptise the project the Train of Ice and Fire, a tribute to Gabriel García Márquez. Remember, 'Many years later, as he faced the firing squad, Colonel Aureliano Buendía was to remember that distant afternoon when his father took him to discover ice.' It's the opening line of *One Hundred Years of Solitude*.

'It took a lot of energy and conviction to get the project off the ground,' recalls Cati.

Finding the sponsors and negotiating with different enterprises would be a long haul. Finance was scarce too. The AFAA, the main donor, put 600,000 francs on the table, that is, about 12% of the estimated cost of the project. It's in Colombia that logistic and financial support would be crucial. Ferrovías lent its workshops and workforce in Facatativá, thirty-five kilometres from Bogotá. The first French technicians arrived in March. With the scrap iron provided, they made the coaches,

Roberto the dragon, and other fabulous machines. Colombian partners like *El Espectador*, Radio Caracol, SFT (the other Colombian rail company), the shipping line Grancolombia, Sofasa-Renault, and Néctar, came on board. So, the team had been offered eighteen colour pages in *El Espectador*, free freight in two containers, a car, a big enough budget to construct the train, buy the necessary wood, paint, and tools, pay the Colombian workers, and cover the costs of everyone involved. Before each stage of the journey, Guillermo Ferreo, a Colombian theatre designer, will meet the various municipalities and get them to provide electricity, petrol, water and ice.

The train shudders. This time, this is it, we're finally off. We leave in total silence, no shouting, no explosions of joy. A contained, almost discreet emotion, individually and collectively, overcomes the ninety-nine people on board.

All, however, are at the windows, on the roofs, on the footplate. Some can't help shedding a few tears. We are moved and astonished to see the impossible gamble become a reality. Our train is on its way, and it's superb. At every curve of the track, heads lean out to admire the convoy. Iván (who I've just learned is the technical director of Ferrovías), who put 'the full weight of his balls on his boss's desk to get this project accepted', is crying like a baby. 'This is a very important moment for Colombia,' he manages to say through his tears.

Maybe so, but that's not what the hundred idealists on the train are thinking. They couldn't give a damn whose interest this is serving. They're there for the dream and its contradictions, it's the impossible adventure that's important, to play before a virgin audience, to communicate with them, and that's all. Don't tell them things like they're 'cultural ambassadors'. They won't pull a gun on you (guns and drugs are the only things prohibited on board), but they hate hypocrisy.

The entertainers of fire and ice aren't being paid a penny, just per diem for food. For some of them, this has been going on for months. They even afforded themselves the luxury of refusing help from a political party who suggested financing the whole tour. The Train of Ice and Fire could have been a first-class propaganda coup. 'The train's going through guerrilla country. If we pass without problems, it'll be because the guerrillas have let us. We have to be neutral, not provoke anyone,' explains Manu. 'That's why we avoid songs that are too political. What we want to do is bring a fiesta to people in small towns that have never seen a show like ours.'

So, on November 15, 1993, carrying a band of artists, acrobats, tattooists, punk-rockers with exotic haircuts and earrings (some looking a bit grubby and cadaverous), technicians and logicians, the Train of Ice and Fire leaves Bogotá. It will follow the route the Conquistadors took from the Andes to the Caribbean coast: three uninterrupted days devouring the 1,000 kilometres of track to reach Santa Marta, and the start of our six-week tour.

The train advances slowly amongst ripples of applause and gestures of friendship: curious bystanders anxious to get a glimpse of Melquíades' gypsies as they pass. The first stop is the station at Facatativá, buzzing with people, to get the route plan and check the brakes. It's looking good. We're off again. This time, for good.

Ten minutes later, the diesel engine reaches its cruising speed, between eighteen and twenty kilometres an hour, up to twenty-five on the flat. But when the locomotive, christened *La Consentida,* goes into kinetic extravaganzas, it rocks, rolls, and risks flying off the rails. We remind ourselves we're not on the Paris–Lyon TGV, and anyway fifteen kilometres an hour is the ideal speed to enjoy the countryside from the roof, or to pee on the track between two carriages. How could we relieve ourselves (number one or number two) if our dear train got up to speeds of 120? And what if we got the '*turista*', in other words, a massive dose of the runs?

The vegetation of the Altiplano, this cold land so far from the tropics rising to 3,500 metres, rolls past our glassless windows. Holstein cows, chewing the cud like in Normandy, stare languidly at us. A battalion of dogs, curs with xylophone ribs, bark pitifully as we pass. From both sides of the train, we wave amicably to astonished Colombians; men, women and children who have never seen a passenger train bespangled with yellow butterflies, and never will again.

To the kids, this extravagant convoy might even seem normal. They'll have to see ordinary trains, at other times in other places, to realise just how magical this caravan of gypsies is. A few years in Europe will suffice for them to recreate the landscapes handed down to them by their patriarchs and discover that their life is just a chronicle foretold. Then these men of maize will only have to write well to get the Nobel Prize for poems of love and songs of despair.

We cross forests of melancholy oaks with mouldy trunks, their branches laden with some hairy parasite. We soon see arborescent passion flowers, beautiful shades of lilacs, fuchsias and elegant arum lilies; as well as gigantic greenhouses.

Colombia is second only to the Netherlands in cultivating flowers. Not everything is coca. And in any case, here they say, 'we only produce coca because the Yanks snort it'. There's tremendous anti-Americanism here, so much so that Colombians would like to turn their country into a vast coca plantation just to satisfy the suicidal urges of the gringos.

We can't see the roses, orchids or carnations hidden inside these interminable hothouses of plastic sheeting. Nor the chrysanthemums that are grown on a huge scale; death is a flowering industry. In these parts, people die very often, and very young. Dying at a ripe old age is a luxury. Almost half the funerals in the South Bogotá cemetery are for victims of violent deaths. The forensic institute has seen its staff increase from 320 to 840 in five years because the number of autopsies it does every day gives them no respite. Not surprisingly, a veritable industry of the macabre has sprung up in Colombia: marble craftsmen, undertakers, priests…the list is long of professions profiting from the violence.

We begin the descent from the Andes at sunset, leaving

behind the Bogotá plateau with its potatoes, pigs, Normandy or Dutch cows. Iván halts the train to reinforce the brakes. The descent looks vertiginous and our miserable metal system will no longer be sufficient. And here's the first tunnel. An explosion of joy breaks out, long contained by tacit agreement. Shouts, cheers, *vivas* — it's pandemonium. People are less inhibited in the dark, it seems. Or maybe because inside the tunnel we detect adventure, we sense the unknown. Everyone is laughing, crying, hugging each other.

It's no secret that the train will cross regions where the guerrillas are well embedded, but nobody seems nervous.

'What kind of PR would it be for a liberation movement to shoot at a group of clowns?' muses Jean-Pierre.

Down steep mountainsides, we descend into the temperate zone. The vegetation changes, so do the smells. A few palm trees appear, *cinchonas* abound, and *befarias* with mutating flowers perfume the forest's edge. But why have they planted pines and eucalyptus that impoverish the earth and look so out of place in this landscape? Like everywhere else, I suppose, to make profits for the cellulose companies.

Half past six, and it's already dark. We light candles, there's no electricity yet. Raph promises to start the troupe's generator. I make a trip to the café. Not much to eat or drink, practically nothing. Yet a couple of Colombians are behind the bar, an innocent-looking girl with protruding tits and her brother, both impeccably dressed. Strange! The organisers are paying two waiters when there's nothing to eat? The two kids rummage about anyway, and offer me a Nescafé. Nescafé in Colombia? I'm told the Americans buy the beans here and ship it back granulated. Before Castro, they used to buy sugar from the Cubans then sold it back to them as lollipops. Worse still in Haiti. The original pigs from the French Antilles, which you can fatten on scraps of any sort, are being replaced by gringo pigs that can't live without the vitamins the Haitians have to buy from the U.S.

The girl with the innocent look and generous tits was at Mano Negra's concert in Bogotá last year, during the Cargo '92 tour. She didn't like the music before, but now she's learning the guitar. Does she want to meet Manu? No way, she'd be too shy.

Everyone goes to bed early, they're worn out. But the indefatigable *Consentida* continues her long march, after her first derailment. Nothing serious, a slight hitch; one carriage lifted back on the rails by Iván's team in three quarters of an hour.

As the train gradually rolls down from the Andes, we take off our jumpers, socks, shirts, trousers. Our bodies become exotic prey to *zancudos*, local mosquitoes which zoom in ferociously on the slightest bit of visible flesh. We all curse and scratch away in our couchettes.

Tuesday 16 November
Destination 'Violencia'

At midnight, the heat is unbearable. The *zancudos* penetrate our most intimate parts, causing horrible swelling. Yet despite the bites and jolting, imaginary rhythms transport us slowly towards sleep.

Blaise Cendrars used to recognise European trains by their literary resonance. Some sound like bad prose, others tap out a more poetic rhythm. In ours, the noise of the wheels on the tracks constantly changes genre and instruments. Monotonous drumming on the flat; Martenot's Waves, melodic humming choirs among the vegetation; until the noise of the sleepy wheels is no more than a sort of silence.

People choose the night to pee from the end of the carriage. Relatively easy for the guys, but more complicated for the girls. They usually go in twos; one relieves herself while the other hangs on to her, to stop her falling knickerless onto the gravel.

Great screeching of wheels, long sigh of brakes, and two of the pissers are nearly sandwiched between the carriages. The train stops just in time. It was a nasty moment. Iván's men stabilise the train again, putting pieces of rail on the ballast and raising the axles with hydraulic levers, as if it were a bicycle chain.

That happened at Utica, to be precise.

As soon as we start, we stop again. Another derailment? Not this time. A goods train is coming in the opposite direction. Drat! We have to wait five or six hours with nothing to eat or drink, before the track is clear again.

We're in Dindal, a hamlet not marked on any map. Here, farmers are even earlier risers. How can you work in this noonday heat?

At seven in the morning we go looking for a café and find a bar-bakery-grocery not far from the station. The owner is at his door with his grown-up son. He welcomes us (is he welcoming us?) with disconcerting indifference. It reminds me of Che Guevara, who in his *Motorcycle Diaries* complained about the Indians' passivity. They certainly don't measure time with a Seiko. It takes fifteen minutes to get our coffee, a cup of liquid cold socks, undrinkable. We swallow the stuff feeling we've disturbed the family nirvana and pay, even though it seems out of place but...they are running a business, aren't they?

Some good soul is waiting for us on the track with real coffee. It's very welcome, but what we really need is a cold shower, and a comfortable WC. People take us off to their toilets, closets or backyards, where we gratefully relieve ourselves and clean up.

Hunger and thirst notwithstanding, we continue our journey beside the Rio Negro, aptly named for its coal-black waters. The vegetation is more luxuriant here, royal palms, coconut palms, bromeliads, tree ferns. The physical types are changing too, we're beginning to see more black people. The locals live in symbiosis with nature. The houses, called *malocas*, are made of juxtaposed tree trunks held together by sun-baked mud, with roofs of palm or iraca leaves. The very same constructions Rodrigo de Bastidas found on his first expedition in 1501. Except that in those days the *malocas* were circular. 'Now they're rectangular,' says Juan Manuel Roca. Five centuries of history and twenty-five years of Kennedy's Alliance for such definitive progress to be made!

The train opens a path through the jungle. We're advised not to lean out, in case we get a papaya in the gob.

It's pouring down when we cross Dorada, the hottest town in Colombia, according to Juan Manuel. On a wall 'Long live the FARC'. We'd forgotten about the '*Violencia*', the people here are so courteous and hospitable. We're entering an area controlled by one of the numerous guerrilla groups that proliferate in this country.

Colombia is at war. It's one of the twenty-five countries in the world in a state of belligerence. *Una guerra sucia* – a dirty war – say the Colombians, who have borrowed the term from the generals in Argentina who murdered their opponents in clandestine prisons. But what's new about this conflict is not the kind of victims or the number, but the difficulty in clearly distinguishing politics from common law, and revolutionary insurgency from the crime industry. The guerrillas kill, but so do the Colombian armed forces, and the multiple paramilitary armies servicing the oligarchy, large landowners, politicians and drug traffickers of every hue.

The FARC (Revolutionary Armed Forces of Colombia), formed in 1964, is the oldest revolutionary movement in Latin America. Relatively low key at first, the FARC expanded during the following decade, especially from 1979 under its charismatic commander Manuel Marulanda Vélez aka 'Tirofijo' (Sureshot), renowned for having lived in the mountains for over thirty years. With a force of 8,000 men split into fifty fronts, the FARC has lost a lot of support since. In order to fill its coffers, it has resorted to kidnapping and imposing ruinous 'revolutionary taxes' that even affect poor farmers. Linked to the Communist Party – though the Party denies it – the FARC was unofficially represented in parliament through the Patriotic Union party until its members were systematically wiped out by the hit men of the big landowners and the drug mafia during the eighties.

Ever since Alonso de Ojeda stepped ashore on its Atlantic coast in 1499, there has been continual war in Colombia, interspersed with the odd period of peace. The struggle for Independence aggravated this traditional phenomenon. The great liberator Simón Bolívar even planned to put to the sword all the inhabitants of the region of Pasto who remained loyal to the monarchy.

The nineteenth century was disfigured by numerous civil wars, the last of which, the 'War of a Thousand Days' (1899), ended with 120,000 dead.

Then came the terrible Bogotazo (the Bogotá riots).

On April 9, 1948, Jorge Eliécer Gaitán, undoubtedly the most famous and revered figure in Colombian history since Bolívar, was assassinated in Bogotá. To this day it's not known whether the poor assassin was a jealous husband, a drugged lunatic or an opponent's hired gun, since ten minutes after the event the wretched man was lynched by the crowd.

Gaitán ran for office under the Liberal Party banner, inflaming the masses with his demagogic rhetoric. After a brilliant career, he had just lost the presidential elections because of divisions within his own party. To some, he was an inspired paternalist, to others a dangerous demagogue, an admirer of Mussolini. The most charitable critic would compare him to Perón at the height of his popularity in Argentina. Like Perón, he sought direct contact with the masses. A genius at improvisation, his rhetoric was purely emotional with little thought for consistency or style, and with constant allusions to his private life. His simplistic and aggressive slogans were rammed home. He called upon the 'heroic rabble', proclaimed 'the people are superior to their leaders', cried 'I'm not a man, I'm the people' and invariably ended his harangues with '¡A la caaarga!' (Chaaaaaarge!).

On that April 9, 1948, the people marched through the streets of the capital but remained relatively calm. And then, suddenly, their pain turned to anger, cleverly manipulated by the radical left. In no time, the city erupted in terrible riots. The masses took to the streets and gleefully set fire to trams, banks, government buildings, elegant shops, churches and schools, in fact a good half of the centre of a capital city that back then had 500,000 inhabitants.

The army tried to restore order with reinforcements from neighbouring regions but for two days Bogotá was the scene of a full-scale battle. There were 3,000 dead in the capital alone. Soon the battle engulfed the whole country claiming 300,000 victims. The photos and films preserved to this day show terrible scenes of devastation and death, with their catalogue of atrocities, displacement, families torn apart, and expropriation of peasant farmers' land.

Eyes gouged out, ears sliced off and castration were common currency. Victims' bodies were drawn and quartered. Gangs signed their actions with particular types of barbarity like 'the monkey' (head in hands covering the sexual organs); 'the necktie' (the tongue pulled out through the open throat); 'the florist' (after decapitation, the four extremities placed in the neck like a bouquet).

In many regions, people bore the terror passively, like a cataclysm, a curse. In other regions they began to resist, and organise. Persecuted by the 'Violencia' in all its forms, they took up arms. A series of symbols – the gun, the machete, the flag, the horse – were celebrated in songs and popular poetry.

These are the tortuous and complex origins of the current situation, the latest phase of an undeclared war.

The rest is part of recent history. But no time to talk of that now because we catch our first glimpse of the Magdalena, mythical river, full of meanders and mud. Everyone rushes to the windows. Described by

Rodríguez Freyle, by Charles Saffray, filmed by Francesco Rossi, seen from the train, the Magdalena does not disappoint. Immense, majestic, swollen by recent rains, its banks hidden by abundant vegetation, it disappears into the horizon.

We cross the Magdalena on an iron bridge.

Heat, humidity and the smell of warm earth, mango and damp. Suddenly, without warning, torrential rain drums on the carriage roofs, penetrates the windows that by now have lost all memory of their panes.

Twenty-four hours travelling and we've barely covered 200 kilometres. We're deep in the Magdalena Medio (the middle sector of the river Magdalena), traditionally marked by the '*Violencia*'.

From 1985 onwards, the simultaneous arrival of the drug barons, the return of the guerrillas to clandestinity after their foray into politics, and the repression by the army, has brought the region back to 1950 levels of violence.

Taking advantage of guerrillas' weaknesses and the decision of the big landowners to combat them, drug traffickers financed and coordinated paramilitary groups who, with the help of instructors from Israel, speedily and bloodily dislodged the FARC from their main bastions.

Hired killers appeared on the scene, as well as paramilitary groups like the MAS (*Muerte a Sequestradores* – Death to Kidnappers). Meanwhile, the drug mafia began buying up large tracts of land, causing the price of land to skyrocket. Peasant farmers, caught between the guerrillas, the army, and the narcos, began selling up and moving to the towns. Large landowners dominate the region now, and the presence of the State is barely noticed.

La Consentida and her convoy stagger along the gravel like pianists in Wild West saloons who keep playing the wrong notes while bottles whizz past them and glasses smash. But no one has the slightest doubt we'll get to Santa Marta on Wednesday the 17th, according to plan. Not the driver, not the tribe of entertainers, no one. Faith can move mountains. But can it speed up trains? Let's see what our main protagonist, our unpredictable *Consentida*, has to say. She stops, this time to take on provisions, at a station called Mexico. The modest station bar is unprepared for the assault of a battalion of guzzlers like us. So only the first fifteen get served. They share with the rest of the troupe, of course, so everyone stays hungry.

It's football and music for dessert. Manu gets his ball out for a match with local kids. Then Gambit, Manu and Xoumoul pick up their instruments for a jam session under the acacias. The little station fills up with rubberneckers, curious to see this strange tribe: the mystical trapezist who walks barefoot on stones and mud, the Belgian tattooist whose body is a veritable advertisement for his art; little skinny white French girls with melancholy eyes, the technicians with the Iroquois haircuts, all of them look as if they've escaped from a film by our long-lamented Fellini. Gambit makes a huge impact. And it's true, this blond giant with bright blue eyes and a body covered with tattoos has the equipment to astonish. Questions rain down. 'Where are you from?'

'Spik eengleech?' In excruciating Spanish, the group manages to convey they're not Yanks. The locals say these musicians are from 'over there'. A boy explains to his little sister that Gambit's double bass is a pregnant guitar. And in fact, Madame Descourt – as Gambit calls his bass – is not a very common instrument in these parts.

Each stop is a meeting of ways rather than a clash of cultures. One discovers the other in mutual astonishment and they fraternise in a celebration of difference.

Three toots of the whistle alert us. We're all used to it by now. All aboard! *La Consentida* moves off at half past one, and ventures into a yawning tunnel. We follow the course of the Magdalena. Against the facades of the houses, even the poorest, even the pre-Colombian, grow bougainvilleas, hibiscus, and *curazaos*, red on green, contrasting colours like a Kandinsky painting. The flora changes again, orange trees, banana trees, *ceibas* and *totumas* – the tree that maracas are made from.

We're going to have to do twenty hours on the trot to make up the twelve hours we've lost. Iván advises us to stock up on food and we stop at a non-scheduled station. But what to buy and where?

The mosquitoes come in clouds. They won't let us sleep, we put our clothes on, get in our sleeping bags, barricade the windows with blankets, but the tiny *jején* that has dislodged the *zancudo* defies our nets, even our jeans, and inflicts extremely painful bites. We use insect repellent, Autan and Citronelle. Some people take Vitamin E: the smell is so awful it scares off friends and lovers, but not the mosquitoes.

Raph and Moussa have been working on the generator and have finally got us some light. We'll have it for three hours. Our faces, pinker now, show the effects of that first day in the sun. We can read and write a few lines. When darkness returns, the musicians organise a candlelit jam session in the bar. Each time we stop — because *La Consentida* has to eat as well — Manu invites the kids that hang around the station onto the train. They nick quite a bit of money off him. '*Cría cuervos*'…as they say in Spain. 'If you raise ravens, they'll peck your eyes out.'

Wednesday 17 November
On the Savannah

Dawn on the savannah. What time is it? In these parts it's always midday. The dogs, dirty Gothic dogs, haven't the breath to bark. The fauna has changed again. The Normandy cows have turned into cebus. Juan Manuel thinks insecticides will soon do away with the *guere-guere*, so that funny little bird will soon only be flying in the José Bravo song:

Hay un guere-guere de allá de la montaña	A *guere-guere* from the mountains
Viene buscando sus querers	Comes to find his love
Pero no lo engañan	But don't deceive him
Ay guere-guere de la tierra mia!	Ay, *guere-guere* from my homeland!

It's not a *guere-guere* but a falcon that follows us to Gamarra. The Train of Ice and Fire has ploughed on through the night, we're in the flood plain of the Magdalena and our drivers aren't even stopping for breakfast. We've crossed the region of Barrancabermeja without a hitch, and at eleven in the morning we're in Gamarra.

The station is crowded. Our arrival was announced for six in the morning. I'm told many people have been waiting since dawn. We're welcomed with firecrackers, which would be cause for rejoicing if Comandante Parmenio wasn't active in this region.

Parmenio is a loose cannon from one of the many loose cannon branches of rebel groups that demand a *vacuna* – a 'vaccine' – from the *campesinos*. ETA, in Spain, call this type of extortion a 'revolutionary tax'. Here they prefer metaphor. If people pay up, there's no problem. The problem is the farmers need an antidote for the acronyms: PRT, FARC, ELN, EPL, PP. And another for the *sicarios*.

Sicarios are teenage gunmen who, for an agreed sum, kill whoever has been fingered. They do it in the street in broad daylight, cocking a snoot at the police or the army and their rather suspect vigilance. Impunity is the name of the game. Going to court takes at least four years, so justice is privatised. A simple motorbike and machine gun does the job that these never-identified 'powerful forces' have confided in them.

The *sicario* has to prove his metal by killing someone of his master's choice or by choosing some unfortunate passer-by himself. Remuneration varies according to the importance of the target. A miserable sum for a *campesino*, 50,000 pesos max. For a journalist, a bit more. César Gaviria could be worth three million pesos, about 25,000 francs. Not very expensive, I hear you say, for the President of the Republic. Apparently Antonio Navarro Wolff, a leader of the demobilised M-19 insurgent movement turned parliamentarian, could bring in even more given that he's quite adept with guns himself and his goons are as well trained as he is.

Until 1989, most of the victims of the violence were poor – *campesinos*, Afro-Colombians, indigenous people. When it started to affect the bourgeoisie, those with political power, that's when the so-called self-defence forces took the law into their own hands. These paramilitaries have killed five times more civilians than the guerrillas. Yet, in November 1992, President Gaviria referred to them as a 'possible solution' to the guerrillas.

Impossible to have a shower in Gamarra. The village water tank is dry. Cati gleans information about the political situation in the area. 'Terrible,' she's told. Daily clashes with the army. Casualties on both sides. 'Do the guerrillas come down as far as the station?' It happens. Not very forthcoming. It's a taboo subject round here and Cati doesn't insist.

Some of us eventually manage to wash: a few at the station, some in the school. Iván, Manu, Juan Manuel, and the writer of this chronicle, in the house of the *cacique*, the local strongman.

'Ice-cream!' someone calls from a street corner. Ice-cream!

The voice is carried on the wind. Outside pass white, black and mestizo silhouettes. But no indigenous people. What's surprising as we go deeper into Colombia is the marked difference between the races, the variety of physical types and their behaviour. Three mountain ranges divide the country into a series of isolated regions that have developed separately and maintain a strong tendency to live according to their own norms, ignorant of and rejecting people from elsewhere.

Most Colombians are mestizo, and find a certain cohesion in this racial mix, even though they want to be seen as white and an ethnic hierarchy exists as clearly as the social hierarchy. You can affectionately call your dark-skinned friend *moreno* (brown) or *negrito* (blackie); a girl whose hair isn't the colour of coal is a *mona* or *rubia* (blondie), a black calls his slightly lighter-skinned mate *blanquito* (whitey). In other words, when friendship – or contempt – come into it, it's impossible to establish proper ethnological distinctions.

'The Colombian aristocracy dreams of being English; the middle class, French; the business class, North American; and ordinary people, Mexican. And they go to the bullfights on Sundays like Spaniards,' says Juan Manuel Roca.

Strange place, Gamarra. Triangular, scattered, desert. Someone gets a drum out and starts to play. It's like cow hide, crocodile or alligator skin, or the belly of a dying dog. The *cacique* sets off fireworks that shoot up very high.

'What about the guerrillas, Juan Manuel?'

'Looks like they're ignoring us.'

'Well, the mayor tells them we're here.'

'And when we're leaving.'

Two hens stretch out in the shade, one with its wings deployed, the other sweeping up the dirt. The shadows of three men in idle mode fall on a wall speckled with whitewash. They discuss cattle, skirmishes, assassinations, the drought. Above their heads is a sign. 'House and ice-cream for sale.'

Two cacti jut out behind the wall. The sun glints off the

corrugated roofs, empty bottles, a workman's pick. One of the hens stretches before disappearing behind a fence. These unfortunate people, what will they do without ice-cream?

We board the train. *La Consentida* gives her three toots. Someone shouts from the crowd, '*Viva Pablito!*'

We set off again, anxious to get to La Gloria. A mulatta walks slowly alongside, at a slight angle, like a jaguar at noon. She leans against a wall, draping herself sensually over it, her red dress moulded to her body, and gives us a penetrating stare. After a few seconds her image disappears, like so many dreams, like landscapes left behind.

The heat is torrid. It's one of the hottest regions of Colombia. Arid savannah and large cebus reminds us of Africa, we expect an elephant or giraffe to appear at any moment.

Not far from here, at Puerto Triunfo, Pablo Escobar has created a zoo at his ranch, called Naples. The drugs tzar has three passions: automobiles, animals and his family. Cars and relatives he had plenty of. To satisfy his third hobby, he imported wild animals from all corners of the earth. Tigers, panthers, lions, elephants, hippopotami, rhinoceroses... He housed them in guilded cages, and opened his animal park to the people. Escobar used pachyderme excrement – in other words, elephant shit – to spread on the packages of cocaine. Apparently it puts police dogs off the scent.

When the State confiscated the zoo, the animals starved. Feeding them isn't part of its budget.

At La Gloria, it's communal showers under the curious eye of the townsfolk. Everyone in underpants, knickers and bras. We make the locals laugh. They must find our bodies strange, in hues from white to bright red. The tattoos and the girls in various stages of undress elicit juicy comments from the Colombians, but nobody gives a damn, this shower is long overdue.

The train cuts its way through two walls of vegetation. Tamarinds, *totuma* trees, almond trees, bananas. We're on a canvas of luxuriant vegetation, modelled on the Uruguayan painter of the same name as the town. Gamarra.

I settle myself in the studio that Radio Caracol has set up in one of the coaches. Sumptuous landscapes roll by, fields of maize, palm trees. A flock of herons suddenly covers the trees in white. The train stops so we can listen to the distant roar of a howler monkey making his extraordinary racket. On a rough boulder, an iguana stretches out in the sun, its green colour turning to gold. A sloth hangs from a branch. And tiny birds, *garrapateros*, pick ticks off the cebus.

At Chiriguana station, there's nothing to eat. We're all hungry. We take taxis to stock up in town, five kilometres away.

Raph has found a stowaway. He's been on the train since Faca, hiding in the ice-wagon, sleeping in the empty mould for the block of ice.

'There were two to start with,' he explains to Cati, 'but the other one got off at Dorada. When I found this one, he was trembling with fright. He was practically naked, I lent him some clothes and gave him something to eat; he'd eaten nothing but bananas. Two days in your underpants, behind a block of ice, with nothing to eat but bananas, I wouldn't wish that on anyone. His Spanish is pretty inadequate, and he says he is 'eighteen or seventeen', he doesn't know exactly. Have you seen the film *Emperor of the North*? It's the story of a stowaway in a train... What do we do with him?'

Cati hasn't seen the film *Emperor of the North*, but she can see Raph has taken a shine to the teenager (his name is Jairo), and taken him under his wing. Raph is the doyen of the team, a little man who doesn't say much and works like a mule. Cati turns a blind eye. There had to be one stowaway, at least.

Félix, one of the train drivers, takes *La Consentida* up to the supersonic speed of twenty-five kilometres an hour. Sleep is impossible. The wheels jolt dangerously, luggage gets dislodged and two or three tattoo merchants fall out of their couchettes. We ask one of the Ferrovías guards to stop the train, we beg Félix to slow down to a reasonable speed. He laughs. There's no danger; we're on the flat and the track is good. But we'd rather be safe than sorry.

Thursday 18 November
Santa Marta

We finally reach Santa Marta (where Simón Bolívar died in 1830), so-called beach resort on the Caribbean, with its bay and cactus-covered mountains. It is picturesque. With its arches, gardens and palm trees, it has the air of an oriental city.

Spanish galleons dropped anchor for the first time here in 1498. About thirty years later, Santa Marta was Spain's main commercial centre in South America. The Conquistadors marvelled at the natural beauty, the magnificent trees, the flowers, the brilliant luminosity of the Caribbean coast, the gentleness of the people. 'If there is a paradise on earth, it is here in this land of Indians,' wrote the chronicler Fray Pedro Simón at the beginning of the sixteenth century.

In 1521, Rodrigo de Bastidas, already a renowned explorer, was charged with founding on terra firma a town that could serve as an operational base for expeditions into the interior. He landed in 1525, near the Indian village of Gaira, on Saint Martha's day, and founded the city that bears that name.

We arrive at eight in the morning. Less than a thousand kilometres, over sixty hours travelling. A day late, it's true, but no major incidents. The press is here, but no crowds. There's no air of celebration at the station, hidden away next to the port. Cati has just found out the amount the Ministry of Culture is putting into the project: 50,000 francs! Less than 1% of the budget! News like that doesn't exactly raise spirits.

The team sets to work unloading the carriages and erecting the stage, surrounded by armed police in combat gear, and guards with rifles. The technicians busy themselves, the artists help. All hands to the pump, unpacking equipment, welding. To one side, the *feria* sideshows are taking shape. Further on, Daniel Seven, known as Dani the Belgian, sets out his tattoo booth, while Jean-Marc Mouligné attempts to awaken the dragon.

Usually so quiet, the station is transformed into a buzzing hive of activity. It's an invasion of foreigners. But the legendary Colombian hospitality is not a myth. They try to talk to the French and manage to understand their rather dubious jumbled Spanish. At thirty degrees in the shade, the air is humid, torsos gleam. With few means at their disposal, these galley slaves are working wonders. 'Everything's held together by string,' says one of them proudly. 'If you can't get what you want, you make do with what you've got.'

And it works!

Amid the general euphoria, however, the usual precautions lapse and it's not long before injuries take their toll. Xoumoul, the French Lovers' guitarist, cuts his finger. Catastrophe! He'll need stitches. He won't be playing in the first few concerts. Soon it's Franck's turn; Mano Negra's lighting man gashes his knee. Philippe Renaud takes him to hospital. Dédé receives a fifty-kilo girder between his thighs and almost loses his crown jewels. You need to be keen!

The concert at Ciénaga has been cancelled. Ciénaga is a small town some fifty kilometres from Santa Marta, scene of the terrible banana massacres in 1928. Not much has changed. The authorities want to give us an army escort during the trip, our stay, and the concerts. Cati refuses. We won't play in Ciénaga in the shadow of bayonets. It's not in the spirit of the train, and the guerrillas might see it as provocation.

We're surprised. According to our information, 'flash points' that could be dodgy are Aracataca, Bosconia and especially Barrancabermeja. The latter, with neighbourhoods it's wise not to venture into, is a xenophobic town where 'cleansers' of homosexuals, drug or tattoo addicts, are extremely active. Yet here we are replacing the Ciénaga show with a second one in Barrancabermeja where our band of gypsies will spend a week.

Friday 19 November
Nerves on Edge

The atmosphere is deteriorating. The symptoms are too obvious not to be taken seriously. A technician is told to leave the train; he's a bad apple, always on the beach while the others are working. Is morale sinking? At closer inspection, it may not be that at all. It might be the exact opposite. Simple fear. Natural apprehension before the big night. Besides, still knocking the set together with the curtain about to rise is enough to make anyone nervous.

Barely a week ago, this motley crew didn't even know each other. Many are working without knowing what the *feria* entails exactly, or what kind of show they are putting together. They set to work without a pecking order, each one allotting themselves an imprecise area that may or may not clash with another equally imprecise area adopted by a workmate. Having said that, nothing explains the aberrant behaviour taking place on a daily basis. Tools are hidden, work is even sabotaged. Apparently it all goes back to when the train was being built in El Corzo, or even as far back as the Royal de Luxe tour of Latin America. Maybe so, this chronicler wasn't there. Now he's told the group is unbearable. He's amazed, because on an individual level he finds them all great. And it's hard for him to see who is working and who isn't. They all seem to be pulling their weight.

There are quite a few problems. Roberto the dragon got damaged on the journey. We need to get aluminium for Jean-Marc's infernal lightning machine, find some way of bartering for bottled gas, make a compressor for the fire-wagon, sort out the soldiers who are apparently here 'to protect us' but who we've caught stealing ventilators.

This morning work seems back on track. The Ice Museum appears, so does the trapezists' scaffolding. Everyone's on the job at six in the morning because it's too hot to work in the sun after eleven. Now the stage is built, the Mano Negra flight cases make their appearance, discreet under their covers.

At noon, the team assembles at Platania, a shady little restaurant, for the set 1,300-peso lunch (about 11 francs). In the afternoon, Mano Negra's keyboard player Tom finds time to paint a voluptuous beauty to decorate the Tattoo Tent.

The same questions recur. What's the show about? What exactly is a *feria*? Where is this famous fifteen-ton cube of ice that appears on all the billboards? Nobody knows! Coco hasn't arrived yet and there is no artistic director. The Climatec machine (with glycolated water) that we've nicknamed the 'DIY machine', isn't plugged in, and the unfortunate Jean-Marc – in racing driver's helmet and goggles, his face blackened by iron filings – is by the furnace arguing with a technician. As for the *feria*, only Filippo knows the answer to that, but he's in a catatonic state and hardly comes on site any more.

The snow machine isn't working. Dédé and his acolytes are attacking it. Régis and Isa, dubbed the King and Queen because of their beauty and imperial serenity, put the finishing touches to a pre-Colombian style backdrop for the stage. Anne-Marie is finishing her Light Tent and building a big bamboo tepee with the help of Jean-Marc who follows her about everywhere.

Amidst all this mess, loud laughter echoes round the station. The two Brazilian *capoeira* masters, Sorriso and Garrincha, have just arrived. And with them, Claudia, a journalist from *El Espectador*, and Fernando. Seeing them again is great, but the news is not. The help promised by Radio Caracol amounts to thirty million pesos in advertising space. Cati is furious. What use is publicity now the train is on its way? If they'd given it in March when she asked for it, she could have turned it into real money. But now? No chance.

All this heralds serious budget problems during the journey. Cati is putting a lot of store on the first show and its impact in the media. Tension is beginning to show on her face too, she feels responsible for all the problems.

Coco has arrived on the same flight. His eye isn't great. He is on antibiotics and under doctor's orders, but the risk of a perforated cornea has disappeared. The group gives him a huge welcome and seems reassured by his presence. 'Tomorrow we'll have a meeting and organise the show,' he decides. That calms spirits but not anxieties. On his rare appearances, Filippo continues to wander about like a zombie, and talks to no one.

That evening, the Mano Negra sound system is set up.

And in the humidity we attend the first rehearsal, with bass guitarist Gambit who is replacing Jo.

Saturday 20 November
More Stowaways

Christine and her brother, the two waiters in the empty café, are crying on the platform. Cati has chucked them out because their parents have made a big fuss in Bogotá. They phoned *El Espectador* and Radio Caracol, threatening to call the police. Their children have been kidnapped and are being held in the Train of Ice and Fire. They have to come home. It's tough on them; they've just got themselves punk haircuts. What will their parents say? Manu, Isa, Jean-Pierre and several others manage to calm Cati down. She speaks to their mother. A fax from her authorises Christine to stay, but her brother has to go home to sit his exams. Christine is the second stowaway to be sorted out.

The whole of Santa Marta knows the acrobats have arrived. To reach the station you now have to force your way through the crowd pressing against the barriers, and the armed soldiers. The Coca-Cola vendors soon run out, to be replaced by those looking for clients for their *tinto*, a very sugary coffee. From now on all vendors need a pass to get into the station, because we've seen lots of crafty little Colombians offering their local wares. Obviously, with coke at 3,000 pesos the gram and the notorious *Punta Roja* (extra-strong ganja from the Sierra Nevada) for almost nothing, simple souls are bound to be tempted. But since the tasteful headline in the French newspaper *Le Jour* ('French artists do a line in Colombia'), the team is a bit paranoid on the subject.

The problems are getting worse: from material going missing, to bits of iron needing welding, to engines needing mending. Our lads, most of them black with grease, are an impressive sight. People have never seen artists under this guise before. Everybody has their shoulder to the wheel, even the girls. But Santa Marta men are hot. They whistle, flirt, and flatter. Even the soldiers try it on, and why not?

To be honest, the soldiers cause us nothing but trouble. This morning, Tom caught another red handed as he tried to steal a walkman through his window. Cati made a stink with the captain or duty sergeant, but to no avail, they're more phlegmatic than the British.

The meeting is held at the end of the day, on the platform. The general atmosphere is not great; the bad blood between some in the team is still there. No one controls the meeting, everyone talks at once, and in French. The Colombians and Brazilians don't understand a thing. As far as the show is concerned, it's decided that all the *feria* sideshows will take place simultaneously. The question 'What is the *feria*?' is back on the table. No one knows what it's supposed to be exactly, nor who is doing what. Lots of things aren't ready, anyway. Filippo suggests explaining everything on site and distributing roles later that night. Then he decides to do nothing, and tomorrow just use the acts that practically work by themselves.

Sunday 21 November
First Night in Santa Marta

D-Day. From three in the afternoon, the road to the station is choc-a-bloc. We know the whole of Santa Marta is coming. Bouchon has deployed soldiers in strategic places but doesn't have much faith in them. There is a feeling of imminent catastrophe. We smile to reassure each other. At five o'clock, Bouchon lets the crowd in and a veritable human wave submerges the soldier-thieves.

People ask where they can buy tickets to visit the attractions and see the show and how much it costs. We are perplexed. Claudia and Fernando came up with the idea that instead of tickets they would distribute slips of paper to be filled in with 'Human Desires' (along the lines of 'Human Rights'); these would then be handed in at the Ice Museum by way of entrance tickets. A monstrous queue has formed in the station forecourt to get these famous slips. Some little villains are selling them to the public for 1,000 pesos. Three hoots from *La Consentida*'s whistle announce the start of the show. Night is falling. The Train of Ice and Fire is illuminated and the mystery of her cargo slowly unfolds. 5,000 people wander from place to place: the 'Beat the Goalie' range, Philippe Mazaud's ice exhibition, the Office of Human Desires, the fire-wagon, the Yeti's grotto (without its inhabitant). People mill around not really knowing what to do. There's pandemonium in the museum-wagon. Impossible to get in, or out. The girls call for help. Anne-Marie's Light Tent is invaded too. It's hard work containing the kids at the entrance to the carriage where Tom and Dani have set out their tattoo stall. The most sought-after designs range from Jesus to the Black Panther, by way of Roberto the Dragon. Fortunately, the trapezists fly overhead and draw the attention of the crowd. It seems happy.

Cati prays to Saint Peter and Divine Providence that it will rain. But the sky is clear. However, seconds later, a few drops fall. The loudspeakers discharge a pretty violent rock. A singer-dancer comes on stage. It's a black kid, Rondelle, a street kid, one of thousands in Colombia. They are youngsters between eight and sixteen, organised in tight clans, living off petty crime, following rules they make themselves and apply without answering to anyone, and without allowing the slightest interference from outside. Either orphans or kids abandoned by their parents, they sleep on the pavements, sniff glue, and are often killed by the 'social cleansing' movements we mentioned before.

This kid sings, dances, rolls on the stage to a clash of cymbals, gets up to drumming, and disappears with the same panache with which he appeared. Sammy Davis Junior eat your heart out.

The real show begins with the Golden Dragonfly marionettes. This story of Pirandellian dolls who rebel against the dictatorship of their handlers pleases both kids and parents who don't catch the implicit danger.

Now on stage, the Brazilian *capoeira* dancers Sorriso and Garrincha bring a touch of exoticism, even to their geographical neighbours.

Finally it rains. We quickly cover everything with tarpaulins. But rain or no rain, Roberto awakens from his slumbers. And here he is, ladies and gentlemen, the *feria's* biggest attraction, Roberto, the world's only *Draconidus Magdalenius*. He is over five metres high: an iguana with a dragon complex, a dragon who wants to be an iguana. When he's disturbed, Roberto gets up, sweeps the crowd with his projector eyes, snorts smoke from his nostrils, and expels a jet of fire ten metres long over the crowd. Every time Roberto opens his mouth, Tomasin roars Roberto's theme out of the synthesiser. The crowd roars many decibels back at him.

In the days of the Conquest, the iguana had been at the centre of a heated debate. Was it flesh or fish? It was a thorny canonic problem for the soldier-priests. Was it a sin for humans to eat it on Fridays? Not a problem for the Indians, of course, who didn't have souls as yet. Flesh or fish, the iguana was very popular with gastronomes. They were hunted (or fished) with nets and the help of specially trained dogs. It's forbidden to hunt them these days but they're still very sought after for cooking and for their skin, and are easily found in the soup kitchens of Valledupar, capital of the Vallenato and roast iguana. Apparently it tastes like chicken.

Carlos Rojas still has two iguanas at home. He used

them as models for Roberto, a symbiosis of iguana and mythical mediaeval dragon. The embryo Roberto was then taken to the workshops of the School of Fine Art in Bogotá where twenty-odd architecture and industrial design students gave him the morphological configuration he was born with.

Jean-Marc Mouligné, film special effects expert, (*The Visitors* for example), is the father of this monster. On August 8, 1993, he wrote to Manu Ciao (sic):

'For the past dozen or so years, I've created many spectacular machines for the cinema that could used be used in the fire-wagon. Remote-controlled fire, of course, but also a lightning machine that emits a dazzling white flame. I can make flame-throwers and I'll create a battle between human flame-throwers dressed in firework-covered asbestos suits. I've just finished – and patented – a sort of repeating cannon that fires fireballs towards a fixed spot in the sky (if you want), a firestorm of two or three bombs per second. In a nutshell, I'd like to bring my ideas and toys to your very lovely project.'

Jean-Marc is a bloody liar. He joined the train in pursuit of a great but only partly requited passion.

It hasn't been easy for Jean-Marc. On October 30, 1993, in the El Corzo workshops, he was very worried about Roberto. 'It was a huge iron skeleton of a flame-throwing dragon with bad diesel breath. To start with he was very heavy. I had to make sure he'd be able to stand up. He was suspended by the crane, with me on his back, when he keeled over and fell on his knees. His whole carcass was prostrate in front of the workshop. He had to be able to open his cage and get up on his own. We couldn't dress him because no one really knew how to do it, and I had already begun to take his innards out to house the smoke machine in his stomach.'

That was Raph's job. And the enormous shell where Roberto sleeps was the work of César González, industrial design student at the National School.

After a rest Roberto is released again. He unfolds out of his shell, majestic and terrifying. Tom, on the synthesiser, works wonders, the dragon emits monstrous cries and roars. The kids in the audience are thrilled. It's the pyrotechnic effects spectacle par excellence and Jean-Marc and Fabrice give it all they've got, even surviving one of Colombia's frequent blackouts. And joy of joys, torrential rain engulfs the town. The Colombians couldn't remember it having rained that hard for years.

When the downpour eases off a little, the French Lovers come on stage. Their generosity and craziness are equalled only by a quality of music rare in French rock. In 1984, Bruno and Captain were at secondary school in Beauvais when, bored with state education, they suddenly decided to go into music. They certainly had the tools: zero in terms of singing, neither played an instrument, no idea of musical scales. Ideal for forming a group.

During a year off in Montreal, Bruno starts to tinker with a guitar. To attract a crowd they engaged two mega chicks and did completely mad stuff. By 1988–89 they were playing with the Négresses Vertes and Casse-pieds. All a pretext to travel. Musically, they were still zero.

Things were going badly, Bruno and Captain were on their own again, with no contracts and no chicks. Their only future was in the Métro. They even considered begging. They needed a double bass to play in Switzerland! They picked up Gambit from the band Hell's Crack, he's another funny stuff specialist. For a second Swiss trip, they dipped into Hell's again. Shuman the drummer goes with them. Two months later, the guitarist Xoumoul joins them for a trip across the Channel. Hence, a very bad and atypical rock group is formed that plays *trashguinguette,* an invention of their own. And it works. The five of them play all over France, with no acoustics, no mic, no amplifier. In bars, in the street, in the Métro, in concert halls, they make a name for themselves, developing their music as they go along. Peter Murray signs them to the Nord–Sud label. A record with Clive Martin. An album, *Dans les rues d'ici.* Olympia, Euro–Festival. Manu was dead keen for them to come to Colombia.

The skies open again. The audience dashes for shelter in the station forecourt, but the French Lovers keep playing the fool, up to their knees in water. The show stops there for today. We breathe a sigh of relief. Mano Negra didn't play but the show went out in a blaze of glory thanks to Roberto.

The scene is indescribable. Tom and Dani finish their tattoos by candlelight, while in the station forecourt, revved up by Néctar *aguardiente* (sponsors of the train), the kids demand and get another set from the French Lovers, who are always ready to dash off one more song.

Manu joins them and the fiesta goes on until four in the morning.

As said before, the Train of Ice and Fire has a delegation from the Office of Human Desires, a complementary organisation to the UN Office of Human Rights. The Office gives out postcards with the train's logo and invites people to write their innermost desires on the back. The postcards go into a draw and the winners can choose between a large poster of the train, t-shirts, caps from *El Espectador* or maps of Colombia.

Messages in the Office of Human Desires in Santa Marta:

Pineapple, lemon, lemonade
If you don't love me
Why do you kiss me?
Damaris, 15

Win the car in the lottery on 17 December, 1993. That we love each other all our lives. And that Colombia wins the World Cup.
Elkin and Patricia, 19 and 18

I wish for peace in Colombia, and that you come back one day with your show, which I think is wonderful. We'll be waiting.
Damaris Blanco, 15

One of my biggest dreams is that there'll be peace in Colombia, and to do that we have to stop the drug traffickers. As for me, I hope that when I'm eighteen I'll have a good job so I can help other people and be a good person.
Illegible signature

One of my dreams is that we'll really have trains for passengers one day. The other is that peace will be the word on everyone's lips next year.

Myriam Silva, 14

Monday 22 November
Ciudad Perdida

Joseph Conrad's most ambitious novel *Nostromo* describes a huge mountain crowned with snow in a tropical country. It's the Sierra Nevada de Santa Marta with its twin 5,775-metre peaks; the Cristóbal Colón and the Simón Bolívar. This Sierra Nevada is the world's highest coastal mountain. In the windy season, because of the downward currents, the mountain helps lower the temperature in the town. And on a clear day, you can see the two snow-covered peaks from the beaches of Santa Marta. In yet another marriage of snow and fire that is the metaphor for our train, the Sierra Nevada inspired the popular song 'I dreamed the snow burned, I dreamed the fire froze'.

Your chronicler and our sound engineer Guillermo Rodríguez are flying over the Sierra Nevada in a Radio Caracol helicopter. At 1,000 metres, we see the first huts amidst enormous ferns, orchids, and different kinds of palms. I can't help thinking of the huts, called *pallozas*, of my native Galicia. The same construction of mud and straw, the same round form, the same conical roof. We ascend amid grandiose mountains through a thick mist that hides the peaks, and after a good deal of manoeuvring at 1,100 metres above the humid vegetation, we land on one of the platforms of the Ciudad Perdida.

The Spanish Conquistadors didn't appreciate the value of these towns, since for them finding the largest amount of treasure possible in this jungle El Dorado overrode every other consideration. Nevertheless, the chroniclers Gonzalo Fernández de Oviedo, Fray Pedro de Aguado and the poet Juan de Castellanos painted an enthusiastic picture of the 'fabulous cities of Tayrona, Pocigueira, Betoma, Tayronaca and Bonda' before they were destroyed. We don't know the indigenous name for the city that was discovered and baptised Ciudad Perdida, the lost city.

The year is 1975. Sepúlveda is a *guaquejo*. That means he digs in ancient ruins and necropolises for gold objects. He stumbles across the lost city by chance and begins digging in secret. But the word gets round among his fellow *guaquejos* and the race is on. It ends badly for Sepúlveda who is killed by his brothers in poverty. By a variety of routes, the rumour reaches the ears of the director of the Bogotá Institute of Anthropology. Another race is on, this time between *guaquejos* and scientists. The contest is solved in a very Colombian way. The archaeologists, paralysed by a lack of funding, work on the site side by side with the looters who have an 'official' association in the good town of Santa Marta. And − irony of ironies − the looters' best customers are the renowned Gold Museum in Bogotá and the Institute of Anthropology who recuperate, one way or another, most of the treasure scavenged by the *guaquejos*.

Getting out of the helicopter, we feel we're profaning a sacred place. But military boots have beaten us to it. They're there waiting for the tourists beside the stubborn archaeologists. A group of surprisingly small barefoot Kogui Indians are resting after a long trek. They are dressed in white tunics. With their long straight black hair falling down their backs they look like a gang of brown-skinned kids.

The commander of the garrison receives us. 'We're here at the Koguis' request, to protect them from marijuana producers,' he says. He shows us the site. The ruins are on terraces clinging to the slopes of Mount Corea, two square kilometres at a height of 900 to 1,200 metres.

No temple, no palace, no statues, the Sierra Nevada ruins are a long way from the grandeur of Machu Picchu, the Mayan Temples of Yucatán, or the pyramids of the Mexican *Meseta*. Yet the way the ruins adapt to, and respect, their physical environment is remarkable; the stone terraces follow the relief perfectly. They resemble the agricultural terracing in Provence but the stonework in Ciudad Perdida is better finished. Some of the platforms are covered by huge sculpted flagstones (iron wasn't in use then). Some 250 different areas are linked by interminable steps, made with little Amerindian feet in mind. A trail leads down the mountainside from the site to the sea. It's five days on foot. At one of the pedestrian crossroads, a huge vertical stone like a menhir has a network of lines engraved on it. Could it have been a map of the city at its most splendid?

Guillermo Pava, Radio Caracol's technician, brings the satellite-case from the helicopter. The other Guillermo gets ready to broadcast our first report. He reminds me of Pedro Camacho, the character in *Aunt Julia and the Scriptwriter* by Mario Vargas Llosa. He has the same feel for radio that the pioneers had, always ready, always on the lookout, backed by super-sophisticated technology and unusually cultured for that kind of journalist. The ease with which he improvises amazes this chronicler, who can't run two words together without a script. This chronicler begins to mistrust this Stakhanovite of the airwaves, as he rushes out one newsflash after another, five in fifteen minutes, even getting ahead of events. 'We're leaving Santa Marta for Ciudad Perdida...what does our guest think?' It so happens that the guest was thinking of something else entirely or nothing at all. He also thinks that if he'd been given advance warning, he wouldn't be looking stupid. All the same, he manages to blurt out what he remembers from reading *Le Monde* or *Géo*.

The Tayronas were originally an agricultural people, industrious, rich and brave. They fought valiantly against the Spaniards, leading Juan de Castellanos to say:

> 'And even now, strange to say,
> no Spaniard has claimed victory.'

The Tayronas lived at the centre of their own world, since they had everything they needed – every type of climate, plant, and bird. At their feet was the ocean, coconut palms, and the burning sun. They believed in the order of the universe, in nature as the supreme being. Their priests told them the earth was 'the mother of all races, men and tribes'. For them, the spirit – that they called Aluna – was everything, and concrete and visible things were only symbols. Coca was grown on the temperate slopes of the mountainside. Its leaves, as big as the tree that produces tea, are smooth, pointed and dark green. The Tayronas recognised the nutritive and medicinal principles of the plant. Chewing it with a small amount of chalk or cinders, meant they were able to bear the exhausting work in the mines, and the forced abstinence of long voyages.

The word *tayrona* in their language meant foundry. And indeed, not far from Santa Marta, was a huge area where they worked the gold from the local mines. They were imprudent enough to offer Rodrigo de Bastidas a large amount of gold to temper his bellicose intentions. Bastidas respected the truce offered, but his moderation didn't fit well with his companions' greed and they killed him. Fray Bartolomé de las Casas, so severe with those who ill-treated the Indians, gave full credit to the exceptional, almost unique, behaviour of Santa Marta's founder. 'I always saw him act very charitably towards the Indians,' said the bishop historian, 'and he was angry with those who didn't treat them well.'

Later on, Captain Vadillo put 500,000 Tayronas to the sword in a vast 'pacification' campaign. He did it with the blessing of the Bishop of Santa Marta: 'Your Majesty knows full well that in these parts there are no Christians, only demons, no servants of God, only traitors to their law and their King.'

The Indians retreated into the mountains to organise resistance. Battles raged until the victory of Captain Pinol who, in 1599, ordered all ears, noses, and lips of male prisoners to be cut off, to wipe away a century of disrespect.

The Koguis claim to be the true descendents of the Tayronas. They live in those strange conical huts. Good hunters, they refuse to use firearms that frighten the game, and they eat maize and manioc. The historian Gregorio García said of the strange language (Kogui) they speak: 'The devil knew that the Bible would be preached in this land. To make it more difficult for the missionaries and prevent the Indians from understanding them, he persuaded the Indians to invent a large number of languages and helped them with that unique talent of his.'

The Koguis obey their priests, their *Mamus*, who tell them of the sky, the moon and the sea. In their cosmography, the earth is a huge body of a woman who feeds and protects; the world is a divine uterus. They have a dual conception of the universe – Good and Evil – and believe that their sole purpose on earth is to protect nature. From time to time, they fill their *mochilas* (woven bags) with the tools they need and leave their hamlets to go and prepare a new piece of land.

A few dozen of them, looking rather miserable, are standing around chewing coca. The archaeologists and army use them as guides.

'What does our guest think?'

There were 6,000 of them in 1950. Now there are less than half that number. They were first affected by the arrival of the marijuana producers. Santa Marta Gold was very sought after in the US. Convoys of 500 mules loaded with bales of the stuff would go down to the coastal ports daily. The traffickers burned their villages, and took their lands in exchange for a few bottles of *aguardiente*.

In the 1980s, coca replaced marijuana in the Sierra, as marijuana began to be grown on the spot in California. Coca fields proliferated, so did the secret laboratories making the pasta base and eventually cocaine. The drug traffickers systematically slaughtered the *Mamus*, depriving the Koguis of their past, and their guides to the future. The Sierra didn't only fall prey to traffickers of all hues, but also to the guerrillas and their internal battles. More active than the FARC on the south-easterly slope of the Sierra Nevada is the ELN, led by a priest called Pérez.

And on the heels of the traffickers came the police, the army and the small planes that spray the coca crops from the air with glyphosate, and at the same time destroy fields of maize and even the huts of the Koguis themselves. The effect of this destruction is terrifying.

From 1950 on, about 2,000 peasant farmers, encouraged by the government, started their long march to this mountain. They were, in the main, families desperate to escape violence elsewhere, hoping to find a peaceful refuge. They came from North and South Santander, where guerrillas of all factions were the law; from Tolima, a violent region if ever there was one; and from Caldas, coffee country with luscious green hills but torn apart by bloody settling of accounts. Blacks, mestizos, *zambos*, creoles. They all knew that life in the mountains was hard. They had to fight their way through the jungle, then clear the land, cutting down trees and digging out roots. The Koguis didn't accept the presence of other people on their land, and settlers and Indians are repeating the same tragic experience as the Conquistadors and the Tayronas of yesteryear. The Conquest has not finished.

Tuesday 23 November
Second Night in Santa Marta

The train has become a veritable camp of cripples. Forced labour and fatigue have taken their toll among the youngsters, most of whom don't usually work in manual trades. Coco takes a turn for the worse. His eye is like a chocolate egg. Off to hospital again.

We're delighted to learn from the press that the concerts by Mano Negra and the French Lovers were amazing. It made us all laugh. Yesterday was a chance to take stock. Filippo announced he was leaving, Bouchon is obviously accident prone, Cati and Manu have written a script for the show.

The team is more relaxed and in principle everyone knows what they have to do. The station doors open from three in the afternoon and again crowds flood in. Kids push to get from wagon to wagon, touching the weird walls of the Yeti-wagon, icy under the tropical sun. Grown-ups go into raptures over the Ice Museum displays: an iron with a frozen bottom 'to get creases out of silk in Siberia'; or the model of 'skyscrapers for Eskimos'. Considering Sunday a wash-out as a rehearsal, the organisers have decided to tighten up the show. But a surprise act appears. It's the governor of the region. If he speaks we're done for. Our show has to be apolitical, any provocation can bring reprisals. On stage are the French Lovers and three of Mano Negra's musicians: Santi on his bongos, Garbancito and Tom on keyboards and samplers. Their mission is to calm things down and provide background music for Roberto's act. But the dragon is being temperamental and doesn't want to come out of his shell.

The tattoo-wagon is being an unheard-of success. The queue at the door is interminable and even the windows have been taken by assault. The trapezists are a sensation too and every time Fabou flies through the air, cries of joy go up from the crowd.

It's time for Roberto. Everyone rallies round, but a power cut stops the dragon in all his fury. Fabrice improvises a dragon-taming routine that wasn't in the script and manages to wake the monster. A bit too well, in fact. The technicians obviously don't know Gratian's maxim: 'good things, if brief, are twice as good'.

And finally it's the long-awaited Mano Negra concert. The group set off like bats out of hell improvising on latino and especially reggae rhythms. Fidel, the Argentine rasta, has joined Mano for all the new pieces like 'Delbor' and 'Rock in Zonzón' by King Daddy Yod. I know this from Mehdi Boukhelf of *Best*, your chronicler not being up to speed on this kind of music. This guy Fidel has an incredible voice, a delivery to make Solaar jealous, and it's in Spanish, which has the kids in the front rows going mad. And, to cap it all, the timbre of his voice marries beautifully with Manu's, a bit like Jamaican DJs and singers.

There are problems with the sound, the back-line; what the audience is hearing isn't what the group is playing. Chino, the sound engineer, goes to his mixing desk again and again to check the connections, while the amplifiers get stronger. The audience doesn't give a stuff, they're totally enthralled. Mano Negra's set ends with a request for 'Sidi H'bibi' and Khaled's 'Ne m'en voulez pas', sung by Garbancito.

Cati is distraught, but for a different reason. When the director of Néctar (the tour's biggest sponsor) and the local governor set foot in 'their' carriage, the lights went out. They cried sabotage and left in a fury. And with them went the troupe's last financial hope.

Who could have done that? Raph, old Raph. An hour earlier, he'd wanted to go into the carriage to check the electrics and was unceremoniously thrown out by the governor's bodyguards.

Mano Negra's groupies have travelled from the port of Barranquilla to see the band they first discovered when the Cargo '92 tour stopped there. They leave ecstatic. But the musicians aren't very happy with their performance. Their new songs need more rehearsing. Manu had to take some songs out of the Colombia tour: one of them, 'Señor Matanza', describes the activities of a Latin American landowner turned patron of hired killers. On the other hand, Mano Negra had the audacity – irresponsibility? – to play a four-minute tape of the slogan of Salvador Allende's Popular Unity party: 'El Pueblo Unido Jamás Será Vencido' (A People United Will Never Be Defeated). Everyone's astonished! They pounce on Manu. Doesn't he know that slogan had been adopted by the FARC?

Apart from that, everything has gone relatively well. The little black kid from yesterday gave us a musical extra on the last chords of the refrain. Manu thinks he's brilliant. He went looking for him yesterday in the streets of Santa Marta, and today found him on stage again, the kid's natural environment.

Messages in the Office of
Human Desires in Santa Marta:

My dream is to have a t-shirt. I need one.
Darío Romero, 15

Peace for Colombia and for the violence in our country
to end. No more crime in Colombia and an end to
drugs.
Arturo Cáceres, 18

Neither narcos or guerrillas in my country. The
government should think about us poor people and
make more job opportunities.
Eliécer Rincón, 42

My dream is for there to be no more drugs so they don't
keep killing our young people.
Luz Amiria Alvarez, 23

Wednesday 24 November
Latest News from the Front

Headlines in the local paper this morning. 'Municipal Councillor Assassinated in Ciénaga'. Ciénaga was going to be our next stop, after the two *ferias* and concerts in Santa Marta. It has been cancelled. The news: 'Lazaro De Andreis, together with his bodyguard and chauffeur, were assassinated yesterday afternoon in the city centre. The authorities have decreed an eleven o'clock curfew.'

We're back in 1928.

Headline in the Bogotá daily *El Espectador*. 'Urabá Under Fire'. The news: 'The FARC have assassinated thirteen People's Liberation Army sympathisers in the banana region.' Commentary-question in Santa Marta paper *El Informador:* 'What will happen to Colombia if all the progressives are assassinated?' A foreigner might be perplexed. Who exactly are the progressives in this case?

The barefoot trapezist has a gash in his forehead. Four stitches. There are ripples of anarchy. Philippe Renaud decides to go back to Paris 'to be true to his principles'. A sibylline phrase. Are we starting to haemorrhage?

Thursday 25 November
Leave Santa Marta. Arrive Aracataca

We were warned. The train would leave at ten o'clock sharp, too bad for any latecomers. They can go to Aracataca by bus. But the Colombian railwaymen have lost the punctuality habit, if they ever had it.

Philippe Renaud, Filippo and Jeff remain on the platform. They are the first to jump ship. To even things up, we've gained some girls, the eternal fan club inherent on musicians' tours.

Guillermo Rodríguez invites your chronicler into his helicopter again, to get some aerial views and do the radio commentary of the departure from Santa Marta. The train snakes along the track, so slowly that from the helicopter it looks as if it has stopped to view each change of scenery. Guillermo gets out his mic, but this time your chronicler will not be caught unawares. He talks about the meeting of cultures and the marriage of opposites. We should have been in Aracataca for the second news report, but the helicopter is still hovering over Santa Marta. So, your chronicler adds a few reflections on the ice of Melquíades and the ice in the train. After thirty years in the radio business, he feels he's finally beginning to master his trade thanks to Guillermo.

After the imaginary voyage to Aracataca, the pilot offers to take us there in real life. He has been so impressed by our description. But an hour in a helicopter is very expensive so Guillermo asks him to take us down to the train. The pilot decides to set us down on the moving convoy, so we have to do a sort of Jean-Paul Belmondo act.

We've only just landed when the train stops, abruptly. We've derailed. Already! Again! The state of the track is quite picturesque. The sleepers are only loosely nailed to the rails, and the rails are completely twisted because they don't dilate very evenly. Sometimes, when we're on the footplate we can see a huge bump where the rail is suspended in the air for about ten metres, thirty centimetres above the ballast. When the train arrives, it flattens the bump. But in the meantime, little stones get under the track and the convoy derails again with a huge shudder from top to tail.

Two hours to get back on track, twenty minutes to reach cruising speed and allow people to scramble onto the roof again. Once we're used to all the shuddering, the view is more and more spectacular.

From our vantage point we look out over the interminable banana plantations, the workers' miserable huts, the gardens arid from the dust and heat. Women in shorts and blue-striped shirts, playing cards under their porches, shout greetings as we go by. Ox-carts laden with bunches of bananas trundle along the dusty roads. In the river young girls leap from boulder to boulder, leaving us with the memory of their magnificent breasts.

These fleeting scenes stop on an old man who is chasing us on a bicycle. He keeps up with us for a good many metres, his right hand clutching the handlebar, and his left raised in a fist. He cries, 'Don't forget there was a massacre of agricultural workers here in 1938!'

The old cyclist is about a decade out. In fact the massacres in the banana plantations took place in 1928, after the gringos took over these lands in the name of United Fruit. With powers hitherto reserved for Divine Providence, they speeded up the harvests, modified the rain cycles, and changed the course of the river, diverting it with its icy water and white boulders from the bed in which it had lain for centuries to the other end of the village, behind the cemetery.

The workers didn't want to have to cut and load bananas on a Sunday, and it seemed such a legitimate demand that Aracataca's illustrious priest, Father Francisco C. Angarita himself, pleaded in its favour because he found it conformed to the will of God.

After five weeks of conflict, faced with firm resistance from the agricultural workers, the Americans and their stooge General Cortés Vargas tried to get the Colombian government to dub the striking workers bandits. The union leaders, who had gone into hiding, suddenly reappeared and organised demonstrations in the villages of the banana region. The police were content just to maintain order. But, the following night, the strike leaders were taken from their homes and sent to Ciénaga prison in five-kilo leg irons.

General Cortés Vargas's arrogance bordered on

dementia. Jorge Eliécer Gaitán, who was then a Liberal Party deputy, famously supported the strikers. He recounted how the Santa Marta football team, home from a victory against Cali, was received with great pomp by the General. The whole town was decorated with garlands and banners saying 'Viva the victory of General Cortés!' Addressing the players magnanimously, he said: 'Ask of me whatever you wish'. These valiant sportsmen asked him to free their family and friends, and their wish was granted.

The strikers' discontent grew when a decree giving the workers a new pay deal was signed in Ciénaga. The workers complained that they weren't paid in money but with coupons they could only use in the United Fruit stores (to buy things like Virginia ham).

Eyewitnesses report an army lieutenant climbing onto the platform of Ciénaga railway station where four machine guns were pointing at the crowd. A bell rang calling for silence. The lieutenant read out a decree: in three clauses totalling eighty words, he called the strikers 'a band of outlaws' and gave the army the power to mow them down.

The army immediately opened fire on the crowd gathered in the main square of the little town of Ciénaga, and then embarked on a ruthless repression of the whole region. Father Francisco C. Angarita sent a detailed report of these atrocities to Jorge Eliécer Gaitán on June 16, 1929.

According to the police, forty people were killed in the banana massacre. The strike leaders put the figure at 1,500.

The train continues its journey, leaving behind the old man, who is by now quite out of breath. Ahead of us lie fields of poppies and the stifling humidity of the plantations. Behind us, dark clouds appear. Suddenly they're upon us. Enormous raindrops drum on the roof and bounce off the carriages.

We travel on through the downpour and a veritable forest of giant cacti before reaching Sevilla. Not very imaginative, these Conquistadors. Sevilla, Córdoba, Pamplona...they nostalgically named the towns they founded in the New World after their birthplaces, without bothering about onomastics.

In Sevilla, we're welcomed with cheers and banners. A woman gestures to us to stay at her house. Kids run behind the train. We lose sight of them but their cries ring in our ears. We pass several stations. Unlike our outward journey, there are people all along the track. They're expecting the train. Thanks to television, newspapers, Caracol...that old devil Guillermo.

Night is falling. It is already dark when we hear children shouting. What godforsaken town are we in now?

'Aracataca!' replies a kid proudly. He sounds like a machine gun.

At that very moment, this little town is shaken by three resounding hoots and the long drawn-out gasp of the exhausted engine. When the shock of the whistle and sigh passes, the inhabitants converge on the station to witness these modern-day gypsies riding atop the engine and carriages, waving their arms, and they discover, dumbfounded, a train decorated all over with flowers and yellow butterflies beside the platform for the first time in twenty years, four hours behind schedule.

From the station, out of the darkness, comes a deafening cacophony, produced by all sorts of musical instruments: maracas, percussion, drums, tambourines, pipes. There are welcoming cheers, fireworks and peels of bells. A Vallenato band drawls its nasal monotony. And a children's choir accompanied by guitars gives a rendering of the Marseillaise. In French, if you please.

This delirious reception takes us by surprise. We don't quite know how to react. It's hard to rise to the occasion. We're not Melquíades: these people already know about ice and fire. And could any of us sing the Colombian national anthem, or even dare join their choir in the Marseillaise? We do, however, don the mantle of false patriotism and murmur a few bars so as not to disappoint.

We get off. People touch us, say a few words in Colombian franglais. Camera flashes and Bergeron's projector split the darkness to reveal over 2,000 people.

'Where's the dragon?'

We have to explain that our family of gypsies has to set up our *feria* in front of the station first. But where? Suddenly two luxury cars drive up. It's the mayor of Fundación, the neighbouring village. He insists we go there. We can't stay in Aracataca because they can't even provide anywhere decent for us to do our show. He gestures to the potholes in the road. It's true that the terrain is a bit dangerous for a *feria*. Beside the mayor are his bodyguards, armed to the teeth, teeth of worrying

94

whiteness. They turn to this chronicler. He explains that for us Aracataca is symbolic: you know, García Márquez, Melquíades, the ice? Rubbish, the Nobel prize-winner has written a load of rubbish, he's a Lefty. But they finally leave. Phew!

We mingle with the crowd again. They compare us to the acrobats and jugglers who brought the ice, all those generations ago. But unlike Melquíades and his tribe, it doesn't take long to prove we're not heroes of progress but vulgar peddlers of pleasure. So, although we show the ice, we do so as a simple circus curiosity, and are careful not to stress its usefulness. And this time we have, among other ingenious inventions, a gigantic iguana that spits fire. But there again, its creators are not presenting it as a pivotal contribution to the history of special effects, but as a clever technical trick.

Soon the problem of violence resurfaces. We say we've been told Aracataca is very dangerous. 'In the mountains, yes...' they gesture vaguely into the darkness, 'things do kick off. But the people here will protect you.'

A light flickers. A neon sign comes on. 'Welcome to Aracataca, global capital of literature.' We can see around us now. There is a soldier for every ten inhabitants. People are fascinated by the tattoos on Gambit, Dani and Bruno; they're veritable walking exhibitions.

'Are you from Montpellier?' 'Is Montpellier nice?'

We're surprised by Montpellier's celebrity. 'Of course, Montpellier is beautiful,' we reply, admiring the beauties descended from Úrsula and Colonel Aureliano Buendía.

The director of the García Márquez museum

welcomes us. If we want to wash and rest, he recommends Señora Herminia's house.

We're desperate to find a hotel. There are no hotels in Aracataca, just two pensions. The more comfortable being the Residencia Montpellier. Now we understand why our beautiful Languedoc town embodies the epitome of French chic. The rooms are acceptable. Clean at least. The proof is a notice asking guests 'not to spit on the walls'. That's a relief. But there is so little space that if you don't spit on the walls, where the hell can you spit? Although the room already has two beds, the host assures us he can fit in several more, for the whole troupe, if necessary. And for the pleasure we will pay 1,000 pesos per extra bed. Two will do nicely, thank you.

The daughter of the house comes up to your chronicler. Her name is Shirley Helena, but since she doesn't like the name Shirley, she calls herself Sirena. She's a mix of white and Indian, chubby, with smooth skin. She's wearing only a very short tight skirt and a bra. It looks good on you, Sirena. She's like a Botero. She has a fresh resounding laugh. Standing a few centimetres from the chronicler, she asks him all sorts of questions about Paris, France, Frenchmen, Frenchwomen, men in general, women in general, his wife and his potential mistresses. Your chronicler forces himself to remember that Sirena is only fifteen and that he's supposed to be the most respectable of the gypsies. We talk about our coming to Aracataca. Is it true we're not being paid? And why here? Nobody ever comes here. I remind her that other gypsies came a very long time ago, they didn't get paid either. She has heard of Melquíades, of Úrsula Iguarán, a whole series of Aurelianos and José Arcadios, the first, the second, and she gets them mixed up like everybody else. Her father knew them. Her father is sixty. His job consists of opening and closing the pension door each time a customer comes in or goes out. Each time, he goes to the kitchen to fetch the key or take it back. I tell him it would be less tiring if he hung the key nearer the door, or if he carried it on him. 'It's my job,' he replies with a smile. Did he know any of the Buendías? The second Aureliano, or perhaps the third? He didn't, but his mother had held Gabito in her arms when he was born. Everybody here calls García Márquez 'Gabito' (diminutive of Gabo, in itself a diminutive of Gabriel). 'Did your mother tell you if Gabito had a pig's tail?' He looks at me in astonishment. 'Is your mother still alive? Can I visit her?' 'Of course, she's ninety-two.' But Sirena's father proceeds to give me very convoluted instructions. 'Next to the cemetery, ask for Señora Fermina, she'll take you to Constancio, and he'll…' I thank him. I can find out if García Márquez has a pig's tail just as easily in Paris.

Everyone's delighted to be in a village at last, it's what we've been dreaming of. Big towns are behind us, the real tour starts now.

But first things first. Team meeting. Everyone on the platform. We need to avoid some of the errors that occurred in Santa Marta.

'We must organise things better, so the public doesn't flock to one attraction. It's a disaster. They don't see anything and they're disappointed.'

'There's no artistic direction, everyone does whatever they feel like.'

Fabrice is criticised for having done the Great Zampano act with the dragon. Manu defends him.

'He's the only person who took any initiative, yet everyone's giving him a hard time.'

'Agreed. All the same, no one mounts Roberto; it's sacrilege.'

'Okay, Fabrice, you wake him up, then you leave him alone.'

'And what about the ice exhibition? People queue for hours and there's nothing to see.'

'Yes, but they all come out smiling.'

Then the unexpected happens. Claude Mattis, from the AFAA, arrives with four million pesos, enough to keep us going till the next stop.

Problems with the army are already written into the programme. The soldiers are nervous because of the guerrillas, who are well dug in around here. A kid has been beaten about the head and turfed out of the station. Cati tells the commander this is a show, not a military front. She orders a troop withdrawal — but doesn't get it.

Friday 26 November
In the Streets of Aracataca

It feels good to set off early in the morning to explore the town.

Aracataca was founded here because of the quality of the soil and its privileged position vis-à-vis the sandbank. It's no longer the village of twenty mud and straw houses beside a diaphanous river running over a bed of polished stones as big as prehistoric eggs that it was in Gabo's day. Modern Aracataca has 40,000 inhabitants. The river is muddy, dirty, a far cry from its ancestor. The houses have kept the same structure, but now they're made of cement or wood. In one of them, the old gypsy Melquíades, always mindful of humanity and progress, left no less an inheritance than the philosopher's stone, the solution to squaring the circle: 'Here we buy like the poor to eat like the rich.'

The primitive hamlet has metamorphosed into a bustling town, with shops, artisans' workshops, and a road with a constant stream of traffic, down which had once come the first Arabs in moleskin slippers, rings in their ears, exchanging glass bead necklaces for parrots.

Herminia's house is one of the most beautiful in town and the others seem to have been made in its image: a spacious brightly lit hall, dining room on the verandah with brightly coloured flowers, two bedrooms, a patio with a giant almond tree, a well-cultivated garden and a pen where goats, chickens and pigs live peacefully together. The only forbidden animals, not only at Herminia's but in all of Aracataca, are fighting cocks.

Near a large pond is a strange-looking tree which former Indian inhabitants and old people of today call a *mocondo*. It looks like our plane tree, especially its branches. At the end of the branches hang little capsules with five membranous wings, fine and resonant like parchment. Close up they look like lanterns made of greaseproof paper.

When the world was so young that many things didn't even have names, and you had to point to them with your finger, José Arcadio Buendía dreamed that on this spot would be built a town full of life and energy, and houses with walls made of mirrors. He asked the name of the town and in his dream the name he was told had a supernatural resonance: Macondo. But Macondo is also the name of a game played with a twelve-sided dice, which is better suited to the town's random destiny.

It was also José Arcadio Buendía who, around that time, decided the streets would be planted with almond trees instead of acacias, and discovered, without ever revealing how, the way to make those trees eternal. Many years later, to this day, the village is a hotchpotch of cement and wooden dwellings, with zinc roofs. The oldest streets still have almond trees, mutilated and covered in dust, but nobody knows who planted them.

News from the station, Franck is leaving. His little boy has been taken to hospital in France and is in a resuscitation unit.

Carine has set up her hairdressing salon — a chair and a pair of scissors — right on the track. Santi is her first customer. A punk cut. The photo does a world tour.

First Night in Aracataca

At six in the morning, birdsong enters the room with the same effrontery as the mosquitoes during the night. A canary atop an electricity pylon raises his head to emit his high-pitched treble. A slightly deeper trill responds from afar.

The streets are filled with blue tits, *turpiales* and robins. Why does birdsong lead me to the village's barber?

It's a large room. In the middle is a single leather armchair. The seat is already occupied and five or six people are waiting their turn. No they're not, they're there to gossip. I go in and the questions start. Where are these gypsies from, what novelties are they bringing, what do the tattoos mean?

The barber, a man of about fifty, is discussing music with his regulars. They're talking about the Vallenato, the music of the region. They say that the embargo imposed on Cuba by the gringos (they've called them that ever since Mister Brown and Mister Herbert descended on the outskirts of the village with a group of engineers, agronomists, hydrologists and surveyors, and spent several weeks exploring the terrain) has had a big influence on the evolution of Caribbean music. There's less Cuban *son*, less rumba, and too much Dominican merengue. There are technological problems too. Cuban recordings aren't good quality because of the embargo, and we don't know what's happening on the island music-wise.

They complain about the way the Vallenato has developed. Initially, Vallenatos told tales lived by their composers, who also sang them. And now, look at this guy Carlos Vives. He trivialises other peoples' poems. The pioneers of Vallenato didn't sing to entertain people but because they felt the need to express themselves, moved by their own experience. For the barber, the real Vallenato is Rafael Escalano, 'with his tender and nostalgic accordion'. 'He is the intellectual of our popular melodies,' he says waxing lyrical, 'the man who moulded and matured them until they reached that state of grace in which music breathed the air of pure poetry.'

And he tells us the anecdote of the notorious Pancho Rada, aka The Pontiff. One day he was arrested. In prison he got out his accordion and started to tell the story of his own arrest, until the local people demanded his freedom. His captor had to leave town. 'Since then, no singer in the Magdalena region is ever jailed with his instrument; it serves both as a Safe Conduct and Get Out of Jail Free.'

It's my turn, and I've already had time to see how my predecessor fared at the hands of this music-loving Figaro. But I've no desire to cross him. I sit down and submit to his clippers, come what may. He tips the chair back and, without so much as a by your leave, begins to shave me. He's obsessed with the blockade on Cuba, unjust, criminal, imposed by the gringos in the same way they've imposed drug trafficking on the Colombians. 'Why can't we sell coca like we sell guavas?' he asks.

The *turista* and dehydration has taken its toll on our troops. We've all got the runs from a mixture of water and tangerine juice we drank at Madame Herminia's. Aracataca water isn't drinkable. We should have boiled it first. We manage to find recycled water in plastic bottles, but it's impossible to get it down our gullets. In this heat we should be drinking litres of it. Jacquot is taken to hospital. Fidel, Puce, Tom, Manu are all ill. We regret not bringing a doctor on the expedition. Gambit gathers up the medicines we have among us and distributes handfuls of Nivarum. We wonder what will happen in the weeks ahead. The hardest part comes after Aracataca, both climate and food-wise, and in terms of political chaos and violence. Bosconia, Gamarra, Barrancabermeja are all hot spots. What does the month before we reach Bogotá have in store? We begin to fear the worst. Desertion, that is. There are already defections in the ranks. We impose draconian rules. No unbottled water (and even that's not totally safe), shakes with milk not water, no ice, and nothing raw. Only boiled vegetables, rice and hot soup. At this point we discover how delicious Colombian soups and broths are, with their unique variety of vegetables and potatoes.

People are complaining. How is it possible that there's still no water, showers, WCs, electricity? Not everyone can afford the Montpellier. Some of the troupe live on the train and have to wash in local people's houses (always hospitable) or in a mate's hotel room.

The station has become the centre of Aracataca. Three of our new young friends, Judith and her sisters, Estrella and Marisa (fifteen, seventeen and twenty respectively) have only known the station as a sad place. Now it's a hive of activity. People talk, romances bloom. It's often not clear what mouths are saying, but hearts translate the strange words. The girls of Aracataca find this new game amusing: they joke, flirt, tremble, and when night falls they recount their adventures as if it were a dream.

As the *feria* is about to open, Judith arrives in floods of tears. One of her friends, Fagid Cure Graaf (Fagidito), a descendent of one of the first Arabs in Aracataca, has just committed suicide. His parents are separated. Fagidito had phoned his mother in Barranquilla beforehand to tell her he loved her and announce his decision to kill himself. Then, he went to see his father, whom he loved deeply, and during all the emotional upheaval, stole his gun. He took the time to wrap up a silk tablecloth for his ex-future mother-in-law. But when his father rushed into the bedroom, he found Fagidito with a hole in his head. On the bed, a letter for his best friend, who was also his partner in some vague cereal venture. Fagidito swore everlasting friendship and left him his part in the business.

The *feria* begins. In actual fact, Aracataca has been one big party ever since the train arrived. The giant block of ice, that wasn't on show in Santa Marta for technical reasons, has been finished *in extremis*. We'll see it for the first time today.

In front of several thousand people, the exhibits of the

Train of Ice and Fire follow one from each other as if by magic. People file into the stalls, the children touch the ice. And then come puppets, trapezists, poets, local musicians, foreign musicians like the French Lovers.

Later that night, to apocalyptic music, the Yeti-wagon opens and a surrealist vision appears. Masked figures hurl themselves onto the ice and break it into a thousand pieces, enveloped in steam, vapour, smoke and light. It's exactly what's needed to wake Roberto. The dragon rises, his eyes flashing lightning, his mouth spitting flames. His sudden movements excite the crowd. The music goes suddenly quiet, only to break out again. Mano Negra come on stage.

Amazed by so many marvellous inventions, the inhabitants of Aracataca don't know how to show their astonishment. A little girl says the ice makes 'her skeleton tremble', a little boy, more conventionally, says 'it burns'. People queue up to see the ice sculptures, spend hours in front of the Yeti and marvel when Roberto fills the air with roars and fire.

In fact, Roberto now has the role played many years ago in Aracataca by Melquíades' ice. The young, and the not so young, open their eyes wide, go into ecstasies, scream blue murder, and recoil with fear every time Roberto sweeps the station with his piercing eyes and blows ten metres of flame, to a deafening crash of sirens and decibels. A little girl wants to take him home 'so he can get rid of the mosquitoes', another would like him 'to recount the legends of his country'.

No Aracataca resident, however, goes near the tattoo

tent. Those who submit their skin to Tom and Dani's patience are all from Fundación, the neighbouring village. Judith explains that people in Aracataca are terrified of marks on their bodies, and that they try, as far as they can, to hide their scars.

How can we forget the seventeen sons of Aureliano Buendía whom Amaranta accompanied to church one Ash Wednesday? More as a joke than out of conviction, they let themselves be lead to the altar where Father Antonio Isabel drew a cross of ashes on their forehead. When they went home, the youngest tried to wash his forehead and realised the mark was indelible. The same thing happened to his brothers. They tried to scrub it with soap and water, with earth, and finally with pumice stone and bleach, but they couldn't wipe away the cross. Amaranta and all the others at the Mass, however, had no trouble getting rid of theirs. Aureliano's seventeen sons were all killed by bullets hitting that target. Toni and Dani have done their best to sell tattoos you can wash off after four days. Fear of the evil eye is so strongly anchored in their spirits that even Judith refuses to sit with the tattoo guys.

Judith is crying again. A second boy, Leonardo Gómez Acosta, the one Fagidito wrote his farewell letter to, has in turn committed suicide. And he also has left a letter, a few words, for his best living friend. The French Lovers are playing 'Dur de Dormir'. Three young girls are listening.:

'What's your name?'

'Mariluz.'

'How old are you?'

'Twelve.'

'Did you come and welcome us at the station?'

'Yes.'

'Did you sing the Marseillaise?'

'The...what?'

'The French national anthem.'

'Ah, yes.'

'Who taught you?'

'Our priest and our teacher.'

'Did you practice...I mean the choir...very often, for a long time?'

'No, not long, for about three months.'

'Do you like the show?'

'Yes, it's very nice.'

'Did you know Fagidito?'

'Yes, I really liked him. He didn't talk much to grown-ups, but with us little girls he was very affectionate.'

'And what's your name?'

'Estrella.'

'Did you like the show, Estrella?'

'Unbelievable. We've never seen anything like it in Aracataca, it was brilliant.'

'Did you know that long ago Melquíades and his gypsies used to come here with a block of ice?'

'Of course, García Márquez wrote all about it in his novel *One Hundred Years of Solitude*.'

'What do you think about what these gypsies brought this time?'

'Marvellous. García Márquez' dream has finally come true.'

'What impressed you the most?'

'The dragon who spits fire.'

'What about the two boys' suicide?'

'I was at Francisco's house just now. There weren't many people there, just the family. People are out having a good time, but I'll go to the funeral tomorrow.'

'What about you, Mariluz? What did you like best?'

'The dragon.'

'Would you like to take him home?'

'Yes, so my dad wouldn't scold me.'

'And after him, what did you like?'

'The music of the boys who played rock.'

'And you, Estrella?'

'I really like the wagon with flames outside and the cold inside. It was great. And also when they sprinkled the snow and everyone ran away.'

'Did you run?'

'No, I stayed so I could get my face wet.'

Messages in the Office of
Human Desires in Aracataca:

I'd like the Little Lord Jesus to bring my papa to spend
Christmas with me and my mama.

X, 7

My name's Felipe, I'm eight and I dream above all of
having a TV set in my room so I can sit in front of it all
day without being hungry and watch cartoons without my
brothers changing the channel.

Manuel Felipe Cruz, 8

My dream is that there will be no need for children or
teenagers to go hungry. Obviously we have to have pain
in our lives, but not so much.

Franklin Muñoz, 13

How beautiful Colombia would be without war! Here a
man loses his life and leaves a wife and children. A rifle
shot ends an existence, mothers cry for their children,
wives cry for their husbands. No more wars, no more
bombs, no more violence. Why does everything have to
end with a rose on the grave?

Rita Santos, 24

Sunday 28 November
Aracataca in Mourning

I go with Caroline Bourgine of *France Culture* and Sylvie
Véran of the *Nouvel Observateur* to visit the García
Márquez Museum. We get there down a very steep path,
interspersed with swampy puddles, full of bits of bamboo
and cactus. All the roads are the same in Aracataca. We
have to ask the way several times, with the result that
when we finally reach the house/museum we are about
half a dozen people, each informant having joined the
party.

Just like the cathedral in Santiago de Compostela,
where a Baroque facade hides that masterpiece of
Roman art, the Pórtico de la Gloria, here they've built a
sort of hut in front of the house where the Nobel Prize
winner was born. The main room of the museum houses
a statue of an Indian woman with a bow and arrows. She
is Ara, the founder of Aracataca. *Cataca* means 'river of
clear waters'. In one corner is a rather peculiar bronze
bust of García Márquez. A suffocating smell of damp
pushes us on towards the director's office, where we
discover a nude statue of Remedios the Beauty, half
hidden behind a pile of old cardboard boxes.

The house of the writer's father, a telegraph operator

by profession, is behind the museum. It's made of wood, and painted white as a dove. The father had refused to paint it blue to celebrate Independence Day, as the local government official ordered. 'If you've come to create chaos by forcing people to paint their houses blue, you can pack your bags and go back to where you've come from,' said he.

In the middle of the little English garden, surrounded by a lawn (exotic in these parts), is the chestnut tree to which José Arcadio Buendía was tied until his death. It took ten men to detain the old man, twenty to drag him to this gigantic tree, fourteen to tie him to it, where he was left barking in a strange language, a green foam round his mouth.

We take a few photos for Tachia, to whom Gabo dedicated *Love in the Time of Cholera*. We all sign the illustrious visitors' book and then go off in search of the past, so present here.

As we turn into a side street, we come across a small crowd of silent children. In the middle of the group, four kids are carrying a tiny white coffin. Minutes later, back at the hotel, we hear the metallic notes of some distant music, coming nearer and nearer. A procession of young girls, dressed in white, comes into view. Some are playing the triangle, others beat drums. In the middle, a girl is squeezing some oppressive repetitive notes from a xylophone. Now they're right in front of us. Behind them is the coffin of one of the boys who committed suicide. Without histrionics, sobs or tears, the cortege walks on in a dignified manner towards the cemetery.

Leaving Aracataca

Three groups start to form. Those who want to go home, and those who want to see the project through. In the middle, are the waverers who'll follow the active majority.

Santi, Garbancito, Jean-Marc and Kropol, in other words, Mano Negra's drummer, percussionist, and two brasses, are leaving for France this morning. There are multiple and complex reasons for this defection. Classic differences between creators and interpreters, artists and instrumentalists. It's been going on for a long time, it only needed a crisis to bring it to a head.

Some members of Mano Negra enjoy the finished article. For them, the important thing is to improve their performance along the same lines. Others, always on the lookout for the unexpected, are no longer comfortable with guaranteed success.

The break-up happened without histrionics, calmly, almost coldly, but after Aracataca, it will be hard for these eight youngsters to carry on as they were.

Is it the end of the band that galvanised French rock? Maybe not. Together or separately they'll begin again, doing who knows what, but something else.

But for the tour, it's a catastrophe. It comes just when

all the press and the secretary of the AFAA are here. The journalists sniff around, trying to find out what's really going on. Cati is demoralised and disgusted, but she has to put on a brave face for the 'officials'. 'No,' she says, 'it's not serious if some of Mano Negra leave. Manu is staying, so is Tom, and Fidel. They'll all be playing, and the French Lovers are still in.'

I take Guillermo Rodríguez to my barber, who I think deserves to feature on Radio Caracol. My good friend receives us dramatically: 'The hundred years of solitude are beginning today!' he cries, pointing his index finger at the sun. 'It's unheard of in Aracataca. The odd suicide here and there, that's normal. But a stream of motiveless deaths? This is a first.' Do you know what the letters say? 'No, the families don't want to divulge them.' What happened to the third boy? 'He threw himself under a tractor. Fortunately, the driver managed to avoid him. But he's in intensive care. What can we do? It's always the same. If one person is happy, someone else has to suffer. Yesterday, the whole village was happy, but at the price of other families suffering.'

Before the train leaves, a first-year student comes up and sits next to us. He's polite, cultured, and is wearing some fancy tortoiseshell glasses.

'Why do you think García Márquez never came back to Aracataca after he won the Nobel Prize?'

'You mean after he left Colombia? Because he received death threats from extreme right-wing groups, for goodness' sake. And he values his kids' lives.'

Rondelle, the little black singer, has left in a huff of hurt feelings. Jean-Marc refused to let him climb on the prototype of a model helicopter that takes off from rail tracks that he's tinkering with. Rondelle got on the first bus to Santa Marta.

The Vallenato group that greeted us is here to see us off. Friends come to say goodbye. A good hundred other people: the shoemaker, the barber, Judith and her sister Estrella, the staff from the Montpellier. It reminds me to ask, 'Why exactly was the pension called Montpellier?'

'Because the great hero of Colombian football, *El Pibe* (The Kid) Valderrama, played two seasons for that French team.'

We'll send them a postcard of the Eiffel Tower, and another of Montpellier.

'Stay another day! Come back!'

We'll meet again, we'll be back. It's a promise. Sure.

The train pulls away in silence, leaving in the station a smell of dust, that acrid smell that will stay in our minds for ever, inseparable from the memory of our friends in Aracataca.

Tuesday 30 November
Arriving in Bosconia

The landscape between Aracataca and Bosconia is one of the most beautiful imaginable. A vast plain flanked in the distance by bluish hills, covered in luminous forest, dissected by a wide waterway seeking sloping ground, forming islands of bamboo, sandy beaches, shining lakes. The sky, a deep blue, is reflected in the transparent waters.

The first houses in Bosconia begin on the other side of the railway, on arid terrain, covered in a fine layer of dust. They are made of wood, with rusty decrepit tin roofs that let the rain in. There are some people at the station, but not a crowd. We're not surprised, we knew Bosconia wasn't a pushover.

The further away we go from the station, the roads are paved, and the houses less miserable.

Bosconia and the land around it used to be a prosperous agricultural region. But between 1976 and 1982, with the exception of rice, production of its main crops (cotton, sorghum, maize and sesame) was in a parlous state. Cotton production has suffered further setbacks lately due to the massive trade in contraband cotton from Venezuela. Local producers have found it impossible to pay their debts. Many have gone out of business. We see huge areas of land lying fallow, and others have been turned over to cattle again.

Bosconia is also at the crossroads of several smuggling routes: Valledupar to Bucaramanga, the Magdalena plain to Santa Marta, Cartagena and Barranquilla. Clothes, domestic appliances, shoes can be bought by the locals at derisory prices. Nothing for tourists or foreigners, on the other hand.

Ridiculous, the sign at the entrance to the town: 'Welcome to Bosconia, Developing Town.'

We are welcomed with more curiosity and less enthusiasm than in other parts. The military presence on the station platform is even more impressive than at previous stops. That doesn't dissuade little Bosconians from taking liberties, climbing on the wagons, trying to get in the carriages. We have to be especially polite and patient so as not to jeopardise our stay from the outset. A local musician offers to participate in our show. 'With pleasure,' we say, 'but there's no money in it. We're all working for nothing.' He disappears. They must think we're made of money.

They look at us as if we're Martians. We reply to the numerous questions with the usual: we're not political; we're not paid; yes, a crazy thing you do once in your life… But we can see it's not enough. The Ferrovías workers tell us that once a month the guerrillas encircle the town and rob the bank, when it happens to be pay day. It's still a hot spot.

Under these suspicious gazes, the train gang sets to

work. There's an incident with little Dario, another kid Gambit has taken under his wing. The kid is always clinging on to someone, obviously cruelly lacking in affection. The incident happened at the station bar. Jean-Marc offered him a Coca-Cola. A few minutes later the owner asks Dario to pay for it. The kid hasn't time to open his mouth when the idiot goes into his kiosk and comes out brandishing a machete. Some of our guys manage to save Dario's head.

The guard at the Palma de Mallorca hotel where I'm staying isn't surprised. Round here, people like us mean trouble. In darkest Colombia, tattoos suggest homos, ex-cons, druggies, crooks. I should be at the station so they can see there are proper people in the group too.

People like me? I put on a clean shirt, rush to the station and install myself opposite *El Espectador*'s carriage. A few minutes later, I receive a visit from two characters: one looks like a left-wing intellectual, the other has an impassive look, obviously Indian. The intellectual asks what's the purpose 'of all this'?

'All what?'

'The train.'

'None. These lads are idealists who want to have fun and give people a good time.'

'Who finances you?'

'Partly the French embassy, partly Ferrovías. But not much. Nobody gets paid. And everything's free for people.'

'Is the army protecting you?'

'Not at all. We have people protecting our equipment

118

against thieves, but only in the stations. We refuse any official presence.'

'How many are you?'

'Let's see, two or three electricians, the same number of welders, a dozen musicians, quite a few layabouts, some of them journalists, two tattoo artists and some kids along for the ride. About sixty of us in all, without counting the Ferrovías workers.'

The mute says: 'And you, who are you?'

I'd like to ask him a question, but it's not the time to play the stereotypical Galician. So, I roll out my whole CV, even the bit about Chevalier of Arts and Letters, you never know, it might help at tricky moments.

They're impressed.

'Our organisation would like to keep in touch with someone so important.'

'Well, come to the *feria* tomorrow, I'll give you my card.'

Group meeting this evening. How to replace the Mano Negra members who've defected? Difficult. Manu would like to play with the French Lovers but he doesn't know their repertoire. In the end, he'll sing with Fidel and Rondelle, who has come back.

The priest in Bosconia arrives at eight o'clock. 'Couldn't we make people pay and give him the takings to speed up repairs to the church?'

'We're agnostic and apolitical.'

Wednesday 1 December
Fiasco in Bosconia

The evening is a total flop. Firstly, there are no puppets.
The two brothers from the Golden Dragonfly have left.
We miss them. It was a good act to start the show off
gently and prove we were putting children first,
something much appreciated in a country campaigning to
protect childhood (but who allow kids to be assassinated
in the street).

After much petty negotiating, the Vallenato musicians
fail to turn up. The ice cannon has deviated from its
functions. It no longer spouts snow, but battles it out with
ice cubes. As if there isn't enough violence in this place.
But worst of all possible luck! Roberto lies inert. He's
depressed. All attempts to lift him are in vain. It seems the
coil is burnt out.

The House of Light, 'Beat the Goalie', 'Jojo's Egg':
none of the games are working. Catastrophe upon
catastrophe, some bit of cable has stuck in the Ice
Museum and nothing is working. A local group hasn't
turned up, and the Mano Negra musicians who are left
can't get little Rondelle off the stage. Tom, Fidel and
Manu are astonished by the cheek of this kid who thinks
he's 'Tarzan's mother' as they say in Panama.

There are also problems with the trapeze. Germain and Fabou have their own adaptation of Borges' Babylon Lottery method: plenty of tumbles, the public loves it. Usually there's not a single triple jump or death spiral that doesn't end up with a body on the ground. But this time, by not concentrating enough, one of them lets Dédé catch him, or hands grip each other instead of slipping down their sweaty arms. In short, they forget to crack their heads open. There are murmurs of disapproval.

Thank Heavens for the circus, with the arrival in the troupe of a real star of the ring, the Great Ramón, the other one, formerly of the Marseilles Opéra.

He's been mad about acrobats ever since he was a kid. He was barely walking when he and a pal climbed the baptismal font in his local church and, defying laws of gravity and morality, both of them pissed in the holy water. Even more difficult, they accomplished this sacrilegious act holding each other's member. True to his promising debut, Ramón climbs, twists, up, down, round, and as a finale, does the flag act on a long stiff rope.

Fortunately there are the French Lovers, they are asked to do two sets. Still without Xoumoul, Manu does some great numbers with them on guitar. All the same, they can't be expected to fill in for everyone.

Working conditions get harsher and harsher. The station is twenty minutes by foot from the centre, so buying the slightest thing means a long walk under an implacable sun. Several people are paralysed by illness. Wounds get infected, so do recent tattoos even though Tom and Dani always warn customers to protect their tattoos with Vaseline and not to expose them to the sun for two weeks. Everyone says we should have had a doctor on board, or a bit of a pharmacy at least. But we don't. Gambit has collected bits and bobs of medicine, and done a few timid surgical interventions with his penknife.

Diarrhoea continues to take its toll. Bouchon, irreplaceable pivot of the whole show, has got either an intestinal infection or sunstroke, the local doctor isn't quite clear. He injects a whole bottle of physiological serum and tells him to rest. Bouchon falls into a deep slumber.

It looks like your chronicler is plagiarising Stanley's journey to find Livingstone, but there's no plagiarism, no invention, in this journal: he's just plying his odious profession.

Jean-Marc is worried.

'It all started when that bloke left in Santa Marta, the one who didn't lift a finger, spent all his time on the beach and talked a load of rubbish. Some people don't want to commit and insist on having a boss. When I hear that word, my heart sinks. What we have in common, what makes us such a spectacular group, is precisely that we don't want bosses, and even rarer still, we can do without them. If we're united by a dream, Coco's dream, it's not today, not at the first obstacle, that we're going to pack up and leave.'

Dismantling the show is done in a hurry. There's a general feeling of embarrassment, and packing up is more like beating a collective retreat.

Messages in the Office of
Human Desires in Bosconia:

I dream of owning a little bit of land to work and feed my
six children so they'll have a better future.
Eduardo Rojo, 53

My main dream in Colombia that is so unhappy because
of the violence, is that we have peace again, like the
Scriptures tell us.
Franklin Danilo Serpa, 27

I dream of peace for Colombia.
Lilibeth, 16

I wish this plague of drugs would end, that it stops
harming the young people of our country.
Luz Miriam Alvarez, 60

Thursday 2 December
Departure from Bosconia
Death of Pablo Escobar

'You okay, Puce?'

It's eight in the morning. The boys and girls have spent a good part of the night dismantling the circus and stacking it in the wagons.

'Psychologically worn out,' he replies, 'last night was rubbish. Everyone does what the hell they feel like, there's no discipline, no direction.'

'Will you see it through to Bogotá?'

'Don't know. At least, it can't get any worse.'

I wouldn't have been surprised if this adventure had lost its charm for the troupe, discouraged by the huge task still ahead, made even harder by the increasing number of desertions. Besides, hadn't we already reached the high point of the journey, the magical stay in Aracataca?

But not a bit of it. No one is thinking of stopping half-way. True, a lot of people have jumped ship, but the hard core is still here: the French Lovers, Jean-Marc, Jean-Pierre, Isa, Carine, Régis, Manu... Cati thinks the same as Puce. 'When you touch rock bottom, the only way is up.' Some good news, Bouchon is better.

And there's still the train. There, at least, despite the

heat, despite the discomfort, in the train we can rest and the scenery is always superb. Someone has made three or four holes in the water cistern pipes so there's a shower of sorts, and that means they can have a good wash before climbing into the cistern and slipping into the two thousand litres of water; Dédé comes back happy. (The waves made by the speeding train give you the impression of being in your mother's womb. Kids...)

And Garrincha and Sorriso are there to raise our spirits. They're always happy, always smiling, each time morale drops they bring out their instruments and raise it with some *capoeira* drumming.

Having left three hours late, we are now crossing a wide valley of pasture, cattle and palm trees. The guitarists keep playing, and yesterday's troubles seem far away.

Suddenly we get news that Pablo Escobar has died. Sorriso and Garrincha improvise a samba:

Vamos fazer festa	Let's have a party
Ao som do meu cavaquinho	To the sound of my guitar
Ouvi dizer que mataram Pablo Escobar	I heard they killed Pablo Escobar
Pois então vamos constatar em Medellín	So let's find out in Medellín

The plan to go to Medellín, strongly advised against by the embassy, is now definitely out.

Some of the Ferrovías railwaymen are in tears. When we stop at La Gloria, we ask the locals. They're prudent. 'He was a human being, we can't rejoice at his death.' Amid the hurly-burly of the station, people are anxiously watching the television. They can see (admittedly from far away and the images aren't very clear) the corpse of the drug baron on a stretcher. The inhabitants of La Gloria are suspicious. 'Why don't they show him properly?' asks the owner of the café. 'As far as I'm concerned, until I see him with my own eyes, he's still alive.'

Escobar came out of clandestinity and entered legend. Things hadn't been going well for the godfather of the drug trade. While he was in hiding, other traffickers had increased and extended their operations. The Cali cartel, headed by the Rodríguez family – much more discreet but more effective than the Medellín cartel – took over 70% of the coke market, especially in Europe where Medellín had formerly controlled 80%. Escobar and the Rodríguez brothers had already fought for control of the California market. The latter had taken the lion's share, but this didn't stop them planning to assassinate their rival in March, 1992.

Escobar's popularity came from his peasant origins, the myth of his generosity to his own kind, and the fact that he had fought governments of greater or lesser levels of corruption for over ten years. But, above all, because he had taken on the United States.

With the Cold War over, the anti-drug war became a pretext for the Americans to militarise the continent, without waging war on drug consumption inside their own territory. But the war on coca may well be lost, just as the wars in Vietnam or Somalia were lost. As long as the US spends a mere 5% of the money devoted to the drug war on promoting alternative crops, the Andean peasant farmer will cultivate coca and support the traffickers. As long as the South American elites indulge in corruption, nepotism and privilege, the road is open for the new bosses of the cartels. And no amount of fanfares celebrating Escobar's assassination will prevent a single kilo of coke from entering Europe and the US.

Ensconced between the Sierra Nevada and the River Magdalena, the town of Gamarra has been waiting for the train to arrive for several hours. Late, as usual, we are welcomed by two crowds: one of friends (we passed through here on our way to Santa Marta), and the other of mosquitoes. There is also a profusion of soldiers in combat gear. It's a proper regiment with orders to protect us in the town, and accompany us to Barrancabermeja. Escobar's death merits certain precautions.

The workmen painting the station in our honour haven't finished. They're still plastering but they'll be done before we leave. Promised.

New and heated discussion among the group. Do we have to accept the company of the soldiers? For some, it's unacceptable since it goes against the spirit of the project. For others, either we accept military protection, or we stop the tour *motu propio*. Interminable discussions, until we notice that Gambit has missed the train in Bosconia. Finally, Cati gives in. Some soldiers will stay in the train to prevent theft. Others will stay in their barracks, on the outskirts of the town. But there's no question of them accompanying us.

Friday 3 December
Gamarra

It's twenty-four hours since we had news of Gambit. The station master has phoned Bosconia, Chiriguana, La Gloria, all the stations and hotels along our itinerary. We're starting to get worried. What should we do? Inform the military?

The *Vanguardia Liberal* in Barranquilla, brings out a special issue on the death of Escobar. Headline: 'Chief Goes to his Grave...What next for the Mafia?' I show the photo to the station master. 'It's Pablito,' he says. 'His death won't solve anything, on the contrary. Now it's serious. They'll react with violence.' He passes the paper to his friends. They all talk about Pablito with affection. They're not convinced by the photo.

We try to phone France, to reassure our families. No chance. The only line in Gamarra has been occupied by Radio Caracol.

Gambit still isn't back. His pals start work on the *feria* again. Roberto's mechanism has been mended. He is being got ready. In the evening, the television shows Pablito's funeral. The coffin is torn from the pall bearers by his devotees, over 5,000 people from the poorest parts of Medellín. 'We see, we sense/Pablito is present' shouts

the crowd to the rhythm of 'The people united/will never be defeated'. The slogan of the victims of Pinochet's repression adapted for all circumstances. But it's painfully clear what happened to the Popular Unity experiment in Chile: the Christian Democrats are in power with Frei's son as president and Pinochet pulling the strings. The people, united or not, have always been defeated, even by those who purport to liberate them.

They want to see, to touch their Pablito. 'There's God, Jesus Christ, and him,' we hear someone say on the TV. The most amazing thing is that mainstream television seems to be contributing to the deification of this *capo* of all the mafias.

There's a profusion of testimonies from among his protégés, who evoke his memory with fervour and passion. Our ears are filled with his good works, we're shown images of Medellín's shanty towns, before and after. Just ten years ago, 2,500 families were squatting on a municipal refuse dump beside the River Aburrá, forgotten by politicians and God. They shared the rubbish and the smells with rats. Scabies, respiratory diseases and malnutrition may have left their mark on the bodies of the inhabitants, but all of them remember Pablito getting out of a Renault 18 to bring them rice, cooking oil, and milk. In 1983, Escobar gave these poor devils 1,000 keys to the same number of nice clean houses, with parks, schools, swimming pool and sports ground, built on a piece of land he owned.

To even things up, the small screen then shows the families of the *capo*'s victims. All high society. Widows of military men, judges, ambassadors, who expressed their dissatisfaction. Has justice really been done by Escobar's death for millions of poor Colombians?

The TV accompanies the images of the coffin with the funeral march from *Siegfried*. We can hardly believe our eyes, or our ears. But it's perhaps not as innocent as that. Is it the sublime recuperation of the nascent myth? What if the propertied classes manage to appropriate the idol of the shanty towns? They've certainly phagocytosed the slogan 'The people united/will never be defeated'.

Each time we arrive at a station, the team needs forty-eight hours to get the show ready. Gamarra is no different. Watched by astonished Gamarrans, Régis, Jean-Pierre, Fred and the whole gang start manoeuvring iron girders, unloading tons of material, plugging in the electrics and erecting the acrobats' frame. Gambit turns up, meanwhile, a bit shamefacedly, in a taxi. He tells a rather confused tale in which some Helvetic lady seems to have played a part. Unearthing a Swiss in Bosconia, is something only Gambit could do.

Saturday 4 December
First Night in Gamarra

Headline in the Barrancabermeja newspaper: 'The Myth Buried'. Underneath is a photo of a tragic beauty; Escobar's sister on the drug baron's coffin. In the background is the shadow of a cross. Antigone and Polynice. Irene Papas in the Sophocles tragedy. This Reuters photo is too beautiful not to be a montage.

Ever since Santa Marta we've heard nothing but Vallenato, served up in all possible flavours. Salsa, samba, tango don't exist. The people here are deaf to any other type of music. Nothing but Vallenato. We're sick to death of Carlos Vives. The barber in Aracataca was right. The Vallenato has lost its soul, it's musically bland now, a simple monotonous rhythm.

But the Vallenato is the only downside to the main square in Gamarra. Otherwise, it's bright and open, shaded only by almond trees. The locals have set up all sorts of stalls selling fruit juices – papaya, *zapote*, guava, passion fruit – all dangerously delicious. With the water and ice, we'll fall victim to the *turista* again.

When we sit in any of the café terraces, we're immediately surrounded by dozens of kids, teenagers, old men and soldiers. Wherever we are, even in the most intimate of places, they come and observe us with touching curiosity. It's uncomfortable, we feel we have to say something, '*hola*, hello, hi,' anything. That's the beginning of the end. They bombard us with every type of question imaginable, the answers to which are often obvious. We have to get rid of our cultural references, improvise a new language, invent coherent explanations for things we've never sought to understand ourselves.

Yesterday afternoon, Franck Ericson of *L'Express*, Philippe Ariagno of AFAA, and myself, came across a couple of Indians in Aguachica, a village about ten minutes from Gamarra. Here people don't talk in terms of kilometres, they calculate distance in time – hours, minutes – and it's up to you to figure out if they mean on foot or by mule. We'd expected to see Indians in Aracataca and buy their *mochilas*, those woven wool bags with geometric designs. But in the end they didn't come down from the mountains. So, in fact, these were the first indigenous people we'd seen in Colombia.

In a nation where 75% of the inhabitants are of Amerindian or African descent, but where indigenous roots are far from admitted by everyone, *indio* is still an insult. Excluded, rejected, displaced for centuries, the indigenous peoples of Colombia have retained their considerable diversity. There are about a hundred ethnic groups in all, speaking seventy-five languages grouped in a dozen linguistic families: Chibcha, Carib, Arawak, Tukan... Having retreated into the most inaccessible areas, and very dispersed, the Indians are divided into two main categories. On the one hand, there are the traditional jungle communities (the Yaguas in the Amazon, the Embera or Katios in the Chocó) who are self sufficient and live off fishing, hunting, growing manioc or bananas. On the other hand, the farming communities whose cultural traditions are disappearing and are more or less integrated into mainstream economic life: Arawaks in the Sierra Nevada, Guambianos in the Cauca highlands, Sinús in the north, Paeces in Tierradentro.

The main square in Gamarra starts filling up around midday. The first *chivos*, those multicoloured buses overflowing with people, arrive at ten from Aguachica and other neighbouring villages. The square is crawling with kids. Why is it you see nothing but kids in Colombia, where are the old people? They install themselves on the esplanade, turning it into a bullring like an Andalucian town.

The locals have come without really knowing what kind of show to expect, nor what time it starts. Those who came in the morning leave disappointed, so that at six in the afternoon the square is half empty again.

Several sideshows aren't ready again. Some of the Ice Museum statues have melted, the snow cannon isn't firing... Roberto is well, despite everything. But when he faces the wind, a gust blows out the wick and the flame-throwers have to get dangerously near his mouth to relight the gas.

There are no local groups. Impossible to get any without paying. It looks as if the Colombian bands want to recover the Bogotá gold they must think stayed in Paris with the Exhibition.

The French Lovers replace Mano Negra with brio. Manu and Fidel join them to play *trashguinguette*, which prevails in the realm of the Vallenato. Having played in the first half, they come on stage again to close the show, and have to do several encores.

The audience refuses to go home. They stay in the square till midnight. It's the first time, the station master tells us, that so many different types of people have come to the square without anyone being killed.

Messages in the Office of Human Desires in Gamarra:

I dream of a very big train travelling in peace with all Colombia's children on board and we can see shows about love where people are affectionate to us.

Erika Johana Quintero, 14

I dream of travelling in a train.

Ana González, 12

My biggest dream, please, is for you to give me an encyclopaedia.

Ivon Julio Vega, 15

Please, let the hope of peace return, especially for Colombia. We need it so very much. Please, may the armed groups put down their machine guns, they do such a lot of harm to people. We don't want any more war or hate.

Antonio Parra, 32

Is This the End?

A dozen or so of us are sleeping on the floor of a school on the outskirts of Gamarra. Not far away, the mountains are crawling with guerrillas. Since our soldier-guards were exiled to outlying neighbourhoods on Cati's orders, there is unexpected promiscuity: the school turns out to be their dormitory too. Although these little soldiers, barely old enough to shave, are not very talkative, we have made friends. They treated us with suspicion at first but softened when we started being nice to them. How do they get on with the guerrillas? No problem, if we don't go after them. Are there a lot of people from Gamarra in the hills? Some of their friends are up there but they wouldn't like to meet them. And the army? They get food and a certain status. Girls go for it.

They'd love Tom or Dani to tattoo them, but they don't have the money. Don't worry, they can get scarred for life for free. Not on the chest, nor on the forehead. On the shoulder, it's painful but not fatal.

That night we take a little soldier to the Tattoo Tent. It's a branch of the salon Dani has in the centre of Bogotá.

Dani is the strangest of all the charming specimens gathered on the train. From Brussels, about forty, he's a

Mephistopheles with a constant grin. After finishing Brussels School of Fine Art, he thought he'd travel around Latin America. It happens all the time. So does falling madly in love with a beautiful Colombian. To win the heart of Amparo and bread for his forthcoming family, Dani decides to go into the only profession as yet inexistent in Colombia: tattooer, or tattooist, or rather 'dermographic artist', a name that works better with conservative mentalities. He learns the rudiments and opens a salon in La Candelaria. The press gives this eccentric Belgian free publicity, and he has already tattooed the crème de la crème of the capital.

Dani went even crazier during Mano Negra's visit to Bogotá last year. When he heard in November that the band was back, with the train, and that the train was leaving the following day, he told his wife, 'I'm packing my bag, Amparo. There'll be no more tattoos in Bogotá this year.'

He tells us, 'Colombians are beginning to appreciate artistic tattooing. They've been doing it for ages, but it was bad tattooing, badly done, nothing but marine or military themes.'

'Is it true it's frowned upon?'

'Yes, that was true for a long time, but now it's become fashionable. People who get tattooed these days aren't on the fringes, they're people who want to be up with the latest craze.'

'How many tattoos have you done in the train?'

'About seventy.'

'What are the most popular designs?'

'Quite a lot of Jesus, lots of Rock stuff, skulls, dragons, Robertos. In fact, Jesus and Roberto are top of the list.'

'Is it mostly young people?'

'Yes, lots of soldiers. But people of forty and fifty too.'

'How much does a tattoo cost on the train?'

'Four times less than in my salon in Bogotá. And we often do them for free, Tom and me, it depends on the person's pocket. The other day a guy came to Tom and offered him a revolver in exchange for a Botero, on his arm I suppose. He hadn't any cash and he put the gun on the table, loaded. He was drunk. Tom said he needed a picture of the Botero. If he came back with one he'd do the tattoo, no problem. The guy didn't come back.'

'Is it a good experience, doing tattoos on the train?'

'It's brilliant, a good vibe. People ask for tattoos in unbelievable places. It's as if doing them in the train takes away their inhibitions.'

'Has anyone asked you to write "souvenir of Constantinople"?'

'No, nobody. I tattoo everywhere, except dicks.'

Fringe, maybe, but one has one's principles.

Dani tattoos you without your realising it. Mainly because he's so charming. You sit down beside him, left sleeve rolled right up, and he sticks the drawing on like a transfer. It still seems like fun, you only start shaking when he starts rummaging in his needle box. You weren't going to let him, you weren't going to agree, the joke has gone on long enough. But he's already drawing the outline of a star with that electric thing. What's it called? The dermograph. It pricks, but nothing like the old

138

techniques: animal bones, fish bones, sharpened stones, bamboo, or tapping with a tiny mallet (oriental style). That's it, I'm done for. It's the point of no return. I watch stoically as he draws the palm of a hand, and then the fingers. Now and again Dani cleans the drawing, or rather the wound, with antiseptic. Everything's confused. What the fuck is he doing to me? I can't stop, about fifteen curious faces are watching me, I have to experience everything on this trip: hunger, thirst, danger, tattoos... It's starting to take shape, the fingers, the tips of the star. It's there for a lifetime. 'What will your wife say?' My wife! Stop, Dani! Too late, it's already indelible. Apparently the Germans have found a way to remove it, but it leaves a burn. Otherwise it's cosmetic surgery and that costs an arm and a leg. Hold your breath. It's not a bed of roses. And you watch, I watch, Dani's pitiless figures colouring the star red with thousands of little pinpricks. Gulliver attacked by Lilliputians. I should call on my compatriot the Duke of Alba to give this giant (Walloon or Flemish?), in any case my torturer, a plaque in the Grande Place in Brussels next to Egmont, whom the Duke beheaded. Manu, the photographer, takes some snaps for posterity. Actually, it's starting to look good, the black hand on a red star, especially since you don't see many red stars these days, they're out of fashion, but they'll be back, time is circular and history progresses in a spiral. Cheer up. Seeing Dani so proud of his masterpiece makes me want to hug him. It's finished, the audience applauds, and the Mano Negra logo is stuck to my skin till my dying day.

We come back to the school to sleep. At around five in the morning, we hear shots. There's shooting everywhere. My Paris nightmares have come true. It's inevitable, the guerrillas would be mad not to attack us, we're such a spectacular and easy prey. Sorriso starts shouting in Portuguese and I barricade myself in my sleeping bag. It goes on for two or three minutes. Then quiet, the muffled buzz of the forest returns, bucolic sounds like canaries, monkeys chattering, snakes hissing.

At dawn, we think we hear the sound of tragedy. We open our eyes cautiously, the door is ajar. We tiptoe to it and peep out. Sleeping soldiers, leaning against the schoolhouse walls, or stretched out on the ground, their guns littering the yard. At Gladys' house, next door, some of the train are arriving for breakfast.

Gladys is the nurse in Gamarra. She feeds us for a modest fee. Her sister Libia combines two functions of the highest order: headmistress and police inspector. In order words, she's top man in Gamarra. This pretty young woman commands the tender Rambos protecting us and lends us places to sleep. 'What happened last night? There was gunfire, were any soldiers killed or injured?' No. Everything's calm, just my imagination playing tricks. The shots I heard, explains Libia after quizzing a little soldier, were fireworks in our honour, howler monkeys, the neighbour's goats. The soldiers sleep on.

One of the train guys hobbles in. We all know each other by sight, but often can't put names to faces. Or rather we learn them in the course of a short conversation and forget them instantly. This lad's name is Nono. He shows us his right foot, it's swollen and purple. He needs to see a doctor, it's an emergency. But Gamarra doesn't do emergencies, nor doctors for that matter. Gladys says there's a healer who lives nearby. Half an hour later she takes us to see Angel, he's the village *sobador*. The verb *sobar* could be roughly translated as manipulate, so let's call him Gamarra's manipulator. He's about sixty, with white hair and a sardonic expression that suggests pre-Hippocratic knowledge.

'That looks very bad,' he says with a tender smile. He goes into his house and comes back with an ointment. Indifferent to the gestures of pain, he massages the tendons, separates the toes, manipulates Nono's foot. The session lasts half an hour. Nothing's broken, but the tendons are damaged. Nono has to come back tomorrow at seven.

Cati and Fernando ask to see me. We have a clandestine meeting in the train.

'The tour can't go on,' begins Cati. 'I've no money. Some sponsors haven't come up with the goods. Radio Caracol is offering us publicity but we have to find the advertisers. I'd need a good week to get them. And anyway, the atmosphere in the team is horrible. I'd rather stop now than expose myself to a shameful stampede later on. One more show tomorrow, then straight to Bogotá. I need the bit of money I have left to pay lawyers. I'll have problems with broken contracts and I'll have to pay Avianca for changing the return flights.'

That seems reasonable to us. We're exhausted and with half the team gone, the workload falls to the rump that is left.

On top of that, there are all the petty individual conflicts that turn into group conflicts: the trapezists clan versus the free base club, the show versus the fair, the passenger-carriage versus the prod-carriage; the cliques are all pulling in their own direction.

Team meeting for tonight's show. A timetable is established. At five o'clock, 'Beat the Goalie' and 'Jojo's Egg' must be open. (This latter game was suggested and built by Jorge, the Ferrovías' electrician. It's a tree trunk with a hole in the middle. Inside is an egg that punters try to hit with a metal ball). At half past five, the Ice Museum opens. At six, the trapezists, followed by Roberto, and after him the polar bear.

'Bear?'

'Yes, our magnificent polar bear,' says Coco.

'Why hasn't he been brought out before, instead of having violent ice battles that are totally superfluous in this country?'

'Because…'

No one wants to get in the bear skin. Apparently it's suffocating in there, you risk fainting and blackouts. Nono forces Raphael to do it.

'And the music?'

'Fidel, Rondelle and Manu will go on after Roberto.'

'Impossible. Rondelle's gone,' says Manu, looking sad.

The kid has left in another huff. Manu misses him. He'd promised him a meteoric music career. He'll be back, Manu, cheer up.

Darío is still with us. There's no way we can get him to go back to Santa Marta. We've tried reasoning with him, telling him that in Bogotá he'll have to sleep in the street, prostitute himself, have his hand chopped off by the capital's 'social cleansers'. Nothing doing. He's determined to follow us. Each time there's a train going down to Santa Marta, the little guy disappears. He obviously guesses we want to send him back. Worse still, he's a model for other kids who try to sneak on the train. We see them lying in wait. But how can we stop them? They're very inventive, not scared of anything. On his first attempt to board, Darío hung on to the bottom of the train as it was going, risking his life. Did he know Gambit had a soft heart?

We can see by Rondelle and Darío's behaviour that they have a certain class. Panache. Style. One of their favourite jokes shows they fancy themselves a bit. It goes like this.

A *gringo* arrives in Bogotá and has his wallet nicked on the bus. When he gets home, he says, 'I'm never going to Bogotá again, they're pretty smart there…' So his friend bets, 'Let's see if they can outsmart me!' He comes to Bogotá. When he gets to Tenth Avenue, he asks a street kid to shine his shoes and says, 'Are you smart?' 'Sure,' replies the kid. The *gringo* laughs and says, 'If you're so smart, try nicking my wallet without stopping shining.' 'Okay,' replies the kid, 'if you suck me off without bending your head.'

Today it's going like clockwork. The French Lovers are on form. So is Roberto.

The idea of building Roberto came from Gérard Guyon, author of *The Illustrious Burattini Family*. The finished article was built by Jean-Marc Mouligné. But it was the Colombian director Carlos Rojas who did the first sketches of this monster who looks like he's straight out of *Jurassic Park*.

'Not at all. He's the exact opposite. Spielberg had the benefit of the most sophisticated technology, whereas we used Third-World methods. Luckily we had Jean-Marc, he managed to forge a personality for Roberto out of scrap iron. We collected all the bits lying around the Ferrovías workshops at El Corzo.'

'Why did you choose a Dragon-Iguana?'

'A traditional dragon wouldn't have meant anything in Colombia, especially in the Magdalena Medio. An iguana, on the other hand, is typical of the Magdalena river banks and the region around it. No need to look to Chinese or Western dragons for a model. I got my inspiration right here. Design students from the Fine Arts School in Bogotá began doing outlines and sketches, not only for Roberto, but for the whole train. We came up with a kind of very complicated automaton that walked with a system of pneumatic jacks, which was too technologically advanced for us. That's when Jean-Marc stepped in.'

'Does the public's response make your efforts worthwhile?'

'Absolutely. Everyone loves Roberto, especially the children.'

'Do they come and tell you?'

'Absolutely, straight away they ask us questions about Roberto. Whether he's alive. He has become quite a legend.'

'How do you think your fellow Colombians see the train?'

'It brings them a fiesta, a bit of joy and peace, things you don't get much of in the regions we're going through, zones very affected by the violence and deplorable social conditions. For me, we've succeeded when someone, young or old, comes up to us with tears in his eyes, and thanks us for coming because they've never seen their village so full of people, getting together peacefully. Nor have they ever seen a show like this.'

'They've got TV.'

'Not all of them. Besides they never dreamed they'd see performers in the flesh, performers from another continent, who talk to them, and let them touch them.'

'So we shouldn't stop?'

'No way! It would be criminal!'

Messages in the Office of
Human Desires in Gamarra:

I dream of having a motorbike!
Shirley Quintero, 18

I want the railway to work well so it will bring peace to
Colombia, and I want the economy to treat us better.
Crisanto Buenahora, 14

I wish my father would come home, and that the
violence ends so I can be happy and have a career.
Yazmín Teresa Rozo, 13

Monday 6 December
We Carry On!

Second session of kino-sorcery. Nono arrives at Glady's house dragging his foot. We go and see Angel. Nono has worked all night, first during the show and then dismantling it. He's still in pain, and his foot is still swollen.

'Not important,' says the manipulator.

I've come as Nono's interpreter. Señor Angel's granddaughter asks him all sorts of questions. I translate. Astonished that she doesn't understand what Nono is saying, she asks me at what age people learn to speak in our country.

The group's morale is at its lowest ebb. Two technicians have gone to Bogotá to fetch their girlfriends. Most people are having a lie in, the usual handful are working. The atmosphere is getting gloomier, nerves are reaching breaking point. That's how Nono hurt his foot. By fooling around fighting. Instead of kicking his friend, Nono kicked the engine.

Ana, the Spanish girl, and her boyfriend Jacquot, return from Aguachica. There were seven murders there today, and three the day before, all because of petty thieving – a watch, earrings, a little money. Ten dead in three days in a small provincial town. From now on, we'll be going to Aguachica in groups.

So, it's possible Gamarra will be our last stop. Those who do the work are fed up, and the lazy bums want to go home. But from the outside, it's very difficult to say which are which: two hours under the burning sun is already a good day's work under union rules in our countries.

Impromptu meeting in the station bar. Cati announces she is leaving. Cati is responsible for the Prod, she has all the contacts and the little money that's left. Without her, the ship goes down.

'I'm leaving and that's that. I'm fed up with meetings where nothing's resolved. Besides, there's no money left. If anyone wants to take over the production, I'll pass them all the contacts.'

Stormy session, direct personal accusations which I won't go into here since they're soon to be forgotten: one's not doing his job, one gave up the ghost long ago, a third and fourth go to Bogotá to get their girlfriends and leave their mates in the shit.

'Individually you're all great, but I hate the group,' bursts out Cati.

Someone replies: 'It's because there's no leadership, no artistic direction!'

'I can't sell our Camelot to advertisers,' retorts Fernando. 'They pay for a ski slope, for Mano Negra, for snowstorms, and we don't do any of that. They could ask for their money back.'

Fernando is Brazilian. He's managing the project with

Cati. He started out as a journalist with Globo TV, then he was the director of the Fundicão Progreso in Rio. His role is to get commercial companies to help us, with goods and services. His job needs tact, understanding Colombian sensibilities (Mobil Oil participation was discarded), trying not to lose his head in the labyrinths of Colombian bureaucracy. Colombia is a paradise for jurists and lawyers: a bottle contains 'about' half a litre of mineral water, a box has 'approximately' forty matches, precautions to be taken to avoid Kafkaesque trials; a person's word is worth nothing, devalued as it has been by smarmy politicians and their never-ending lies. Colombians are stuck in the mire of administrative jargon that only benefits the *tinterillos*, sort of public scribes who sit with their typewriters at the ready in front of all government buildings, filling out tax returns, pension applications, social security forms. This pile of paperwork is the only face of the government the majority of Colombians ever see. Their only knowledge of the State is the law of *el embudo*, the funnel, 'the wide end for them, the narrow end for us'. Otherwise known as 'one law for the rich, another for the poor'.

'I don't want any more herpes or haemorrhages,' Cati continues, 'we stop the tour, go back to Bogotá, and I hire a lawyer to help us limit the damage with our partners.'

The refusenik front reacts, Jean-Marc, Jean-Pierre, Manu, Dani the Tattoo, the French Lovers. They insist on a real meeting with everybody, including the Colombians, the Ferrovías railwaymen.

Okay, this evening at seven o'clock.

It's Jean-Marc, the crazy scrap-iron man, who leads the debate. First, he asks those who want to quit to catch the first bus to Bogotá. Hands up anyone who does? Nobody. Who wants to continue? A good half.

Cati insists. 'We've no more money and no way of getting any. I'm exhausted, and I'm sick of the lot of you. For me, it's over.'

'You can't pack it in just like that.'

'Can't I? Bouchon fell apart, and I have the right to quit. You too, Manu. Four of your group have gone home and you've stopped playing.'

'Yes, but I'm still here. I do other things.'

Jean-Marc proposes that people give up their per diem, 7,000 pesos a day (about 50 francs). Carried. But the debts are so enormous that it doesn't resolve much.

'Besides,' continues Cati, 'there's a disaster waiting to happen. Yesterday, Fabrice gave the flame-thrower four times too much electricity. Carlos burned himself with aluminotherm, a thousand degrees on his arm. No, thanks.'

'Cati can't take decisions alone. *Locovía* is all of us,' Jean-Marc butts in. 'There's no boss, and there's not going to be one. We don't want a saviour, and that goes for production too. Let's make it as much fun as we can, let the fatigue and hardship of the week ahead give us the chance to stop all the backbiting, intrigues, cabals, gossiping and petty aggression that's going on. First, there's work to do, and plenty of it. It's a hard slog. And second, we tend to forget that we're living the craziest adventure of our lives.'

Tomasín, Manu and your chronicler act as interpreters for the Ferrovías workers who want to join in the discussion.

First, Jorge: 'If you stop now, it will be an insult to Colombia. They're waiting for us in Barrancabermeja. It'll be dangerous to creep past the station like thieves, without stopping. We won't go through alone, that's for sure. The people there don't mess about. They'll be furious, and it's the most violent place in Colombia.'

Then Diablito: 'You don't realise the hope this train brings to the villages we go through. It makes them dream of peace, of developing the country. Disappointing them will do a lot of harm. It would have been better not to start.'

It's the voice of the people. No need to vote. We pass straight to reorganising the show. We have to improve it, put on different acts. A third railwayman gives us a lesson in *mise en scène*:

'You don't all understand Spanish, so you don't know how people react. I can tell you that the audience is always very happy. So, now's not the time to improvise. Just make sure everything works properly. The queue for the Ice Museum is too long. Put a couple of people on to control it. Same goes for the Light Tent. It's a children's show. Explain to adults, make them let the kids go first. And most important, the train should arrive at the station with the last carriage in flames and with music blaring. It's the best way to respond to the warm welcome.'

All that's left is to group people into teams. The railwaymen offer to lend a hand. The discussion is practically over. Before we leave, Diablito speaks again:

'Careful, everyone. No partying after the show in Barrancabermeja. Gamarra is the sticks, but we'll be in a residential area in Barranca. And there, people don't call the police, they call the *sicarios*.'

He means the paid assassins, the hit men. We take his point. We agree to meet tomorrow at ten.

To get to our dormitory, we have to pass the soldiers. They're all asleep. Some on the ground, some in hammocks with mosquito nets. Their rifles are still littering the patio. Lucky for them no guerrillas are about to give them a fright!

Tuesday 7 December
Nono Exorcised

Nono should have been here at eight o'clock to see the healer. He's late, he apologises, but he doesn't want to continue this magic therapy. The pain is getting worse. I go and see Señor Angel alone. He suggests making the sign of the cross over the poorly foot while saying some prayers. It even works with cows, and at long distance. In other words, the owner of the cow describes where the animal is: 'go out of the house, first road on the left, then first right after the post, carry on for ten minutes, you get to a dirt road leading to a palm plantation, there the cow is chained to a chestnut tree, like José Arcadio Buendía.' Señor Angel can miraculously send a prayer to the cow.

'Fantasic! But why didn't he suggest that to start with?'

'We only invoke God as a last resort.'

'Okay then, let's do it!'

In any case, like the cows, Nono doesn't have to know about the therapy that's curing him. And it doesn't cost him anything. I pay for the previous manipulation and massages, and in advance, for the divine intervention.

The ten o'clock meeting is exemplary. It should have been like this from the start, daily. Certain people have been made responsible for distributing the workload.

There will be a general rehearsal at six. Dinner at eight, and then, on stage.

Final question: what to do with the kids? Rondelle hasn't come back, but the immovable Darío is still here and two other kids are trying to join the expedition. If it continues, we'll be taking an orphanage to Bogotá. If we try to leave them at the station, they'll only get on board again. Let's leave the station master to sort it out. He can keep them until the train has gone. Today, 7 December, is the start of the Christmas festivities in Colombia. The Ferrovías guys collect money to buy candles. That evening the neighbourhood round the station is carpeted in lights. They look like fireflies.

Leave Gamarra, Arrive in Barranca

Fireworks, fireworks, and more fireworks. Every day, starting with our arrival, in the early morning, and now for our departure: always fireworks. Libia and Amparito, her little sister, are crying. Will we see each other again one day? Of course, we'll send you the photos we've taken. Will we be getting a luxury train? Well, yes, Ferrovías has plans to put certain trains back in service now that it has been privatised. But from there to building the American Express is a long haul, my girl.

We get the feeling the younger one wants to follow us. One word of encouragement and she'll be on the train like a street kid. But what would we do with her in Paris? We're aware of the hopes we raise among these forgotten people of Colombia. Yet we're all so busy with our petty bickering, our settling of scores, wondering whether we'll spend Christmas with our families, will we stop the tour, will we go on!

Little Darío was put on a goods train to Bosconia earlier in the day. Our guardian angels with machine guns saw to it that he was shut in an office with the two other kids prowling around the station. But the train still has squatters. Now we have a Colombian hippie. She spends her time threading bead necklaces to sell in the *ferias*. Then she spends the money in ways that could be dangerous for us. She should be packed off with the street kids. But we're not cops, are we?

We leave Gamarra at eleven thirty, after almost a week. We're leaving lots of friends, lots of hopes and, last but not least, the station newly painted with Miró-style rings and colours: red, blue and yellow.

But the girls are right. Out of sight, out of mind. Next month in Paris, when we develop the films, their names will come back to us. And maybe we'll send the photos with a postcard of the Eiffel Tower.

Twenty-five kilometres from Gamarra to Barranca-bermeja, ten hours scheduled for the journey. But at four in the afternoon, Diablito announces that we're half an hour away from our destination. So, we stop to light the fire-wagon, put garlands and multicoloured streamers round the engine, set up the sound system and blast out the jingle Tom has composed for us. Patrick is in charge of turning the resolutions we took the day before yesterday into reality, and making sure the train arrives in a blaze of glory. The effect is spectacular. The people of Barranca are amazed. Why didn't we do it in Santa Marta, Aracataca, Bosconia?

Because the railwaymen had not taken over the artistic direction.

Thursday 9 December
Barrancabermeja

Headlines of the Barrancabermeja *Vanguardia Liberal* this morning. 'Forty-four Thousand Families Without Electricity in the Province of Santander.' But our hotel has a phone and a fax. We can phone Paris reverse charge. We've travelled from the candlelit age to the electronic age. In this town, one of the most important in Colombia, cocks crow at six in the morning in the patio of a luxury hotel. The offices of Ecopetrol, Colombia's largest oil refinery, are surrounded by shanty towns.

So here we are in modern Colombia, inexplicable in its complexity and contrasts. A country whose riches are lauded by economic experts from Harvard and Yale, yet is hostage to the monstrous phenomena of street kids and hired killers.

In Barranca we find riches and poverty, strong union militancy and an active presence of all the armed groups that devastate the country. A huge banner, spanning the main street, invites: 'Private Defence. Join Our Action.'

At the same time, Barranca has a long Liberal tradition. The town declared itself a 'Popular Republic' in 1948, during the terrible violence that followed the assassination of Jorge Eliécer Gaitán. It has become a cliché to call Barrancabermeja the capital of abstract, gratuitous violence, lodged in the genes of its inhabitants.

The people indigenous to Barranca, the Yariguis, were the most aggressive tribe of the region at the time of the Spanish Conquest. Any enemy who fell into their hands was cut into pieces, grilled and eaten. Their thighs were hung in Yarigui huts like smoked hams. There was oil in abundance, and before battles Chief Pipaton would smother himself in oil to give himself courage. So much blood was spilt that the Spaniards called this land *bermeja* (red). Hence Barrancabermeja – Red Cliff – although the indigenous name was Tora, 'summit that dominates the river'.

The atavistic violence in Barranca began again at the turn of the century with the rush for the black gold. Like in Texas, people from all corners and classes converged on the region. Any cultural identity the town might have had was slowly erased. Oil money brought new European fashions and novelties via the port of Barranquilla up the River Magdalena. Barranca had cosmopolitan whorehouses filled with Italian and French prostitutes. Other regions of Colombia developed more slowly, even harmoniously, with musical instruments that created a folkloric tradition, like the harp in the Llanos or the accordion on the Atlantic Coast. But the new rich of Barranca imported mechanical pianolas from abroad to enliven the nights in the cabarets and brothels. And that stifled the creation of a culture of their own.

As for the train, it's bliss. Monday's psychodrama was a success, everyone loves one another. Even your chronicler, who started the trip with so many prejudices, finds himself two or three times a day hugging the girls, Anne-Marie, Charlotte, Carine…and especially the boys, Nono, Gambit, Captain, Manu…as if they were all his children. The people of Barranca could not be gentler or nicer and, carried away by the euphoria, we decide to offer them two shows.

The gypsies spread out round the town. They know there are neighbourhoods it's best to avoid, that the town is swarming with groups whose mission it is to rid the streets of undesirables – the destitute, the unproductive. They're everywhere, these groups. Their names often evoke their prey. Medellín has the largest number, many devoted to eliminating youngsters in the shanty towns: 'Complete Cleansing', 'Alpha 83', 'Love for Medellín'; Cali has the 'Kan-Kil', and 'Death to Homosexuals'; Bogotá is home to the 'Vampires', and 'Trigger' and in several places 'Mano Negra' (no kidding, Mano Negra!). Tramps, the homeless, street kids, homosexuals, are killed in bloody night-time safaris.

Guerrilla territory begins just around the corner from the station. Straying soldiers, lost tourists, are easy targets. And the station just happens to be our flock's headquarters. 'Don't worry, nothing will happen to them,' the editor of *Vanguardia Liberal* tells me, 'people are very grateful to you for coming.'

If only they knew…

The guerrillas come to get information from the horse's mouth. They ask questions, especially of me, your chronicler. I assume because I'm no spring chicken. The same questions as in Bosconia. There's a monotony about oft-repeated replies. Then it's my turn to ask questions:

'Why are you with the guerrillas?'

'Because they pay me.'

'Doesn't it cause you moral problems?'

'Everyone kills here.'

'Not everybody; a taxi driver just told me that in Barranca you only kill if you disagree with the person you're talking to. Don't you agree with your victims?'

'There are guerrillas everywhere. You have them in France as well.'

'In France?'

'Yes, on an island. Like in Ireland.'

'Do you think you can beat the State?'

'It's not to do with winning, just living.'

'Do you know where the money you earn comes from?'

'Not exactly. Some people say it's from drugs. I prefer to think it's a revolutionary tax on big companies.'

'Ecopetrol?'

'I don't know. But where do you think the money comes from to pay those who exploit our country? From the people.'

In the areas they occupy, the guerrillas are the law. They run a parallel State: administration, tax collection, the police and judiciary. When they're victorious, they kill a pig and dance salsa. The guerrilla I'm talking to has just got married. Like many guerrillas in Barranca, he lives in the town, goes to work every morning and comes back at night, except when he's out doing overtime.

Nono is much better. He's no longer limping. Bouchon took him to hospital where they gave him an anti-inflammatory injection. We'll always wonder about the treatment though. What if it really was Señor Angel's prayers?

That evening, the National Liberation Army (ELN) blows up an oil pipeline on the outskirts of town. Tom saw the whole spectacle from a taxi. Massive flames. Like ten Robertos. The driver was very proud of the guerrillas' exploits.

Little Darío is back. Like a bad penny. He's sitting at Isa and Régis' table, all smiles, explaining that when they left him in Bosconia, he took the next goods train back in the opposite direction. Now we won't be rid of him before Bogotá for certain. And what then, will he swim after us to France?'

Friday 10 December
First Night at Barranca

On the road leading to the station is the headquarters of
the Unión Sindical Obrera (USO), the main trades union
organisation. On the front of the building hangs a
enormous banner: 'No to Union Repression. Free our
Imprisioned Comrades.' What's more, the first three pages
of today's paper are all about massacres of banana workers
in the Urabá region: over twenty-seven dead in seventy-
two hours. Sound familiar? Any different from the
situation in 1928?

The pride of today's show is a ten-ton block of ice
with an Indian's head carved in the middle, all enclosed
in a flaming wagon. Coco wanted to encrust a huge
sword in the ice, like Merlin the Wizard's. What Coco
didn't know was that some years ago Bolívar's sword had
been stolen from the Palace of Justice by the M-19
guerrilla group. It hasn't been heard of since. So Coco's
idea could cause misunderstandings. He was advised to
freeze his own balls rather than the symbol of Colombian
Independence. It's a pity. At this stage of the journey, it's
obvious our youngsters are sailing blithely over all
dangers. Like Alice in Guerrilla-land.

If this continues, the show will be perfect for the final

performance in Bogotá, which is now scheduled for the 30th. The Ferrovías railwaymen are the heroes of the hour. The success of the operation is primarily down to them. They replaced to good effect the defectors from the production team and even those from the artistic direction. Félix organises the queues in front of the Museum, Diablito looks after 'Beat the Goalie', Gustavo replaces 'Jojo's Egg', Jorge compensates for the absence of Radio Caracol's compère.

The crowd is huge. The queue to visit the Ice Museum is monstrous as usual. Pépète works wonders. She tells a fantasmagorical tale about the origins of ice. Some people are terrified and make the sign of the cross before going in. Who are these good people? A lot of them come from the shanty towns on the outskirts of Barranca, the so-called *barrios enfermos*, or sick neighbourhoods, where the presence of the State is totally absent. These marginal people – unemployed, underemployed, or doing odd jobs when they can – stoically endure the queues and accept the caprices of Roberto (today the victim of a power cut), and patiently wait to dance to the French Lovers' rock music as if it was Vallenato and not the brutal pogo of the Cigale Club.

Today is the debut of the Yeti, masterpiece of Coco, the hot and cold specialist.

'The Yeti is Roberto's friend and, like him, lives in the flaming wagon. The Yeti is asleep. To enable him to sleep we have to keep him cold. So we've built a block of ice about five metres long, a metre and a half wide and one metre twenty high. He has horns on his head which stick out of the ice.' Coco spoils and pampers his creature. He adds little blocks of ice here and there to make paws, fins, the finishing touches.

Messages in the Office of
Human Desires in Barrancabermeja:

I'd like a government that is sincere with the people, and stops deceiving us with false promises.
Nancy, 16

I wish we'd take more care of nature and that the Ice Train keeps going for years.
Jaime Alberto Tabales, 10

I want the train to come back and give new life to the county and more work.
Julio César Rojas, 17

I'd like us to stop polluting the earth, and for every one of us to plant a tree so that our children have a better future in a healthy world.
Dora, 21

The dream I have is for children to stop being kidnapped, that there be peace in the world, and that there be no more guerrillas in my country.
Anonymous

Saturday 11 December
Second Night at Barranca

I read in the paper this morning: 'The Health Minister has launched a campaign against obesity.'

Colombians no longer want those bronzed rounded Botero bodies that Parisians could touch in the Champs-Elysées. Main target: cellulitis. The paper advises a series of physical exercises, massages, slimming creams, in order to become svelte. And more fruit and vegetables, less starch and fats. What on earth will the Boteros eat?

Thirty-nine degrees in the shade. We walk down the main street, picking our way through the shops, clothes stalls, vendors of all types, many of them children. We resist the temptation of fruit juices, and refuse the numerous sirens who offer us their wares, touch us, and pronounce themselves *a la orden, a la orden* – at our service. We cross the market and, down the hill again, we begin to smell pineapple, orange, apple and the sea, before we finally reach the river of a thousand legends.

At this spot, the River Yuma – actually it's not the Yuma now but the Magdalena – must be about a kilometre wide. Its slow sad waters carry rubbish, and sometimes corpses. A launch approaches the quayside, making waves. It's the quay of a real port, with its restaurants serving fish stew, abandoned cargo ships, rusting cranes, and bars without dockers. On the other side is the jungle. Nearby, to the right, the famous refinery, which has turned this formerly virginal waterway into one of the most polluted rivers on earth. I am disappointed.

When I get back to the station, however, my spirits are lifted. A tenor canary from Barranquilla, a certain Domingo, has just been named national king of the high trills. We see him on television, and hear him chirp. The Colombian school of singing canaries is one of the most important in the world. Its pioneer, Malibrán, learned his scales in Italy under the baton of the famous Caruso, world champion at all registers in 1988. The Colombians are hopeful of winning the world championship, to be held in Germany in early 1994, with a male team. Female canaries – as any serious ornithologist will tell you – only groan.

While still waiting to win the football World Cup, Colombia boasts several world records. This country of thirty-two million inhabitants has the largest number of reigning queens. As well as ordinary beauty queens, they elect onion queens, corn queens, coconut queens, bean queens, sovereigns of machetes, *mamoncillos* (small exotic fruit), hammocks and ivy. It is also true that we've never seen so many beauties per square kilometre. They say the most beautiful women come from Cali, but if we had to choose Miss Ice Express, without a doubt, we'd go and look for her in Aracataca.

Yesterday, our electrics failed and everybody's nerves were on edge. But the panic's over. Tonight, we'll connect up to the local power supply. The public turns out again in force, as big a crowd as last night but maybe more tense. Although they're as young as yesterday, and still plebian.

Half of them are guerrillas, jokes Miguel of Ferrovías. And why not? They're camped 200 metres from here, and they have the right to enjoy themselves without their weapons. Tom and Dani have set up shop in a corner of the café El Vagón. A guerrilla came to get tattooed. He explains to anyone who wants to listen that he joined the rebels because they were the only ones who gave him medicine for his sick child.

Very moving is the presence of 350 children from neighbouring hamlets, kids who've never even set foot in a town. The priest who is accompanying them wants to regroup his flock because the girls on the train are too provocative. We show him that they're no more or less dressed that Colombian girls in general.

'Yes, but they're French!' he cries.

You're right, dear priest. Grass is always greener... Look at the Colombians in Barranca. While we go mad for the local girls, they tease our girls, flatter them, chat them up, let their hands wander. But the French Lovers lower the tension by getting the kids to sing Christmas carols to rock rhythms.

The dusty avenue of almond trees leading to the hotel is lined with discos, bars, night clubs, and some private houses. People dance and sweat inside and out on the pavement, with the music at full blast. One Vallenato merges into another Vallenato every ten metres, a musical chain of nasal voices that dissolves into a single kilometre-long Vallenato.

Messages in the Office of
Human Desires in Barrancabermeja:

I dream of being able to save up and help the street kids
in Medellín and Barranca.
Luzmila Zapata Díaz, 19

I dream of the earth being less contaminated. I suggest
educating people about rubbish. And factories shouldn't
give out so much smoke and bad smells. They should find
a new technique for car exhausts.
Adela Fiallo, 24

I dream that there will be work for everyone who needs
it in Barranca. I'd like it for poor children.
Yuli Gómez, 8

Sunday 12 December
Arrival at Dorada

Stormy weather this morning. We planned to leave at ten
o'clock. We head off at midday. The locomotive advances
cautiously at twenty kilometres an hour.

'Why aren't we going quicker?' we ask the driver, 'the
track is good.'

'Because if there's a bomb under the rail, I'll get it
right in the face.'

Houses with corrugated iron roofs, lit by petrol lamps.
Predominant shade everywhere is meadow green. On the
track, facing us, is a curious contraption called a *diablo*
(devil) loaded with vegetables. The driver jams on the
brake, his dog howls. He just has time to get out of the
way.

The *diablo* is found all over the Third World. It can only
exist in countries where railways have been abandoned.
It's a sort of cart with four vertical ball-bearings wheels to
slide over the rails and four horizontal ones which guide
it along, with a few millimetres' play since the rails don't
always have the same distance between them. You propel
yourself along with a sort of rudder, like a gondola, and
it's used to transport both goods and animals.

We pass several abandoned stations. Cuatro Bocas, La

Vizcaína, Pulpapol. A monument marks the 1970 attack on a convoy protected by ten soldiers that was carrying money to pay railway workers' salaries. They were stopped by a gang who only wanted their guns. The only bullet in the ambush was fired at Ricardo Coronel, because of his name.

We advance very slowly. Time is measured in sleepers. We watch them pass one after another. Ten, fifteen per second. And then five climbing up to Carare, a big station apparently no longer in use. It was taken out of our schedule on the advice of the Ferrovías technicians, not for our own safety, but that of the inhabitants of Carare. The army might use our presence as a pretext for 'cleansing' the area, known to be a guerrilla provisioning centre. Official or not, there are still people waiting. Fireworks, cheers, the smell of gunpowder. Now we see it would have been brilliant to hold the *feria* in this immense station. Never listen to the voices of doom and gloom.

Mario Vargas Llosa, the most Flaubert-like of Latin American novelists, writes in today's *Espectador* about the case of the child murderers in Liverpool. His article, as long as the end of the world, is entitled 'Wild Beasts Freed'. A few pages further on, we learn that last year, in Bogotá alone, 164 murders were committed by children. Gambit comments, 'He's making a meal of it.' A translation of Ho Chi Minh's 'Ten dead in Europe, it's a tragedy; a thousand dead in Asia, it's news.'

At midnight, *La Consentida* pulls into a deserted platform. We're in Dorada, but there's not a soul to welcome us. Have we been forgotten? We, the saviours of the Colombian railways? We hang about, still sleepy, on a bit of muddy ground, then head for some vague lights a few hundred metres further on. We get to a miserable hall. Only beer. No food, no rooms. Welcome to Dorada!

We take taxis, six or seven of us to a car. Dorada is five minutes away. We find the town in full swing. Juice sellers press oranges, thirst turns to delicious freshness, hunger is calmed on beautifully served tables, and loudspeakers blast out guajiras, rumbas and salsas. We're apparently in a Vallenato-free zone.

After dinner, we check into the Hotel Rosita, a large patio full of flowers with monastic cells on four sides. Twelve francs a room. For six or seven days, it's the most welcoming palace of our whole journey.

Monday 13 December
Free Day in Dorada

The train has changed stations. It is now next to the main square, on the banks of the Magdalena.

It is here, beside the omnipresent river, that the greatest of Colombian demagogues learned the art of sophistry.

Paris, summer of 1926. Boulevard Raspail. In the apartment of the American Daré Francis, Russian princesses expelled by the Bolsheviks, Scandinavian ladies from Oslo and Stockholm, Van Dongen models, receive three dark-skinned Colombians.

Alejandro Vallejo, Rómulo Rozo and Jorge Eliécer Gaitán arouse general curiosity.

'We are ferocious savages, *mesdames*,' explains Gaitán, 'come to France to study Western civilisation. We have purchased these oppressive suits so we may visit you in your home, but at home we're always naked.'

Rozo introduces himself as a tamer of big cats, and Gaitán as the high priest of a mysterious pre-Colombian region, as yet undiscovered by Claude Lévi-Strauss. 'Each morning, at dawn, I ride round my domain on the back of the most majestic of crocodiles, and all the wild beasts of the River Yuma follow us in procession.'

'But how do you make them follow you? Do you feed them?'

'Madame, I give them nothing. I talk to them.'

'And what do you say?'

'Nothing. The important thing is to talk to them. It is the talking, not the content, that attracts animals.'

That phrase cost Colombia 300,000 lives.

Tuesday 14 December
Wandering Around Dorada

The train people wander around town. Are they bored? Have they had enough rest? Imagined perils (kidnapping, theft, mugging, damaged material), and past suffering (diarrhoea, heat, mosquitoes, workload and Vallenato), seem to have added spice to the adventure. The comforts of Dorada soften bodies and raise spirits. Some people even abandon the no-star hotels and go back to the train. A comfortable odyssey in a luxury train with showers and WC would not leave such an indelible tattoo on our lives.

There is a vague but unanimous desire to make this journey last for ever. No more bad feeling, bad faith, or bitterness. No one is counting the days any more. People who ten days ago in Gamarra wanted to pack it in, are now asking for new stops to be added. Why aren't we going to Utica, Villeta? Because there's no more money. Cati used this argument in the past to apply an electric shock to an angry team. But now the coffers are well and truly empty. Without a miracle – a deluge of millions – the schedule won't be modified. Friday 17 Dorada, Thursday 23 Facatativá, Thursday 30 Bogotá. And that's it.

Wednesday 15 December
Visit to Armero

We leave at six in the morning with Guillermo Rodríguez and the Radio Caracol gang for a visit to Armero.

Remember...Mariquita, Chinchina, Guayabal, Armero. These pretty names still toll like a bell, a funereal litany of horror, death, and despair that has haunted this Andean highland valley for eight years.

What a contrast. After a two-hour journey through amazingly beautiful landscapes, and a descent into a promised land of bounty – rice, cotton, maize, sorghum, fruit of every kind, rich pastures – we come to this buried town.

Our first sight is of a few ruined houses. Then, in a crescendo of desolation, we reach what had been the town centre.

'What does our guest think?'

Nothing, there's nothing left. There used to be a couple of dozen schools, banks, a building society, three convents, two churches. And over 27,000 inhabitants. No schools now, nor churches, nothing. And yet, in the middle of this strange bare terrain that used to be Armero, stands, like a silent symbol, the strongroom of the National Bank of Colombia. It has withstood everything, even attempts to force open its bullet-proof door. A hole had to be blown in the concrete to recover jewellery deposited and several million pesos. A few days after the tragedy, the soldiers responsible for protecting it, were caught with their hands in the till, so to speak, trying to empty the strongroom.

25,000 dead. This mountain town was totally destroyed by a huge mudslide. A double eruption of the volcano Nevado del Ruiz, at 5,400 metres, melted the snow and ice covering its slopes. The River Lagunilla swelled and broke its banks. Within minutes, a torrent of lava and water cascaded down the mountainside carrying everything before it. The mudslide began its assault on Armero. The inhabitants, surprised as they slept, hadn't time to escape and died buried under the debris of their houses.

'What impression...?'

It's not like Pompeii or Herculaneum, where several centuries later, petrified people were discovered eating, working and loving under the ruins. Nothing of the sort will be found in Armero. Eight years on, the site is covered with fig trees, almond trees, and *veraniegas*, a tree that flowers in the summer, hence all year round here. No hand has planted them. The few survivors have remade their lives. Eduardo Rojas lost twenty-seven members of his family, including his wife and children. He's in charge of cultural affairs in the new Armero. Pedro Martínez runs a service station. His wife and children were swept away by the lava. Neither of them has forgotten, but they have had to move on. They are trying to get companies to invest in Armero, to create new jobs.

In perfect symbiosis with its inhabitants, nature performs its daily task. Even the crosses and gravestones that mark where the houses stood are covered in vegetation. Surviving along with the bank strongroom will be the arch erected in memory of the policemen who died. A list of their names is engraved on the marble. At the top, the commander, then three brigadiers, and so on, down to the ordinary recruits in alphabetical order. Eternal respect for hierarchy.

There is also the tender memory of little Omaira, who came to symbolise the tragedy for the whole world. How can we forget that little twelve-year-old girl, trapped in the mud, dying on camera, expressing her wonderful words of hope and love? Trapped in the ruins of her home by an enormous piece of timber, her head and body sticking out of the dark mass of mud, Omaira fought for three days, talking to her rescuers, worried about the effect the catastrophe would have on her school work. By the time the hydraulic pump arrived from Bogotá to save her, it was too late.

Japanese children erected a monument with a series of innocent haikus on the spot where Omaira died.

The dead will never know that the tragedy could have been averted, that the danger of an eruption had been known for months, that a Swiss specialist had gone to the region to organise evacuation plans. On the very morning of the disaster, after the first cinders starting falling, the local authorities assured the population of Armero that there was no risk, and in the evening, when the tragedy had already begun, the governor admonished the mayor because he had woken him at an inappropriate hour. The governor is still running.

Thursday 16 December
Visit to the Whorehouse

Carlos Rojas and the French Lovers are patrolling the streets of Dorada.

'Are you from the Ice Train?' ask two young women. Superfluous question, you only have to look at them.

'When are you playing?'

'Tomorrow at six in the evening. And who are you?'

'We're whores.'

'Pardon?'

'We're whores, that house there is a brothel. Come and play this evening.'

Early that morning we'd been on a boat trip on the Magdalena. Another dispatch for Caracol. Guillermo and his damned satellite. 'Live from the Magdalena...are European rivers as polluted as this one?'

Your chronicler has to improvise a similarity between the Magdalena and the Thames, the Seine and that trickle called the Manzanares in Madrid. At this point, the majestic Magdalena is clogged up with tons of old clothes and plastic from Bogotá. What have become of the manatís, those sirens so loved by the Conquistadors?

Ten o'clock that night. Only a privileged few were party to the visit to the whorehouse. But by the time we set off, there are a good forty of us, of whom about a dozen are girls. It's like taking fridges to the North Pole.

Leading the way are the French Lovers with their instruments, Carlos posing as their manager, and myself, to chronicle the evening, naturally. So, all in all, about fifty people walk along the railway track towards the house of ill repute.

'There are the tarts!' shouts Gambit.

But they're not ours. We turn down a dirt road. From behind the third door that we stick our noses in, out comes an explosion of joy. The girls tumble out into the street. There are about twelve of them. One is wearing a white tutu like a ballet dancer, another is poured into a sequinned number, a third shows off her tits in a two-piece 'sporty-whore' outfit.

The girls set out chairs in the street. We all sit down, waiting for the French Lovers to begin. Our hostesses request Vallenatos. Poor old French! But these valiant guys always come up with the goods, even in risky situations like these. Indefatigable, they keep the girls spellbound for half an hour. At the end, the job done, they put away their instruments and accept a beer, and hopefully more.

It's midnight. The bulk of the expedition goes home. Only the most well-heeled and intrepid stay. One of the girls is terrified. She asks me, in my role as *paterfamilias*, how these French barbarians make love. What happens next is not known, your chronicler having failed in his professional duty.

Visit to Fresno. First Night in Dorada

This morning, there's an outing with the Caracol people to broadcast from Fresno, capital of coffee production.

Fresno is an hour and a half by car from Dorada. We leave from 275 metres above sea level at seven in the morning. It's already hot. Fresno awaits us at 2,300 metres with Parisian cold. In seventy kilometres, we cross a whole gamut of landscapes, vegetation and temperatures, as is often the way in Colombia.

Fresno's main square looks like the *plaza mayor* of any Castillian town. The same one-storey houses, the same bandstand surrounded by a bit of garden, the same white church dominating everything. But, here, coffee is grown everywhere, even on the rooftops.

Until the end of the last century, Fresno lived off its gold mines. The people were rich, and the men depraved, until the mines closed in 1904. In full economic depression, the good Lord saw fit to appoint as parish priest Juan B. Cortés, otherwise known as the Visionary.

How could he retrieve his flock and restore the town's fortunes at the same time? His solution was to let sin bear fruit. The priest made all the townspeople go to confession at least once a week. Instead of unproductive punishments, he'd tell them to sow between ten and three-thousand coffee plants, or between two and four-hundred bananas. The number depended more on the economic status of the sinner than on the gravity of the sin. So, thanks to the visionary Cortés, Fresno became one of Colombia's main coffee producing centres.

The area between Dorada and Fresno is known as Colombia's Switzerland. There are immense haciendas growing fruit trees, cereals and vines. There are even ranches raising fighting bulls.

Some of these lands were supposed to be part of a land reform package and distributed to peasant farmers. But on the contrary, the '*Violencia*' and the entry of drug traffickers into the agricultural sector meant that the land became concentrated in even fewer hands. According to the weekly magazine *Semana*, the mafia bought more land in two years (a million hectares) than was distributed in a quarter century of land reform.

Once this 'counter land reform' was carried out, the narcos, directly or through intermediaries, brought in their private armies to cleanse the region. The extermination of Communists, trades unionists, and left-wing politicians reassured investors and contributed to making the land profitable.

The landowning class, with its own position now secured, was also transformed. It brought in technological innovations (mainly in cattle ranching); electricity in the haciendas, technical equipment in the barns, and the massive influx of prime reproductive stock from abroad.

The evidence suggests that this process was initiated by drug traffickers, who had the capital to provide investment on such a scale. So, since this investment doesn't respond to any overall planning but to the need to launder drug money and increase their wealth, it will continue as long as the drug business continues. That's why the government's war on drugs irritates these new landowners.

Despite being up to its neck in problems, Colombia has often been cited as a model. It has maintained a steady growth rate, without excessive inflation, in a continent wracked with instability, and with internal conflict. 'The country is in a bad way, but the economy's going well,' has been an oft-heard saying. 45% of Colombians still live below the poverty line and the big cities are all ringed by appalling shanty towns, but the country reacted well to economic crisis.

Colombia is lucky enough to have infinite resources. Its subsoil has emeralds and other precious stones, huge reserves of bauxite, potassium and copper. Oil exports started in 1986, with an annual production of eighteen million tons, and have increased ever since.

The Colombian economic miracle is also in part that of drugs. This barely subterranean activity irrigates the country. But the idea that Colombia's economy is based mainly on cocaine is false. Only a fraction of the final profit from sales in external markets benefits Colombia. During the marijuana boom, it barely reached 3%. Most of the huge profits from the drug trade are put in Swiss or Panamanian bank accounts and return to the United States. One of the successes of the drug traffickers' propaganda has been to make Colombians think their fortunes are reinvested in their country.

Colombia has other unusual characteristics. Unlike other countries in Latin America, Colombia has not been ruled by bloodthirsty tyrants of different hues. The last to try it, Rojas Pinilla, did not long survive the opposition of the two traditional parties, and was deposed in 1957. Furthermore, the Colombian ruling elite is educated in its own excellent universities. Bogotá is still considered the Athens of Latin America. Even the chauvinistic Argentines and Mexicans readily admit it.

The Liberal and Conservative parties have shared power since the end of the last century, alternating governments in a way that makes Mexico (the most perfect dictatorship in the world) pale with envy, according to Mario Vargas Llosa. They dispose of well-oiled mechanisms supervised by the oligarchy.

Understandably, this political game is not to the liking of all Colombia's citizens and turnout for elections is very low. Any new political force has a huge problem making its voice heard, if it doesn't do so inside one of the two big parties. The M-19 guerrilla movement, for instance, came out of clandestinity to join in the game of 'restricted democracy'. Legalised in 1991, it made an amazing impact on the elections for the Constituent Assembly in that same year. Some people even thought that it embodied that mythical third force capable of shattering the Liberal-Conservative duopoly. Alas, the former guerrillas got involved in all sorts of political shenanigans and many hopes were dashed.

Back from Fresno, we go straight to the station. It is two in the afternoon. The sound system is set up. Money has arrived from Bogotá. One more problem solved. The *feria* in Dorada begins an hour late. Malfunctions are now par for the course. This time, it's the turn of the electrics. But the boys are used to Colombia and everything works out in the end.

Tonight, it's brilliant. There's a big crowd at the station. It's a classy audience. Dorada is the geographical centre of the country, so people have come from Bogotá, Medellín and Cali. The other Ramón is increasingly inspired on his rope. Germain and Fabou fly like angels on the high trapeze, caught by Dédé, but they forget the slips and tumbles, which is a pity because it takes away all the suspense. Roberto is on great form. He has understood that he can't be 'unwell' in front of an audience like this.

It's a real musical feast. Fans from previous shows, as well as the girls from the night before (warm and loyal), galvanise the French Lovers. They go berserk. After a month on tour, they're increasingly confident, masters of the stage.

The crowd calls for Mano Negra. Many have come hundreds of kilometres to see them. They wear t-shirts with King of Bongo, got from God knows where. So Fidel, Tom and Mano make a sound system with a synthesiser that resembles the group in its heyday.

The show ends with the joyful cacophony of a *papayera* band. Just wind and percussion instruments. Vibrant binary rhythms: the *bunde*, the *guabina*, the *pasillo*, the *pasodoble*. A fusion of Spanish, Caribbean, and mountain

Chibcha cultures; grass-roots music in its virgin state that would have delighted Charles Ives.

Messages in the Office of
Human Desires in Dorada:

I dream passionately of peace for my country, to see my family united and for my father-in-law to stop drinking.
Anonymous

I dream of travelling and seeing countries, because you foreigners have left a very beautiful souvenir in our Colombia.
Fidelina Rojas, 32

I dream of finishing my studies, and above all of getting out of poverty.
Felisa Bustos, 22

I dream of winning the lottery and buying a car.
Anonymous

I dream of having peace in my soul so I can pass it to my neighbour and help this world be a better place.
Alexandra Pinzón,
La Voz de Dorada, 23

Fire on Board. Eroticism at Last!

'The train of fire is on fire!'

The sprinkler sprinkled. The carriage where Isa, Régis, the French Lovers, Jojo, Manu, Fidel and Nono were dossing, went up in flames. Nono's room flared up, like marijuana. It wasn't a short circuit, because there's no current. A fag end or a candle, then? A mystery. Fire extinguishers, zero. Firemen, ditto. It's not their fault. They got their hoses out but the water was cut off.

No deaths to lament, but clothes, cassettes and Captain's hat in cinders. Joking aside, we were scared, especially for Nono who lost his passport, air ticket and all his money – the 2,000 francs he brought from France.

Nono was saved by Bouchon, his soul brother. They'd had a row the night before, brought on by an excessive dose of alcohol. Feeling guilty, Bouchon came by at six in the morning to patch things up.

'I had to shake him several times to wake him up, and we went for a coffee. Half an hour later his room was in flames.'

Philosophers have told us *ad nauseum* that there's no such thing as chance, and every encounter is a rendez-vous.

The mayor of Dorada invites us all to lunch: train

people, journalists and photographers. We gather on the quayside to go to Picapiedra, on the other bank of the Magdalena.

The mayor is amazing. Far from typical. He's black for a start (which away from the Caribbean coast is not a good electioneering gambit), he owns neither house nor car, does not seem to have a woman in his life, and has never hidden his penchant in this direction anyway. Although a member of the Liberal Party, ideology is absent from his brief platform of 'promise nothing and take action'. And because he's as good as his word, he is much loved by his people.

The boat rocks dangerously, and we almost end up in the gruesome waters of the Magdalena thanks to the other Ramón, our baptismal font acrobat. In just one week, Ramón has become the life and soul of the train. A barge for fifteen passengers, but with thirty on board, is paradise for him. And hell for us. Will someone please sit on him during the crossing!

A *guingette* on the Marne. To right and left, tropical rainforest. Before us, the impetuous Magdalena. In the distance, the houses of Dorada, the park, the station, and the white church, silhouetted against the blue sky.

The mayor welcomes us with great pomp: bare feet, flowery shirt and Bermudas. He bids us welcome and invites us to partake of the barbecue. Everyone's there, everyone's happy. Now that the end of the tour is in sight, we all say it's a shame we're leaving, just when we're beginning to understand each other, and the show has finally gelled.

The other Ramón, like a bullfighter in the ring, his long hair caught up in a ponytail, struts his stuff on the dance floor to the strident chords of a Spanish *pasodoble*. He is wearing only his black silk briefs. The mayor, tempted by the music, joins in the dance, each adapting to the other's movements. Ramón stamps out the Andalusian rhythm, while the chief executive of Dorada shows he is no slouch as a dancer. The teacher lets himself go, his ponytail waving aloft, his hands playing his own personal strings. Together they offer the erotic spectacle the tour has been cruelly lacking.

Licking our fingers (the ritual of the barbecue does not include napkins), we re-embark. The mayor remains on the quayside waving his white scarf.

'I hope you're writing all this down,' says the other Ramón on the boat.

'I don't think it will interest the readers.'

'That depends on you, you have to know how to use your imagination.'

'And to write. Tell me, what has moved you most on the journey?'

'For me it's the train, crossing the countryside, arriving in these towns and villages where people have never, or hardly ever, seen a show. I love seeing their reaction, the warmth of their welcome, the sadness when we leave. I'll never forget them, and I hope they won't forget us either.'

'And your own experiences?'

'I wasn't afraid, despite passing through frankly dangerous areas. I think people imposed moments of peace and offered them to us. In Barranca, for example, before we arrived various people were killed, but while we were there it was calm. And I've just seen in the paper that there was an attack as soon as we left. We had that type of relationship with the people. We offered them part of a dream, they offered us moments of peace. Colombians are super generous. At the end of the show, the audience calls you by your first name, they stop you in the street, they touch you, it's a bit tiresome, and after a while it's hard to cope, but there's no way you'd tell them to leave you alone. They are so nice you can't resist them. That's clear.'

Quite clear, Ramón.

In the evening, we go back to Picapiedra for a French Lovers concert. We chum up with Marina, twenty, and Isabel, twenty-three. They want to come on the train with us to Bogotá and even further, Paris, Marseilles, anywhere. Isabel is a secretary-receptionist in a local bank. Her boyfriend is there, drinking beer with us and wearing a smile of resignation. With her full lips, limpid eyes and plunging neckline, Isabel suggests sending me her CV (here the term is much more poetic, 'page of life'), and coming to Paris if I can find work for her.

Marina troubles me: twenty years old with a 'page of life' which could very well be virgin. She falls in love with your chronicler, who could be her father, or even a precocious grandfather. This desire to escape is disconcerting, we see it everywhere. Not only the young boys and street kids, but also girls who don't have any real problems. They all want to leave their boyfriends, their homes, their families and towns. Just leave.

Cati won't let them on the train. It's completely full, especially since the fire in the dormitory coach.

It's a pity, because the expedition is now largely made up of stowaways whose situation has been 'normalised'. Some even get expenses, having proved themselves more enthusiastic workers than some of the regulars.

'Yes, that's happened several times,' says Jean-Pierre. 'It's surprising really because your first reaction is to throw them off. You say if you let one, then you'll soon have fifteen or thirty. But, in fact, it's produced very interesting situations. Like Jairo, the stowaway who got on right at the start at Villeta.'

Jairo was an 'undesirable' until the day he hid in the first wagon of a train whose destination he didn't know.

'Now, Jairo is a mate. He swears that when he learns to read and write, he'll write the history of the train. And I believe him, because he's bright and has picked up a whole load of things.'

What an example! It's not just anyone who has to learn to write, and especially to read, before launching himself on a literary career.

'In a month, Jairo's a different person. He has put on five kilos (when we're all losing weight), and he speaks more coherently, even if he mixes lots of French words with Spanish now.'

Jairo has an aim in life: to find his father who abandoned him before he was born. But in the days he has spent with us, he has planned another kind of vengeance. He knows that if he becomes rich and famous, his father will come looking for him. Writing seems to him the best way of getting fame and wealth. The chronicler encourages him. It's exactly what happened to the Spanish writer Juan Marsé. Jairo will learn to read. But for the time being, he's busy fixing the lighting.

It's two in the morning and your chronicler is dozing off. The French Lovers, except for Captain who is irresistibly taken with Isabel, are still playing. I make my escape, but Marina catches up with me on the quayside. Crossing the river, she tells me her life story. Her parents are separated. Her mother sells lottery tickets in the street. She's doing a course to be able to work in a travel agency. Silence as far as her father is concerned. However, she does have an aunt in Bogotá, so she'll come and see me when we're there.

Dorada is all dark. I can't possibly let a girl of twenty walk through dark and dangerous streets on her own. I accompany Marina to her house like a true gentleman. Twenty shadowy minutes through sordid back streets. Her mother is waiting, accompanied by several indignant, threatening and aggressive neighbours. How can I explain? And what about me? Who will accompany me to the hotel with these guys at my back?

Sunday 19 December
Leave Dorada and Return to Dorada

Drama on the tracks at half past six in the morning. A mother is screaming. She wants her son back, we must give him back.

'Where was your son?'

It appears he was at Picapiedra last night.

'How old is your son? What does he look like?'

The mother puts him at twenty-two. Her description matches that of an ephebe we glimpsed last night at Picapiedra, in the shadows with the other Ramón. We wake up the rope man.

'Ramón, don't be stupid. Tell us where you've hidden this kid. There'll be a shitload of trouble.'

But this time, Ramón appears to be innocent. Cati invites the lady onto the train to look for her son, but she refuses. She's scared she'll meet the Devil himself. The cops arrive. The mother now says her son is eighteen but, unfortunately for her, still an adult. We're off the hook.

We were set to leave at seven o'clock. A miracle. The engine emits its three statutory whistles a few seconds early. Tom, his girlfriend Charlotte, Tomasín, Fidel and Manu, and other latecomers, are left in Dorada. Let them manage best they can. For once, the schedule is the schedule.

We take our leave of Dorada with tears in our eyes. Leandro has dragged himself here to say goodbye. He first turned up the day we arrived, leaning on his two crutches. After that, he was always hanging around the train. Jean-Marc took him to the hospital to get the nauseous wound on his leg looked at.

The hospital wouldn't admit him. No money. However, they did prescribe antibiotics he'll never be able to buy. No money. So he'll need to have his leg amputated. No money. Moussa remembers we have a metal saw in the wagon-workshop. Patrice (finally a doctor on the train when we've learned to take care of ourselves!) asks who'll look after him and get him the antibiotics he'll need.

Leandro will keep his putrid leg the time it takes to catch septicaemia, because he has no money.

We've covered ten kilometres in an hour. The engine stops. What amazing energy maternal love gives! On the track is this morning's mother still in tears. She has run all the way and now she wants to search Ramón's pad.

Chino chases dragonflies. We discover marijuana shoots on the running board of one of the coaches. How generous is Colombian nature!

Half an hour later, the Ferrovías men inform us that a convoy of fifteen wagons has derailed in front of us. It'll take time for the rescue brigade to arrive and clear the track. Indeterminate wait and return to Dorada. Meanwhile, the prodigal son having returned to the fold, the Brechtian mother apologises to the other Ramón.

'If only it had been true,' he says with a sigh.

We wait on the platform for fourteen hours. People come back to see us. Are we doing another show? Impossible, we could be leaving at any time, as soon as the track is cleared. Isabel and Marina, the two girls who want to spread their wings, arrive by motor scooter. 'Have you come back to get us?' Alas, no. They stay with us anyway until two in the morning.

A smell of humidity wafts through the windows, the stars and the fireflies wink at us. In the train, the night music begins.

Monday 20 December
Leave from Puerto Salgar. Arrive in Faca

We wake at seven o'clock, following the Rio Negro, a river of coal-black waters. The vegetation has lost its exuberance. Fewer coconut trees, fewer palms; ferns and bromeliads are disappearing. We arrive in Utica where we had originally planned to perform. 200 people are waiting for us on the platform. How can we explain that we've no money to do a show? It's free, isn't it? Yes, but to serve you up a dream, good people, capitalist enterprises have to drop us a few crumbs from their table.

Dialogue in the station hall:

'I've never been on a train, have you?'

'Yes, I have.'

'Often?'

'Yes.'

'Do you like getting on a train?'

'I prefer watching it pass.'

'I've seen them pass, but I've never been on one.'

'We lived near a stop.'

'Like this?'

'No, this is a station. Where we were, it didn't always stop, only when passengers got off. We went every day to sell figs. When the train didn't stop, we ate the figs ourselves.'

'So, wasn't it better if the train didn't stop?'

'No, because when it stopped we sold figs and that meant we had coffee for two or three days.'

'I like figs better than coffee. Don't you?'

'I don't know. It's so long since I ate figs and so many mornings that we haven't had coffee I've forgotten the difference.'

'What were the figs like?'

'Big and fleshy, and full of pips inside.'

'What were the trains like?'

'They were long and joyful, and when they didn't stop people waved at us from the carriages. It was brilliant.'

'The only train I've ever seen is the one in Puerto Colombia, but it's really small and I didn't see it moving. When trains aren't moving, people don't wave, do they?'

'No, they don't wave. They look, that's all.'

Past Utica, the long climb up to the Altiplano begins. The changing flowers of the *befarias* illuminate the edges of the forests. There are even fewer palms and *chinchonas*. The mosquitoes disappear, and we gradually start putting on shirts, jumpers and jeans again.

The train splits into two halves. A second engine is waiting to help us climb the 3,000 metres up the *cordillera* of the Andes. Despite the cold, we lean out of the windows to watch the slow transition from tropical vegetation to that of the cold lands of the Altiplano. The Holsteins glance desultorily at us, and return to their grass; the xylophone-ribbed curs spit out their barks. On both sides of the track, Colombians, men, women and children, thank us for having shown them a passenger train decorated with yellow butterflies.

We reach the arborescent passion flowers, the beautiful lilac colours, the fuchsias, and cross the sad forests of oaks hung with parasites of trailing hair.

On a hill, at the entrance to Alban, we see a cemetery in the shape of a chess board. They're lucky, these Albanians, some plots are empty. In Sahagún, the necropolis has a 'full' sign up. No more room for corpses, it says in the newspaper. Actually, there are plots but they belong to poor folk who refuse to rent or sell their place in the sweet hereafter.

'You're joking, my friend. If I rent it now and my mother-in-law croaks tomorrow, what do I do with her? Where do I put her? Should I pack her in salt and keep her at home for ever?'

All the same, being offered 200,000 pesos is food for thought. Many people do rent their eternal resting place. You can buy a house and eat while you're still amongst the living. After that, who knows?

In the village there's a medicine man who specialises in predicting funerals. He can tell if a rich or poor person is going to die by listening to bird songs. If he's woken in the night by an owl hooting, the defunct will be a pauper. If the owl hoots twice, that's two impecunious corpses. But if the trilling comes from a nocturnal *marimbero*, a bird of seductive plumage, the necromancy expert leaps from his hammock to attend the moribund who is unquestionably a millionaire.

Between two tombs, children play at waking the dead with a game of *tejo*, a sort of Colombian *petanque*. The game consists of throwing a metal disc at a firework.

We keep climbing towards Facatativá. Soon (which in train time means four or five hours), we reach the vast 100 square-kilometre plateau that is the Sabana de Bogotá. There is not a tree in sight. It is sown with European cereals and dotted with villages.

This plateau is the dried bed of Lake Funza, important in the mythology of the Muisca Indians, the indigenous people of the region. The source of evil, the moon, conjured up a wave of sins that created the lake. But Bochica, the sun, the source of good, broke the rock Tequendama (where the famous waterfall is now), Lake Funza burst through it, and the inhabitants of the region, who had fled to the neighbouring mountains during the flood, returned to their plain. After giving the Muisca people a political constitution and laws similar to those of the Incas, Bochica went to live in the temple of Sogamoso. He lived there for 2,000 years and then returned to the sun.

We reach Facatativá at nightfall, twenty-four hours late, and leave for Bogotá straight away in a minibus.

Bogotá. Altitude 2,600 metres. Centre of a population explosion. A million inhabitants in 1950, four and a half million in 1993, double that by the end of the next decade if growth continues at its present rate. Contained to the east and soon to the south by mountains, this human wave is spreading out to the west and especially to the north over larger and larger areas. The living conditions of the majority of the population of Bogotá are totally sub-human, worse even than other Latin American capital cities.

Apart from coping with the rarefied air at this altitude, we're nearly asphyxiated by the pollution, the car exhausts, the dust and the crowds in the main streets. As we speak, Bogotá is literally in the shit. The bin men are on strike, as if the city wasn't dirty enough. The minibus leaves us at San Victorino, in the centre, the warmest place in the city, according to Claudia, who is putting us up at her place.

Avoiding buses that think they're racing cars, and trucks that play at being tanks, we make it onto the pavement. With every step we bump into street vendors, shoeshine boys, rubbish rummagers, many of whom are only kids. Whole businesses are contained in little boxes, or folding trays. Their wares are cigarettes, matches, sweets, razor blades, lottery tickets and newspapers.

These wretched vendors are a thorn in the side of the authorities, because they demonstrate all too clearly the failure of the system and the scale of unemployment. From time to time, the capital's mayor accuses them of hindering traffic, of competing with honest traders who pay taxes, of being smugglers and thieves, in short, as they say here, antisocials. They slap prohibition orders on them and send the police in to get them off the streets.

Among the cigarette, chewing gum and lottery ticket vendors, Otavalo Indians (in white trousers, blue ponchos, black hats covering their long tresses) try to sell tourists phoney arts and crafts made in Guayaquil. Clowns standing on chairs, their faces white with flour, like lighthouses above the crowd, inveigle customers into restaurants, shops with sales on, or boutiques with leather goods from Antioquia.

I've got my computer and printer on me. Hugo is loaded down with the dozen walkie-talkies from the train, Garrincha and Sorriso are trailing their *birimbau* and *atabaque*, and all their clobber. Attractive booty, indeed. Enough for several banquets for any petty thief. We close ranks. Taxis pass but don't stop. We form a circle, treasure in the middle. Finally a taxi, our saviour. The five of us, and all our baggage? We'll pay double, triple, and then some.

Finally the taxi takes us to La Candelaria. It's the colonial part of Bogotá. Artists have moved in, but it still has a grass-roots feel. There's a lot of security because President Gaviria's residence is not far from here. We can sleep peacefully in our beds.

Tuesday 21 December
We Go Back to Faca. Another Meeting

Fernando, his friend Hugo and I are keen to get back to Facatativá. We get up early. We descend the steep streets of La Candelaria in search of a taxi. At the bottom of the old colonial town, are the government and administrative buildings, a legacy of the eighteenth century when the landowning aristocracy and the liberal oligarchy tried to establish a State in order to end their secular civil war.

A sign of the times is that the big financial octopuses have abandoned the neoclassical buildings of Avenue Jiménez. In their place stand a barrage of proud towers, advertising (in the image of their American brothers) the power and wealth of the companies that built them. We discover the names of the new owners of the country: Banco de Colombia, Grancolombia, Bavaria, flanked by the inevitable Hilton.

No one is prophet in his own country, we realise that when we arrive at Faca. The Train of Ice and Fire was born here, as was Roberto and the whole infrastructure of the *feria*. So why are the station staff so disagreeable? Bouchon has politely asked the boss if we can use the WC. 'There isn't one,' he growled. Yet Bouchon saw blokes going in and out of some room doing up their flies.

'Look, señor, I really need to shit.' Bouchon takes his trousers down. 'And if you haven't a shithouse,' he leaps onto a chair, 'I'm going to do it on your desk.' He squats on the table.

Following this outburst, the heat is taken out of the situation. Ferrovías brings a young Turk from Bogotá to help sort out this kind of problem.

A bed, a wooden table, and a shower and WC in a corner. At first sight, the Hotel Central in Faca seems all right. But we soon discover there's no hot water. And when we stretch out on a crumpled sheet that has obviously served several generations of commercial travellers, without a top sheet, the body in direct contact with a rough blanket, we're immediately assailed by legions of fleas. The hotel is declared disgusting. And this is where the nabobs of the group are staying! The other penniless bunch is still huddling in the cold carriages. It's in this hotel that the meeting to decide the future of the tour is to be held.

The tour managers owe the sponsors three more shows, one of which has to be in Bogotá (Bogote as my gypsies call it in their slang). Except that we realised ages ago that things could go badly wrong in Bogotá without Mano Negra. Young people are expecting them, and we haven't told the press they've split. The Prod weren't going to announce it twenty days ago, they were too afraid the funders would pull the plug. But now there's total panic. Cati demands a statement from Manu. He says it's up to the organisers to announce the programme, not the artists. He is, however, prepared to explain to the press. But nobody does anything.

The big dilemma remains: are we or are we not going to Bogotá?

Everyone agrees the project has been a success. Despite all the difficulties, the serious internal problems, the numerous defections (of the ninety-nine who left Facatativá five weeks ago, about forty of us are back here), and the fact that we didn't do half of the things we planned and promised, the important thing is that in the small towns, out in the countryside, the crowd loved it, there was joy, hope, and above all, proof that they can enjoy themselves together in peace. It took us a long time to understand this, but it happened and nothing can stop us now. Besides, we have plenty of aces up our sleeve thanks to the valiant publicity, that's within a whisker of being tedious, by *El Espectador* and Radio Caracol. Same thing in France, from the feedback we're getting. There have been numerous articles and reports by special envoys from the most memorable stops, notably in Santa Marta and Aracataca, where Mano Negra were still operational.

But go to Bogote? Not without Mano Negra. The show can't cope with big crowds. 200,000 people are waiting there, the queues to get in will be huge, with serious risks of violence. Cati doesn't want any deaths on her CV. 'That would be the limit, crossing the whole of the Magdalena without a single incident, not even a drunken brawl, and ending up with a full-scale drama in Bogotá! No, thanks.'

We'll do three shows in Faca. But even here, we have to announce Mano Negra won't be playing.

Our people are by now seriously broke. They haven't had their per diem for three days. Many are living off loans, others frankly are charity cases. We keep this to ourselves, of course, because in the street outside there's a lot of competition. By the way, none of our youngsters are indifferent to an outstretched hand. They always give something and don't say, as people do at home, that charity degrades those who give and those who receive, and that poverty is a problem only for the State. People at the bottom of the heap don't even know the State exists, or if it does, it's certainly not there to help them.

Since I decided to be everyone's dad, it's normal for them all to come to papa, but papa can't cater for the needs of such a large family. So I'm the most broke of all.

Wednesday 22 December
Facatativá (Part II)

We explore Facatativá, a dormitory town forty kilometres to the north-east of Bogotá. Prosperous in its time, when the railways established their workshops here, the people of Faca now live from small businesses and many of them travel to the capital every day to work.

Faca doesn't have the charm of Gamarra, nor the economic power of Dorada. That doesn't stop the local authorities considering it 'an expanding town', one of the modest pensions calling itself the Hotel Hilton (Family Atmosphere), nor the only men's clothing store being called Onan.

In the 'station café test' with which we amuse our tiny minds, Aracataca comes top because of the magic of the place, the welcome we got, and the beauty of its young ladies. Gamarra and Dorada come joint second, while a minority go for Barranca. We've apparently forgotten about Santa Marta, as if the first stop was only a dress rehearsal.

Anyway, people have been paid again, but only from last night and without back expenses for the previous days.

Thursday 23 December
Polar Bear on the Altiplano

Seven in the morning and devoured by fleas! These insects have managed to burrow their way through the sleeping bags we barricaded ourselves in with.

I speak in the plural, because can you imagine that at half past three in the morning someone knocks on my door. Divine surprise, before my very eyes little Isabel from Dorada! I didn't have time to rejoice or remember that Captain thought he had scored with her, because her boyfriend also entered my field of vision. What else could I do but offer to share the fleas? We finished the night all three of us in the room, the fiancé, like Tristan's sword, between Isabel and me, naturally.

On this subject, I have to say that after five weeks of abstinence and everyone now with a bunch of Spanish words at their disposal, we begin to see our Frenchmen arm in arm with Colombian girls. But this won't happen to Isabel and Captain since her bloke has her under constant surveillance.

At half past five a bus deposits Marina, she for whom your chronicler risked his skin in Dorada. Marina has come, as promised. Did she promise something?

The show starts three quarters of an hour late, due to

an unfortunate handling of the electrical system that blew all the fuses.

Politics raises its ugly head again. Since the interference of the governor in Santa Marta, we have managed to prevent any would-be takeovers by local potentates. But here is the governor of the region of Cundinamarca butting in with a load of electioneering hot air. It's true that the audience greeted him with a barrage of whistles but he doesn't care, what's important is getting in the papers the next day.

Garrincha and Sorriso have never been as brilliant. The other Ramón twirls on the end of his rope above the stage to some pretty violent rock, while Germain and Fabrice launch themselves into the void between two flights of the trapeze to be caught infallibly by Dédé.

Meanwhile back in the Tattoo Tent, the two girls from Dorada want an indelible memory of their escapade. Tom draws a black hand on Isabel's shoulder, while her fiancé looks on dumbfounded, and Dani traces a scorpion on Marina's left breast. Your chronicler takes some quick photos before going off to do his act.

Getting inside a polar bear skin is no small beer. It's as hot as hell in there. Even on a winter's night on the Altiplano.

The costume is made in France, as seen on TV in a duvet advert. It's lined with a five-centimetre-thick layer of foam. Impossible to get into it by yourself, you need to smother it in Vaseline. Jojo and Fantasio (one of the stowaways now on per diem) come to my aid. 'Take off your shoes, put the mitts on, turn round, lower your head, look through this hole, don't show your face, don't forget to walk slowly.' Coco demonstrates by staggering around like a slow-motion film. Okay, the bear is ready. Four men dressed in black come out carrying flame-throwers. The audience recoils. The men walk over to the shell where Roberto is sleeping. With a roar, the dragon pulls himself up to his full height, his yellow eyes menacing, and fire spewing from his mouth.

At this point, the masked pyromaniacs begin their assault on the huge wall of ice that obstructs the entrance to the polar bear's igloo. Inside, Jojo and Régis keep up their instructions. 'Show your head, try to get out of your grotto when your attackers approach.' Will the flames be deflected in time? 'Come on out!' It's not that easy in this paraphernalia. The attackers aim their flames at the half-melted block of ice. Once the ice wall has dissolved, the bear has to slide down the ramp from the wagon on its bum. Its imposing stature and beady black stare scare off the four arsonists. The children cheer. 'Try to play with them gently, it'll be fine while they're frightened.' Easy enough to say for anyone who doesn't know kids: their natural curiosity comes galloping back and the poor bear only has Coco's slow-motion gestures to defend himself with. In Ice Train memory, no polar bear has ever risked going this far into the crowd. He may be a bear but he's not stupid, he ignores the kids and clasps Claudia to his hairy bosom. Emotion, time inside the skin, rarefied air at this altitude, all conspire to suffocate a bear already close to asphyxiation. Anxiety and claustrophobia take over, he calls for help, fears he's getting a nose bleed. Help! Air!

Get me out of here! But the foam muffles all cries as hundreds of screaming kids surround him. Claudia, the only friend he can count on, is also overcome by events. He blacks out for ten or fifteen seconds before summoning enough strength to lash out with his claws willy-nilly: less out of vengeance than instinct. He was a kid once, and he still is one at heart. The act finishes and the polar bear disappears behind the big door, arm in arm with his little friend Claudia. The kids shout '*otro, otro*' as if a bear that came in from the cold had the energy of a French Lover. This age knows no pity!

We got word that a gang of fascists were coming from Bogotá. These skinheads are easy to spot. They try to provoke a fight but the French Lovers unmask them as soon as they come on stage. Captain points them out with his finger, inviting the audience to boo them. Easily aborted, it was the one and only incident in the whole tour that might have been dangerous.

The French Lovers bring this extraordinary night to an end. The group gets better and better. Within their own style, their music has acquired a whole new dimension. Manu sings two songs with them. '*Otro, otro*,' demand the big kids as well.

The governor's intervention at the beginning of the show has got Manu all worked up. After all, he can't denounce the activities of one Señor Matanza (prototype of the drug-trafficking local strongman in one of Manu's songs) and have the crowd held hostage by another one. The governor and ten of his gorillas, armed to the teeth, de facto took over the stage, and have such power, that...

All the same... As a reprisal, Tom plays the tape that had caused such dismay in Santa Marta: *El pueblo unido jamás sera vencido.* This time no one says a thing. It's responding to the governor's provocation. An eye for an eye.

That night, I let the three visitors from Dorada have my room and I go and sleep in the train. It's like the North Pole.

Prediction for 1994 in *El Tiempo:*

A Colombian victory in the World Cup in the United States
A Colombian victory in the 1994 Miss Universe Contest
Increase in Colombian foreign trade figures
Improvement of Colombia's international image

Messages in the Office of
Human Desires in Facatativá:

What I hope for most is for Colombia to live in peace, because we're all victims of a deadly violence. I hope that one day we can open *El Espectador* and read some good news.

Jorge Beltrán, 21

My most sincere hope is that the violence against children will stop.

Lorena Patricia Vargas, 9

My dream? That they'll open the railway again, it's the cheapest form of transport for poor people. I also hope we'll have peace in our country.

Carlos Campos, 21

It would be wonderful if Colombians could realise the paradise they have had the good fortune to be born in. Why don't they treat it with respect, and care for its flora and fauna. In this beautiful country we don't even have to work the land for it to give us its fruits? Why can't we accept this gift? Are we blind?

Anonymous

Friday 24 December
Christmas Eve in La Candelaria

It's Christmas. 1,700 soldiers are on the trail of Commandante Pérez, who is somewhere in the mountains of San Lucas. The TV offers a programme about him and the movement he leads. Soldiers are being deprived of their family and religious celebrations because of a priest!

Son of humble peasant farmers from Zaragoza in Spain, Manuel Pérez studied theology in Rome where he took holy orders in 1966 from Pope Paul VI. The day of the solemn ceremony, he arrived at the Vatican in jeans. He then worked in Paris with Abbé Pierre and travelled to Cuba in 1965 where he became a committed follower of Che Guevara.

Why stay in Europe? All his former colleagues in the seminary have gone off to Guatemala, El Salvador or Nicaragua. He goes to the Dominican Republic before opting for Colombia.

In 1980, there is a serious internal crisis in the ELN. 'We succumbed to a militaristic interpretation of the situation,' declared Father Pérez at the time, 'our leadership was no longer collective. These problems have now been resolved.' This is a Jesuitical way of saying that

Fabio Vásquez, founder of the ELN, had been packed off back to his studies in Cuba, and that from now on a new group was in charge of the movement, lead by Father Pérez.

As a Christian and a Marxist, in his own way he reconciles ice and fire, death and eternal life. 'We do not reject the teachings of Che on the validity of the armed struggle and the concept of the New Man that he embodies, but we are trying to define a political line more in keeping with Colombian reality.'

The guerrilla-priest is going through a bad patch at the moment. His moderate wing recommends negotiating with the government. But peace, even at Christmas, interests neither the military nor the priest: the mediators are received with bullets by the army.

We wander the streets of Faca. We go back and forth to Bogotá for no real reason. The hour and a half in the extraordinary *chivas* is worth the journey. These decrepit buses from the fifties are adorned with velvet, lights, garlands, with their deafening music – salsa, Mexican *corridas*, Vallenatos, a bit of rock from Medellín – wailing children, numerous customer-called stops, friendships cemented along the way.

We get off at the Sabana bus station. Big mistake. We should have got off two stops earlier, the Sabana neighbourhood being – yet another one – 'the most dangerous in Bogotá'. We start walking, try to hail a taxi, or get another bus that takes us nearer La Candelaria. Like all *gringos*, we are assailed by emerald touts who offer us pretty green stones wrapped in tissue paper, under the permissive eyes of policemen. This corner of town is the centre of emerald dealing. In the elegant cafés, the touts' bosses, podgy intermediaries with their phalanxes covered in stones the size of casino chips, exchange merchandise, suck emeralds as if to taste them and hold them up to the light.

Christmas party in 'the office', an old house in La Candelaria rented by the Prod that has even put aside 5,000 pesos to buy fireworks. They're pure dynamite in the hands of Bouchon, Fantasio, Tom, Coco, the other Ramón and the trapezists, who lark about like guerrillas. There's even money left for a nostalgic Christmas. Bread, cheese, salami, beer, rum and a bit of whisky to raise the spirits.

Still another week of living together but we're already feeling the pangs of separation. The idea of going home doesn't appeal. Would you do it again? Absolutely, everyone would take off for Santa Marta again. It has been really important for the Colombian people...!

We begin to swap addresses. But we're worried about the train. What will happen to it? Several ideas are circulating about how to keep it going. But without us...? And what about Roberto? Roberto stays, of course. He was born in the El Corzo workshops. He's Colombian. Okay, then...

The family party over, some want to carry on in the salsa discos. Others are staying in the house to sleep, that's one way of putting it. Bodies lie higgledy-piggledy on boxes, in hammocks, on tables, anywhere and everywhere, most of them shivering with cold. Tom,

Charlotte, Puce, Fantasio and myself choose to go back to Faca.

Christmas Eve, three in the morning, looking for a taxi in the streets of Bogotá, in full dustbin men war, in a Siberian cold. That takes the biscuit. Locals are burning their rubbish on every street corner. We walk for half an hour. The sky is alight with rockets and fireworks, the streets full of drunks. A bottle of water costs twice as much as a can of beer. A kid tries to help his dad stand up. 'If you want me to live, give me death,' sings a band of boozers. It's a Saint Teresa of Avila Vallenato, in the biting Bogote night.

The pavements of Seventh Avenue offer Colombia's finest cripples, torsos on wheels, festering sores, ragged children, all begging with grimaces worthy of Valle Inclán. On Christmas morning, at dawn, Jean-Marc strayed into this court of miracles. 'I didn't think this had happened since the Middle Ages,' he said. He saw an old man robbed at gunpoint, trembling with fear. Beside him, night owls step indifferently over a warm body on a pile of rubbish.

We finally find a taxi. He can't take us. Faca is outside his zone. But he stops another taxi. They get in a huddle and whisper. Okay, they'll take us to Faca, but we have to hire both taxis and pay double. What can we do? We agree.

As usual, our taxi driver turns out to be very friendly. He adores Spain: Chantada, Lugo…! Of course, Chantada and Lugo are on a par with Montpellier, but has he been to Toledo, Granada, Aranjuez? No, those towns weren't on his organised tour.

The story about being outside his zone was a load of rubbish. It turns out the taxi was afraid to go to Faca alone. Not because of us, but because of bandits. It's like this: two cars roar up, one goes in front, the other behind, and the victim, caught in a sandwich, has to stop. It's the car the thieves are after. They take it, and then, to avoid problems, they slit your throat. The taxi makes a horizontal gesture with his hand.

If there's one area in which Bogotá deserves its reputation, that's certainly it. A car left a couple of minutes unattended is a car that is lost, even if the owner hasn't already lost it. At night and on Sundays the streets are empty, if not of vehicles, at least of stationary vehicles. Thieves cross deserted squares, walk endless pavements. When they see a car on its own, they regard it as a legitimate prey. Sooner or later, it will give a little cry – a moo or a bark – of alarm.

Our taxis burn all the red lights, so street kids don't rip off their sidelights or wipers. As old as the New World, like characters out of Spanish picaresque novels, these modern street kids are as skilful as those *lazarillos* (rascals) who came with the Conquistadors. Like them, they live off their wits in a hostile society. They form groups to face danger. In twos, threes, tens, they feel stronger. Educated by brutal contact with life, they scour the city, their eyes always on the lookout, dirty, frightening, and every day they stake out a neighbourhood and make it their hunting ground. They steal something here, take something there, lark about climbing on car mudguards. At night, to keep warm, they huddle up together to sleep, with their dogs, like rats at dawn.

But a street kid is not just a kid who begs, nor a little tramp, nor a little thief, nor an abandoned child living off odd jobs, nor a rebel who sleeps in the streets. He is all those things rolled into one, simultaneously or alternately.

'The *Violencia*, it's always the *Violencia*. That's why taxis are so expensive,' says our driver. 'The *Violencia* justifies everything. If me and my colleague agreed to take you, it's because we saw you wandering about in one of Bogotá's most dangerous areas.' All areas of Bogotá are dangerous.

We finally arrive in Faca. The obligatory life insurance has cost us two times 20,000 pesos, a week's per diem for the five of us.

Saturday 25 December
An Evening in Faca

We spend Christmas Day quietly in Faca. Fabrice has been attacked. It's the first time it's happened to any of us. He was at a table with his girlfriend eating disgusting lasagne. Two big skinheads sat beside them, pushing them against the wall. 'You're not Colombian, yet you can travel in our country, and we don't even know it.' Fabrice and his girlfriend get up to leave, but no way. 'Go back to France, you've no fucking business here.' All the same, Fabrice invites them to the next *feria*.

'What's it cost?'

'It's free.'

'And why is it free?'

Not easy to explain.

One of them puts his Doc Marten's on the table. 'I'm going to stick them in your fucking face.' The other customers and the waiters appear not to see anything, even when the visitors order something to drink. 'Beer and whisky on the foreigners.' They're served. Fabrice wants to call the police. 'There's no police in Facatativá,' he's told. Fabrice pushes the guy next to him, gets up, his girlfriend too. The fight starts. They're both held by the shoulders. Fabrice, brave but frightened, offers another round of beers. To cap it all, the guys at the pizzeria rip them off.

'Not very glorious, all the same,' admits Fabrice once he has recovered from the shock. Attacked, not by guerrillas, nor in the jungle, but in a pizzeria in Faca by two skinheads from Bogote.

Sunday 26 December
Escobar's Inheritance

The press wonders: 'Who will be Escobar's heir?' A huge
court case is about to start. The family and lawyers of the
Mafioso who died about twenty days ago are now locked
in litigation with the State. 'Can goods and property
acquired to the detriment of public morality be claimed?'
His fortune is estimated at three billion dollars. His men
of straw, his paper heirs, have the most to lose. They hold
95% of the drug lord's wealth, his family will share the
other 5%. It's still a considerable amount. The list of
ranches, office blocks, houses, cars, planes, hotels, discos,
is impressive. The houses on the River Aburra, in
Medellín, are not in the catalogue. Escobar gave them to
their occupants in 1982. Otherwise, they could have
risked the same fate as the animals in the Puerto Triunfo
zoo.

Monday 27 December
Reception at the French Embassy

Tonight the French embassy is giving a cocktail party for everyone on the tour. The troupe bristles at the mention of the embassy. Embassy, ministry, chief, editor, director, church, Christmas, military, are words that make the hairs stand up on the back of the necks of our train's 'undesirables'. We understand the invitation has given rise to some robust polemics. 'Don't give a fuck about the embassy,' say some. The less intransigent agree to go on condition there are no speeches. However, the *saucisson*, *Camembert*, and *vin rouge* on the menu exert a strong influence on even the most radical. It's obvious we've all lost an average of five kilos, twice that for the French Lovers: Bruno, Captain and Gambit are unrecognisable.

And so, being homesick and skint drives most of us to the main square in Faca where the buses leave for the capital.

With Claudia, and Annie Gasnier of Radio France Internationale, I discover the market in Bogotá to buy some presents. We're told to guard our money with our lives and even to put notes in our shoes. We've heard a million anecdotes about theft. If car drivers wear their watches on their right wrist, it because the left is too exposed when the window is lowered. It's best not to open the windows anyway. Even sensible people are afraid of getting snakes or rats on their passenger seats. Startled motorists get out of their cars, a motorcyclist following behind will get off his bike, sit behind the wheel, and roar off with the car.

'Don't show you're afraid,' advises Claudia.

We go down the hill in La Candelaria. At the bottom of the old colonial quarter, around Avenue Caracas, lies an area of tiny narrow streets. Some are just a mess of rubble and rubbish, but most of the others buzz with people, shops, carts of vegetables and fruit, ice, stands with corn on the cob. Down a side street, are the stalls of the flea market. Not much variety in the clothes, scruffy and dull like everything else. But people shop here to replace worn-out clothes not to get dolled up in the latest flea-market fashion like in Paris. As for the other merchandise, poverty and penury are absolute.

The French embassy is in North Bogotá, the bourgeois neighbourhoods where rich businessmen, liberal professionals, industrialists, landowners, and politicians, live. What they call '*los doctores*'. For ordinary people, being a *doctor* isn't a question of what you know, or having a university degree, it's a question of social position. The car, the house, the office, and *voilà*, you're a *doctor*. On the lips of a secretary, the porter or the servant, the nuance is a mark of respect. For a street kid, it's an easy, half-ironic way of getting a few pesos out of well-dressed people. In intellectual circles, however, it's pejorative: the *petite bourgeoisie* and politicians are *doctorcitos*, little doctors.

In the chic parts of Bogotá are luxury department stores, like the Unicentro, where they sell absolutely everything, including bottled mineral water imported from France. When I think how difficult it was to find drinking water on our journey! Water and electricity both. It's a rule in these sorts of places, as stupid as it is universally respected, that you have to have all the lights on in the house as soon as night falls, to show 'that there's someone at home'. Seen from the plane, North Bogotá looks like a gigantic Christmas tree and the south like a huge dark void. In fact, you could say the same about the whole country, where a good half of homes have no electricity. Whole neighbourhoods are being militarised, especially the areas near the mountains, above Seventh Avenue, where the super-rich live with their corteges of maids, cooks and valets. All over the place, you bump into blokes in uniforms, carrying guns. Security guards are everywhere, in the gardens, the garages, at the entrances to apartment blocks.

Some of the most unyielding members of the troupe ignore the embassy invitation and prefer red beans and rice in a cheapo restaurant. More's the pity, the embassy buffet is first rate, or at least that's what it seems like after six weeks of famine. The inevitable speech was very charming, nobody can criticise the words of Pierre-Jean Vandoorne.

Luis Bernardo Villegas, the director of Ferrovías, was the main beneficiary of the expedition's success. He tells us:

'When the project was first presented to me, I thought

it was completely mad. Many Colombians think the idea of rehabilitating the railways in our country is mad. Now I say that if the first folly has succeeded, there's no reason for the second not to succeed as well. For Ferrovías, it's very important. The welcome the Ice Train received everywhere reinforces our belief that the train is an indispensable means of transport for the new Colombian economy.'

'You could say that they've become indispensable since the railways have been privatised!' says your chronicler.

'Yes, it's much better. Two years ago, the situation was pitiful. The trains were doing less than ten kilometres per hour and derailed all the time. This year, we've carried ten million tons of merchandise and we hope to do even better in the future.'

'And passenger trains?'

'For the moment, they're not competitive. To give you an example, the journey between Bogotá and Santa Marta by road takes twenty hours, while the train can take up to forty-four hours.'

'Even up to seventy. So, you're interested in developing goods trains between Bogotá and the coast. And what about the huge hopes the passenger train raised among the people we met?'

'What we really want is to create a link between Bogotá and Medellín, Colombia's industrial centres, and the ports. For that we have to create a means of transport that is both efficient and cheap. I hope that in 1997, the train can transport twenty million tons of goods, that's already good for our country.'

'In all the towns we went through, we saw that people are waiting for the passenger train like a Christmas present.'

'The railways have never been part of Colombia's development like they were in France, or the US. The people who live beside our railway tracks are very poor and uneducated. That's why they waited so impatiently for the train and why they were so sad when it left.'

'The train was made by Colombians and French together, and was decorated by students from the School of Fine Arts in Bogotá. It's yours now. What's going to happen to it? What will be the fate of Roberto and the other wagons, with their store of rich stories?'

'We want Colombians to use it. The Cultural Institute wants to keep doing shows with Colombian artists on the same track, so the people who were so affected by the experience can see it again.'

Dénis Vène was first secretary at the embassy when the first contacts were made. He then played a decisive part in bringing the project to fruition.

'From our point of view, it's strengthened the idea of bringing French theatre to the people. Of course, we'll still keep taking the *Comédie Française* to the Colón Theatre in Buenos Aires for people who know about it because they have the money to fly to Paris. But we also have to find ways of reaching the people who can't travel. I thought the idea of the train was fabulous, we should use it again for other countries. We've already talked about the Trans-Siberian railway. Mexico would also like a show like this in its villages round the countryside.'

'The incredible thing about the train is that it went to areas that are completely outside the traditional cultural orbit.'

'As you know, you can't say a spectacle is cultural or not. There are two sides to the equation. If country people who have never seen anything suddenly see a dragon spouting flames, it's obviously going to have a big effect. But if you put on a play by Audiberti, they're not going to understand anything. So, it's logical to use the spirit of the train in a country like Colombia, but maybe in other countries we could use other forms of culture, culture in inverted commas, that is.'

'Are you surprised the train was able to cross regions as dangerous as the Magdelena Medio? Did you have talks beforehand with the guerrillas, or the paramilitaries?'

'I think it was all down to the fact that the team on the train acted so responsibly, they were absolutely neutral and reacted to each situation in the most appropriate way. They told the army they didn't need them, that they weren't to set foot on the train. When they tried to, Cati, who is a very brave person with boundless energy, made them get off. Those who could have complained didn't have the chance to, and theatre in the countryside isn't an easy enemy to take on. So, the guerrillas, and the narcos and paramilitaries, who had no financial interest, or any other, in stopping a train of this sort, left it alone. Anyway, it would have been very unpopular. Why run the risk?'

The evening ended in the best possible way, with a concert by the French Lovers.

Tuesday 28 December
In Faca with Manu

Manu had been to Cali.

'So, how was the *feria*?'

'The bullfights weren't great. But Cali's the capital of salsa, so...'

'Why did you say you'd get involved with this train?'

'Because Coco asked me to, and Coco's my mate. Even before we knew what it entailed, I said he could count on us. He's really something, Coco. He always has mad schemes, like this one, but hey, it's going really well.'

'What about your group?'

'No problem. Everyone was ready for an adventure like that.'

'You were on the Cargo '92 tour last year. What differences are there between that and the Ice Train? Do you see it as a logical extension of Cargo?'

'Not really. Cargo concentrated on the big cities, in Colombia and other places. What we wanted to do with the train was to get out into the countryside, to the little towns in the Magdalena Medio where they'd never seen anything like what we were offering. This is a show on small stages, not on a huge structure for 60,000 people, like we did in the Plaza Bolívar in Bogotá in 1992. This time we went right into the backwoods in Colombia. The important thing was that the concerts were free and that we played in the stations, which are usually on the outskirts of town. When the concert ends, in ten minutes you make friends who take you back to their homes and offer you whatever they've got. In Latin America, if you make people pay ten francs entry fee, you've already lost 95% of the population.'

'So it was worth it?'

'Yes, fantastic. It was a shock for us to discover that our whole way of life, of dressing, our culture in general was so different from our audience. But the contact always went beyond mere comprehension, and into deep affection. I'd even go as far as to say that's why we continued despite all the problems we had. In spite of everything, each time we left a village, we were so buoyed up for the next, just from the warmth of the goodbyes. That didn't mean we didn't have to break the ice again at each stop. Especially in the Magdalena Medio, where they are suspicious of people from outside. Lots of people in Bogotá told us it was collective suicide to go and play in Barrancabermeja.'

'You must have been sympathetic to the guerrillas with that slogan *El pueblo unido jamás sera vencido.*'

'I admit that was a mistake. It was gratuitous provocation, but I still think it's a great sentiment. Except that here it takes on a different dimension. We trotted it out at Santa Marta because the local senator had tried to muscle in. The atmosphere changed straight away! You must have noticed that the next day the papers talked about the train, but not a word about Mano Negra. I toned down some of our songs in Spanish, they were too political for the context. But you also have to look at the way the guy wanted to hijack the show, that's more dangerous than the slogan. The compère introduced the senator as the train organiser, and there were guerrillas in the audience. Just picture it. In Colombia, in any gathering of more than 6,000 people, there are always knifings and shootings, it always ends up like that. In Barranca, three quarters of the guys who came to see us, whether they were twenty or seventy, had a gun in his pocket. That's one of the things that most amazed the Colombians, that there were no incidents.'

'Is that what struck you the most?'

'No. I was struck most by the poverty in Bogotá. I've been here several times and the poverty is always there, right in your face. The horror of it. It disgusts you at every step you take. In Bogotá, I spent time with the street kids who risk getting murdered. Life's hell for them. But despite everything, they're more cheerful than you or me. They're twelve years old, drugged to the gills, and not one of them's a virgin. When they go to sleep at night, they don't know if they're going to wake up. A plastic bag over the head, in the boot of a car, over the mountain and, pow, a bullet in the brain.'

'You do a lot of jamming with local musicians. What's that like?'

'It never stops. We're always finding new rhythms, new melodies. And even if we don't learn them – I never ask people to explain the chords, I don't dissect them, it's just for the fun of playing – it stays in your head anyway, and I know that some time or other it'll pop out, in Paris or somewhere, and I won't know exactly where it comes from.'

'Half of Mano Negra quit after Aracataca. Is that the end of the group?'

'Hey, not so fast. The group hasn't split up. We don't have a manager, our next disc was slow in coming out, someone had to go back to France and sort it out. Having said that, Daniel, Tonio and Jo more or less left at the end of the Cargo '92 tour. Others came in. But we've never had fights in Mano Negra, no shouting matches or anything. Anyone who's left or come back is still a friend. There's never been anything nasty, and we're proud of that. We spent four years together, and separated. Living with Mano Negra isn't easy, especially on tour, you have to put your family life on hold. But I know when we get back to France, the new record will come out and we'll start again, with some old members, some new, and without others who don't want to go on doing the same old thing. It's impossible to have lived this experience and carry on as if it hadn't happened. We'll go back to Europe and offer people something different. The group has new members and we're experimenting with stuff. I don't know if our show in France will be the same as on the train.'

'You've got attached to the little black kid...'

'Yes, Rondelle. This kid's destined to be a star, if he carries on in music. He's exceptionally talented, as a singer and dancer.'

'Are you thinking of bringing him into the group?'

'Mano Negra doesn't need a kid of ten. It's the last thing that would have occurred to me. But I don't want to talk too much about his future; we'll see what we can do with him. Maybe he can play with us, but I don't know if he can be a new member of the group. He's gone back to Santa Marta, but I'll go and get him and arrange a passport to bring him to France.'

'We also saw Fidel, the Argentine, with you.'

'We met Fidel in Argentina. We did a thing on television and the first person to come to the hotel and congratulate us was Fidel. His group was on the first part of our tour and we started collaborating then. When we recorded the album, we missed Fidel, so we got him to come over to France. He played with us for three months. Now he's part of the family too.'

'What's the future of the Ice Train?'

'What I hope is that there will be passenger trains, that's what the people are expecting, not just goods trains. Having said that, I don't think that we, with what we've done, can revolutionise the history of the Colombian railways. But what's important is for this train to keep travelling with Colombian entertainers on it.'

Wednesday 29 December
Second Night at Faca

The other Ramón is ill. Tonight, the show goes on without him. The other acts — trapeze, bear, Roberto — will have to make up for his absence.

In the event, they don't even have to. From the very start, the *feria* bursts into life. In front of the station is the same interminable queue for the House of Light where young spirits are illuminated with special effects and tricks of light. Next to it, kids try to score a goal past the wooden goalie who turns on his pivot and doesn't stop anything. Further on, trapezists fly back and forth in the air.

At the end of the track, the water cannon is getting ready. The war of fire and ice is about to break out. The two enormous ice cubes thrown onto the rails are attacked by men in black with flame-throwers. The water canon rolls out to help them, Roberto pulls himself up to his full four-metre height and shoots flames from his mouth. Against a background of unearthly music, fire and ice battle it out for a good quarter of an hour, with a tempest of lightning, flashing, and thundering. The fight ends in a draw with the public in a state of shock.

Inside the bear, your chronicler is learning to breathe a

bit better. He has gone from playing with the kids for five minutes last week, to fifteen this week. He claws at a sweet little soldier. Even in disguise, the bear's primal anti-militarism gets the better of him.

For the rest, the French Lovers – the most idiotic group on the planet – are as wonderful as ever, and the audience very enthusiastic.

Thursday 30 December
Last Night at Faca

I have to keep up this journal so that I don't look bad vis-à-vis my boys who never stop working. True, I don't participate in mantling and dismantling the *feria* (although I try to be useful as the bear) but an average of five or six pages a day, rubbish or not, is still a hefty bit of work. All this is by way of saying that your chronicler isn't just having a good time, and that he'd completely forgotten Marina's gratuitous promise to come back to Faca for the last night party.

She arrives around midnight without Isabel – much to Captain's disappointment although he no longer has any illusions due to the bodyguard-boyfriend. The first thing Marina wants after a bus journey is a hot bath. I let her have the permanently cold shower to herself, although God knows I'm dying to see if the tattoo is still there. I leave discreetly to install myself in that other Faca gem, the Hilton (Family Atmosphere).

A very fruitful day for your chronicler in terms of pages written due to being cooped up in his room.

At seven o'clock, the last *feria* of the tour begins. The skinheads who attacked Fabrice and his girlfriend want to get tattooed. Nothing doing if they don't apologise, say

Tom and Dani. No sooner said than done. What's more, an adequate excuse is found. They'd taken them for a couple of *gringos*.

As for the show, there's nothing to say, except that for the last night of the tour we expect nothing less than perfection. Roberto, the trapezists, the other Ramón, are all superb. On his third outing, the bear has the kids spellbound for at least twenty minutes, and your chronicler can see, from his hairy hidey-hole, little Marina searching desperately for him.

Manu plays just one number with the French Lovers. The crowd — because today too, there's a huge crowd — goes wild. All Bogotá skinheads have become *trash-guingette* fans; they get up on the stage, launch themselves at the audience. But these are very special skinheads. Apart from their ultra-nationalism and their shaved heads, they don't differ much from our ecologists. At the moment, their *bête noire* is César Rondón, Colombia's most famous bullfighter. They're leading a violent campaign against bullfighting and there's good reason to. Coco, Fabrice, Bouchon, Annie Gasnier and myself went to a *corrida* in the Bogotá bullring the other day. Impossible to describe, or even imagine, such carnage.

The concert seems like it's never going to end. Everyone's dancing on stage, everyone's singing, people are tearing the train posters down, the French Lovers play their repertoire over and over again. They finish with a bang, and I admire them from the studio of Radio Caracol. It was an enormous challenge for them to take over from Mano Negra, one they never expected. And they were a great success, these amazing guys. Awesome!

The audience leaves, exhausted, but the troupe still has work to do: take down the stalls, dismantle the trapeze structure, put away all the material. The temperature has fallen to minus six. Nobody thought of bringing appropriate equipment, so the layer of ice on the speakers sticks to fingers. But there's no question of missing the trip planned for tomorrow morning round the outskirts of Bogotá.

By four o'clock everything is stashed away. The chronicler makes his way to his Family Hilton where the bed is damp and the room icy. He can't help dreaming of the warmth of his former pad, the Hotel Central, where Marina is!

And he tells himself that all the patriarchal saints, and all the anchorites in the desert, had less virtue triumphing over sin than he, because the women sent to seduce them weren't Colombian, or their granddaughter's age.

Friday 31 December
Tour of Bogotá

We have to get all our stuff out of the train, all our summer clothes, the things we didn't need last week in Faca. The train is leaving this morning for Bogotá, but only with the carriages needed for the show. I pass by the Hotel Central to pay for Marina's room. Will she have already left? I ask the owner.

'Yes, at seven this morning. She wrote you a note.'

Thank you for everything, thank you for giving me the feeling of being loved and of letting me enter your world and share your best moments, they were unforgettable. I pray to God not to forget you and that you won't forget me either. You make this world a universe of peace and love. Being near you is being in a world where violence, envy and falsity don't exist, and each one of you will take a piece of my heart with you. You are wonderful people and wherever you go, you will leave culture, adventure, friendship, love, peace and kindness.

I hope God will protect you wherever you go and that you will stand beside us in the fight to make this world a better place and win the battle against violence, because only God is almighty.

I hope you'll enjoy good health. All of us together should say no to drugs, no to alcohol, no to violence and yes to life.

Very best wishes, wonderful people. Don't forget me. Marina

Your chronicler pays for the room and tells himself that, in all truthfulness, such innocence wasn't meant for him.

The tour today is the result of a real mix-up of, let's call them commitments, between the Prod and the sponsors, the embassy and the Prod, the mayor's office and the embassy, the sponsors and the embassy. Not surprising, then, that once again the rock-susceptibles aren't too impressed.

To honour our contracts, we're making a grand entrance into the Capital...but only on the outskirts. In other words, we're going to Bogotá without going to the city centre because the mayor refuses to cough up.

It's beautiful weather at ten in the morning. Everyone climbs onto the roof of the train, officials and gypsies together. Jean Digne and Brigitte Proucelle of the AFAA, Pierre-Jean Vandoorne, the embassy chargé d'affaires and Jean-Marc Stricker of France-Inter, Yves Berton of *Le Parisien*, and the photographers, rub shoulders with Anne-Marie, Dani, Patrice, and Jeff who has come back from Paris.

Patrick sets fire to the last wagon, on the footplate the French Lovers attack their first song, and the train is off.

The train sets off, but we miss the valiant rust bucket that derailed every twenty kilometres along the River Magdalena, that inflicted draconian alimentary regimes on us, and that stopped for hours in the bush under an infernal sun. The train we loved has been castrated, it's more shameful parts having been cut off: the dormitory-carriages, the mosquito-carriages, the pissing-carriages, that gave it character, and life. Our unforgettable train has become sanitised.

We pass through Fontibón, a middle-class town. Naturally the people are astonished. Men give us the thumbs up, women wave from their windows, children chase us.

After Fontibón, the railway runs parallel to the road. The cars slow down to the rhythm of the train, causing an almighty traffic jam. A van goes up to the footplate and gives the musicians beer. The French Lovers and Manu begin to play in time to car horns. Above us, in a shiny white crematorium, a funeral procession forgets its mourning and dances a waltz in time to our passing, as a last farewell.

To our right, we begin to see the excavations of San Cristóbal, one of the many shanty towns around Bogotá that spring up overnight on wasteland.

Massive displacement has turned Bogotá into a city-refugee camp, and the overpopulation brings with it inequalities, accentuates social segregation, the rich in the north, the poor to the south. The most destitute squat on the mountainsides in shacks without running water or drains. If ever theft could be seen as one of the manifestations of the fight for life, it's in a society (not clandestine but parallel) where you begin by pirating water and electricity.

All along our route we see signs on walls saying 'This land is not for sale. For further information...' followed by a phone number. Con men sell land that isn't theirs to gullible *campesinos* at low prices. Colossal fortunes are built fast by preying on this misery.

Around 1,500 people per day pour into these shanty towns. Displaced by aerial spraying of the coca crop by the military, massacres by paramilitaries, the guerrillas and their 'vaccine', or the arrival of drug traffickers, these are the victims in the wars that plague the countryside all round the world. Bogotá spreads out horizontally because no one wants to live in tower blocks. Unable to adapt to the city, the *campesinos* cling to their past. They yearn for gardens, chickens and trees. Being displaced from lush tropical vegetation to the freezing arid highlands is like being doubly punished.

As the train approaches, tethered cows tug at their halters, goats nibble the sparse grass sown beside the tracks, pigs pull on the ropes tying them to their sties.

Three out of four city dwellers are the children or grandchildren of *campesinos*. Sons of the earth, a thousand and one tiny things give their origins away.

The lucky ones manage to get construction work, where there are more jobs than in industry, but since most of the building sites are in the north (buildings go up where's there's money), their women cross the city to take them their lunch. Among all the hustle and bustle of traffic, they sit on embankments under a tree or in the angle of two walls, and watch their husbands or adult sons eat the staple meal of the poor: beans, rice, fried potato or plantain. It's the menu we've had served up to us the whole journey.

The sun beats down. Brigitte, Proucelle and Jean-Marc

Stricker turn bright pink, our music shocks old grannies, a hi-fi shop advertises 'exotic sounds', the traffic jam trails back into the distance, the beer van is back, and roosters, ducks, and hens spray the air with feathers as we pass.

These *campesinos* are so needy they'll grow anything. No question of cultivating crops, buying any patch of land is precarious, and the ground is packed too hard. Many of them have chickens, and a fair number of cows can be seen in downtown Bogotá, grazing on the tiniest corners of grass beside the provocative buildings of the financial centre. Their owners are called 'farmers without land'.

These poor farmers still cling to their superstitions, their affinity for sorcery and other quackeries. The churches are full to bursting and during religious festivals, their womenfolk drag themselves sobbing along the pavement to touch a statue of Christ or some saint with the clothes of a sick child or a runaway husband.

We had lost the van at one point, but we catch up with it on a level crossing. We get fresh beers from the six occupants. What luck!

We reach El Chico, a traditional bourgeois neighbourhood. Brick houses, with gardens and terraces. And guards everywhere. They're obviously afraid of their shanty-town neighbours just down the road. The obsession with security which attacks the oligarchy is contagious, and has reached the middle classes. In these new neighbourhoods, whole apartment blocks are stuck behind bars and a sentry box installed at the only entrance. The fashion for intercoms has caught on everywhere.

We arrive at La Caro, end of the outward journey. We get a bite to eat at a café, just time for the train to do a few manoeuvres.

We're now on our way back, after a thirty minute stopover. Still on the roof of the train, it's starting to get chilly. Beside the track the same goats, the same pigs in the front yards. To our left is one of the most reputed boarding schools in Latin America, with its monumental church and luxurious sports grounds.

Frozen stiff, our teeth are chattering.

The people who cheered us on the way there, wave at us. Cordially, of course, but it's already déjà vu. We're old hat. The train is taking us to the *El Espectador* building. 'Another hour,' says Claudia. *La Consentida* isn't in a hurry to get there. More cows, more hens. The corpse at the crematorium has had more than enough time to burn, his family have left. Thirty years ago, the bourgeoisie relaxed at aristocratic clubs like the Gun Club or the Jockey Club, where the men played bridge and conversed in their best Castillian. But nowadays, the new rich have built other clubs with leisure centres. Bang up against the shanty towns, Bogotá boasts no less than a dozen golf clubs, among them the superb Lagartos Club and the Country Club, home of the Colombian Open. One detail of chic: these clubs import turf straight from England and the fairways are softer than the velvet Her Gracious Majesty wears when she goes riding.

The French Lovers have stopped playing, they kept it up for the whole day. The El Chico neighbourhood again and the shanty towns beside it. We get our pullovers out.

Then, suddenly…

'Everybody off!'

What? We haven't got to *El Espectador*!

'It's over. We're going back to Faca non-stop. Anyone who wants to come can.'

Quick, we run along the gravel to the tattoo-wagon to get our sleeping bags. But surely this isn't the place to say our goodbyes! We're a bit disorientated. Which way is Bogotá? Diablito comes up and it's hugs all round.

'We won't forget you, Diablito.'

'Me neither. It's been an honour for me to have been chosen to accompany you. Staggering.'

We have to hurry, there will be no taxis left. We hug Diablito. Quick. Jeff and Claudia help me drag my stuff along the gravel.

From time to time, we turn and look back at the train.

Postscript
An Afternoon with Ramón

June 2008 and Ramón Chao is sitting in a café on the South Bank of the River Thames in London. A few hundred metres across the river, President George W Bush is in Downing Street on his farewell tour of Europe. Ramón is patiently answering questions about the legacy of the Train of Ice and Fire.

Have you been back to Colombia since the trip and did you ever hear from Rondelle again?

Yes, I've been back twice. People still remembered the train, but there was no sign of Rondelle. He'd been taken in by an organisation that helps young people but when I wanted to see him, he'd gone awol the previous week. He escaped regularly. Manu had started the process of adopting him and bringing him to France, but nobody could find him. Just as well, I'd say, because the kid might not have fitted into a society like the French. I don't know where he is. Anything could have happened to him since we know what the paramilitaries get up to.

What about the legacy of the train in Colombia, do you know of anything that happened after you left?

Manu wanted nothing less than to bring passenger trains back to Colombia. The railways had stopped carrying passengers about twenty years before he turned up. He noticed there were still railway lines but much of the track was covered by undergrowth. The road haulage monopoly was owned by private airlines and they weren't interested in seeing people travelling by train again. So on the journey we were almost more afraid of the lorry drivers than we were of the guerrillas.

Needless to say, the expedition produced no concrete results, only dreams. Roberto ended his days as scrap iron at Facatativá station. A year later, a friend of mine, a journalist from a Barcelona radio station, went to Barrancabermeja. I asked her to take some of my books to give to the people I'd met at the station. She was surrounded by six men and taken to an old hangar.

'What are you doing here?' they asked.

'I'm a journalist, I have this book for the stationmaster.'

'There's no railway here,' they said threateningly.

The girl took out the book and showed them what I'd written about Barrancabermeja. One of the men recognised himself as the guerrilla who had questioned me about the train, and they let her go. Not surprisingly, the girl took the first plane home.

The other part of the legacy of course is what impression the tour left on you and the others on the train. What happened after you left Colombia?

One clear result of the tour was the break-up of Mano Negra. Most of the band jumped ship before the journey ended, and others left in Paris. On the other hand, some of the French Lovers, like Gambit and the accordionist, joined Radio Bemba, the band Manu formed after he emerged from months of depression. In the end, Manu was revitalised by a trip we made together – him on a Yamaha 500, me on a modest Vespa 125 – from Paris to Finisterre in Galicia, following Bishop Prisciliano of Compostela's footsteps, not the Camino de Santiago which is a farce, an invention.

Former members of Mano Negra ended up more or less as follows: my son Antoine first worked with a theatre company in Nantes, then as musical director of Radio Latina, and now as a journalist on Daniel Mermet's programme *Là-bas si j'y suis* for Radio France. My nephew Santi is a businessman, an important executive of the private television channel France 1. It supports Sarkozy. Thomas, the keyboard player, was very involved in Cuba and Mexico; he formed a group called Les Mariatchis, I don't know if it lasted.

I came home hardened by the trip and was soon off on the adventure with Manu that I mentioned before; return trip Paris–Finisterre. After what we went through and suffered in Colombia, everything was easy.

From your account, many things came to a head in Aracataca, including the disintegration of Mano Negra. This was a moment of great change for your family. How do you feel when you look back at your time in Aracataca, has the resonance of those events grown over the years?

You could say this adventure changed my life, and maybe it did, but I don't notice these things. I think life changes gradually, and the Train of Ice and Fire was yet one more link in the chain. Another was the brain haemorrhage I survived eight years ago. The Colombia thing was very important, and so was my trip through Spain with Manu.

The importance of adventure and journeys reoccurs in your books. Clearly you have made important journeys in your life, what is it that keeps bringing you back to this theme?

That's right, but I don't do it consciously. In my very first novel, *El Lago de Como*, I write about my first trip to Paris...and its consequences. In *Son Adelfas*, published in France, I go to Mallorca, then there are *Las Travesías de Luis Gontán*, *Las Andaduras del Che* and *Prisciliano de Compostela*, all about journeys. Of course there's this train book, of which we'll say no more. I'd rather write locked in a room and travel in my head. It's easier to write about journeys, but my books have action and characters too. At the moment, I'm working on a novel about the cathedral in Santiago de Compostela, and again it will centre on pilgrims. Yes, journeys...

There are easier ways to write a book than to travel on an old rickety train through Colombia with a troupe of young rock and rollers. Did you get seduced by the rock and roll lifestyle at all?

I didn't actually turn into a rocker. At my age it would be difficult, but I did try. On December the 24th, Manu had gone to a bullfight in Cali, and we were celebrating Christmas Eve in the organisation's house. It was rumoured there was a special dessert, a marijuana cake. I had never smoked, not even normal cigarettes when I was kid. But I let myself be tempted. I tried a piece of cake, and since it didn't seem to be having any effect, I had another, and another. I carried on until I suddenly felt some other guests picking me up off the floor. Apparently I'd just keeled over and looked like I was asleep for half an hour. I was in the clouds and totally out of it for two days. When Manu got back from Cali someone told him, and he said, 'Honestly, Papa, I can't leave you anywhere.'

Having a tattoo was also quite rock and roll. How do you feel about your tattoo all these years later?

After the Colombia tattoo, I went on adding a tattoo for each of my books, at first retrospectively, and then as they were published. The idea came from a rather macabre conversation I had with Juan Carlos Onetti, the Uruguayan writer I'd written a book about. We were very close friends. When he was very ill, about to die, *Le Monde* asked me to write his obituary. I did it and since I had to go to Madrid, I showed it to Onetti. He read it and said, 'Okay, if you've written it, it must be true.' I went back to Paris and gave it to *Le Monde*, signed: 'Ramón Chao, with the approval of the deceased.' The newspaper censored the bit about the deceased because it obviously seemed a bit risqué to them.

But I had also asked Onetti, and this did get published, what he thought about dying. He said, 'I'm very calm, because when it happens I'll summon my characters – Larsen, Angelica, Petrus – and they'll all comfort me and say goodbye to me.' Afterwards I thought, instead of summoning my characters, I'd go one better than Onetti, I'd carry them with me... I've got fourteen tattoos now, originals by great painters, like Antonio Saura, Wozniak, and the next will be by Miguel Barceló. So my skin is already worth quite a bit, and I'm thinking of donating it, post mortem of course, to a museum or art gallery.

For further information on this book,
and for Route's full book programme
please visit:

www.route-online.com